"It's a book that will make you think. Clinical researche
how upbringing may influence psychosis provide a to
recommended."

– **Professor Daniel Freeman,** University of Oxford

ATTACHMENT THEORY AND PSYCHOSIS

Attachment Theory and Psychosis: Current Perspectives and Future Directions is the first book to provide a practical guide to using attachment theory in the assessment, formulation and treatment of a range of psychological problems that can arise as a result of experiencing psychosis.

Katherine Berry, Sandra Bucci and Adam N. Danquah, along with an international selection of contributors, expertly explore how attachment theory can inform theoretical understanding of the development of psychosis, psychological therapy and mental health practice in service users with psychosis. In the first section of the book, contributors describe the application of attachment theory to the understanding of paranoia, voice-hearing, negative symptoms and relationship difficulties in psychosis. In the second section of the book, the contributors consider different approaches to working therapeutically with psychosis and demonstrate how these approaches draw on the key principles of attachment theory. In the final section, contributors address individual and wider organisation perspectives, including a voice-hearer perspective on formulating the relationship between voices and life history, how attachment principles can be used to organise the provision of mental health services, and the influence of mental health workers' own attachment experiences on therapeutic work. The book ends by summarising current perspectives and highlighting future directions.

Written by leading mental health practitioners and researchers, covering a diverse range of professional backgrounds, topics and theoretical schools, this book is significant in guiding clinicians, managers and commissioners in how attachment theory can inform everyday practice. *Attachment Theory and Psychosis: Current Perspectives and Future Directions* will be an invaluable resource for mental health professionals, especially psychologists and other clinicians focusing on humanistic treatments, as well as postgraduate students training in these areas.

Katherine Berry is a professor in clinical psychology at the University of Manchester, UK, and Co-Director of the Complex Trauma and Resilience Research Unit within Greater Manchester Mental Health NHS Foundation

Trust. She has carried out extensive research into the psychological and social causes of psychosis and has published a large body of work on attachment theory over the past decade. She is co-editor of *Attachment Theory in Adult Mental Health* with Adam N. Danquah (Routledge).

Sandra Bucci is a professor in clinical psychology at the University of Manchester, UK and Co-Director of the Complex Trauma and Resilience Research unit within Greater Manchester Mental Health NHS Foundation Trust. Her research is focused on understanding the putative psychological mechanisms involved in the development and maintenance of psychotic experiences.

Adam N. Danquah is a senior lecturer at the University of Manchester, UK, and practicing clinical psychologist and psychodynamic psychotherapist. As well as attachment, his research and teaching focus on intercultural approaches and helping practitioners and practitioners in training deal with the impact of patient care.

THE INTERNATIONAL SOCIETY FOR PSYCHOLOGICAL AND SOCIAL APPROACHES TO PSYCHOSIS BOOK SERIES

Series editors: Anna Lavis and Andrew Shepherd

Series advisor for the monograph strand: Andrew Moskowitz

ISPS's core aim is to promote psychological and social approaches to understanding and treating psychosis. Recognising the humanitarian and therapeutic potential of these perspectives, ISPS embraces a wide spectrum of therapeutic approaches from psychodynamic, systemic, cognitive and arts therapies, to need-adapted and dialogical approaches, family and group therapies and residential therapeutic communities. A further ambition is to draw together diverse viewpoints on psychosis and to foster discussion and debate across the biomedical and social sciences, including establishing meaningful dialogue with practitioners and researchers who are more familiar with biological-based approaches. Such discussion is now increasingly supported by empirical evidence of the interaction of genes and biology with the emotional and social environment especially in the fields of trauma, attachment, social relationships and therapy.

A global society active in at least 20 countries, ISPS is composed of a diverse range of individuals, networks and institutional members. Key to its ethos is that individuals with personal experience of psychosis, and their families and friends, are fully involved alongside practitioners and researchers, and that all benefit from this collaboration.

For more information about ISPS, email isps@isps.org or visit our website, www.isps.org.

ART THERAPY FOR PSYCHOSIS
Theory and Practice
Katherine Killick

CBT FOR PSYCHOSIS
Process-orientated Therapies and the Third Wave
Caroline Cupitt

PERSONAL EXPERIENCES OF PSYCHOLOGICAL THERAPY FOR PSYCHOSIS AND RELATED EXPERIENCES
Peter Taylor, Olympia Gianfrancesco and Naomi Fisher

THE INTERNATIONAL SOCIETY FOR PSYCHOLOGICAL AND SOCIAL APPROACHES TO PSYCHOSIS RESEARCH SERIES

Series advisor: Andrew Moskowitz

PSYCHOSIS, PSYCHOANALYSIS AND PSYCHIATRY
IN POSTWAR USA
On the borderland of madness
Orna Ophir

MEANING, MADNESS AND POLITICAL SUBJECTIVITY
A study of schizophrenia and culture in Turkey
Sadeq Rahimi

RECONCEPTUALIZING SCHIZOPHRENIA
A transcultural, phenomenological introduction to homelessness
Sarah Kamens

For more information about this series, please visit:
www.routledge.com/ISPS-Research/book-series/ISPS

ATTACHMENT THEORY AND PSYCHOSIS

Current Perspectives and Future Directions

Edited by Katherine Berry,
Sandra Bucci and Adam N. Danquah

Routledge
Taylor & Francis Group

LONDON AND NEW YORK

First published 2020
by Routledge
2 Park Square, Milton Park, Abingdon, Oxon OX14 4RN

and by Routledge
52 Vanderbilt Avenue, New York, NY 10017

Routledge is an imprint of the Taylor & Francis Group, an informa business

British Library Cataloguing-in-Publication Data
A catalogue record for this book is available from the British Library

Library of Congress Cataloging-in-Publication Data
A catalog record has been requested for this book

ISBN: 978-1-138-95674-2 (hbk)
ISBN: 978-1-138-95675-9 (pbk)
ISBN: 978-1-315-66557-3 (ebk)

Typeset in Times New Roman
by Newgen Publishing UK

KATHERINE: FOR JACOB, ETHAN AND
BENJAMIN

SANDRA: FOR JAMES AND SOPHIA

ADAM: FOR THE BOYS, PATRICK,
IVAN AND STANLEY

CONTENTS

CONTENTS

CONTENTS

FOREWORD

Written reports of studies often describe the demographic details of the sample: we tend to skim over them, but actually they tell us a very interesting and important story. They describe a group of people who are young at the onset of psychosis; who rarely marry or form long-term relationships; and whose adolescence is often characterised by interpersonal difficulty and social withdrawal. The disease model of psychosis casts these simply as epiphenomena of the developing disorder and, once psychosis is manifest, of the way persecutory and related delusions can undermine trust in others and how negative symptoms affect the capacity to form emotional bonds. Cure the psychosis and all this will go away.

Early applications of Bowlby's attachment theory to psychosis met with the same fate. The high level of *dismissing attachment* observed (up to 70%), where adults tend to deactivate emotions and attention to mental states of self and other, and prefer to keep others at a distance, was seen as a kind of collateral damage arising from a common neurobiological process; links unearthed between severity of psychotic symptoms and dismissive attachment, were viewed as hard evidence of this. Meanwhile in 'mainstream' attachment research early experience of child abuse, neglect and indifference had been robustly linked to the development of personality disorders, problems of affect regulation and interpersonal ambivalence or withdrawal.

I think there was a turning point in psychosis when Bowlby's attachment theory and its role in psychosis were rediscovered. I would trace it to the discovery of robust epidemiological gradients and social risk factors for psychosis. Here, population cohort studies showed repeatedly that child abuse, neglect, deprivation, inequality and social marginalisation are powerful risk factors for psychosis; and in populations with multiple such factors, the risk of psychosis is raised by a factor of 5 or more. These social risk factors are not specific to psychosis of course, but are shared with many affective disorders, first demonstrated in the classic studies of Brown and Harris (1978). This came full circle with the realisation that psychosis, far from being a 'non-affective' psychosis, is replete with affective disturbance, often of a long-standing nature, including depression, social anxiety disorder and PTSD.

In trying to make sense of this incongruent state of affairs, I proposed that there are several pathways to emotional dysfunction in psychosis (Birchwood, 2003) and in common with others, argued that insecure attachment is one mechanism. In early work, myself and others demonstrated that insecure attachment can have multiple consequences, including poor engagement with services and a 'sealing over' recovery style (Drayton, Birchwood and Trower, 1998; Tait, Birchwood and Trower, 2003).

The importance of attachment theory to understanding the complexities of psychosis (affective disturbance, personality disorders), the positive symptoms and 'table one' in research studies described above (marital status, social isolation etc.) is laid out in this outstanding edited volume. Leading researchers in attachment theory and psychosis, from centres in the UK and internationally, take us on an extraordinary journey from theory, links with psychosis and its risk factors, anomalous developmental trajectories through to innovative therapeutic approaches for psychosis and specific symptoms. [On a personal note, I was delighted and impressed to see how Berry, Bucci and colleagues have taken forward the cognitive model of voices using attachment theory to understand the subordinate relationship with 'omnipotent' voices].

CBT for psychosis is now into its second generation of studies, with greater emphasis on single symptoms and targeted mechanisms. In this book, we can see the *third generation* taking shape, involving greater attention to interpersonal processes, regulation of affect and exploration of the therapeutic opportunities that attachment theory can bring. Katherine Berry, Sandra Bucci and Adam N. Danquah are to be congratulated on their pioneering work and for bringing together world-leading authorities in this volume and showing us the future of psychotherapy for psychosis.

Max Birchwood,
Professor of Youth Mental Health
University of Warwick, UK
August 2018

References

Birchwood, M. (2003). Pathways to emotional dysfunction in first-episode psychosis. *British Journal of Psychiatry.* May; 182: 373–375.

Brown, G. & Harris, T. (1978). *Social Origins of Depression.* Tavistock: London.

Drayton, M., Birchwood, M. & Trower, P. (1998). Early attachment experience and recovery from psychosis. *British Journal of Clinical Psychology.* Sep; 37: 269–284.

Tait, L., Birchwood, M. & Trower, P. (2003). Predicting engagement with services for psychosis: insight, symptoms and recovery style. *British Journal of Psychiatry.* Feb; 182: 123–128.

1

INTRODUCTION

Katherine Berry, Sandra Bucci and Adam N. Danquah

Background

Attachment theory is a life span theory, which proposes that early relationships with significant others have a profound impact on later interpersonal relationships (Bowlby, 1969). The theory is based on the assumption that early experiences lead to the formation of what John Bowlby, the theory's founder, termed 'internal working models', consisting of mental representations of the self, others and relationships with those others. Individuals interpret experiences in light of these working models, which guide and influence the way they interact with, and behave towards, others. Attachment is embedded in the evolutionary need for safety and security (Bowlby, 1969). From an evolutionary perspective, caregiving relationships, and closeness to the caregiver in particular, ensure protection in a dangerous world, and thus promote safety and a felt sense of security. There is evidence that childhood experiences influence attachments to others in adult life, and that adult attachment style predicts social functioning, interpersonal difficulties and mental health (Bartholomew & Horowitz, 1991; Berry, Wearden, Barrowclough & Liversidge, 2006; Platts, Tyson & Mason, 2002).

Given the role of attachment in interpersonal functioning and mental health problems, a number of researchers have argued that attachment theory can help extend existing models and conceptualisations of psychosis (Berry, Wearden & Barrowclough, 2007; Gumley, Barker, Schwannauer & Lawrie, 2015; Korver-Nieberg et al., 2015; Read & Gumley, 2008; Berry & Bucci, 2016; Berry, Varese & Bucci, 2017). When asked about the relevance of attachment theory to understanding psychosis, Bowlby replied it, 'had nothing to contribute to schizophrenia' (Khar, 2012, p. 10). Whether this statement reflected the modesty of a man whose work is so central to the understanding of mental health and personality development or thinking from different times, it is clear that thinking has moved on within the field. The link between developmental adversity and psychosis is well established (Varese et al., 2012) and attachment has been identified as a key potential mediating factor in this relationship (Berry, Barrowclough, & Wearden, 2008; Read & Gumley, 2008).

The well-known attachment theorist Jeremy Holmes (personal communication) suggests that attachment theory can be an invaluable framework for conceptualising psychosis. He observed that the kinds of insecure attachment – i.e. dismissiveness, preoccupation and disorganisation – in their extreme form, can respectively tip into paranoia, confusion and fragmentation. With such a framework, we are moved from a description of symptoms to the developmental origin and relational function of otherwise inexplicable behaviour. Increasing understanding of the mediating role dissociation plays between psychosis and its traumatic origins (Pearce et al., 2017) is proving a particularly promising line of enquiry regarding the contribution of attachment, so closely tied are dissociative or psychotic phenomena and the processes of disorganised attachment (Liotti & Gumley, 2008).

Although the empirical evidence for the role of attachment difficulties in psychosis has lagged behind these theoretical speculations, over the past decade there has been an exceptional growth in research measuring attachment styles or patterns in psychosis. Studies show an association between insecure attachment and psychotic phenomena (Berry, Barrowclough & Wearden, 2008) and, moreover, that dismissing and disorganised patterns predominate (Harder, 2014). A number of hypotheses have been proposed to account for these relationships (e.g. Liotti & Gumley, 2008), though the area is still contested. What is now less controversial is the relational dimension to psychosis. Apart from contributing to re-humanising psychotic experience, more light is being shed on how to engage with people whose early attempts at connection have been thwarted and yet who – it is now clear – continue to try to connect all the same. In line with such understanding, there has been increased interest in using attachment theory to inform psychological therapies and mental health care more generally for people with psychosis. Given these developments, it is timely to synthesise and showcase current thinking in the field by drawing together theories, research findings and therapeutic work from a range of well-established researchers and clinicians. In this introductory chapter, we aim to provide an outline of the structure of the book and summarise the content of each chapter. Before doing so, we will describe the basic concepts of attachment theory in order to provide a context for the chapters that follow.

Basic concepts

Attachment relationships are distinguished from other types of social relationships in that there is a persistent and emotionally significant affectional bond, which is formed with a specific person, who is approached in times of distress. Theorists have suggested that caregivers' mental representations about their own childhood attachment experiences are important in influencing the quality of the attachment relationship formed with their own child (Main, Kaplan & Cassidy, 1985). Attachment relationships can be distinguished from other types of relationships and are defined in terms of both a desire for close proximity to the attachment figure and evidence of distress following involuntary separation (Bowlby, 1973; 1980; 1982; Weiss, 1991). Attachment behaviours are defined as any form of behaviour that results in the individual regaining or retaining contact with his or her attachment figure; such behaviours can be triggered by environmental threats, distress, illness, or fatigue (Bowlby, 1973; 1980; 1982). The attachment relationship is further hypothesised to provide a 'secure base', which enables one to engage in exploration, develop and gain independence (Ainsworth, Blehar, Waters & Wall, 1978).

Bowlby (1973; 1980; 1982) proposed that as a result of their interactions with caregivers during infancy and childhood, individuals develop mental representations of the self in relation to significant others and expectations about how others behave in social relationships. These working models are hypothesised to guide attention, interpretation, memory and predictions about future interpersonal interactions. They are characterised in terms of cognitive elements, which reflect beliefs about whether the individual him or herself is worthy of attention and whether other people are reliable, and also represent emotions associated with interpersonal experiences, such as happiness, fear and anger.

The Strange Situation procedure for assessing attachment security in infancy was crucial in providing empirical support for Bowlby's theory and measuring individual differences in the quality of attachment relationships. The procedure involves a laboratory-based observation of the infant's response to two brief separations from, and reunions with, his or her caregiver (Ainsworth et al., 1978). Responses are traditionally classified in terms of three patterns of behaviours: secure, insecure-avoidant and insecure-ambivalent. The different patterns of responses are hypothesised to relate to different attachment working models and methods of regulating distress (Ainsworth et al., 1978). The caregiver's sensitivity to distress appears to be a significant factor in determining attachment classification (Weinfield, Sroufe, Egeland & Carlson, 1999). In the case of insecure attachment, the child's emotions are ineffective in eliciting contingent responses in caregivers, so the child learns to either inhibit (avoidant attachment) or exaggerate their emotional needs and expressions (ambivalent attachment). The sensitivity of the caregiver has been associated with a number of factors including: his or her own mental health; sources of stress and support inside and outside the family (Belsky & Nezworski, 1988; Cummings & Cicchetti, 1990); his or her own attachment style (van Ijzendoorn, 1995); and infant characteristics, such as temperament (Rutter, 1995; Weinfield et al., 1999).

In addition to the three categories of attachment originally identified by Ainsworth, Main and Soloman (1986) noted that some infants displayed disorganised and disoriented responses to separation and reunion from caregivers that appeared contradictory and inconsistent with the 'organised' attachment patterns such as avoidant or ambivalent attachment. This disorganisation of the attachment system was conceptualised as the outcome of interactions in which the infant experiences the attachment figure as frightening, frightened, or dissociated in times of stress. The caregiver might act in ways that are confusing and unpredictable for the infant, rendering it difficult for them to develop an 'organised' pattern of self-protection. According to Liotti (2004), the infant experiences 'fright without solution' at being confronted with the biological paradox that the attachment figure, the primary source of safety and protection, is also the source of infant distress. There is evidence of associations between attachment disorganisation and parental maltreatment (Lyons-Ruth & Jacobvitz, 1999), but the development of a disorganised attachment pattern could also be influenced by more subtle (but frequent or pervasive) disruptions in parental attunement, possibly caused by a range of adverse conditions and circumstances (e.g. parental poor mental health, trauma and experiences of loss (Cyr, Euser, Bakermans-Kranenburg & van Ijzendoorn, 2010; Hesse & Main, 2006; Lyons-Ruth & Jacobvitz, 1999; van Ijzendoorn, 1995; 1999).

Bowlby emphasised that attachment is an integral part of human behaviour *'from the cradle to the grave'* (Bowlby, 1979, p. 208). In order to provide a clearer picture of the attachment literature and different models of adult attachment, which we know is complex, we present the different models in Table 1. The Table illustrates how the different categories of attachment style in adulthood developed by different theorists map onto each other, as well as attachment categories commonly described in the childhood literature.

The Adult Attachment Interview

Main and colleagues argued that individual differences in attachment in adulthood relate to the organisation of representations of earlier attachment figures and developed the Adult Attachment Interview (AAI; Main & Goldwyn, 1984) to measure attachment representations and the quality of caregiver-infant attachment relationships, or 'attachment states of mind'. The AAI is a semi-structured interview that focuses on parent-child relationships during childhood. It consists of around twenty questions and takes approximately an hour to complete. Questions focus on earlier experiences of being parented, including asking people to identify five adjectives to describe each parent. Individuals are assigned to one of three primary categories: secure-autonomous, dismissing, or preoccupied, on the basis of their descriptions of their relationships with parents, and the coherence of their narrative in terms of quality, quantity, relevance and manner of delivery (Crowell, Fraley & Shaver, 1999; Hesse, 1999). Individuals who fall in the dismissing and preoccupied categories are deemed to be insecure, while individuals who fall in the autonomous category are deemed to be secure. The narrative of securely attached individuals is characterised as coherent in that their description and

Table 1.1 Summary and comparison between different models of attachment

Authors associated with model or system of classifying attachment	Method of assessing attachment	Attachment patterns identified*				
		Secure	Ambivalent/Resistant	Avoidant	NA	Disorganised
Ainsworth et al., (1978) Main & Soloman (1986)	Strange Situation test in infancy A laboratory-based observation of the infant's response to two brief separations from, and reunions with, his or her caregiver	Children feel confident that the attachment figure will be available, responsive and helpful in such a way that the caregiver easily soothes them in times of distress. They also use their caregiver as a safe base to explore their environment. The child will feel positive and loved as their caregiver will present as 'sensitive' to the child's needs.	Children will exaggerate their needs and expressions towards the attachment figure, but will reject their attempts to engage and comfort. Children are unable to use caregivers as a secure base to explore novel surroundings. This is as a result of inconsistent responses from their caregiver at times of need, meaning the child is unable to develop feelings of attachment security.	Children are very independent of the caregiver in both the physical sense, when exploring the environment, and emotionally. They will not seek help from the caregiver and inhibit their emotional needs. The caregiver often presents as insensitive and not responsive to their needs due to withdrawing at distressing times or not being available.	NA	Children appear afraid of their caregiver who presents in a manner that is confusing and unpredictable for the child, therefore not facilitating an 'organised' pattern of self-protection. Children may display behaviours such as overt displays of fear; contradictory behaviours or affects occurring simultaneously or sequentially; stereotypic, asymmetric, misdirected or jerky movements; or freezing and apparent dissociation.

(continued)

Table 1.1 (Cont.)

Authors associated with model or system of classifying attachment	*Method of assessing attachment*	*Attachment patterns identified**				
Main & Goldwyn (1984)	Adult Attachment Interview in adulthood	*Autonomous*	*Preoccupied*	*NA*	*Dismissing*	*Unresolved*
	A semi-structured interview focusing on earlier experiences of being parented, including asking people to identify five adjectives to describe each parent.	Individuals have a coherent and collaborative narrative when discussing earlier attachment experiences. They may have had positive or negative childhood experiences, but hold an understanding perspective of their own and others contributions to such experiences.	Individuals may appear overwhelmed, confused and preoccupied with details of past attachment experiences without taking an objective perspective. Their narratives in describing attachment experiences often seem long, incoherent and unable to maintain focus, while sometimes seeming vague or angry.		The individual minimises or even fails to consider attachment experiences. When they actually provide details of such experiences, significant feelings are dismissed or are often short and generalised.	The individual's narrative is disorganised when discussing and reasoning about experiences concerning attachment loss or trauma. They may appear confused or unaware of the interview context by not completing sentences or changing to inappropriate tenses.

Authors associated with model or system of classifying attachment	Method of assessing attachment	Attachment patterns identified*				
Hazan & Shaver (1987)	Self-report measure in adulthood (e.g. 3-item Relationship Questionnaire)	*Secure* Individuals describe themselves as being comfortable with intimacy and able to depend on their partners. They also report high self-confidence, self-esteem and trust in others.	*Ambivalent/anxious* Individuals describe themselves as having a strong desire for closeness with and dependence on others. Their reported behaviour often consists of emotional highs and lows triggered by relationship experiences.	*Avoidant* Individuals describe feeling uncomfortable being close to others and difficulty trusting others.	*NA*	*NA*
Bartholomew (1990; 1997)	Self-report measures in adulthood (e.g. 4-item Relationship Questionnaire or Relationship Scales Questionnaire)	*Secure* Individuals report positive beliefs about the self and others, indicating a sense of worthiness and lovability. This includes an expectation that others are accepting and responsive in times of distress.	*Preoccupied* Individuals report negative beliefs about the self, but positive beliefs about others, indicating a sense of unworthiness but a positive evaluation of others. They report a tendency to strive for self-acceptance by gaining the acceptance of valued others.	*Dismissing* Individuals report positive beliefs about the self but negative beliefs about others, indicating a sense of self-worthiness with a negative disposition towards other people.	*Fearful* Individuals report negative beliefs about the self and others, indicating a sense of unworthiness and an expectation that others will be untrustworthy and rejecting.	*NA*

(continued)

Table 1.1 (Cont.)

Authors associated with model or system of classifying attachment	Method of assessing attachment	Attachment patterns identified*			
			They report a tendency to avoid close relationships, as they expect other people to be unavailable and insensitive.	NA	They report a tendency to avoid close relationship to protect themselves from anticipated rejection by others.
Fraley & Shaver (2000)	Self-report measures in adulthood (e.g. Experiences of Close Relationships Scale)	Secure: Low levels of both attachment anxiety and avoidance. Individuals have a secure attachment and appropriate thresholds for detecting the unavailability of the attachment figure and appropriately seek contact with attachment figures when needed.	Preoccupied: High levels of attachment Anxiety, but low levels of attachment avoidance. Individuals have a predominant anxious attachment style and low thresholds for detecting cues which signal the unavailability of the attachment figure. They will seek contact with attachment figures when stress is triggered.	Dismissing: High levels of attachment avoidance, but low levels of attachment anxiety. Individuals have a predominant avoidant attachment style and have high thresholds for detecting cues which signal the unavailability of the attachment figure. They will withdraw and attempt to cope with situations alone.	Fearful: High levels of both attachment anxiety and avoidance. Individuals have low thresholds for detecting cues which signal the unavailability of the attachment figure, but will withdraw and attempt to cope with situations alone.

* The patterns described within each column are conceptually similar to each other, although not synonymous.

evaluation of attachment-related experiences is consistent, whether experiences were favourable or unfavourable. Individuals who are classified as dismissing with respect to attachment minimise the significance of attachment-related experiences and their narrative is incoherent, with generalised representations of attachment history that are unsupported or contradicted. For example, individuals may describe their parent in global positive terms, but report instances of neglect or negative interactions. Individuals who are classified as being preoccupied with respect to attachment appear overwhelmed by attachment-related experiences and find it difficult to maintain focus or contain their responses to specific questions (Hesse, 1999). Adults can be assigned to a secondary attachment category, termed unresolved/disoriented, if, when prompted about experiences of loss or abuse, there is evidence of disorganisation or disorientation when discussing these experiences (Crowell et al., 1999). Evidence for a disorganised response to related questions includes: i) lapses in discourse, where the individual no longer appears appropriately aware of the interview context (e.g. silence mid-sentence, failing to finish the sentence, making no reference to the silence when resuming to speak); and ii) lapses in reasoning (e.g. speaking of a deceased person as though they still currently relate to them; Main et al., 2002). The AAI measure has good reliability and predictive validity (Hesse, 1999), but requires extensive training and is time consuming to administer and score (Crowell et al., 1999).

Self-report measures of attachment

Independent of the development of the AAI method to assessing and classifying attachment, social psychologists began to assess attachment styles through the use of self-report measures. This approach developed from the work of Hazan and Shaver (1987), who conceptualised romantic love as an attachment process and translated Ainsworth et al.'s (1978) three categories into three adult attachment styles: secure, ambivalent and avoidant attachment. Several multi-item continuous self-report measures have since been developed by various research groups (e.g. Collins & Read, 1990; Simpson, 1990; Collins, 1996; Simpson & Rholes, 1998).

One important development in the self-report tradition of attachment measurement was Bartholomew's attempt to integrate the two paradigms of attachment research (the AAI approach and the self-report approach; Bartholomew, 1990; 1997; Bartholomew & Horowitz, 1991; Bartholomew & Shaver, 1998). Bartholomew (1990) argued that Main and colleagues, and Hazan and Shaver, were measuring different types of avoidance, which were respectively motivated by defensive self-sufficiency and avoidance of rejection. Bartholomew's (1990; 1997) model incorporates both types of avoidance labelled as dismissing-avoidant and fearful-avoidant and describes four attachment prototypes (secure, preoccupied, dismissing and fearful). These prototypes are described in terms of positive and negative beliefs about self and others (see Figure 1.1). According to Bartholomew (1990; 1997), secure individuals are characterised in terms of positive beliefs about the self (such as "I am worthy", "I am loveable") and positive beliefs about others (such as "Other people are trustworthy", "Other people care about me"). Securely attached individuals are hypothesised to be comfortable with both autonomy and intimacy, and utilise others as a source of support in times of distress (Bartholomew, 1990; 1997). Preoccupied individuals are characterised by negative beliefs about the self and positive beliefs about others. This attachment style is hypothesised to develop as a result of inconsistent parenting, typified by over intrusiveness and overt expressions of devotion, followed by neglect. Individuals with preoccupied attachment styles are characterised as being highly focused on relationships, dependent on others, and are hypothesised to seek personal validation through gaining others' acceptance and approval (Bartholomew, 1990; 1997).

Individuals with both fearful and dismissing attachment styles are characterised as having negative beliefs about others as uncaring and unavailable, which develop as a result of consistent rejection from attachment figures and lead to subsequent avoidance of close relationships. However, according to Bartholomew's model, these individuals differ in terms of their own self-worth, with fearful individuals believing that they are unlovable and avoiding others due to a fear of rejection, and dismissing individuals believing that they are self-reliant and invulnerable to the rejection of others (Bartholomew, 1990; 1997).

In support of Bartholomew's model, the four prototypes are correlated with theoretically relevant variables relating to self-concept and interpersonal functioning, for example, both preoccupied and fearful attachment have been associated with low self-esteem and dismissive and fearful attachment have been associated with withdrawal from social relationships (Bartholomew & Horowitz, 1991). Despite the popularity of Bartholomew's model of attachment, it has also been criticised for excluding important individual differences in attachment. For example, the model has been criticised for characterising individual differences in attachment in terms of beliefs, and neglecting individual differences in affective and behavioural regulation processes (Crowell et al., 1999; Fraley & Shaver, 2000; Pietromonaco & Feldman Barrett, 2000).

In an attempt to address the above criticisms of Bartholomew's model, Fraley and Shaver (2000) developed an alternative model of adult attachment (Fraley & Shaver, 2000; Shaver, Gillath & Mikulincer, 2002a). Within this model, attachment is conceptualised in terms of two dimensions: attachment anxiety and attachment avoidance. Individuals can be scored on both dimensions and the combined scores from each continuum represent the person's attachment style. According to the model, one dimension or component of the attachment system involves monitoring the psychological proximity of the attachment figure and is related to individual differences in attachment anxiety. For example, individuals who are high in attachment anxiety are hyper vigilant to attachment-relevant cues, as the attachment figure is inconsistently available; individuals who are low in anxiety are less vigilant, as the attachment figure is perceived to be either available or irrelevant for personal safety. The model also proposes that the attachment system has a second component or dimension that is responsible for the regulation of attachment behaviour and is associated with individual differences on attachment avoidance. For example, to regulate attachment-related anxiety, individuals both withdraw and attempt to handle situations alone, or alternatively seek contact with the attachment figure (Crowell et al., 1999). The former avoidant strategy is associated with a history of consistent neglect or negative responses from attachment figures, and the latter non-avoidant strategy is associated with a history of obtaining positive responses from attachment figures or at least obtaining positive responses on some occasions. Fraley and Shaver (2000) argue that Bartholomew's (1990) four prototypes can be re-conceptualised in terms of two dimensions: attachment anxiety and avoidance. In terms of the 'attachment anxiety' component of the system, individuals with secure and dismissing attachment styles have high thresholds for detecting cues which signal the unavailability of the attachment figure, whereas individuals with preoccupied and fearful attachment styles have low thresholds for detecting such cues. In terms of the 'attachment avoidance' component of the system, they argue that individuals with secure and preoccupied attachment styles seek contact with attachment figures, while individuals with dismissing and fearful attachment styles withdraw and attempt to cope with situations alone. Within Fraley and Shaver's model, fearful attachment represents a breakdown in the use of avoidance or other forms of defence in the face of threat (Shaver, Gillath & Mikulincer, 2002a). This conceptualisation of fearful attachment has been criticised for failing to capture the dysregulation of the attachment system, which is a core feature of disorganised attachment in the Strange Situation in infancy and unresolved attachment on the AAI (George & West, 1999; Simpson & Rholes, 2002). However, as Shaver, Gillath & Mikulincer (2002b) point out, the model which depicts individuals with fearful attachment styles as both withdrawing from relationships, yet continuing to experience anxiety about the availability of attachment figures, helps to explain why a person might appear disorganised.

As the above summary suggests, there are a number of different ways of conceptualising and measuring attachment that make it difficult to hold a clear picture of the literature in mind and make comparisons between studies from different paradigms and with different measures. It must also be borne in mind that while the measurement of attachment has become a highly sophisticated, if contested field, the application of such measures to routine work is not unproblematic. Apart from the time and (sometimes) cost required for in-depth training, administration, scoring and interpretation, the research focus on classification may result in 'a failure to appreciate the complexity and depth of attachment processes as they are manifest within the clinical domain' (Slade, 2008, p. 91).

Clinical utility

Understanding the role of attachment in psychosis allows us to make the fundamental shift from treating psychosis to working with a person with pronounced interpersonal difficulties. The latter involves a focus on establishing safety, promoting emotional regulation and stability, working with the relational meaning of symptoms and the fundamental importance of the therapeutic relationship as the agent of therapeutic change. These are easy things to say, but not so easy to uphold in the context of fear, mistrust, confusion and the realities of social inequality and deprivation. Interpersonal trauma leaves a terrible legacy and the work to engage with and change the damaging patterns of relating that people are left with is certainly demanding and sometimes demoralising. In order to provide thoughtful and safe care for the service user, the clinician has to ensure his or her own mental health is being looked after, such can be the impact of the work. Much of this book, then, is about how trauma can be contained by and explored safely within the context of therapeutic relationships. There is, moreover, also a recognition that such a relationship is affected by organisational and sociocultural contexts, which have to be engaged with as part of the work.

Outline of book

This volume of chapters addresses how attachment theory can inform theoretical understandings of the development of psychosis, psychological therapy and mental health practice with service users with psychosis. The first part of the book describes the application of attachment theory to the understanding of paranoia, voice-hearing, negative symptoms and relationship difficulties in adulthood, including social relationships more generally and parenting in particular. This section of the book concludes with a chapter summarising the neurobiological basis of the attachment system and how disturbances in this system might increase the risk of developing psychosis. The second part of the book considers different approaches to working therapeutically with symptoms of psychosis and demonstrates how these approaches draw on the key principles of attachment theory in terms of assessment, formulation and intervention. Therapeutic approaches that are considered include psychodynamic therapy, cognitive behavioural interpersonal therapy, cognitive analytic therapy, compassion-focused therapy and cognitive-behavioural family work. The final chapters in the third part address wider systemic issues, such as voice-hearer perspectives on formulating the relationship between voices and life history and show how attachment principles can be used to inform the organisation and provision of mental health services, and demonstrate the influence of mental health workers' own attachment experiences. The contributors throughout the book are all mental health practitioners and researchers who have studied the clinical applications of attachment theory to psychosis and routinely apply the theory in their own clinical or research work.

In Chapter 2, Richard Bentall and Katarzyna Sitko consider the role of attachment in paranoid delusions, perhaps the most common symptom of psychosis. In the authors' recent research, different social risk factors in childhood have been found to be associated with different kinds of psychotic experiences in adulthood, with attachment threatening events such as being raised in a children's home and emotional neglect specifically associated with paranoia. Also, in healthy participants stratified for psychotic experiences, the authors have found that insecure attachment styles are specifically associated with paranoid symptoms. Experiences of victimisation are also associated with paranoia, as is exposure in adulthood to harsh inner-city environments. The authors present these findings and propose that insecure attachment experiences in childhood lead to sensitisation to threatening environments, and the consequent over-anticipation of threat that is the defining feature of paranoia. In doing so, the authors will argue that this process involves a dysfunction of a threat-avoidance mechanism.

Similarly to Chapter 2, Chapter 3 focuses on the experience of voice hearing, another commonly reported and potentially distressing symptom of psychosis. Katherine Berry, Sandra Bucci, Filippo Varese and John Read begin the chapter with an overview of a cognitive model of voice-hearing, which proposes that the way individuals appraise their voices influences their emotional and behavioural reactions to these experiences. This is followed by a discussion of studies exploring the role of trauma and insecure attachment in relation to voice-hearing, including longitudinal research suggesting that childhood adversity plays a causal role in the development of voices. The chapter then presents the traumagenic neurodevelopmental model of psychosis and the cognitive attachment model of voices (CAV). The traumagenic neurodevelopmental model of psychosis integrates the biological and psychological sequelae of early adversity in relation to psychosis through highlighting the similarities between brain abnormalities of abused children and adults who receive a diagnosis of schizophrenia. The CAV model integrates cognitive, dissociative and attachment processes to explain the maintenance and development of distressing voices. The proposed CAV model emphasises how attachment theory and the concept of disorganised attachment in particular can enhance the cognitive conceptualisation of voice-hearing. The chapter concludes by outlining clinical implications of theories of attachment and voice-hearing.

Although psychosis has typically been characterised by positive symptoms such as delusions and hallucinations, longitudinal studies have shown that negative symptoms, such as avolition-apathy, anhedonia and asociality can be evident very early in the course of psychosis and for a significant number of people these symptoms can predate psychosis onset by a considerable margin. In Chapter 4, Helen Griffiths and Hamish McLeod argue that developmental risk factors that modify the likelihood of negative symptom expression are beginning to be understood and it seems that early relational and interpersonal environments have a distinct influence. This chapter reviews evidence addressing the early developmental pathways that may contribute to negative symptom development with a particular emphasis on mentalisation, meta-cognition and the differential expression of attachment states of mind. This provides a platform for discussing and integrating more complex and multi-faceted accounts of negative symptom development, expression and maintenance. From within this framework, the authors consider the limitations of pure deficit models of negative symptoms. Contemporary models of negative symptoms are examined and a case is made for elaborating these to incorporate attachment theory concepts and processes in treatment formulations.

Difficulties in social relations are one of the hallmarks of psychosis. In Chapter 5, Jasper Palmier-Claus, Nikie Korver-Nieberg, Anne-Kathrin Fett and Shannon Couture outline the importance of social and interpersonal functioning in psychosis, including decreased social networks and difficulties in engagement with services. The authors highlight the importance of social cognition in psychosis and propose that social cognition is a potential mediating concept between insecure attachment and social functioning outcomes. The chapter summarises research investigating attachment and social relationships in psychosis in addition to the emerging literature examining attachment and social cognitive processes. The chapter concludes with a case example illustrating how attachment theory can be used to understand social withdrawal and disengagement from services in the context of psychosis.

In Chapter 6, Susanne Harder and Kirstine Davidsen build on the previous chapter on social relationships to focus on how a person's own attachment history affects their parenting capacities. The chapter starts with a theoretical introduction to the field of parenting in people with mental health problems and psychosis from an attachment perspective, focusing on theories of the impact of parental mental illness, parental attachment, caregiving representation and parent-infant interaction. Following this, the authors summarise empirical knowledge of parenting in psychosis and infant outcomes. The authors argue that the attachment approach has rarely been applied to empirical studies of parenting and child development in psychosis. The chapter ends with a focus on preventive interventions to support families where the mother has psychosis. Several studies indicate that it is possible to improve parenting skills in these families by provision of practical parenting support and focusing on improving the relationship between parent and infant.

In the seventh and concluding chapter of the first theoretical section of the book, Benjamin Brent, Martin Debbané and Peter Fonagy present the neuro-biological basis of the attachment system. The chapter begins by reviewing the neural underpinnings of the attachment system. This is followed by a discussion of how disruptions within the neural circuitry mediating attachment might interact with the neurobiology of the symptoms and social cognitive deficits of psychosis. Finally, the authors present the therapeutic implications of the neurobiological interconnections between disturbances of the attachment system and the phenomenology of 'schizophrenia'.

In the second section of the book, Chapter 8 focuses on psychodynamic approaches to working with people who experience psychosis. Alison Summers and Gwen Adshead begin this chapter by arguing that, from Bowlby's perspective, attachment theory was an offshoot of a branch of psychodynamic theory but in relation to therapy with psychosis, attachment theory and psychodynamic theory can inappropriately be seen as separate and distinct. The authors use an object relations model to describe how attachment theory relates to some contemporary psychodynamic thinking on the nature and development of psychosis, especially in relation to supporting recovery and therapy for psychosis. The authors include a clinical vignette to illustrate how supportive psychodynamic psychotherapy (SPP) may address attachment related difficulties in someone experiencing psychosis. They propose that there is much common ground between attachment theory and psychodynamic therapy and conclude that there is a strong case for greater dialogue between the two perspectives.

In Chapter 9, Angus MacBeth, Andrew Gumley and Matthias Schwannauer present a summary of the key components of their Cognitive Interpersonal Therapy for Psychosis. The authors' formulation-driven approach is grounded in a developmental perspective on help-seeking and adaptation to psychosis. The authors argue that integral to this model is the importance of understanding attachment as the developmental context in which the individual's understanding of self and others emerges. This in turn creates the psychological architecture implicated in cognitive and interpersonal responses to the experience of both onset and relapse in psychosis. The authors describe how Cognitive Interpersonal Therapy aims to support adaptation and self-reorganisation after acute psychosis, taking into account the effect of attachment organisation and disorganisation. The chapter outlines current theoretical and empirical evidence supporting key components of the model and illustrates the therapeutic principles through a case vignette.

The tenth chapter focuses on cognitive analytic therapy (CAT), which is widely used in the UK for a range of difficulties, including depression, anxiety and personality disorder-type problems. More recently, there has also been a growing interest in the use of CAT for individuals with experiences of psychosis. Peter Taylor and Claire Seddon argue that CAT is an integrative model of psychotherapy, which draws from a variety of sources including object relations theory, social developmental theory and cognitive theory. The authors propose that CAT and attachment theory approaches to therapy share a number of common elements, including a focus on early interpersonal relationships in shaping the way an individual perceives and interacts with their social world. Nonetheless, they highlight that there is some debate about the extent to which attachment theory and CAT can be integrated and some argue that important distinctions remain between these frameworks. The chapter draws on case material to illustrate the CAT approach with someone with experience of psychosis and concludes that CAT may be a particularly helpful way of applying some of the principles of attachment theory to individuals with psychosis.

In Chapter 11, Charles Heriot-Maitland and Angela Kennedy present compassion-focused therapy for psychosis. They argue that compassion-focused therapy is an integrative therapeutic model, which harnesses the person's own caring motivations towards themselves and builds resilience through the application of scientific knowledge regarding neurobiological regulation. The chapter outlines the relevance of attachment processes and socially-related emotional learning to psychotic presentations. The authors highlight the value of a compassionate focus to work with psychosis and report on the principles of the approach with this client group. They use a case example to illustrate a compassion-focused approach to working with someone with psychosis and difficulties in attachment relationships.

Chapter 12 focuses on the importance of considering cultural factors in attachment-based therapeutic work and specifically focuses on family work with those from African-Caribbean backgrounds to illustrate an example. Amy Degnan, Lucy Shattock and Dawn Edge present strong evidence for the increased rates of psychosis amongst African-Caribbean people in the UK and outline psychological and social theories for this phenomenon including attachment theory. The authors then highlight the potential importance of family work in building supportive social ties for this group and present a case illustration that highlights how an attachment lens helps to understand the development of psychosis and problematic relating to services.

Chapter 13 focuses on a voice-hearer perspective to formulating the relationship between voices and life history. In this chapter, Eleanor Longden and Dirk Corstens describe a method of psychological formulation to explore the relationship between the content and characteristics of voices and experienced adversity in the life of the voice-hearer. They argue that this systematic process of enquiry, termed 'a construct' by Marius Romme and Sandra Escher, is designed to explore who or what might the voices represent in terms of social, emotional and/or attachment-related conflicts. They go on to describe how the resulting information provides the basis for an individualised psychotherapeutic recovery plan that examines the influence of interpersonal stress in creating vulnerability for emotional crises (i.e., psychological predisposition) and the personally significant events that cluster before onset or relapse (i.e., the actual stressors which provoke voice onset or continuance). The authors present case material using this method, as well as empirical research on the applicability of this approach. The role of safe attachment relationships in supporting voice hearers is also considered, including: the therapeutic alliance and family and peer-support. Recommendations are also made for how mental health services can be structured to better establish safe, healing environments and a 'secure base' for working with distressing voices.

The majority of chapters within the book focus on using ideas within psychotherapy. In Chapter 14, Sandra Bucci, Katherine Berry, Adam N. Danquah and Lucy Johnstone argue that attachment theory also provides a useful framework to inform the design and delivery of general mental health services. The authors describe how attachment theory should inform service policy and evaluation, decisions regading referrals and discharge, the process of assessment and formulation, the delivery and form of psychological interventions, and support services and mechanisms for staff and informal carers.

In Chapter 15, the final chapter of the book, Mark Linington highlights the importance of considering the mental health worker's own attachment experiences and how these play out in therapeutic encounters. The author provides a case vignette from his own clinical practice, which illustrates how his own attachment history shaped therapy with a client with psychosis and how he managed the consequent emotional and behavioural responses.

In the concluding chapter, we as editors draw together material from the preceding chapters and conclude by summarising key implications for clinical practice, health service policy and future research.

References

Ainsworth, M. D. S., Blehar, M. C., Waters, E., & Wall, S. (1978). *Patterns of Attachment: A Psychological Study of the Strange Situation.* Oxford, England: Lawrence Erlbaum.

Bartholomew, K. (1990). Avoidance of intimacy: an attachment perspective. *Journal of Social and Personal Relationships, 7*(2), 147–178. Doi: https://doi.org/10.1177/0265407590072001

Bartholomew, K. & Horowitz, L. M. (1991). Attachment styles among young adults: a test of a four-category model. *Journal of Personality and Social Psychology, 61*(2), 226–244. Doi: http://dx.doi.org/10.1037/0022-3514.61.2.226

Bartholomew, K. (1997). Adult Attachment processes: individual and couple perspectives. *British Journal of Medical Psychology, 70*(30), 249–263. Doi:10.1111/j.2044-8341.1997.tb01903.x

Bartholomew, K., & Shaver, P. R. (1998). Methods of assessing adult attachment: Do they converge? In J. A. Simpson & W. S. Rholes (Eds.) *Attachment Theory and Close Relationships.* New York, USA: Guildford.

Belsky, J., & Nezworski, T. (1988). Clinical Implications of Attachment. *Child Psychology. Clinical Implications of Attachment.* New Jersey, USA: Lawrence Erlbaum Associates, Inc.

Berry, K., Barrowclough, C., & Wearden, A. (2008). Attachment theory: a framework for understanding symptoms and interpersonal relationships in psychosis. *Behaviour Research and Therapy, 46*(12), 1275–1282. Doi: https://doi.org/10.1016/j.brat.2008.08.009

Berry, K. & Bucci, S. (2016). What does attachment theory tell us about working with distressing voices? *Psychosis, 8*(1), 60–71. Doi: 10.1080/17522439.2015.1070370

Berry, K., Varese, F., & Bucci, S. (2017). Cognitive Attachment Model of Voices: Evidence base and future implications. *Frontiers in Psychiatry.* Doi: https://doi.org/10.3389/fpsyt.2017.00111

Berry, K., Wearden, A., & Barrowclough, C. (2007). Adult attachment styles and psychosis: an investigation of associations between general attachment styles and attachment relationships with specific others. *Social Psychiatry and Psychiatric Epidemiology, 42*(12), 972–976. Doi: https://doi.org/10.1007/s00127-007-0261-5

Berry, K., Wearden, A., Barrowclough, C., & Liversidge, T. (2006). Attachment styles, interpersonal relationships and psychotic phenomena in a non-clinical student sample. *Personality and Individual Differences, 41*(4), 707–718. Doi: https://doi.org/10.1016/j.paid.2006.03.009

Bowlby, J. (1969). *Attachment and Loss* (2nd ed.) New York: Basic Books.

Bowlby, J. (1973). *Attachment and Loss: Volume II, Separation Anxiety and Anger.* New York, USA: Basic Books.

Bowlby, J. (1980). *Attachment and Loss: Volume III, Loss, Sadness and Depression.* New York, USA: Basic Books.

Bowlby, J. (1982). Attachment and loss: retrospect and prospect. *American Journal of Orthopsychiatry, 52,* 664–678. Doi:10.1111/j.1939-0025.1982.tb01456.x

Cicchetti, D. and Toth, S. L. (2016). Child maltreatment and developmental psychopathology: a multilevel perspective. Retrieved from: https://onlinelibrary.wiley.com/doi/pdf/10.1002/9781119125556.devpsy311

Collins, N. L. & Read, S. J. (1990). Adult attachment, working models, and relationship quality in dating couples. *Journal of Personality and Social Psychology, 58*(4), 644–663. Retrieved from: https://labs.psych.ucsb.edu/collins/nancy/UCSB_Close_Relationships_Lab/Publications_files/Collins%20and%20Read,%201990.pdf

Collins, N. L. (1996). Working models of attachment: implications for explanation, emotion, and behavior. *Journal of Personality and Social Psychology, 71*(4), 810–832. Retrieved from: https://pdfs.semanticscholar.org/8c13/e4de36a71cd354b06295ea8a2823d5189d20.pdf

Crowell, J. A., Fraley, R. C., & Shaver, P. R. (1999). Measurement of individual differences in adolescent and adult attachment. In J. Cassidy & P. R. Shaver (Eds.), *Handbook of Attachment: Theory, Research, and Clinical Applications* (pp. 434–465). New York, USA: The Guilford Press.

Cummings, E. M., & Cicchetti, D. (1990). Toward a transactional model of relations between attachment and depression. In M. T. Greenberg, D. Cicchetti, & E. M. Cummings (Eds.), *The John D. and Catherine T. MacArthur Foundation series on Mental Health and Development. Attachment In the Preschool Years: Theory, Research, and Intervention* (pp. 339–372). Chicago, IL: University of Chicago Press.

Cyr, C., Euser, E. M., Bakermans-Kranenburg, M. J., & van Ijzendoorn, M. H. (2010). Attachment security and disorganization in maltreating and high-risk families: a series of meta-analyses. *Development and Psychopathology, 22*(1), 87–108. Doi: 10.1017/S0954579409990289.

Fraley, R. C., & Shaver, P. R. (2000). Adult romantic attachment: theoretical developments, emerging controversies, and unanswered questions. *Review of General Psychology, 4,* 132–154.

Gumley, A., Barker V., Schwannauer, M., & Lawrie, S. (2015). An integrated biopsychosocial model of childhood maltreatment and psychosis. *British Journal of Psychiatry, 206*(3), 177–180. Doi: 10.1192/bjp.bp.113.143578

Hazan, C., & Shaver, P. (1987). Romantic love conceptualized as an attachment process. *Journal of Personality and Social Psychology, 52*(3), 511–524.

Hesse, E. (1999). The Adult Attachment interview: historical and current perspectives. In J. Cassidy & P. R. Shaver (Eds.), *Handbook of Attachment: Theory, Research, and Clinical Applications* (pp. 395–433). New York, NY: The Guilford Press.

Hesse, E., & Main, M. (2006). Frightened, threatening, and dissociative parental behavior in low-risk samples: description, discussion, and interpretations. *Development and Psychopathology, 18*(2), 309–343. Doi: 10.1017/S0954579406060172

Korver-Nieberg, N., Berry, K., Meijer, C., de Haan, L., & Ponizovsky, A. M. (2015). Associations between attachment and psychopathology dimensions in a large sample of patients with psychosis. *Psychiatry Research, 228*(1). Doi: https://doi.org/10.1016/j.psychres.2015.04.018

Liotti, G. (2004). Trauma, dissociation, and disorganized attachment: three strands of a single braid. *Psychotherapy: Theory, Research, Practice, Training, 41*(4), 472–486. Doi: http://dx.doi.org/10.1037/0033-3204.41.4.472

Liotti, G., & Gumley, A. (2008). An attachment perspective on schizophrenia: the role of disorganized attachment, dissociation and mentalization. In A. Moskowitz, I. Schäfer, & M. J. Dorahy (Eds.), *Psychosis, Trauma and Dissociation: Emerging Perspectives on Severe Psychopathology* (pp. 117–133). Doi: http://dx.doi.org/10.1002/9780470699652.ch9

Main, M., & Goldwyn, R. (1984). Predicting rejection of her infant from mother's representation of her own experience: implications for the abused-abusing intergenerational cycle. *Child Abuse & Neglect, 8*(2), 203–217. Doi: http://dx.doi.org/10.1016/0145-2134(84)90009-7

Main, M., Goldwyn, R., & Hesse, E. (2002). *An Adult Attachment Classification and Rating System.* Unpublished Manual. University of California, Berkeley.

Main, M., Kaplan, N., & Cassidy, J. (1985). Security in infancy, childhood, and adulthood: A move to the level of representation. *Monographs of the Society for Research in Child Development, 50*(1–2), 66–104. Doi: http://dx.doi.org/10.2307/3333827

Main, M., & Solomon, J. (1986). Discovery of an insecure-disorganized/disoriented attachment pattern. In T. B. Brazelton & M. W. Yogman (Eds.), *Affective Development in Infancy* (pp. 95–124). Westport, CT: Ablex Publishing.

Mikulincer, M., Gillath, O., & Shaver, P. R. (2002). Activation of the attachment system in adulthood: threat-related primes increase the accessibility of mental representations of attachment figures. *Journal of Personality and Social Psychology, 83*(4), 881–895. Doi: http://dx.doi.org/10.1037/0022-3514.83.4.881

Palmier-Claus, J., Berry, K., Darrell-Berry, H., Emsley, R., Parker, S., Drake, R., & Bucci, S. (2016). Childhood adversity and social sunctioning in psychosis: exploring clinical cnd cognitive mediators. *Psychiatry Research, 238,* 25–32. Doi: https://doi.org/10.1016/j.psychres.2016.02.004

Pietromonaco, P. R., & Barrett, L. F. (2000). Attachment Theory as an orrganizing framework: a view from different levels of analysis. *Review of General Psychology*, *4*(2), 107–110. Doi: http://dx.doi.org/10.1037/1089-2680.4.2.107

Platts, H., Tyson, M., & Mason, O. (2002). Adult attachment style and core beliefs: Are they linked? *Clinical Psychology & Psychotherapy*, *9*(5), 332–348. Doi: http://dx.doi.org/10.1002/cpp.345

Read, J. & Gumley, A. (2008). Can attachment theory help explain the relationship between childhood adversity and psychosis? *Attachment: New Directions in Psychotherapy and Relational Psychoanalysis*, *2*, 1–35.

Rutter, M. (1995). Clinical implications of attachment concepts: retrospect and prospect. *Journal of Child Psychology and Psychiatry*, *36*, 549–571. Doi: 10.1111/j.1469–7610.1995.tb02314.x

Simpson, J. A. (1990). Influence of attachment styles on romantic relationships. *Journal of Personality and Social Psychology*, *59*(5), 971–980. Doi: http://dx.doi.org/10.1037/0022-3514.59.5.971

Simpson, J. A., & Rholes, W. S. (2002). Fearful-avoidance, disorganization, and multiple working models: some directions for future theory and research. *Attachment & Human Development*, *4*(2), 223–229. Doi: http://dx.doi.org/10.1080/14616730210154207

Simpson, J. A., & Rholes, W. S. (Eds.) (1998). *Attachment Theory and Close Relationships*. New York, USA: Guilford Press.

Slade, A. (2008). The implications of attachment theory and research for adult psychotherapy: research and clinical perspectives. In J. Cassidy & P. R. Shaver (Eds.), *Handbook of Attachment: Theory, Research, and Clinical Applications* (pp. 762–782). New York, USA: The Guilford Press.

Varese, F., Smeets, F., Drukker, M., Lieverse, R., Lataster, T., Viechtbauer, W., Read, R., van Os, J., & Bentall, P. (2012). Childhood adversities increase the risk of psychosis: a meta-analysis of patient-control, prospective- and cross-sectional cohort studies. *Schizophrenia Bulletin*, *38*(4), 661–671. Doi: 10.1093/schbul/sbs05

van Ijzendoorn, M. H. (1995). Adult attachment representations, parental responsiveness, and infant attachment: a meta-analysis on the predictive validity of the Adult Attachment Interview. *Psychological Bulletin*, *117*(3) 387–403. Doi: 10.1037/0033-2909.117.3.387.

van Ijzendoorn, M. H., Schuengel, C., & Bakermans-Kranenburg, T. (1999). Disorganized attachment in early childhood: meta-analysis of precursors, concomitants, and sequelae. *Development and Psychopathology*, *11*(2), 225–249. Retrieved from: www.ncbi.nlm.nih.gov/pubmed/16506532

Weinfield, N. S., Sroufe, L. A., Egeland, B., & Carlson, E. A. (1999). The nature of individual differences in infant–caregiver attachment. In J. Cassidy & P. R. Shaver (Eds.), *Handbook of Attachment: Theory, Research, and Clinical Applications* (pp. 68–88). New York, USA: The Guilford Press.

Weiss, R. S. (1991). The attachment bond in childhood and adulthood. In C. M. Parkes, J. Stevenson-Hinde, & P. Marris (Eds.), *Attachment Across the Life Cycle* (pp. 66–76). New York, USA: Tavistock/Routledge.

West, M. & George, C. (1999). Abuse and violence in intimate adult relationships: new perspectives from Attachment Theory. *Attachment & Human Development*, *1*(2), 137–156, Doi: 10.1080/14616739900134201

Part I

SYMPTOMS, FUNCTIONING AND AETIOLOGY

2

THE SPECIFIC ROLE OF INSECURE ATTACHMENT IN PARANOID DELUSIONS

Richard P. Bentall and Katarzyna Sitko

In the half century since the British psychiatrist John Bowlby (1965, 1969) first began to articulate his ideas about the developmental impact of early relationships between infants and caregivers, attachment theory has developed into a powerful conceptual framework for understanding the interplay between interpersonal processes and emotional adjustment in later life. Although recent applications of attachment theory have focused on a range of psychotic phenomena, in this chapter, we make the case that attachment processes are particularly important in the case of one specific type of psychotic experience, namely paranoid (persecutory) delusions. Our argument falls into four parts. First, we briefly review the scientific literature on psychiatric taxonomy (the classification of psychiatric symptoms and disorders) in order to suggest that it is unlikely that the same psychological processes are implicated in all of the symptoms of psychosis, which is, after all, a highly heterogeneous phenomenon. Second, we review existing psychological models of paranoia, which implicate core negative beliefs about the self and others in the onset and maintenance of persecutory beliefs. In the third section we examine studies that show specific associations between insecure attachment styles and paranoia. Finally, we review epidemiological studies, which suggest that attachment-disrupting experiences in early life are specifically associated with the development of paranoid beliefs in adulthood.

The picture that emerges is of a developmental pathway that leads from attachment adversity in early childhood to paranoia in adult life (although we, of course, acknowledge that factors other than attachment affect this pathway, and also that attachment processes may impact – either directly or indirectly – on other types of psychotic experience).

The place of paranoia in the psychosis spectrum

The heterogeneity of psychosis

According to conventional diagnostic criteria such as those in the American Psychiatric Association's Diagnostic and Statistical Manual (APA, 2013) or the

World Health Organization's International Classification of Disease (WHO, 1992), people who experience psychotic symptoms such as hallucinations and delusions most commonly receive diagnoses within the schizophrenia spectrum, such as schizophrenia, schizoaffective disorder or delusional disorder. However, these symptoms are by no means restricted to these diagnoses and are also sometimes reported, for example, by people diagnosed as suffering from bipolar disorder or major depression (Goodwin & Jamison, 2007; Lattuada et al., 1999) or, indeed, sometimes by people who do not meet the criteria for a psychiatric disorder according to conventional diagnostic criteria.

This kind of symptom overlap is one reason why diagnostic categories within the psychosis spectrum have long been contested (Bentall, 2003). Another reason is the poor reliability of psychiatric diagnoses, which has not improved with the publication of the most recent diagnostic manuals (Regier et al., 2013). In an attempt to resolve these problems, increasingly sophisticated analytical techniques have been brought to bear in the hope of discovering the true structure of psychopathology (see Bentall, 2014). The idea behind this approach is to use methods such as confirmatory factor analysis (Brown, 2006) to examine the extent to which different symptoms co-occur, and to thereby identify naturally occurring patterns of symptoms that potentially indicate underlying disorders. However, this research in so-called empirical taxonomy has yielded complex findings, which offer no hope for those who would like to divide psychiatric conditions into discrete diagnostic categories.

Those studies which have focused on the comorbidity between conventional diagnoses (the extent to which, for example, an individual with a diagnosis of schizophrenia is likely to meet the criteria for other diagnoses such as bipolar disorder or depression) suggest that there are just three major spectra of psychiatric phenomena: the internalising disorders involving moods such as depression and anxiety, externalising disorders associated with impulsive and antisocial behaviour, and a single psychosis syndrome (Kotov et al., 2011; Wright et al., 2013). On the other hand, factor-analytic studies of symptoms in the psychosis spectrum which seek to identify underlying subgroups of symptoms have converged on five independent symptom dimensions of positive symptoms (hallucinations and delusions), negative symptoms (such as avolition and flat affect), cognitive disorganisation, depression and mania (Emsley et al., 2003). It has recently become apparent that these two models can be reconciled in a hierarchical structure (known as a bifactor model), which combines a superordinate psychosis syndrome and the five dimensions (Reininghaus et al., 2015; Reininghaus et al., 2013; Shevlin et al., 2016). In this kind of model, symptom expression is the product of the latent (or underlying) processes responsible for the five symptom dimensions identified using conventional factor-analytic techniques, and a general psychosis factor that, independently of the factors underlying the five dimensions, influences all psychotic symptoms.

The picture that emerges from this kind of research suggests that psychosis is a highly heterogeneous phenomenon that will defy any single explanatory model. Furthermore, the dimensional and bi-factor models of psychosis have two common features that are particularly important in the present context. First, it seems clear that the positive symptoms occur relatively independently of symptoms belonging to the other dimensions of psychosis (whether or not a person has hallucinations or delusions is a weak predictor of whether they experience negative symptoms, for example) and, second, one of the most consistent findings from empirical taxonomy is that hallucinations and delusions often occur together.

The close association between delusions and hallucinations bears careful consideration. Although it is tempting to assume that the co-occurrence of these two symptoms implies that they are the consequence of common causal processes, it seems unlikely that this is the case. Symptoms can coalesce into syndromes as a consequence of networks of causal pathways between symptoms (so that one symptom leads to another, which leads to another, and so on) rather than because they are caused by the same underlying disease process (Borsboom & Cramer, 2013). It seems likely that some of these causal influences are bidirectional. In the case of hallucinations and delusions, for example, it has been suggested that some delusions arise as a consequence of efforts to explain anomalous (including hallucinatory) experiences (Maher, 1988) but also that beliefs and expectations about the nature of reality play a role in the generation of hallucinatory experiences (Al-Issa, 1995; Haddock et al., 1995). Hence, the occurrence of either one of these symptoms is likely to increase the probability that the other will be experienced (Bentall, 2003).

It has been reported that, in people with first-episode psychosis, delusions sometimes occur in the absence of hallucinations but that hallucinations in the absence of delusions are very rare (Compton et al., 2012). Moreover, in a large experience sampling study (in which people diagnosed with psychosis were asked about their experiences at multiple time points over several days), it was found that the onset of hallucinations was typically preceded by an increase in paranoid thinking (Oorschot et al., 2012). Hence, it seems likely that the causal path leading from delusional thinking to hallucinations is stronger than the path leading from hallucinations to delusions.

This analysis has the important implication that, when we isolate the psychological mechanisms involved in the different symptoms of psychosis, we should expect them to be different, so that, for example, attachment processes are likely to be more important in some symptoms than others. Given the interpersonal nature of paranoid delusions and the mistrust of others that is a central feature of this kind of belief (see below), it seems likely that these processes may play an especially important role in this symptom.

A second important implication follows from the common co-occurrence of delusions and hallucinations: when attempting to understand the role of attachment or any other kind of psychological process in either of these two symptoms it will be important to use appropriate statistical techniques to take this co-occurrence into account. We would argue that the failure to do so might result in misleading findings.

The paranoid continuum

The term 'paranoia' is used clinically, and also in everyday language, to describe the tendency of some individuals to irrationally believe themselves to be the victim of persecution by others. In delusional form, it is perhaps the most common symptom of psychosis (Brakoulias & Starcevic, 2008; Moutoussis et al., 2007). However, epidemiological research has revealed that paranoid beliefs are also quite common in the general population. For example, in the Dunedin birth cohort study, which followed 1000 New Zealand children into adulthood, 12 per cent were judged to show some evidence of paranoia when assessed in their mid-twenties (Poulton et al., 2000). Perhaps for this reason, many researchers have tried to formulate criteria for distinguishing between the delusional beliefs of people diagnosed with mental health problems and other kinds of tenaciously held beliefs and attitudes with similar content. For example, the phenomenologist Karl Jaspers, (1913/1963), noted that the abnormal beliefs of people diagnosed with mental health problems are held with great conviction, are resistant to counter-argument, and appear bizarre to others but further argued that these criteria were not enough to distinguish between true delusions and what he termed 'delusion-like ideas'. The former, Jaspers suggested, were 'ununderstandable' in the sense that they were inaccessible to the clinician's empathetic attempts to see the world from the patient's point of view, and hence could not be attributed to the patient's personality and life experiences.

Other researchers, inspired by phenomenological observations (for example, that the onset of delusions is sometimes preceded by an experience of *das trema* or something impending), have argued true delusions arise from subtle distortions in the way that the individual experiences themselves in the world (Bovet & Parnas, 1993). Although, these kinds of experiences undoubtedly merit further research, at present it is not clear whether they can be used to distinguish between the apparently delusional beliefs of people with psychosis and more widely accepted explanatory belief systems such as extremist political and religious ideologies (Bentall, 2015). Indeed, anomalous experiences of this kind are not uncommon in the narratives of people experiencing religious conversion (James, 1902).

The evidence that paranoid beliefs are frequently observed in the general population suggests that it may be difficult to draw an unambiguous dividing line between clinical and non-clinical paranoia, and that it might be better to think of it as existing on a continuum with healthy functioning. Freeman et al. (2005) conducted a preliminary attempt to test this idea using an online survey, and reported a spectrum of paranoid belief, in which ordinary beliefs of suspicion are very frequent, whereas increasingly severe paranoid beliefs are exponentially less common. A similar finding was observed in an analysis of data from the Adult Psychiatric Morbidity Survey, a UK epidemiological sample (Bebbington et al., 2013). This study identified four sub-factors of paranoia: interpersonal sensitivity, mistrust, ideas of reference and ideas of persecution, Elahi et al. (2017) recently analysed paranoia questionnaire scores from over 600 people with schizophrenia spectrum diagnoses or prodromal psychotic symptoms and over 2000 healthy controls, using taxometric methods which are designed to detect qualitative differences within a spectrum of psychopathology; the findings supported a full continuum model of paranoia.

Psychological models of paranoia

Paranoia as the over-anticipation of social threat

In order to survive, all but the most simple organisms require the ability to anticipate harmful events in order to avoid them. In non-human vertebrates, this ability is facilitated by the conditioned avoidance mechanism, which has been much studied in animal species. There is evidence that the basal ganglia dopamine system (long thought to be implicated in psychosis; Howes et al., 2012, Howes & Murray, 2013) plays an important role in this mechanism (Moutoussis et al., 2008) and animal studies suggest that this system is sensitised by chronic victimization experiences (Selten & Cantor-Graae, 2005). Psychological studies show that paranoid fears are often viewed as adaptive by the people who experience them, precisely because they think that taking a paranoid stance to the world helps them to stay safe (Morrison et al., 2005). These observations are all consistent with the idea that paranoia co-opts normal threat detection and avoidance mechanisms that promote adaptive wariness in unsafe environments. In human beings, this threat detection and avoidance system is likely modulated by higher order cognitive mechanisms (e.g. appraisals), and therefore it makes sense to examine these kinds of processes in the hope of understanding why, in people with paranoia, social threats are over-estimated.

The role of self-esteem

Following earlier psychoanalytic models (Colby, 1977) and research on the way that people with paranoia construct explanations for hypothetical events (e.g. Kaney & Bentall, 1989), Bentall and colleagues (Bentall et al., 1994;

Bentall et al., 2001; Kinderman & Bentall, 1997) proposed that people with paranoia have fragile self-esteem, but avoid negative feelings about themselves by learning to attribute failure experiences to causes that are external to themselves (other-blaming), global (likely to affect all areas of life) and stable (likely to be present in the foreseeable future). The idea behind this model is that, by systematically explaining negative experiences in this way, a person with paranoia gradually builds up a delusional world-view.

A criticism of this defensive model is that it seems to imply that self-esteem should be preserved in people with paranoia. In fact, empirical studies show that people who have this kind of belief often have low self-esteem (Freeman et al., 1998). One possible explanation for this observation is that preserved self-esteem is found only in a subgroup of people with paranoia. Chadwick et al. (2005) have proposed that paranoia falls into two types: 'poor-me' in which persecution is believed to be entirely undeserved and self-esteem is high, and 'bad-me' in which persecution is believed to be deserved and self-esteem is low. Although the former type of paranoia appears to be by far the most common in acutely ill psychiatric patients (Fornells-Ambrojo & Garety, 2005), at present it is unclear whether these are two distinct phenomena. Indeed, subsequent research has shown that self-esteem is highly unstable in people with paranoia and often fluctuates between high and low (Thewissen et al., 2008), and that these kinds of fluctuations often occur as people switch from poor-me to bad-me beliefs or vice-versa (Melo & Bentall, 2013, Udachina et al., 2012).

An alternative approach to the defensive model has been developed over many years by Freeman and his colleagues (Freeman, 2007, Freeman et al., 2002). This model presumes that paranoid beliefs develop when people with low self-esteem and pre-existing feelings of vulnerability experience anomalous events (for example, hallucinatory experiences, or more subtle perceptual distortions caused by lack of sleep or illicit drugs), which provoke a search for meaning. Under these circumstances, the paranoid person's interpretation of events is affected by a number of cognitive biases, including the explanatory bias emphasised in the defensive model (Kaney & Bentall, 1989), but also other cognitive limitations such as a difficulty in understanding the mental states and intentions of others (Corcoran et al., 1995) and, most importantly, a tendency to jump to conclusions when trying to make sense of sequentially experienced information (Garety et al., 1991).

A comprehensive review of the large amount of research that has been conducted to test these models is beyond the scope of this chapter. However, there is very strong evidence that problems of self-esteem and impairments of those cognitive functions essential for reasoning about social situations (including the jumping to conclusions bias and a difficulty in understanding others' mental states) make separate and independent contributions to paranoid thinking (Bentall et al., 2009). A more difficult to resolve issue is how these processes interact but, on balance, it seems reasonable to say the evidence at present more strongly favours the direct model of paranoia as proposed by Freeman and colleagues, rather than the defensive model. However, it is worth noting some important features that are common to the two approaches. Both assume that the over-anticipation of social threat is the final common pathway that leads to paranoid beliefs; that this, over-anticipation is modulated by cognitive biases, and that negative beliefs about the self (low self-esteem) play an important role in paranoid thinking.

In relation to this last point, although, as already noted, evidence suggests that self-esteem in paranoia is highly unstable over time, cross-sectional studies have shown that negative beliefs about the self are strongly associated with paranoia in diverse clinical groups (Bentall et al., 2008). Moreover, in experience sampling studies, the onset of paranoid thoughts is typically preceded by a decrease in self-esteem (Thewissen et al. 2007; Udachina et al., 2009, 2012). Perhaps unsurprisingly, paranoia is also associated with negative beliefs about the attitudes of others towards the self (Fowler et al., 2006, Kinderman & Bentall, 1996). Hence, despite some differences in the way that current psychological models interpret the evidence about the role of specific processes in paranoia, there is broad agreement that core negative beliefs about the self and others play a central role in the onset and maintenance of paranoid delusions.

Attachment and paranoia

Attachment style and paranoid symptoms

Attachment theory provides a suitable framework for understanding the development of these kinds of core beliefs about the self and others, explaining how they affect interpersonal strategies across the lifespan, ultimately leading to paranoia in some cases. As articulated by Bowlby, (1965, 1969), internalised mental models (cognitive schemas) established during early life in the context of relationships with caregivers govern expectations about relationships with others in the future, leading to either secure or insecure attachment styles. Hence, an adequate relationship with a caregiver provides a secure base from which exploration of the world and engagement with others becomes possible. Children who are less fortunate because their caregivers are neglectful, emotionally withdrawn or abusive may develop attachment styles governed by avoidance, anxiety or both.

Integrating this theory into a social psychological framework, Bartholomew and Horowitz (1991) have proposed that attachment anxiety is associated with a negative internal model of the self whereas attachment avoidance is associated with a negative model of others. These two dimensions are reflected in the characteristics of the four most commonly observed attachment styles. According to this model, the secure style reflects a positive view of the self and others and the fearful style reflects a negative view of both. The preoccupied

29

style reflects a negative view of the self and a positive view of others, whereas the dismissing style reflects a positive view of the self and a negative view of others.

Empirical studies have consistently reported associations between insecure attachment and psychosis in general. For example, in a large epidemiological study Mickelson et al. (1997) found that insecure adult attachment was associated with schizophrenia symptoms, a finding that has been replicated in both clinical (e.g. Berry et al., 2007; Korver-Nieberg et al., 2015a; Korver-Nieberg et al., 2015b) and non-clinical samples (e.g. Berry et al., 2006). In a systematic review, Gumley et al., (2014) found strong evidence of an association between avoidant attachment and positive symptoms, and modest evidence of an association between anxious attachment and positive symptoms. More recently, Bucci, Emsley and Berry (2017) analysed attachment scores collected from over 500 people with psychosis, finding that those with both high levels of avoidant and anxious attachment experienced more severe positive symptoms.

Recently, a number of studies have considered associations between insecure attachment and specific psychotic symptoms. In non-clinical samples for example, Meins et al. (2008) found that anxious attachment was associated with paranoia, while Berry et al. (2006) found that attachment anxiety and attachment avoidance were both associated with both paranoia and hallucinations. Comparable findings have also been obtained in clinical samples. For example, Dozier et al. (1991) found that individuals with a schizophrenia diagnosis, who experienced paranoia, had a dismissing-avoidant attachment style, whilst Ponizovsky et al. (2013) found that pre-occupied and fearful-avoidant attachment styles were associated with higher scores for paranoia and hallucinations and affective symptoms, whereas the dismissing-avoidant style was associated only with anxiety.

In a study of a very large clinical sample of more than 500 people diagnosed with schizophrenia spectrum disorders, created by combining data from samples in the Netherlands, United Kingdom and Israel, Korver-Nieberg et al. (2015a) showed that attachment anxiety and avoidance were both associated with severity of hallucinations and paranoia, while Berry et al. (2012) found that avoidant attachment was associated with auditory hallucinations. To our knowledge, only one study has failed to find an association between attachment styles and psychotic symptoms (MacBeth et al., 2011); however, the sample size was relatively small (34), possibly limiting the ability to detect such associations using correlational methods.

One problem with many of these studies is that they did not statistically control for the co-occurrence of symptoms. As noted earlier in this chapter, because both paranoid delusions and hallucinations belong to the positive syndrome of psychosis, and often co-occur, failure to do this limits the ability to detect specific attachment-symptom associations. When

appropriate statistical controls for co-occurrence have been carried out, insecure attachment has been found to be more strongly associated with paranoia
than hallucinations.

In the first study of this kind, carried out by Pickering et al. (2008),
550 students from the UK completed questionnaires eliciting responses
about paranoid thinking, hallucinatory experiences, and attachment style
and both the anxious and avoidant attachment dimensions specifically
predicted paranoia and not hallucinations. Additionally, it was shown that
the relationship between the attachment dimensions and paranoia was
partially mediated by negative self-esteem, the perception that others are
powerful, and the anticipation of threat. (Partial mediation implies that
some but not all of the association between the attachment variables and
paranoia can be explained by the impact of attachment on these inter-
mediate mechanisms.)

In a subsequent clinical study of 176 individuals with psychosis-spectrum
diagnoses, whose symptoms were assessed using the Positive and Negative
Syndrome Scale (PANSS; Kay & Opler, 1987), it was similarly demonstrated
that both the anxious and avoidant attachment dimensions predicted paranoia
and not hallucinations (Wickham et al., 2015). In a comparable mediation analysis to that carried out by Pickering et al. (2008) the association between the
anxious attachment dimension and paranoia was partially mediated by low self-
esteem, while the association between the avoidant attachment dimension and
paranoia was fully mediated by low self-esteem (see Figure 2.1).

Although the studies we have so far considered suggest that insecure
attachment (no doubt in conjunction with other factors) can lead to paranoia, the studies are cross-sectional and it might be argued that the direction
of causality runs actually in reverse, so that paranoia leads to an insecure
attachment style. Evidence from studies conducted over more than one time
period can help to resolve this question. Berry et al. (2008), for example,
suggested that the maintenance of psychotic symptoms could be understood
within an attachment framework. In a longitudinal analysis, which looked
at data over time, they found that attachment styles remained stable over six
months, although an increase in attachment anxiety over time was modestly
associated with an increase in total symptom scores (although not with any
particular type of symptom).

Although most of the literature treats attachment styles as trait-like, it is
known that they can change in the long-term (Pinquart et al., 2013) and it
seems likely that, even though a particular style may predominate within each
individual, attachment attitudes and behaviours might also fluctuate more
rapidly in response to the challenges of daily life. Indeed, some accounts have
emphasised the extent to which attachment behaviours are dynamic strategies
that change in response to circumstances (Crittenden, 2006; Davila et al.,
1997). Hence, a more intensive, fine-grained assessment of these phenomena

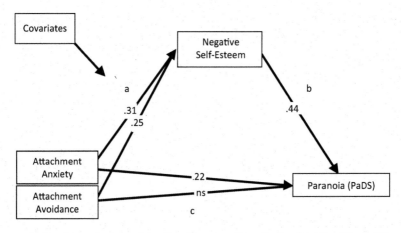

Attachment Anxious – Negative self-esteem – Paranoia, ß = .14, SE = .03, p < .001
Attachment Avoidant – Negative self-esteem – Paranoia, ß = .11, SE = .03, p = .001

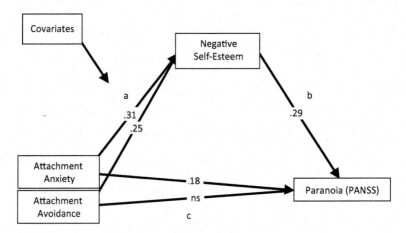

Attachment Anxious – Negative self-esteem – Paranoia, ß = .09, SE = .03, p = .006
Attachment Avoidant – Negative self-esteem – Paranoia, ß = .07, SE = .03, p = .010

Figure 2.1 Visual representation of relationships between attachment anxiety and attachment avoidance (Relationship Questionnaire) using the Persecution and Deservedness Scale (PaDS) (a) and the Positive and Negative Syndrome Scale (PANSS) (b) for paranoia as the dependent variable and with negative self-esteem (Self-Esteem Ratings Scale) as a mediator (from Wickham et al. 2015). The sample consisted of 176 schizophrenia spectrum patients. The model controlled for age, sex and hallucinatory experiences (covariates) in all paths of the model. N.S., Non-significant.

S. Wickham, K. Sitko, R. P. Bentall, Insecure attachment is associated with paranoia but not hallucinations in psychotic patients: the mediating role of negative self-esteem, *Psychological Medicine*, 45, 7, 1495–1507, reproduced with permission.

in the flow of everyday life seems warranted, for which the experience sampling method seems ideally suited.

In a recent study by Sitko et al. (2016), 20 clinical (psychosis spectrum diagnosis) and 20 control participants completed experience sampling diary entries up to ten times a day over a span of six days prompted by beeps from electronic devices. The diaries included questions about current mood, paranoid and hallucinatory experiences and self-esteem. However, there were also questions about attachment representations, which were adapted from the Adult Attachment Style (AAS) questionnaire (Collins & Read, 1990) ("I have found it difficult to depend on others", "I have found myself wanting to maintain a distance from others", "I have found it difficult to trust others completely", "The thought that others might leave me was constantly on my mind", "I am not worthy of others' attention and affection", "I worry that others don't really want to be close to me"). On factor analysis, these questions yielded a single factor of attachment security/insecurity, which meant that it was not possible to use them to distinguish between different kinds of insecurity. However, mean attachment insecurity scores on these questions over the assessment period correlated significantly and in the expected directions with all four subscales of Bartholomew and Horrowitz's Relationship Questionnaire administered at baseline (so, for example, high ESM insecurity was associated with low secure attachment ratings on the RQ), suggesting some degree of validity.

As the data had a temporal structure it was possible to examine whether underlying psychological mechanisms, such as attachment representations, preceded subsequent psychotic symptoms. It was found that, in comparison to the control sample, the clinical sample showed significantly greater fluctuations in their attachment representations. More importantly for the present discussion, in both the psychiatric service users and the controls, increased levels of paranoia were preceded by elevated levels of attachment insecurity (when attachment insecurity increased, paranoid thoughts followed). This kind of effect was not observed for hallucinatory experiences, which did not fluctuate in relation to attachment fluctuations. Furthermore, despite the previous evidence that paranoia is associated with low and unstable self-esteem, the effect of insecure attachment on paranoia remained even when self-esteem was controlled for, which suggests that self-esteem mediates the relationship between attachment insecurity and paranoia as previously observed in cross-sectional studies.

It is possible to interpret these findings within a framework proposed by Davila et al. (1997), who suggested that stability of attachment may be an important individual difference variable, and that people will be prone to fluctuation when they hold tentative and unstable beliefs about the self and others. The overall picture that emerges is that attachment insecurity increases the risk of paranoia, and that activation of insecure attachment-related thoughts precipitates the activation of negative beliefs about the self, which in turn leads to paranoid thoughts.

The social origins of paranoia: the role of early life events

One limitation of the studies considered so far is that they have examined attachment styles in adulthood. Moreover, in many cases the measures employed (e.g. the Relationship Questionnaire) have assessed attitudes towards romantic attachment, rather than attachment to parents. We should, therefore, be cautious about assuming that these results, as they stand, reflect early relationship difficulties with caregivers.

However, in recent years, there has been emerging evidence that environmental and social risk factors, especially in early life, indeed play an important role in the development of psychotic symptoms. These include exposure to urban environments (Vassos et al., 2012) and social deprivation (Wickham et al., 2014), especially in childhood (Pedersen & Mortensen, 2001; Wicks et al., 2010); childhood traumas such as sexual or physical abuse or separation from a parent at an early age (Varese et al., 2012); migration (Cantor-Graee & Selten, 2005), again especially in childhood (Velling et al., 2011); and severe life events in adulthood (Beards et al., 2013). By far the majority of research in this area has employed broad diagnostic concepts such as 'schizophrenia' or 'psychosis'.

If paranoid symptoms are specifically associated with an insecure attachment style, it might be expected that they should also be associated with disruption of early attachment relationships. In fact, there are a number of indicators in the psychosis literature that point to this possibility. For example, in an analysis of data from a Finnish birth cohort study by Myhrman et al. (1996) it was found that children who were born after an unwanted pregnancy (as determined by questioning prospective mothers) were at increased risk of psychosis more than 20 years later. In an analysis of data from the British AESOP study of first episode psychosis in different ethnic groups, Morgan et al. (2007) found that separation from, or the death of, a parent before the age of 16 was associated with a two- to three-fold increase in the risk of psychosis. While the effect was found for all ethnic groups, there was an increased risk of early separation in the Black Caribbean population, partially accounting for the well-replicated increase risk of psychosis in this group.

As is the case when investigating the role of psychological processes in psychosis, care must be taken to consider the co-occurrence of symptoms when attempting to understand the relationship between specific symptoms and specific kinds of adversity. In an analysis of data from the UK Adult Psychiatric Morbidity Survey by Bentall et al. (2012), it was found that being brought up in institutional care was specifically associated with paranoia, while being sexually abused was specifically associated with hallucinations. Very similar findings were subsequently reported from a survey of psychiatric morbidity and early experience in a large British prison sample (Shevlin et al., 2015); that specific associations were observed in this sample was all the more remarkable for the fact that, at the time of interview, the prisoners were all living in very traumatic circumstances.

Comparable findings were also reported in a study using a large US epidemiological sample, the National Comorbidity Survey (NCS), although childhood experiences of institutional care were not measured in this study. In this sample, experiences of neglect in childhood were specifically associated with paranoia, while experiences of rape and sexual molestation in childhood were specifically associated with hallucinations (Sitko et al., 2014). Similarly, in a recent study of a sample of people with psychosis, childhood emotional neglect was found to significantly predict paranoia when hallucinations were controlled for but failed to predict hallucinations when paranoia was controlled for. In this sample, childhood sexual abuse predicted hallucinations when paranoia was controlled for but failed to predict paranoid beliefs when hallucination was controlled for (Wickham & Bentall, 2016).

The study by Sitko et al. (2014) also examined whether the associations between childhood adversity and symptoms in the NCS could be explained by attachment styles (classified as anxious, avoidant, and secure in the survey) and it was found that the association between neglect and paranoia was fully mediated by both anxious and avoidant attachment. Anxious attachment also partially mediated the relationship between childhood rape and hallucinations, although the effect of less severe forms of sexual molestation on hallucinations was independent of attachment style. However, when depression was also included as a mediator, the pathway from childhood rape through attachment to hallucinations was no longer significant; the pathways from neglect through attachment to paranoia were unaffected.

The overall picture that emerges from these studies is a pathway leading from disrupted early attachment relationships, through attachment styles in adulthood to negative beliefs about the self and paranoid symptoms.

Conclusions and caveats

In this chapter, we have argued that attachment theory provides a framework for understanding the development of paranoid beliefs. We have reviewed evidence that suggests that damaged early attachment relationships promote insecure attachment styles which, in turn, lead to the kind of beliefs about self and other that fuel paranoid thinking. We are not arguing that attachment is the only process involved in paranoid delusions. Indeed, as we have noted, there is good evidence that cognitive impairment (Bentall et al., 2009), including problems in the cognitive skills required to understand the intentions of others (Frith & Corcoran, 1996), and difficulties in reasoning about sequential information (Garety et al., 1991) also contribute to paranoid thinking. However, the attachment data fit well with existing cognitive models of paranoia, perhaps especially the direct model proposed by Freeman and colleagues (Freeman, 2007; Freeman et al., 2002), which also incorporate these processes.

Coltheart (2007) has suggested that any model of delusional beliefs needs to include two components: an emotional component that explains the content of delusions and a cognitive component which explains why individuals cannot persuade themselves out of their delusional beliefs and, indeed, as we have seen, there is evidence that these two components are largely independent (Bentall et al., 2009). Attachment seems to provide the key to the emotional component.

We think that the findings reviewed in this chapter have a number of important implications. In terms of methodology, the studies we have reviewed highlight the importance of statistically controlling for the co-occurrence of symptoms when attempting to identify symptom-specific causal pathways. From the point of research, the findings highlight the need to pursue a developmental approach to psychosis, which includes both emotional and neurocognitive elements; doing so will require the use of longitudinal designs, which encompass a considerable portion of the human life span (an arduous undertaking).

At a clinical level, the findings reviewed here suggest that psychological therapists should pay particular attention to attachment-related issues when offering therapy to people with paranoia. It seems to us that existing psychological therapies for psychosis; for example, cognitive-behaviour therapy, could be enhanced by incorporating an attachment perspective. One way in which this might be achieved might be by focusing therapy on unresolved attachment issues, and how the person manages these; our experience is that preoccupation with such issues can be addressed by acceptance-based strategies such as those developed by Hayes and colleagues (Hayes et al., 1999). Given a recent finding that the quality of the therapeutic relationship plays a major role in determining the effectiveness of cognitive-behaviour therapy, and that a poor therapeutic relationship can lead to a poor outcome (Goldsmith et al. 2015), future clinical studies might consider how this relationship is affected by people's attachment styles and investigate specific techniques for managing attachment anxiety and avoidance within the therapeutic setting.

References

Al-Issa, I. (1995). The illusion of reality or the reality of an illusion: Hallucinations and culture. *British Journal of Psychiatry, 166*, 368–373.
American Psychiatric Association (2013). *Diagnostic and statistical manual for mental disorders, 5th edition*. Author: Washington DC.
Bartholomew, K. & Horowitz, L. M. (1991). Attachment styles among young adults: A test of a four-category model. *Journal of Personality and Social Psychology 61*, 226–244.

Beards, S., Gayer-Anderson, C., Borges, S., Dewey, M. E., Fisher, H. L. & Morgan, C. (2013). Life events and psychosis: A review and meta-analysis. *Schizophrenia Bulletin, 39*, 740–747.

Bebbington, P., McBride, O., Steel, C., Kuipers, E., Radovanovič, M., Brugha, T., Jenkins, R., Meltzer, H. I. & Freeman, D. (2013). The structure of paranoia in the general population. *British Journal of Psychiatry, 202*, 419–427.

Bentall, R. P. (2003). *Madness Explained: Psychosis and human nature*. Penguin: London.

Bentall, R. P. (2014). The search for elusive structure: A promiscuous realist case for researching specific psychotic experiences such as hallucinations. *Schizophrenia Bulletin, 40, Suppl 4*, S198–S201.

Bentall, R. P. (2015). Prospects and problems for a phenomenological approach to delusions. *World Psychiatry, 14*, 113–115.

Bentall, R. P., Corcoran, R., Howard, R., Blackwood, N. & Kinderman, P. (2001). Persecutory delusions: A review and theoretical integration. *Clinical Psychology Review, 21*, 1143–1192.

Bentall, R. P., Kinderman, P., Howard, R., Blackwood, N., Cummins, S., Rowse, G., Knowles, R. & Corcoran, R. (2008). Paranoid delusions in schizophrenia and depression: The transdiagnostic role of expectations of negative events and negative self-esteem. *Journal of Nervous and Mental Disease, 196*, 375–383.

Bentall, R. P., Kinderman, P. & Kaney, S. (1994). The self, attributional processes and abnormal beliefs: Towards a model of persecutory delusions. *Behaviour Research and Therapy, 32*, 331–341.

Bentall, R. P., Rowse, G., Shryane, N., Kinderman, P., Howard, R., Blackwood, N., Moore, R. & Corcoran, R. (2009). The cognitive and affective structure of paranoid delusions: A transdiagnostic investigation of patients with schizophrenia spectrum disorders and depression. *Archives of General Psychiatry, 66*, 236–247.

Bentall, R. P., Wickham, S., Shevlin, M. & Varese, F. (2012). Do specific early life adversities lead to specific symptoms of psychosis? A study from the 2007 The Adult Psychiatric Morbidity Survey. *Schizophrenia Bulletin, 38*, 734–740.

Berry, K., Barrowclough, C. & Wearden, A. (2007). A review of the role of adult attachment style in psychosis: Unexplored issues and questions for further research. *Clinical Psychology Review, 27*, 458–475.

Berry, K., Barrowclough, C. & Wearden, A. (2008). Attachment theory: A framework for understanding symptoms and interpersonal relationships in psychosis. *Behavior Research and Therapy, 46*, 1275–1282.

Berry, K., Wearden, A., Barrowclough, C. & Liversidge, T. (2006). Attachment styles, interpersonal relationships and psychotic phenomena in a non-clinical student sample. *Personality and Individual Differences, 41*, 707–718.

Berry, K., Wearden, A., Barrowclough, C., Oakland, L. & Bradley, J. (2012). An investigation of adult attachment and the nature of relationships with voices. *British Journal of Clinical Psychology, 51*, 280–291.

Borsboom, D. & Cramer, A. O. J. (2013). Network analysis: An integrative approach to the structure of psychopathology. *Annual Review of Clinical Psychology, 9*, 91–121.

Bovet, P. & Parnas, J. (1993). Schizophrenic delusions: A phenomenological approach. *Schizophrenia Bulletin, 19*, 579–597.

Bowlby, J. (1965). *Childcare and the Growth of Love*. Penguin: Harmondsworth.

Bowlby, J. (1969). *Attachment and Loss: Vol 1 – Attachment*. Hogarth Press: London.

Brakoulias, V. & Starcevic, V. (2008). A cross-sectional survey of the frequency and characteristics of delusions in acute psychiatric wards. *Australasian Psychiatry, 16*, 87–91.

Brown, T. A. (2006). *Confirmatory Factor Analysis for Applied Research.* New York: Guilford Press.

Bucci, S., Emsley, R., & Berry, K. (2017). Attachment in psychosis: A latent profile analysis of attachment styles and association with symptoms in a large psychosis cohort. *Psychiatry Research, 247*, 243–249.

Cantor-Graee, E. & Selten, J. P. (2005). Schizophrenia and migration: A meta-analysis and review. *American Journal of Psychiatry, 163*, 478–487.

Chadwick, P., Trower, P., Juusti-Butler, T.-M. & Maguire, N. (2005). Phenomenological evidence for two types of paranoia. *Psychopathology, 38*, 327–333.

Colby, K. M. (1977). Appraisal of four psychological theories of paranoid phenomena. *Journal of Abnormal Psychology, 86*, 54–59.

Collins, N. L. & Read, S. J. (1990). Adult attachment, working models of others, and relationship quality in dating couples. *Journal of Personality and Social Psychology, 58*, 644–663.

Coltheart, M. (2007). The 33rd Sir Frederick Bartlett Lecture: Cognitive neuropsychiatry and delusional beliefs. *The Quarterly Journal of Experimental Psychology, 60*, 1041–1062.

Compton, M. T., Potts, A. A., Wan, C. R. & Ionesc (2012). Which came first, delusions or hallucinations? An exploration of clinical differences among patients with first-episode psychosis based on patterns of emergence of positive symptoms. *Psychiatry Research, 20*, 702–707.

Corcoran, R., Mercer, G. & Frith, C. D. (1995). Schizophrenia, symptomatology and social inference: Investigating 'theory of mind' in people with schizophrenia. *Schizophrenia Research, 17*, 5–13.

Crittenden, P. M. (2006). A dynamic-maturational model of attachment. *Australian and New Zealand Journal of Family Therapy, 27*, 105–115.

Davila, J., Burge, D. & Hammen, C. (1997). Why does attachment style change? *Journal of Personality and Social Psychology, 73*, 826–838.

Dozier, M., Stevenson, A. L., Lee, S. W. & Velligan, D. I. (1991). Attachment organization and familiar overinvolvement for adults with serious psychopathological disorders. *Development and Psychopathology, 3*, 475–489.

Emsley, R., Rabinowitz, J. & Torreman, M. (2003). The factor structure for the Positive and Negative Syndrome Scale (PANSS) in recent-onset psychosis. *Schizophrenia Research, 61*, 47–57.

Fornells-Ambrojo, M. & Garety, P. (2005). Bad me paranoia in early psychosis: A relatively rare phenomenon. *British Journal of Clinical Psychology, 44*, 521–528.

Fowler, D., Freeman, D., Smith, B., Kuipers, E., Bebbington, P., Bashforth, H., Coker, S., Hodgekins, J., Gracie, A., Dunn, G. & Garety, P. (2006). The Brief Core Schema Scales (BCSS): Psychometric properties and associations with paranoia and grandiosity in non-clinical and clinical samples. *Psychological Medicine, 36*, 749–759.

Freeman, D. (2007). Suspicious minds: The psychology of persecutory delusions. *Clinical Psychology Review, 27*, 425–457.

Freeman, D., Garety, P., Fowler, D., Kuipers, E., Dunn, G., Bebbington, P. & Hadley, C. (1998). The London-East Anglia randomized controlled trial of cognitive-behaviour therapy for psychosis IV: Self-esteem and persecutory delusions. *British Journal of Clinical Psychology*, *37*, 415–430.

Freeman, D., Garety, P. A., Bebbington, P. E., Smith, B., Rollinson, R., Fowler, D., Kuipers, E., Ray, K. & Dunn, G. (2005). Psychological investigation of the structure of paranoia in a non-clinical population. *British Journal of Psychiatry*, *186*, 427–435.

Freeman, D., Garety, P. A., Kuipers, E., Fowler, D. & Bebbington, P. E. (2002). A cognitive model of persecutory delusions. *British Journal of Clinical Psychology*, *41*, 331–347.

Frith, C. & Corcoran, R. (1996). Exploring 'theory of mind' in people with schizophrenia. *Psychological Medicine*, *26*, 521–530.

Garety, P. A., Hemsley, D. R. & Wessely, S. (1991). Reasoning in deluded schizophrenic and paranoid patients. *Journal of Nervous and Mental Disease*, *179*, 194–201.

Goldsmith, L.P., Lewis, S.W., Dunn, G., & Bentall, R.P. (2015). Psychological treatments for early psychosis can be beneficial or harmful, depending on the therapeutic alliance: An instrumental variable analysis. *Psychological Medicine*, *45*, 2365–2373.

Goodwin, F. K. & Jamison, K. R. (2007). *Manic Depressive Illness: Bipolar disorders and recurrent depression*. Oxford University Press: Oxford.

Gumley, A. I., Taylor, H. E. F., Schwannauer, M. & MacBeth, A. (2014). A systematic review of attachment and psychosis: Measurement, construct validity and outcomes. *Acta Psychiatrica Scandinavica*, *129*, 257–274.

Haddock, G., Slade, P. D. & Bentall, R. P. (1995). Auditory hallucinations and the verbal transformation effect: The role of suggestions. *Personality and Individual Differences*, *19*, 301–306.

Hayes, S.C., Strosahl, K.D., & Wilson, K.G. (1999). *Acceptance and Commitment Therapy: An experiential approach to behavior change*. New York: Guilford.

Howes, O. D., Kambeitz, J., Kim, E., Stahl, D., Slifstein, M., Abi-Dargham, A. & Kapur, S. (2012). The nature of dopamine dysfunction in schizophrenia and what this means for treatment. *Archives of General Psychiatry*, *69*, 776–786.

James, W. (1902). *The Varieties of Religious Experience*. Penguin Press: London.

Jaspers, K. (1913/1963). *General Psychopathology*. Manchester University Press: Manchester.

Kaney, S. & Bentall, R. P. (1989). Persecutory delusions and attributional style. *British Journal of Medical Psychology*, *62*, 191–198.

Kay, S. R. & Opler, L. A. (1987). The Positive and Negative Syndrome Scale (PANSS) for schizophrenia. *Schizophrenia Bulletin*, *13*, 507–518.

Kinderman, P. & Bentall, R. P. (1996). Self-discrepancies and persecutory delusions: Evidence for a defensive model of paranoid ideation. *Journal of Abnormal Psychology*, *105*, 106–114.

Kinderman, P. & Bentall, R. P. (1997). Causal attributions in paranoia: Internal, personal and situational attributions for negative events. *Journal of Abnormal Psychology*, *106*, 341–345.

Korver-Nieberg, N., Meijer, C., de Haan, L., Berry, K. & Ponizovsky, A. M. (2015b). Associations between attachment and psychopathology dimensions in a large sample of patients with psychosis. *Psychiatry Research*, *228*, 83–88.

Kotov, R., Chang, S. W., Fochtmann, L. J., Mojtabai, R., Carlson, G. A., Sedler, M. J. & Bromet, E. J. (2011). Schizophrenia in the internalizing-externalizing framework: a third dimension? *Schizophrenia Bulletin*, *37*, 1168–1178.

Lattuada, E., Serretti, A., Cusin, C., Gasperini, M. & Smeraldi, E. (1999). Symptomatologic analysis of psychotic and non-psychotic depression. *Journal of Affective Disorders, 54*, 183–187.

MacBeth, A., Gumley, A., Schwannauer, M. & Fisher, R. (2011). Attachment states of mind, mentalization, and their correlates in a first-episode psychosis sample. *Psychology & Psychotherapy – Theory, Research and Practice, 84*, 42–57.

Maher, B. A. (1988). Anomalous experience and delusional thinking: The logic of explanations. In *Delusional Beliefs* (ed. T. F. Oltmanns and B. A. Maher), pp. 15–33. Wiley: New York.

Meins, E., Jones, S. R., Fernyhough, C., Hurndall, S. & Koronis, P. (2008). Attachment dimensions and schizotypy in a non-clinical sample. *Personality and Individual Differences, 44*, 1000–1011.

Melo, S. S. & Bentall, R. P. (2013). 'Poor me' vs. 'Bad me' paranoia: The association between self-beliefs and the instability of persecutory ideation. *Psychology & Psychotherapy: Theory, Research and Practice, 86*, 146–163.

Mickelson, K. D., Kessler, R. C. & Shaver, P. R. (1997). Adult attachment in a nationally representative sample. *Journal of Personality and Social Psychology, 73*, 1092–1106.

Morgan, C., Kirkbride, J., Leff, J., Craig, T., Hutchinson, G., McKenzie, K., Morgan, K., Dazzan, P., Doody, G. A., Jones, P., Miurray, R. & Fearon, P. (2007). Parental separation, loss and psychosis in different ethnic groups: A case-control study. *Psychological Medicine, 37*, 495–503.

Morrison, A. P., Gumley, A., Schwannauer, M., Campbell, M., Gleeson, A., Griffin, E. & Gillan, K. (2005). The Beliefs About Paranoia Scale: Preliminary validation of a metacognitive approach to conceptualizing paranoia. *Behavioural and Cognitive Psychotherapy, 33*, 153–164.

Moutoussis, M., Bentall, R. P., Williams, J. & Dayan, P. (2008). A temporal difference account of avoidance learning. *Network: Computation in Neural Systems, 19*, 137–160.

Moutoussis, M., Williams, J., Dayan, P. & Bentall, R. P. (2007). Persecutory delusions and the conditioned avoidance paradigm: Towards an integration of the psychology and biology of paranoia. *Cognitive Neuropsychiatry, 12*, 495–510.

Myhrman, A., Rantakallio, P., Isohanni, M. & Jones, P. (1996). Unwantedness of preganancy and schizophrenia in the child. *British Journal of Psychiatry, 169*, 637–640.

Oorschot, M., Lataster, T., Thewissen, V., Bentall, R. P., Delespaul, P. & Myin-Germeys, I. (2012). Temporal dynamics of visual and auditory hallucinations. *Schizophrenia Research, 140*, 77–82.

Pedersen, C. B. & Mortensen, P. B. (2001). Evidence of a dose-response relationship between urbanicity during upbringing and schizophrenia risk. *Archives of General Psychiatry, 58*, 1039–1046.

Pickering, L., Simpson, J. & Bentall, R. P. (2008). Insecure attachment predicts proneness to paranoia but not hallucinations. *Personality and Individual Differences, 44*, 1212–1224.

Pinquart, M., Feußner, C. & Ahnert, L. (2013). Meta-analytic evidence for stability in attachments from infancy to early adulthood. *Attachment and Human Development, 15*, 189–218.

Ponizovsky, A. M., Vitenberg, E., Baumgarten-Katz, I. & Grinshpoon, A. (2013). Attachment styles and affect regulation among outpatients with schizophrenia: Relationships to symptomatology and emotional distress. *Psychology and Psychotherapy: Theory, Practice, Research, 86*, 164–182.

Poulton, R., Caspi, A., Moffitt, T. E., Cannon, M., Murray, R. & Harrington, H. (2000). Children's self-reported psychotic symptoms and adult schizophreniform disorder: A 15-year longitudinal study. *Archives of General Psychiatry, 57*, 1053–1058.

Regier, D. A., Narrow, W. E., Clarke, D. E., Kraemer, H. C., Kuramoto, S. J., Kuhl, E. A. & Kupfer, D. J. (2013). DSM-5 field trials in the United States and Canada, Part II: Test-retest reliability of selected categorical diagnoses. *American Journal of Psychiatry, 170*, 59–70.

Reininghaus, U., Böhnke, J. R., Hosang, G. M., Farmer, A., Burns, T., McGuffin, P. & Bentall, R. P. (2015). Probing the boundaries of the Kraepelinian dichotomy: Evidence for a bifactor model reveals psychosis spectrum encompassing schizophrenia and bipolar disorder. *British Journal of Psychiatry*.

Reininghaus, U., Priebe, S. & Bentall, R. P. (2013). Testing the psychopathology of psychosis: Evidence for a general psychosis dimension. *Schizophrenia Bulletin, 39*, 884–895.

Selten, J.-P. & Cantor-Graae, E. (2005). Social defeat: Risk factor for psychosis? *British Journal of Psychiatry, 187*, 101–102.

Shevlin, M., McAnee, G., Bentall, R. P. & Murphy, K. (2015). Specificity of association between adversities and the occurrence and co-occurrence paranoia and hallucinations: Evaluating the stability of risk in an adverse adult environment. *Psychosis, 7*, 206–216.

Sitko, K., Bentall, R. P., Shevlin, M., O'Sullivan, N. & Sellwood, W. (2014). Associations between specific psychotic symptoms and specific childhood adversities are mediated by attachment styles: An analysis of the National Comorbidity Survey. *Psychiatry Research, 217*, 202–209.

Sitko, K., Varese, F. & Bentall, R. P. (2016). Paranoia and attachment in daily life: An experience sampling study. *Psychiatry Research, 246*, 32–38.

Thewissen, V., Bentall, R. P., Lecomte, T., van Os, J. & Myin-Germeys, I. (2008). Fluctuations in self-esteem and paranoia in the context of everyday life. *Journal of Abnormal Psychology, 117*, 143–153.

Udachina, A., Thewissen, V., Myin-Germeys, I., Fitzpatrick, S., O'Kane, A. & Bentall, R. P. (2009). Self-esteem, experiential avoidance and paranoia. *Journal of Nervous and Mental Disease, 197*, 661–668.

Udachina, A., Varese, F., Oorschot, M., Myin-Germeys, I. & Bentall, R. P. (2012). Dynamics of self-esteem in 'poor-me' and 'bad-me' paranoia. *Journal of Nervous and Mental Disease, 200*, 777–783.

Varese, F., Smeets, F., Drukker, M., Lieverse, R., Lataster, T., Viechtbauer, W., Read, J., van Os, J. & Bentall, R. P. (2012). Childhood adversities increase the risk of psychosis: A meta-analysis of patient-control, prospective and cross-sectional cohort studies. *Schizophrenia Bulletin, 38*, 661–671.

Vassos, E., Pedersen, C. B., Murray, R. M., Collier, D. A. & Lewis, C. M. (2012). Meta-analysis of the association of urbanicity with schizophrenia. *Schizophrenia Bulletin, 38*, 1118–1123.

Velling, W., Hoek, H. W., Selten, J.-P. & Susser, E. (2011). Age at migration and future risk of psychotic disorders among immigrants in the Netherlands: A 7-Year incidence study. *American Journal of Psychiatry, 168,* 1278–1285.

Wickham, S. & Bentall, R. P. (2016). Are specific early-life experiences associated with specific symptoms of psychosis: A patients study considering just world beliefs as a mediator. *Journal of Nervous & Mental Disease, 204,* 606–613.

Wickham, S., Sitko, K. & Bentall, R. P. (2015). Insecure attachment is associated with paranoia but not hallucinations in psychotic patients: The mediating role of negative self esteem. *Psychological Medicine, 45,* 1495–1507.

Wickham, S., Taylor, P., Shevlin, M. & Bentall, R. P. (2014). The impact of social deprivation on paranoia, hallucinations, mania and depression: The role of discrimination, social support, stress and trust. *Plos One, 9,* e105140.

Wicks, S., Hjern, A. & Daman, C. (2010). Social risk or genetic liability for psychosis? A study of children born in Sweden and reared by adoptive parents. *American Journal of Psychiatry, 167,* 1240–1246.

World Health Organization (1992). *ICD-10: International Statistical Classification of Diseases and Related Health Problems.* World Health Organization: Geneva.

Wright, A. G. C., Krueger, R. F., Hobbs, M. J., Markon, K. E., Eaton, C. B. & Slade, T. (2013). The structure of psychopathology: Towards an expnded quantitative empirical model. *Journal of Abnormal Psychology, 122,* 281–294.

3

HOW ATTACHMENT THEORY CAN DEVELOP UNDERSTANDINGS OF, AND THERAPY FOR, DISTRESSING VOICES

Katherine Berry, John Read, Filippo Varese and Sandra Bucci

Introduction

Auditory verbal hallucinations or experiences of "hearing voices" have been defined as the experience of hearing a voice in the absence of an appropriate external stimulus (Stanghellini & Cutting, 2003). Although not intrinsically pathological, with well-established evidence that voice-hearing is far more common than often thought and that most voice-hearers do not require mental health services, (Beavan et al., 2011), voices are sometimes associated with significant distress (Hatzipetrou & Oei, 2010) and are reported by approximately 70 per cent of people who experience psychosis (Waters et al., 2012).

Interpersonal trauma is a well-established vulnerability factor for the development of voices, with evidence of strong links between hallucinations or hallucination-proneness and several types of adverse childhood experience, such as childhood sexual, emotional and physical abuse, neglect and bullying (Read et al., 2005; Varese et al., 2012; Bentall et al., 2012). The role of trauma in voice-hearing has led us in both our research and clinical practice to consider the potential importance of attachment theory to understanding the voice-hearing experience. In this chapter we present two models, which draw on attachment theory in explaining voice-hearing: The Cognitive Attachment model of Voices and The Traumagenic Neurodevelopmental model. We follow this with discussion of empirical studies that have explored associations between voices and attachment and the clinical implications of using attachment theory to understand voices.

Cognitive Attachment model of Voice-hearing (CAV)

Over the years, a number of theoretical models have been proposed to account for either the development or maintenance of voice-hearing. Vulnerability accounts of voice-hearing which explain why people develop voices in the first place have been informed by cognitive theory. These accounts identify the cognitive and psychological processes involved in the development of voice-hearing experiences, including self-monitoring (Waters et al., 2012) and source-monitoring (Bentall, 1990) difficulties and dissociative processes (Longden et al., 2012). However, causes of voice-hearing remain largely unknown. What maintains distress, once distressing voices develop, has been another area of research focus. The most well-established model proposed to explain why some individuals experience voices as distressing and others do not is the cognitive model of voices, which suggests that the way individuals appraise their voices influences their emotional and behavioural reactions to these experiences (Chadwick & Birchwood, 1994; Morrison, 1998). Until recently, both development and maintenance accounts of voice-hearing have not integrated the different processes that are thought to be involved in distressing voice-hearing into an integrative framework.

In an attempt to think more systematically and integratively about how attachment theory and other important psychological processes might inform current understanding of distressing voice-hearing, Berry and Bucci (2015) proposed the Cognitive Attachment model of Voice-hearing (CAV). The CAV draws on cognitive, dissociative and attachment processes to account for the development and maintenance of voice-hearing in a single framework (see Figure 3.1). In particular, the CAV draws on attachment theory to integrate previous vulnerability accounts of voice-hearing (trauma-related dissociation and source monitoring accounts) with cognitive and relational models of distress exacerbation and maintenance. We will now describe the vulnerability and distress maintenance aspects of the CAV model. Consistent with cognitive models (Chadwick & Birchwood, 1994; Morrison, 1998), the CAV proposes that the way individuals make sense of their voices influences their emotional reactions to and ways of dealing with these experiences. However, the unique aspect of the CAV relates to the role of disorganised attachment and dissociative processes in explaining the link between trauma and voice-hearing, and the role of insecure attachment in influencing appraisal processes, emotional regulation strategies and interpersonal relationships with both others in the social world and voices, once voices develop.

Vulnerability aspect of the CAV (see Figure 3.1)

As with previous accounts of distressing voice-hearing, the CAV proposes that voices can be understood as dissociated aspects of the self or compartmentalised trauma-related intrusive memories (e.g. Longden et al., 2012; Bentall & Fernyhough, 2008; Moskowitz et al., 2009). In some cases, these events are experienced as external and current rather then internal and memory-based, which may occur as a result of source-monitoring problems (referring to difficulties in the ability to recognise whether experiences are internally or externally generated (Varese, Barkus & Bentall, 2012). Central

44

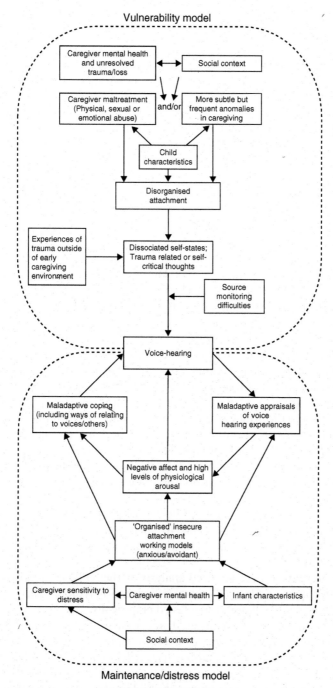

Vulnerability model

Caregiver mental health and unresolved trauma/loss

Social context

Caregiver maltreatment (Physical, sexual or emotional abuse)

and/or

More subtle but frequent anomalies in caregiving

Child characteristics

Disorganised attachment

Experiences of trauma outside of early caregiving environment

Dissociated self-states; Trauma related or self-critical thoughts

Source monitoring difficulties

Voice-hearing

Maladaptive coping (including ways of relating to voices/others)

Maladaptive appraisals of voice hearing experiences

Negative affect and high levels of physiological arousal

'Organised' insecure attachment working models (anxious/avoidant)

Caregiver sensitivity to distress

Caregiver mental health

Infant characteristics

Social context

Maintenance/distress model

Figure 3.1 Berry, K., Varese, F. and Bucci, S. (2017) Cognitive Attachment Model of Voices: Evidence Base and Future Implications. *Front. Psychiatry* 8:111. doi: 10.3389/fpsyt.2017.00411. Used with permissions.

to the model is the role of disorganised attachment. Disorganised attachment is the outcome of interactions whereby an infant experiences the attachment figure as frightening, frightened or dissociated in times of stress. According to Liotti (2004), the infant experiences 'fright without solution' at being confronted with the paradox that the attachment figure, the primary source of safety and protection, is also the source of the infant distress. There are multiple pathways to the development of disorganised attachment. There is evidence of associations between attachment disorganisation and parental maltreatment and unresolved parental trauma (Lyons-Ruth & Jacobvitz, 1999), as well as other adverse conditions and circumstances (e.g. parental poor mental health, sexual, physical, emotional abuse and experiences of loss; Cyr et al., 2010; Lyons-Ruth & Jacobvitz, 1999; Lyons-Ruth et al., 2005; van Ijzendoorn, 1995; 1999).

Individuals who display a disorganised attachment style are also more likely to dissociate in the context of ongoing or later relational trauma. In this way, disorganised attachment has been shown to be a developmental antecedent of dissociation (Carlson, 1998; Dutra et al., 2009; Liotti, 2004; Ogawa et al., 1997), which itself has been shown to be important in the development of voice-hearing (e.g. Pilton, Varese, Berry & Bucci, 2015).

In its most general form, dissociation is characterised by a breakdown in mental integration. Traditional conceptualisations have often regarded dissociation as a unitary construct characterised by a disruption of normal integrative functions, which are qualitatively similar and fall on a continuum. However, the concept of a dissociative continuum has been criticised in recent years. It has been argued that the continuum model appears overly generic, and that dissociation may in fact comprise phenomena presenting fundamental differences in phenomenology and underlying mechanisms (Brown, 2006). Holmes et al., (2005) propose two qualitatively different kinds of dissociation: detachment (an altered state of consciousness characterised by a sense of separation from aspects of everyday experience caused by hard-wired neurobiological response to threat; Sierra & Berrios, 1998) and compartmentalisation (a deficit in the ability to deliberately control processes or actions that would normally be amenable to such control resulting from subtle disturbances in the processes underlying consciousness and mental control; Brown, 2013).

Space prevents a more nuanced analysis of the hallucination-dissociation link in this chapter, and which aspect of dissociation is more clearly associated with voice-hearing will need to be tested empirically. However, in support of the role of dissociative mechanisms, dissociation is a common post-traumatic response that is also experienced among people who hear voices, in both clinical and non-clinical populations (e.g. Kilcommons et al., 2008; Perona-Garcelán et al., 2012). There is also growing empirical evidence that dissociation mediates the relationship between childhood trauma and hearing voices (Perona-Garcelán et al. 2012; Varese et al., 2012). Varese and colleagues (2012) provide evidence to support the role of dissociative processes in mediating the relationship between previous trauma and hallucinations and propose a 'two-hit' model, in which dissociation triggers voices in those vulnerable to impaired reality discrimination or source monitoring.

Distress maintenance aspect of the CAV (see Figure 3.1)

According to the CAV model, disorganised attachment increases vulnerability to hearing voices and the secondary organised attachment states of mind determine the perception of, and relationships with, voices. There is a consensus amongst cognitive behavioural theorists that the way individuals appraise voice(s) influences emotional and behavioural reactions to these experiences (Chadwick & Birchwood, 1994; Morrison, 1998). There is also evidence that higher levels of voice-related distress are associated with beliefs about voices as malevolent or powerful, having personal acquaintance with the individual, and disapproval and rejection by voices (Mawson et al., 2010). There is also evidence that the way in which individuals relate to voices mirrors their ways of relating to others in the external social world (Birchwood et al., 2004). In this way we propose that, once voices develop, insecure attachment styles influence how voices are appraised, how voice-hearers relate to their voices and the strategies they draw on to cope with these experiences.[1]

The CAV model makes a number of predictions about how an individual's adult attachment representations might affect beliefs about voices, ways of relating to voices and coping with voice-related distress. Although these predictions need to be tested empirically in voice-hearers, they are based on an extensive literature on associations between adult attachment, beliefs about self and others, interpersonal relating and coping. As discussed in the following section, there is some preliminary evidence from research with voice-hearers to support these ideas. For those with a preoccupied/anxious attachment, the voice-hearer relationship is likely to be characterised by voice dominance and hearer dependence. Those with access to alternative attachment figures in the external social world will also increase proximity to, and dependence on, these individuals in response to voice-hearing related distress. A preoccupied/anxious attachment would be associated with more negative appraisals about the individual's ability to cope with voices. In contrast, individuals with avoidant-dismissing attachment will hold negative beliefs about voices and will distance themselves from voices, with this avoidant response ultimately maintaining negative beliefs and voices over time. An avoidant-dismissing attachment may serve to maintain voice-related distress by reducing the likelihood that individuals will develop new attachments or utilise available social supports to help cope with distress. In summary, there are two pathways in terms of how attachment style might influence the maintenance of voices: i) an engagement route (anxiously attached voice-hearers may tend to "actively seek" the voices); ii) a suppression route (people employing different suppression strategies that ultimately fail via rebound effects).

Traumagenic neurodevelopmental model

Although not specific to voice-hearing, a related model that draws on attachment theory to account for symptoms of psychosis is the Traumagenic Neurodevelopment model of psychosis (Read et al., 2014). This model, which has much animal and human research to support it, identifies the effects of trauma on the developing brain (see Read et al., 2014 for a comprehensive review of supporting literature). The model proposes that the heightened sensitivity to stress consistently found in people diagnosed with psychotic disorders including schizophrenia originates, for many service users, in neurodevelopmental changes to the brain caused by relational trauma in the early years. Of particular relevance to attachment theory, the model highlights the adverse, sometimes long-lasting effects on the stress and emotion regulation mechanisms located in the hypothalamic–pituitary–adrenal (HPA) axis, which is part of the biological substrate of the attachment system (for further details of the biological basis of the attachment system see Chapter 7.

There are clear overlaps between the CAV and the Traumagenic Neurodevelopment, most importantly the role of earlier relational trauma in the development of difficulties in stress and emotional regulation, which can increase vulnerability to symptoms of psychosis. However, it would be fair to say that the Traumagenic Neurodevelopment model is more explicit in identifying the biological mechanisms underlying the trauma and psychosis link. On the other hand, the CAV, due to its explicit focus on voices, is more clear in articulating the psychological processes involved in the maintenance of distress and in particular, the role of attachment working models and associated beliefs in shaping how people respond to the experiences of voices.

Studies investigating attachment and voice-hearing

Few studies have examined associations between attachment and experiences of voices. Ponizovsky et al. (2013) and Berry et al. (2008) investigated adult attachment and symptoms in participants diagnosed with schizophrenia or related psychoses. Both research groups found associations between attachment anxiety and voices and Ponizovsky and colleagues (2013) also found associations between attachment avoidance and voices.

Berry et al. (2012) explored associations between attachment and the nature of the person's relationship with voices. The authors found evidence of associations between avoidance in attachment relationships and themes of rejection, criticism and threat in relationships with voices. Although this study was novel in investigating attachment and voice-hearing, it was limited by the fact that themes from symptom assessments were used to derive the content of voices; participants were not specifically asked about the nature of their relationships with voices. More recently, Robson and Mason (2014) examined associations between voice-hearers' attachment styles and measures of beliefs about voices as well as ways of relating to voices. The authors found that insecure-avoidant attachment was associated with voice-intrusiveness (voice perceived by hearer as intrusive) and hearer-distance (hearer relates to their voice from a position of distance), and insecure-anxious attachment was related to voice-intrusiveness and hearer-dependence (hearer relates to their voice from a dependent position). Furthermore, the relationship between insecure-attachment and voice-related distress was mediated by voice-malevolence and omnipotence.

Using data from the 2007 Adult Psychiatric Morbidity Survey, Bentall et al. (2012) explored the issue of symptom specificity by examining associations between childhood adversities and both paranoia and hallucinations. Once paranoia and hallucinations were entered into the same regression model, childhood rape was associated with hallucinations whilst being brought up in institutional care was associated with paranoia. As discussed in Chapter 2 the authors suggest that severe trauma (not attachment) increases vulnerability to voice-hearing, whilst disrupted attachment increases vulnerability to paranoia. Wickham et al. (2014) examined the relationship between attachment, paranoia and hallucinatory experiences in people diagnosed with a schizophrenia-spectrum disorder and healthy controls, using a self-report measure of attachment. Again, attachment was not correlated with hallucinations when controlling for paranoia in a regression analysis.

However, a study of 251 attenders of New Zealand community mental health centres found that the total number of types of childhood adversity, but not specific type of adversity, was significantly related to hallucinations in general and to voice-hearing specifically, as well as to delusions in general and to paranoid delusions specifically. A hypothesised specificity between sexual abuse and hallucinations, and physical abuse and delusions, was not found. The two adversities showing the largest number of associations with psychotic symptoms were poverty and, of great significance from an attachment perspective, being fostered/adopted, the latter of which most researchers have ignored. The researchers concluded that the findings were consistent with a model of global and cumulative adversity, in which multiple exposures may intensify psychosis risk beyond the impact of single events (Longden et al., 2015).

Using a covariance modelling approach to explore associations between attachment and non-clinical psychotic phenomena, MacBeth et al. (2011) found that paranoia was predicted by an 'organised' model consisting of attachment anxiety, avoidance and interpersonal distancing strategies, whereas hallucinations were predicted by a more complex model represented by a combination of attachment anxiety and interpersonal affiliating strategies with attachment avoidance and interpersonal distancing strategies within the same individual. The authors argue that the hallucinations model is characterised by the contradictory and competing interpersonal strategies of a disorganised attachment pattern. In the largest study examining attachment profiles in psychosis to date, data from 588 participants who met criteria for non-affective psychosis showed that a disorganised attachment pattern was associated with a higher likelihood of sexual and physical abuse and more severe positive symptoms compared to other attachment patterns (Bucci, Emsley & Berry, 2017), suggesting that disorganised attachment may be more important in terms of understanding positive symptoms than other types of attachment.

Research examining specific mechanisms underlying psychotic symptoms is complex (Read & Gumley, 2008; MacBeth et al., 2008), partly because many people experience both paranoia and distressing voices. However, the experience of trauma, particularly if the perpetrator is a caregiver or if the caregiver fails to protect/appropriately support the victim, is also likely to influence the individual's attachment system given that the functioning of the attachment system is so closely determined by relationships with early caregivers. The relationships between adversity, attachment and voice-hearing should be more precisely examined in order to clarify the range of variables implicated in the adversity, attachment and voice-hearing relationship. Further research is needed to investigate associations between specific childhood adversities and attachment, using established measures of attachment, to determine how these interact to influence specific symptoms. Such studies should include: i) a measure of disorganised/unresolved attachment, which is often not captured by simple self-report measures; ii) a measure of dissociation, which is a key proposed mechanism in explaining associations between trauma and hallucinations; iii) an attempt to determine which particular aspects of the multifaceted concept of dissociation are important for disorganised attachment in adulthood and the experience of voice-hearing; and vi) multi-dimensional measures of voices, which assess voice-related severity and distress as well as other important factors, including beliefs about, and ways of relating to, voices.

Clinical implications

The clinical implications of the relationships among trauma, attachment and psychosis in general have been discussed before (Benamer, 2010; Berry & Bucci, 2015; Read & Gumley, 2008). In this section we describe a case example based on an amalgamation of a number of different clients we have each worked with over the years to illustrate how an attachment lens could inform clinical practice in relation to voice-hearing.

Vignette

David was 23 years old when first referred to the psychological services team by his GP. He was described in the referral letter as low in mood, irritable and socially withdrawn. The letter also stated that he lived at home with his mother who was finding it increasingly difficult to motivate David to leave his room and she reported that she could hear him shouting to himself. Further information included the fact that David had a 5-year-old son, but the child's mother was reluctant for David to have any contact with the child due to David's history of mental health problems. Finally, the letter documented that David had also experienced an episode of psychosis following the birth of his son and had been admitted to hospital following threats to harm himself in an attempt to escape the 'torture of voices' who were commanding him to harm himself and members of his family. The GP speculated that David was currently experiencing another psychotic episode.

Assessment and formulation

During clinical assessment, attachment theory highlights the importance of asking voice-hearers about their experiences of trauma (Read et al., 2005), attachment relationships (Berry & Drake, 2010) and dissociation (Newman-Taylor & Sambrook, 2013). This process enables discussion around psycho-social explanations of voice-hearing, recognising that voice-hearing might indeed be an expected reaction to abnormal stress (Dillon, 2010). To aid this process, therapists might utilise questionnaires including the Childhood Trauma Questionnaire (Berstein et al., 1994), Psychosis Attachment Measure (Berry et al., 2008) and Dissociative Experiences Scale II (Carlson & Putnam, 1993). However, these instruments should not substitute for sensitively conducted comprehensive interviews tailored to the client's level of comfort in disclosing potentially distressing experiences.

Following an initial period of engagement in which the therapist focused on David's current worries and problems as well as strengths and resources, the therapist began to inquire about David's earlier experiences. The therapist started this process by asking very general questions about what it had been like for David growing up and positive and negative memories. As is often the case in the context of attachment difficulties, David found it very difficult to pinpoint specific memories, but reported his childhood was 'nothing special' and not relevant to his current problems. Given the potentially important causal role of trauma in voice-hearing, the therapist made the decision to probe about experiences of abuse. The therapist inquired how discipline had been handled at home when David was growing up and David revealed that his father would hit him if he misbehaved and that on several occasions his father had beaten him to the extent that he had bruises. Due to the particularly sensitive nature of sexual abuse, prior to asking directly about David's

51

own experiences, she informed David that a lot of people that she worked with had experienced unwanted sexual experiences. David disclosed that he had been sexually abused by his father and his father's friends between the ages of 8 and 13 years, when his father was arrested for armed robbery and sent to prison. He had not seen his father since and following David's father's release from prison five years ago, he had not attempted to contact David or David's mother. David was unsure whether or not his mother was aware of the abuse, but he reported that he did not tell her as he was worried about burdening her. David's mother had a history of problems with her mental health and substance misuse and David reported that she had spent several 'periods' of time in hospital when he was a child following attempts to take her own life. The therapist asked David how he had dealt with the abuse and he described mentally shutting down during the acts and blocking out memories where possible.

Information regarding traumatic, attachment and dissociative experiences should inform individualised formulations regarding the development and maintenance of distressing voices. An attachment-informed formulation of voice-hearing would consider how earlier caregiving experiences (in terms of both caregiver maltreatment and more subtle but frequent insensitive parenting behaviours) might increase vulnerability to voices via disorganised attachment patterns and associated dissociative processes. For example, it was hypothesised that due to their own difficulties, David's parents had not been able to provide sensitive and attuned care giving. Paradoxically, David may have experienced both his mother (as a result of her mental health and substance misuse problems) and his father (as a result of the abuse) as sources of threat as opposed to a source of comfort from threat. It was hypothesised that David may therefore have developed a disorganised attachment pattern and experienced dissociative states in the context of the later abuse. As a result of David's disorganised attachment system and associated use of dissociation, fragmented aspects of his self-identity and memories of abuse may intrude into his awareness and be attributed to external sources. The therapist hypothesised that the birth of David's son had activated unresolved trauma memories associated with his own childhood and triggered the onset of voices and initial psychotic breakdown. It was hypothesised that ongoing difficulties in David's relationship with his ex-partner and disputes over David's access to his son had resulted in the recent deterioration in David's mental health.

Attachment informed formulations would also consider how adult attachment styles influence ways of coping with voices and any associated emotional distress, including how individuals seek help and support. Dissociation, stemming from a disorganised attachment pattern, was conceptualised as David's habitual response to overwhelming stressful situations and particularly those involving intense intimate, attachment-invoking circumstances, including the therapeutic relationship. However, it was also hypothesised that David had developed a secondary avoidant attachment strategy, which helped him function. This avoidant attachment style would lead him to have negative beliefs about voices and relate to them with resistance and withdrawal. It was also hypothesised that David's avoidant attachment style might make it difficult for him to seek help in relation to any distress he experiences and even lead him to lack awareness of his emotional needs in the first place. Additionally, for some individuals, voices might be formulated as attachment figures upon which voice-hearers depend. For example, David reported that he had a more positive relationship with one of his voices and described how at times the voice could be a source of comfort and provide reassurance in the face of more menacing voice-hearing experiences.

Attachment and the therapeutic relationship

Bowlby (1982) conceptualised the therapeutic relationship as an attachment relationship and argued that therapist sensitivity, responsiveness, reliability and consistency are fundamental to the establishment of a 'secure base' in therapy. This is particularly important in the context of voice-hearing experiences and psychosis, as the individual's experiences of psychosis and its negative social context, including exposure to traumatic events, such as hospitalisation, loss of social role and rank and post-psychotic depression, can themselves be threatening and highly distressing (Berry et al., 2013). Once a 'secure base' has been established clients may feel more comfortable in exploring and processing the links between previous relationships and relationships with voices. For example, in working with David it was especially important that the therapist was attuned and sensitive to David's needs and that she made an effort to continue to be a reliable and consistent figure in his life, despite David's initial attempts to shut her out. It was only at the point that David had developed trust in the therapist that she was able to start to explore his history and ask him in more detail about his experiences of voice-hearing. Even when a degree of trust had been established it was still important for the therapist to be alert to the possibility that David might interpret her actions in a negative way due to the potential preconception that other people let you down and cannot be trusted, or the possibility that David might dissociate in response to more extreme interpersonal threat or the experience of highly charged affect.

Parallels between relationships with voices and relationships in the external world

An attachment model of voice-hearing emphasises the overlap between relationships with voices and broader social relationships. As McCarthy-Jones and Davidson (2013) highlight, recovery from voice-hearing involves re-establishing or developing attachment relationships with people in the outside world, including relationships with mental health professionals and relationships with friends and family. In line with attachment-informed thera-peutic work, therapists might also consider using the nature and dynamics of the therapeutic relationship to draw parallels with an individual's external interpersonal world. For example, although it was evident from David's non-verbal behaviour that he sometimes felt annoyed with the therapist, for example, when she had to cancel a session due to ill health or when she was on holiday, it was very difficult for him to articulate his negative feelings. The ther-apist therefore normalised David's potential annoyance and encouraged him to express how he was feeling to her, whilst she acknowledged and empathised with the way that he felt. David and the therapist also practised responding to other people in David's life in an assertive way. For example, David was having problems gaining access to his son and attempts to negotiate access with his ex-partner often culminated in arguments due to David losing his temper and being aggressive. The therapist and David therefore role played negotiating access in an assertive rather than an aggressive manner. Later in therapy, David and the therapist used similar strategies to relate to his voices, starting with the less threatening voices and then building up to responding more assertively to more threatening command hallucinations.

Focus on strengths

Conceptualising voice-hearing through an attachment lens highlights the functional nature of the individual's methods of coping with distress. Insecure attachment strategies develop to help infants survive in suboptimal care environments by reducing threat. These self-protective strategies are carried through into later life where they are used to cope with threatening situations and those where threat is misperceived. The emphasis that attachment places on self-protection and self-survival has the potential to help de-stigmatise psy-chopathology and offer a strengths-based approach to treating voice-related distress, as opposed to one organised around vulnerability. Attachment theory suggests that those with insecure attachment patterns are not 'mad', but highly competent in dealing with threat (Crittenden, 2005). This message is especially important to communicate to voice-hearers and is consistent with an approach that normalises psychotic experiences. For example, early on in therapy, the therapist emphasised that David's dissociation had helped him to cope with the abuse and that his use of secondary avoidant attachment strategies had kept him safe in the context of a toxic earlier environment. Later on in therapy, David and the therapist also reflected on the difficulties his own parents may have faced in parenting him given their own attachment histories and problems.

Different approaches for different styles

Attachment theory suggests that people with different attachment styles may benefit from different therapeutic approaches. For example, individuals with avoidant attachment strategies need treatments that help them to access and express negative feelings. Conversely, individuals with anxious attachment strategies may be overwhelmed by negative affect and need therapies that help them to contain emotions (Crittenden, 2005). Similarly, there is some evidence that clients and therapists may work better together if, after having formed a strong therapeutic alliance, they have opposing attachment styles. For instance, avoidant therapists due to their natural inclination towards withdrawal from emotional intimacy may be better placed to contain clients with high levels of attachment anxiety who easily become overwhelmed by affect; whereas, anxious therapists, due to their increased emotional sensitivity and desire for close bonds with others, may be more proactive in engaging withdrawn and emotionally distant avoidant clients (Bucci et al., 2015). These theories are based on the idea that therapy, or more precisely the therapeutic relationship, provides a corrective interpersonal experience whereby the client is given the opportunity to develop a broader range of interpersonal behaviours and ways of regulating affect. However, as we discuss below, therapists with secure attachment styles might be better placed than those with insecure styles to flexibly move between complementing or opposing the client's natural style depending on the stage of therapy and or the client's needs at that particular point in time.

We agree with the notion that therapy can provide a corrective experience and there is good evidence that attachment security can increase during therapy (Taylor et al., 2014). However, we advocate that a skilled therapist can tailor specific therapeutic techniques in accordance with the person's attachment strategies and or methods of regulating distress and needs at that point in time. In order to facilitate the development of a good therapeutic alliance, therapists may need to initially 'match' their approach to clients' attachment needs. For example, a therapist might initially allow those with avoidant attachment patterns some 'emotional distance' whilst allowing those with anxious attachment patterns an opportunity to freely express high levels of affect (Mallinckrodt, 2010). Once the therapeutic alliance is secured (as much as is possible), therapists should consider working in a way that is non-complementary to the client's attachment patterns so as to provide a corrective experience, whilst being mindful of the potential to be pulled into responding to the client's interpersonal orientation in a complementary way.

We argue that clients with disorganised or unresolved attachment patterns, which are associated with trauma and characterised by dissociation, may present particular challenges in therapy. Established Cognitive Behavioural Therapy approaches to the treatment of voices and other psychotic experiences (Morrison et al., 2003) may be specifically adapted to include therapeutic techniques suitable for individuals with trauma, disrupted attachment and dissociative experiences. The therapist should be alert to dissociation in this group and rely on grounding techniques which are an essential prerequisite to developing sufficient focus to enable emotional processing of past traumas and integration of traumatic experiences and dissociated affects. The development of distress tolerance and low arousal behavioural strategies should also be considered in early therapeutic work, with a view to increasing perceived control over dissociative experiences (Newman et al., 2013). Furthermore, developing a trusting therapeutic relationship is fundamental for working with people with disorganised attachment patterns. Therapists must be prepared to work especially hard at repairing frequent alliance ruptures and tolerate missing sessions, drops outs, and still proactively try to engage voice-hearers until they are ready to proceed with therapy. A trauma-focused and relational approach informed by the ideas presented in this chapter and related work may help improve outcomes in CT for distressing voices (Thomas et al., 2014).

The therapist hypothesised that David had a disorganised attachment style but also had developed a secondary avoidant attachment strategy. The therapist was therefore mindful of focusing too early on emotive issues, but instead attempted to engage David in more practical strategies for managing his low mood and coping with voices, such as activity scheduling and distraction. As therapy progressed and David's trust in her developed, she was able to ask David to pay more attention to his feelings in the present moment but also stay with difficult feelings from his past. Throughout this work, the therapist was alert to signs that David might be dissociating and gave him tools for grounding himself. David also frequently misconstrued the therapist's intentions, often leading him to miss the subsequent session. The therapist had to work hard to encourage David to re-engage following missed appointments and articulate to her how he was feeling. David and the therapist discussed the pros and cons of imagery and re-scripting work around his past abuse, but David did not feel that he was ready to embark on this work as he had recently been able to establish contact with his son and did not want to jeopardise this relationship.

The importance of therapist attachment

Parents' attachment styles predict their ability to be sensitive and responsive caregivers for their children (van Ijzendoorn et al., 1999). Similarly, one would expect therapist attachment patterns to influence their capacity to act as effective attachment figures and establish secure therapeutic relationships with their clients. In support of this assertion, a growing number of studies have explored associations between therapists' attachment styles and both therapeutic alliance and outcomes (Degnan et al., 2014). Although studies thus far are limited by cross-sectional designs and small sample sizes, a recent literature review concluded that there is sufficient evidence to suggest that therapists need to pay attention to the influence of their own attachment style in therapy (Degnan et al., 2014). In fact, as discussed previously, it may be the *interaction* between therapists' and clients' attachment styles that is particularly important in understanding the development of alliance and therapeutic outcomes (Bucci et al., 2015). We advocate that all therapists be open to their own attachment style and attachment history. We further encourage therapists to reflect on the impact of these experiences on the therapeutic relationship through their training and ongoing supervision, particularly when therapists are working with clients with distressing voices and complex trauma and attachment histories. The therapist found David's history extremely distressing but at the same time she was aware that due to her own slightly avoidant attachment style, she might be inclined to reinforce David's avoidance of negative affect and discussion of his abuse history. The therapist therefore used session recordings in supervision to increase her own awareness of times when she might reinforce David's avoidance. The use of supervision was also particularly pertinent when deciding with David about the possibility of exploring his past experiences of trauma, as the therapist wanted to ensure that she was not discouraging David from embarking on the work due to her own discomfort.

Caveats and conclusions

Voices are likely to develop as a result of complex interactions between risk and resilience factors, and individualised formulations are needed to understand relevant factors and their interactions for each person. There are some important caveats in applying attachment-informed therapeutic work with distressing voices. First, patterns of insecure attachment are common in people who do not hear voices; in particular, we need to be cautious about pathologising typical, organised patterns of insecure attachments. Second, attachment theory does not in itself offer an adequate account of the complexity and subtlety of the development of voices or voice-related distress; attachment theory alone does not explain all instances of voice-hearing. However, regardless of the underlying cause of voices, we argue that, once voices develop, attachment style is one aspect of an individual's self-identity that will impact on his or her relationship with voices. Third, as with many other accounts of the trauma-hallucination link, the proposed model is unable to account for the 'lag' between early trauma exposure and onset of voices and other psychotic symptoms. Attachment theory may, however, offer insight into this 'lag' effect: the onset of psychosis commonly occurs at a time of separation and individuation from early caregivers or during other important transitions in attachment relationships such as the breakdown in relationships and/loss of significant others. Fourth, before interventions based on attachment theory are routinely made available to clients with distressing voices, research should be carried out to examine the efficacy and added value of an attachment-informed therapy. Relatedly, research should investigate the specificity of the hypothesised mechanisms of any change in distress (e.g. reduction of dissociation and increased control over dissociative experiences). Finally, this chapter has focused on the implications of attachment theory for those who already experience distressing voices. Perhaps most importantly, the potential role of attachment in explaining voice-hearing highlights the benefits of preventative interventions which help children develop secure attachments and therefore greater resilience to voice-hearing (Cicchetti et al., 2006).

Note

1 We acknowledge that there is considerable overlap between attachment patterns and that allocating individuals into attachment categories is somewhat artificial; individuals can display characteristics associated with various attachment patterns (Fraley & Waller, 1998).

References

Beaven, V., Read, J., & Cartwright, C. (2011). The prevalence of voice-hearers in the general population: A literature review. *Journal of Mental Health, 20*(3), 281–292.

Bentall, R. P. (1990). The illusion of reality: a review and integration of psychological research on hallucinations. *Psychological Bulletin, 107*(1), 82–95.

Bentall, R. P., & Fernyhough, C. (2008). Social predictors of psychotic experiences: specificity and psychological mechanisms. *Schizophrenia Bulletin, 34*(6), 1012–1020.

Bentall, R. P., Wickham, S., Shevlin, M., & Varese, F. (2012). Do specific early-life adversities lead to specific symptoms of Psychosis? A study from the 2007 the adult psychiatric morbidity survey. *Schizophrenia Bulletin, 38*(4), 734–740.

Bernstein, D., Fink, L., Handelsman, L., Foote, J., Lovejoy, M., Wenzel, K., Sapereto, E., & Ruggiero, M. (1994). Initial reliability and validity of a new retrospective measure of child abuse and neglect. *American Journal of Psychiatry, 151*(8), 1132–1136.

Berry, K., Barrowclough, C., & Wearden, A. (2008). Attachment theory: A framework for understanding symptoms and interpersonal relationships in psychosis. *Behaviour Research and Therapy, 46*(12), 1275–1282.

Berry, K., & Drake, R. (2010). Attachment theory in psychiatric rehabilitation: Informing clinical practice. *Advances in Psychiatric Treatment, 16*(4), 308–315.

Berry, K., Ford, S., Jellicoe-Jones, L., & Haddock, G. (2013). PTSD symptoms associated with the experiences of psychosis and hospitalisation: A review of the literature. *Clinical Psychology Review, 33*(4), 526–538.

Berry, K., Wearden, A., Barrowclough, C., Oakland, L., & Bradley, J. (2011). An investigation of adult attachment and the nature of relationships with voices. *British Journal of Clinical Psychology, 51*(3), 280–291.

Birchwood, M., Gilbert, P., Gilbert, J., Trowler, P., Meaden, A., Hay, J.,Murray, E., Miles, J. (2004). Interpersonal and role-related schema influence the relationship with the dominant 'voice' in schizophrenia: A comparison of three models. *Psychological Medicine, 34*(8), 1571.

Bowlby, J. (1982). Attachment and loss: Retrospect and prospect. *American Journal of Orthopsychiatry, 52*(4), 664–678.

Brown, R. J. (2004). Psychological mechanisms of medically unexplained symptoms: An integrative conceptual model. *Psychological Bulletin, 130*(5), 793–812.

Brown, R. J. (2006). Different types of 'Dissociation' have different psychological mechanisms. *Journal of Trauma & Dissociation*, 7(4), 7–28.

Brown, R. (2013). Explaining the unexplained. *The Psychologist*, 26, 868–872.

Carlson, E. A. (1998). A prospective longitudinal study of attachment disorganization/disorientation. *Child Development*, 69(4), 1107–1128.

Carlson, E., & Putnam, F. (1993). An update on the Dissociative Experiences Scale. *Dissociation: Progress in the Dissociative Disorders*, 6(1), 16–27.

Chadwick, P., & Birchwood, M. (1994). The omnipotence of voices. A cognitive approach to auditory hallucinations. *British Journal of Psychiatry*, 164(2), 190–201.

Cicchetti, D., Rogosch, F., & Toth, S. (2006). Fostering secure attachment in infants in maltreating families through preventive interventions. *Development and Psychopathology*, 18(3), 623–649.

Crittenden, P. (2005). Attachment theory, psychopathology and psychotherapy: the dynamic-maturational approach. *Psicoterapia*, 30, 171–182.

Cyr, C., Euser, E. M., Bakermans-Kranenburg, M. J., & van Ijzendoorn, M. H. (2010). Attachment security and disorganization in maltreating and high-risk families: A series of meta-analyses. *Development and Psychopathology*, 22(1), 87–108.

Dillon, J. (2010). The tale of an ordinary little girl. *Psychosis*, 2(1), 79–83.

Gumley, A., Schwannauer, M., MacBeth, A. & Read, J. (2008). Emotional recovery and staying well after psychosis: An attachment-based conceptualisation. *Attachment: New Directions in Psychotherapy and Relational Psychoanalysis*, 2, 127–148.

Hatzipetrou, L., & Oei, T. P. (2010). Coping with psychological distress associated to positive symptoms of schizophrenia: A brief cognitive behavioral intervention. *Clinical Case Studies*, 9(5), 339–352.

Hesse, E., & van Ijzendoorn, M. H. (1998). Parental loss of close family members and propensities towards absorption in offspring. *Developmental Science*, 1(2), 299–305.

Holmes, E., Brown, R., Mansell, W., Fearon, R., Hunter, E., Frasquilho, F., & Oakley, D. (2005). Are there two qualitatively distinct forms of dissociation? A review and some clinical implications. *Clinical Psychology Review*, 25(1), 1–23.

Kilcommons, A. M., Morrison, A. P., Knight, A., & Lobban, F. (2008). Psychotic experiences in people who have been sexually assaulted. *Social Psychiatry and Psychiatric Epidemiology*, 43(8), 602–611.

Liotti, G. (1992). Disorganized/disoriented attachment in the etiology of the dissociative disorders. *Dissociation: Progress in the Dissociative Disorders*, 5(4), 196–204.

Liotti, G. (2004). Trauma, dissociation, and disorganized attachment: Three strands of a single braid. *Psychotherapy: Theory, Research, Practice, Training*, 41(4), 472.

Longden, E., Madill, A., & Waterman, M. G. (2012). Dissociation, trauma, and the role of lived experience: Toward a new conceptualization of voice hearing. *Psychological Bulletin*, 138(1), 28–76.

Lyons-Ruth, K., & Jacobvitz, D. (1999). *Attachment Disorganization: Unresolved loss, relational violence, and lapses in behavioral and attentional strategies*. New York, NY: Guilford Press.

Lyons–Ruth, K., Yellin, C., Melnick, S., & Atwood, G. (2005). Expanding the concept of unresolved mental states: Hostile/helpless states of mind on the Adult Attachment Interview are associated with disrupted mother–infant communication and infant disorganization. *Development and Psychopathology*, 17(1), 1–23.

MacBeth, A., Gumley, A., Schwannauer, M., & Fisher, R. (2011). Attachment states of mind, mentalization, and their correlates in a first-episode psychosis sample. *Psychology and Psychotherapy: Theory, Research and Practice*, *84*(1), 42–57.

MacBeth, A., Schwannauer, M., & Gumley, A. (2008). The association between attachment style, social mentalities, and paranoid ideation: An analogue study. *Psychology and Psychotherapy: Theory, Research and Practice*, *81*(1), 79–93.

Mallinckrodt, B. (2010). The psychotherapy relationship as attachment: Evidence and implications. *Journal of Social and Personal Relationships*, *27*(2), 262–270.

Mawson, A., Cohen, K., & Berry, K. (2010). Reviewing evidence for the cognitive model of auditory hallucinations: The relationship between cognitive voice appraisals and distress during psychosis. *Clinical Psychology Review*, *30*(2), 248–258.

McCarthy-Jones, S., & Davidson, L. (2013). When soft voices die: Auditory verbal hallucinations and a four letter word (love). *Mental Health, Religion & Culture*, *16*(4), 367–383.

Morrison, A. (1998). A cognitive analysis of the maintenance of auditory hallucinations: Are voices to schizophrenia what bodily sensations are to panic? *Behavioural and Cognitive Psychotherapy*, *26*(4), 289–302.

Morrison, A. P., Frame, L., & Larkin, W. (2003). Relationships between trauma and psychosis: A review and integration. *British Journal of Clinical Psychology*, *42*(4), 331–353.

Moskowitz, A., Read, J., Farrelly, S., Rudegeair, T., & Williams, O. (2009). Are psychotic symptoms traumatic in origin and dissociative in kind? In P. F Dell & J. A O'Neill (Eds.). *Dissociation and the Dissociative Disorders: DSM-V and beyond* (El). New York: Routledge.

Newman- Taylor, K., & Sambrook, S. (2013). The role of dissociation in psychosis; implications for clinical practice. In F. C. Kennedy, H. Kennerley, & D. Pearson (Eds.), *Cognitive Behavioural Approaches to the Understanding and Treatment of Dissociation*. Oxford: Taylor & Francis.

Ogawa, J. R., Sroufe, L. A., Weinfield, N. S., Carlson, E. A., & Egeland, B. (1997). Development and the fragmented self: Longitudinal study of dissociative symptomatology in a nonclinical sample. *Development and Psychopathology*, *9*(4), 855–879.

Perona-Garcelán, S., Carrascoso- López, F., García-Montes, J., Ductor-Recuerda, M., López Jiménez, A., Vallina-Fernández, O., Pérez-Álvarez, M., Gómez-Gómez, M. (2012). Dissociative experiences as mediators between childhood trauma and auditory hallucinations. *Journal of Traumatic Stress*, *25*(3), 323–329.

Pilton, M., Bucci, S., McManus, J., Hayward, M., Emsley, R., & Berry, K. (2016). Does insecure attachment mediate the relationship between trauma and voice-hearing in psychosis? *Psychiatry Research*, *246*, 776–782.

Ponizovsky, A. M., Vitenberg, E., Baumgarten-Katz, I., & Grinshpoon, A. (2011). Attachment styles and affect regulation among outpatients with schizophrenia: Relationships to symptomatology and emotional distress. *Psychology and Psychotherapy: Theory, Research and Practice*, *86*(2), 164–182.

Read, J., & Gumley, A. (2008). Can attachment theory help explain the relationship between childhood adversity and psychosis? *Attachment: New Directions in Psychotherapy and Relational Psychoanalysis*, *2*(1), 1–35.

Read, J., Fosse, R., Moskowitz, A., & Perry, B. (2014). The traumagenic neurodevelopmental model of psychosis revisited. *Neuropsychiatry*, *4*(1), 65–79.

Read, J., van Os, J., Morrison, A., & Ross, C. (2005). Childhood trauma, psychosis and schizophrenia: A literature review with theoretical and clinical implications. *Acta Psychiatrica Scandinavica, 112*(5), 330–350.

Sierra, M., & Berrios, G. E. (1998). Depersonalization: Neurobiological perspectives. *Biological Psychiatry, 44*(9), 898–908.

Stanghellini, G., & Cutting, J. (2003). Auditory verbal hallucinations – breaking the silence of inner dialogue. *Psychopathology, 36*(3), 120–128.

Taylor, P. J., Rietzschel, J., Danquah, A. N., & Berry, K. (2014). The role of attachment style, attachment to therapist, and working alliance in response to psychological therapy. *Psychology and Psychotherapy: Theory, Research and Practice, 88*(3), 240–253.

Thomas, N., Hayward, M., Peters, E., van der Gaag, M., Bentall, R., Jenner, J., Strauss, C., Sommer, I., Johns, L., Varese, F., Garcia-Montes, J., Waters, F., Dogdson, G., & McCarthy-Jones, S. (2014). Psychological therapies for Auditory hallucinations (voices): Current status and key directions for future research. *Schizophrenia Bulletin, 40*(Suppl 4), S202–S212.

van Ijzendoorn, M. H. (1995). Adult attachment representations, parental responsiveness and infant attachment: A meta-analysis on the predictive validity of the Adult Attachment Interview. *Psychological Bulletin, 117*, 387–403.

van Ijzendoorn, M. H., Schuengel, C., & Bakerman–Kranenburg, M. J. (1999). Disorganized attachment in early childhood: Meta-analysis of precursors, concomitants, and sequelae. *Development and Psychopathology, 11*(2), 225–250.

Varese, F., Barkus, E., & Bentall, R. P. (2012). Dissociation mediates the relationship between childhood trauma and hallucination-proneness. *Psychological Medicine, 42*(5), 1025–1036.

Varese, F., Smeets, F., Drukker, M., Lieverse, R., Lataster, T., Viechtbauer, W., ... & Bentall, R. P. (2012). Childhood adversities increase the risk of psychosis: a meta-analysis of patient-control, prospective-and cross-sectional cohort studies. *Schizophrenia Bulletin, 8*(4), 661–671.

Waters, F., Allen, P., Aleman, A., Fernyhough, C., Woodward, T., Badcock, J., Barkus, E., Johns, L., Varese, F., Menon, M., Vercammen, A., & Laroi, F. (2012). Auditory hallucinations in schizophrenia and Nonschizophrenia populations: A review and integrated model of cognitive mechanisms. *Schizophrenia Bulletin, 38*(4), 683–693.

Wickham, S., Sitko, K., & Bentall, R. (2014). Insecure attachment is associated with paranoia but not hallucinations in psychotic patients: The mediating role of negative self-esteem. *Psychological Medicine, 45*(7), 1495–1507.

4

PROMOTING RECOVERY
FROM NEGATIVE SYMPTOMS

An attachment theory perspective

Helen Griffiths and Hamish McLeod

Individuals characterised as having the negative symptoms of psychosis participate less in constructive or pleasurable activity and often appear disengaged from interpersonal situations. This group of people also experience less positive emotion, heightened levels of negative affect, and often present as devoid of emotional expression. Their speech can appear impoverished and corresponding mental experiences can be profoundly disrupted. Such difficulties are associated with significant impairments in psychosocial functioning (Hunter & Barry, 2012), lower quality of life (Ho et al., 1998) and poorer recovery (Milev et al., 2005). Response to both pharmacotherapy and psychological interventions appears limited (Fusar-Polis et al., 2014; Velthorst et al., 2015). Furthermore, the diversity of the techniques employed in psychological treatment trials makes it difficult to ascertain potential ingredients that bring about improvement (Thomas, 2015).

To date, many theoretical frameworks underpinning both pharmacological and psychological treatments have mainly reflected the historical understanding of negative symptoms as diminished or absent behaviour, functioning and experience (Aleman et al., 2016). We argue that, seen through the lens of attachment theory, negative symptoms can be at least partially understood within a developmental framework of adaptation and resilience, as indicators of a learned coping response in the face of overwhelming life adversity that includes both externally experienced events and painful affects that are avoided (Lysaker et al., 2016). Hence, negative symptoms may be seen as responses involving emotional and social withdrawal that emerge from threats to self-security. This alternative perspective may enrich recovery-orientated approaches by supporting attempts to re-engage with life.

The nature of negative symptoms

Even the most severe negative symptoms are known to fluctuate (Ventura et al., 2004). Current cognitive behavioural therapy (CBT) models propose that variations in negative symptoms relate to changes in self-defeating beliefs (Grant & Beck, 2009; Rector et al., 2005). A recent meta-analysis examining changes in negative symptoms in outpatient populations challenges the view that there is limited improvement over time (Savill et al., 2014). Instead, the results suggest that most patients exhibit some recovery of negative symptoms over time. So, rather than viewing negative symptoms as unresponsive to treatment and predictive of an inevitably chronic illness course, the rate of recovery may be helped by developing more refined psychosocial interventions.

Negative symptoms can be observed in individuals at high risk of developing psychosis (Piskulic et al., 2012), they predict likelihood of transition to psychosis (Demjaha et al., 2012, Piskulic et al., 2012) and can feature during first episode presentations (Lyne et al., 2012). Importantly, early difficulties in adjustment and psychosocial functioning link to greater severity of negative symptoms in both first episode and chronic populations (MacBeth & Gumley, 2008). Whilst it has been argued that problems with poor premorbid functioning and the early manifestation of negative symptoms reflect a neurodevelopmental disorder that becomes evident during adolescence (e.g. Fenton & McGlashan, 1991), it has also been established that exposure to socioeconomic deprivation (Drukker et al., 2006), discrimination (Janssen et al., 2003), childhood abuse, neglect and bullying (Varese et al., 2012), and attachment-related disruptions to secure attachments elevate the risk of psychosis. As MacBeth and Gumley (2008) point out, it would be reasonable to expect that early adversity impacts not only on risk for psychosis, but will also affect premorbid adjustment prior to the development of psychosis. Thus, the difficulty in distinguishing problems in premorbid adjustment, functioning and quality of life from negative symptoms (Malla & Payne, 2005) may be explained within a developmental framework focused on how life experience and learned self-regulatory processes are key risk mechanisms implicated in the early ontogeny of negative symptoms. It has also been proposed that negative symptoms can reflect protective responses to overwhelming life experience including psychosis itself (e.g. Read et al., 2001; Stampfer, 1990). In line with this, psychological adjustment following psychosis, expressed as recovery style, has been shown to be both independent and predictive of poorer outcome on a range of variables, including negative symptoms. For example, individuals with a sealing-over recovery style – a way of coping that minimises the significance of symptoms and their impact – had worse negative symptom and quality of life scores at 12 months than those characterised as having integrative or mixed recovery styles (Tait et al., 2003; Thompson et al., 2003).

Attachment, mentalisation and negative symptoms

Against this background, the emerging evidence that attachment insecurity is associated with negative symptoms is of considerable interest. The impact of early attachment experience on interpersonal functioning and relationships, emotion regulation, and identity formation is well established. Insecure attachment classifications, specifically dismissing/avoidant attachment, appear to be overrepresented in psychosis (Gumley et al., 2014). Moreover, avoidant attachment, characterised by affective deactivation, interpersonal distancing and difficulty recalling emotive memories of past experiences, has been specifically associated with negative symptoms in non-clinical and clinical populations (see Table 4.1). Given that self-report measures may be subject to biases arising from the activation of the attachment system whereby individuals with avoidant attachment styles can tend to report their attachment as secure (e.g. Gumley et al., 2014), these may be underestimates. Recent evidence shows that attachment security, evaluated using the narrative-based Adult Attachment Interview classification system, predicts recovery from negative symptoms at 12 months after controlling for relevant baseline variables (Gumley et al., 2014). There are also particular associations between attachment avoidance and specific negative symptom subtypes such as a loss of the ability to experience pleasure (anhedonia), or social and emotional withdrawal (e.g. Berry et al., 2006, 2007; Wilson & Costanzo, 1996; Korver-Nieberg et al., 2015). In summary, individuals with avoidant attachment style demonstrate restrictions of social-cognitive-affective experience, a pattern frequently observed in people diagnosed with schizophrenia (Gumley, 2011). We propose that these early emotional adaptation processes confer a significant risk for the subsequent emergence of negative symptoms such as asociality, affective flattening, reduced experience of thoughts, diminished motivation and anhedonia.

It has also been suggested that negative symptoms may develop as a consequence of reduced capacity for mentalisation (Gumley et al., 2014; Harder, 2014). Mentalisation is conceptually related to other social cognition capacities that have received considerable attention. For example, Frith's (1992) cognitive neurophysiological model of schizophrenia proposed that difficulties with thinking about mental states (Theory of Mind), including monitoring one's own intentional acts, contribute substantially to the development of negative symptoms. The notion that understanding of one's own mind and the mind of others are central to understanding negative symptoms has been corroborated by studies associating Theory of Mind and other social cognition impairments with behavioural indicators of negative symptoms (Sprong et al., 2007), negative/disorganisation symptoms (Ventura et al., 2013) and social/functional outcomes (Bora et al., 2009; Fett et al., 2010). It is now known that social cognition interacts with negative self-concepts, such as those related to interpersonal competence, to influence negative symptom expression (Lincoln et al., 2011). In summary, social interaction can be affected by very specific processes (e.g. reading facial expressions) as well as much more complex and integrated processes (e.g. combining multiple sources of information into complex and flexible understandings of the reasons for one's own behaviour and the behaviour of others).

Table 4.1 Attachment status and negative symptoms

Study	Design	Sample characteristics	Key measures	Key findings
i. NON-CLINICAL SAMPLES				
Wilson & Costanzo (1996)	Cross-sectional study of attachment style and sub-clinical psychotic phenomena (schizotypy, attentional impairment, psychosis proneness).	273 university students	Adult Attachment Scale Scale of Attitudes and Experiences (schizotypy)	Insecure-avoidant attachment style associated with negative schizotypy. Secure attachment protects individuals from anhedonia (r^2=between .06 and .14 for different assessments)
Berry et al. (2006)	Cross-sectional study of attachment style and sub-clinical psychotic phenomena	323 university students	PAM Social Anhedonia Scale	Insecure-avoidant attachment patterns were associated with social anhedonia (r=.44)
Berry et al (2007)	Cross-sectional analogue study of attachment, negative life events and schizotypy	304 university students	PAM Oxford-Liverpool Inventory of Feelings and Experiences scale (introvertive anhedonia)	Attachment avoidance associated with introvertive anhedonia (r=.50)
ii. CLINICAL SAMPLE STUDIES				
Ponizovsky et al. (2007)	Cross-sectional with, between and within groups comparisons	30 male inpatients diagnosed with schizophrenia spectrum disorders and 30 age and gender matched controls	Hazan & Shaver questionnaire measure of attachment PANSS	Patients with high PANSS negative symptom scale scores also showed higher rates of insecure-avoidant attachment

(continued)

Table 4.1 (Cont.)

Study	Design	Sample characteristics	Key measures	Key findings
Berry et al. (2008)	Prospective study with follow up at 6 months	96 individuals diagnosed with schizophrenia spectrum diagnoses.	PAM PANSS	PANSS negative symptoms were positively correlated with insecure-avoidant attachment at baseline (r=.24)
Kvrgic et al (2011)	Cross-sectional	127 individuals diagnosed with chronic schizophrenia or schizoaffective disorder	PAM PANSS	No association between attachment avoidance and negative symptoms
Gumley et al. (2014)	12-month longitudinal study with assessments at 6 month intervals	58 first episode psychosis service users in specialist public mental health services	Adult Attachment Interview PANSS	68% of the sample exhibited an insecure attachment style (48.1% dismissing, 20.4% preoccupied). Attachment at baseline predicted negative symptom recovery at 6 and 12 months.
Korver-Nieberg et al (2015)	Cross-sectional study of people diagnosed with schizophrenia spectrum disorders	500 patients	Relationship Questionnaire PANSS	Attachment avoidance was not associated with overall negative symptom scores but there was evidence of associations with social and emotional withdrawal

Notes
PAM – Psychosis Assessment Measure; PANSS – Positive and Negative Syndrome Scale

Mentalisation and metacognition have at times been used in the psychosis literature more or less interchangeably to refer to the complex representation of mental states of self and others (e.g. Semerari et al., 2003; Lysaker et al., 2013). We emphasise mentalisation's focus on the way in which these psychological competencies are learnt in attachment or relational contexts. As conceptualised by Peter Fonagy and colleagues, mentalisation "describes the way humans make sense of their social world by imagining the *mental states* (e.g., beliefs, motives, emotions, desires, and needs) that underpin their own and others' behaviors in interpersonal interactions" (Choi-Kain & Gunderson, 2008, p.1127). Mentalisation capacity is facilitated through early attachment experience and a caregiver's contingent mirroring of the infant's affective states, and is consequently intrinsically linked to an individual's capacity to employ affect regulation strategies. Secure attachments provide the psychosocial foundations for acquiring the capacity to develop adequate understanding of one's own and others' minds. Effective mentalisation allows the individual to organise changing social information in a way that regulates emotions, provides a guide to action and supports the person's ability to act independently as an agent of their own destiny. When attachment is disrupted, the ability to have complex thoughts about the self and the world can be adversely affected and this results in less resilience when faced with conflicts and dilemmas relating to social interactions or making sense of one's internal experiences (Fonagy & Target, 1997).

Mentalisation is more severely compromised in dismissing as opposed to secure or preoccupied attachment states of mind in individuals with psychosis (MacBeth et al., 2011). We identified 14 studies suggesting links between self/other mental state processing and negative symptoms (Buck et al., 2014; Hamm et al., 2012; Lysaker et al., 2005, 2010, 2011, 2015; MacBeth et al., 2011, 2014, 2016; McLeod et al., 2014; Minor & Lysaker, 2014; Mitchell et al., 2012; Nicolo et al., 2012; Rabin et al., 2014). These relationships extend across cognitive, emotional and integrative aspects of mentalising processes (MacBeth et al., 2016). The majority of studies are cross-sectional, but three indicate that the relationship is linked to the expression of negative symptoms over time in both first episode samples and samples with more established diagnoses populations (Hamm et al., 2012; Lysaker et al., 2015; McLeod et al., 2014). More refined studies could describe and clarify these relationships in terms of specific metacognitive processes and/or negative symptom subtypes. For example, there is evidence that reduced ability to form and use complex ideas about self and others can exacerbate anhedonia, even in the absence of depressed mood (Buck et al., 2014).

In summary, there is evidence that both avoidant attachment and reduced capacity for mentaliation are implicated in negative symptom expression in both early and later stage psychosis. In Figure 4.1, we propose an explanatory framework, expanding on previous proposals by Gumley et al. (2014) and Harder (2014), which suggests how attachment theory could inform

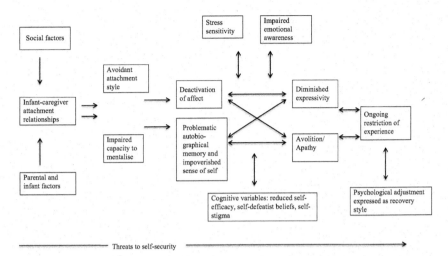

Figure 4.1 Psychological variables implicated in the development and maintenance of negative symptoms

our understanding of negative symptoms. In the sections below, we describe potential roles of affect regulation mechanisms and autobiographical memory, considering how these may inform the emergence and maintenance of negative symptoms such as diminished expressivity and avolition/apathy.

Affect regulation

Flat affect, characterised by unchanging facial expression and paucity of gesture, is prominent during first episode and more established presentations (Evensen et al., 2012). However, there is a marked contrast between the emotional experience and expression of individuals diagnosed with schizophrenia, who consistently report less experience of positive affect but greater intensity of negative affect than people included as comparison participants. It is further known that individuals with psychosis have problems with emotion recognition, likely to be present before psychosis onset (Amminger et al., 2012), and linked to social dysfunction, (Kimhy et al., 2012, 2014) and metacognition (Hamm et al., 2012). A recent study of people diagnosed with psychotic disorder demonstrated that this impaired ability to be aware of and to tolerate distressing emotions was associated with increased stress, as measured by both self-report and skin conductance levels (Lincoln et al., 2015). Interestingly, an altered, heightened sensitivity to stress has previously been established as a risk mechanism for psychosis (Myin-Germeys & van Os, 2007). Furthermore, impaired stress tolerance has been associated with negative as well as other symptoms in individuals at high clinical risk of developing psychosis (DeVylder et al., 2013). Although people with psychosis may experience but be less aware of heightened negative affect, they use similar emotion regulation strategies to individuals with anxiety and depressive disorders (Livingstone et al., 2009). However, they use more dysfunctional regulation strategies (e.g. suppression) than non-patient controls (O'Driscoll et al., 2014). To summarise, individuals prone to psychosis demonstrate emotional reactivity in conjunction with a diminished awareness of their own affective state, but use normal, if ultimately maladaptive, regulatory processes to deal with emotional arousal. This style of dealing with emotional information might shape negative symptom expression.

Adults with dismissing attachment states of mind direct their attention away from emotion and complex mental states, possibly reflecting a developmental adaptation to persistent rejection from caregivers at times of distress. Consistent with this, the degree of critical comments from family members was more strongly associated with negative symptoms than positive symptoms (Barrowclough et al., 2003; for a broader discussion of attachment and expressed emotion see Patterson elsewhere in this volume). At the core of mentalisation is 'mentalized affectivity' (Fonagy et al., 2002), the capacity to reflect upon the meaning of one's emotional states as they unfold. The inability to reflect upon emotional distress and its psychosocial causation is not only likely to result in diminished expressivity, but may also block social behaviour, given that distress fails to be communicated. Possible links between unhelpful self-focus (e.g. rumination) and the use of emotional avoidance and withdrawal strategies to deal with interpersonal difficulties have been demonstrated (e.g. McLeod et al., 2014).

The reduced capacity to experience *positive* affect is also likely to play a key role in the development and maintenance of negative symptoms. It is unsurprising that there is little opportunity for positive affect if an individual finds their own or others' minds confusing and/or threatening and uses emotional, behavioural and social avoidance as primary regulatory strategies. Low expectations of pleasure and success lead to further lost opportunities for meaningful engagement in activity, and become a self-fulfilling prophecy (Rector et al., 2005) that consolidates the maintenance cycle. Although *anticipation* of pleasure may be impaired, individuals with a high level of anhedonia can still experience a normal enjoyment response once they are engaged in a pleasurable activity (Gard et al., 2007).

Autobiographical memory and personal identity

The impact of early attachment experience, particularly the ability to recall and reflect on its significance, has long been associated with the development of the sense of self (Cole & Putnam, 1992; Briere, 2002; Conway & Pleydell-Pearce, 2000). The contribution of autobiographical memory to the self is, however, known to be tempered by the need for a coherent and consistent sense of one's self and identity (Conway et al., 2004). For example, when an individual is overwhelmed by life experience, the drive for returning to a stable sense of self identity is given priority over the integration of threatening personal information that goes against one's values or that is inconsistent with one's self-view. In such circumstances, individuals with a dismissing/avoidant attachment style appear to restrict attention to attachment experience, providing sparse personal life-stories in which difficulties appear downplayed. More broadly, this so-called 'overgeneral memory' is considered to be a strategic attempt to control affect associated with specific negative events (Williams et al., 1999). Within various clinical groups, including individuals diagnosed with schizophrenia, lack of specificity in personal memory recall seems to have an adaptive function in the prevention of suicidality (Taylor et al., 2010).

Such self-regulation may come at considerable personal expense. The personal narratives of individuals with dismissing attachment states of mind typically fail to articulate emotional experience, appearing remote and abstract, fragmented, undeveloped and inflexible. Coupled with the ongoing disruption of mentalisation, this distorted recall of key life experience may confer risk for negative symptoms. Attempts to dampen down emotional fluctuations may not only result in restricted expression of affective experience, but also impact on goal-directed activity. In Conway and Pleydell-Pearces's (2000) self-memory system framework, autobiographical memories are seen as forms of mental models that are distinct by virtue of containing self-knowledge and memories for specific episodes experienced in one's life. Importantly, the self-memory system also includes the self's working goals. In this way, autobiographical memory and the sense of oneself as being able to actively influence one's life are intrinsically linked: autobiographical memory 'constrains what the self is, has been and can be' (Conway, 2005). Restricting access to autobiographical memory in order to preserve self-coherence may therefore come about at the expense of engagement in goal-directed activity, and associated development of avolition/apathy.

It has been well documented that people with a diagnosis of schizophrenia have problematic recall of personal past events (Berna et al., 2015). The impact of this may be particularly evident during a crucial period for identity formation i.e. late adolescence (Cuervo-Lombard et al., 2006). Difficulty recalling autobiographical memories or reduced memory specificity is not, of course, specific to schizophrenia, but present in various mental health problems including depression (Liu et al., 2013) and post-traumatic stress (Moore & Zoellner, 2007). Childhood trauma is linked to impairments of memory for earlier life experiences across diagnoses, including in people who have received a diagnosis of schizophrenia (Shannon et al., 2011). Such experiences have been hypothesised to play a specific role in the development of negative symptoms (Read et al., 2001). Relationships have been identified between negative symptoms and autobiographical memory performance (Aleman et al., 1999; Schmid et al., 2011) and specifically with traumatic memories (McLeod et al., 2006). In a small study exploring the relationships between negative symptoms and autobiographical memory, those with more negative symptoms retrieved fewer specific autobiographical memories and negative symptoms were significantly predicted by both avoidance of traumatic memories and lack of specificity of autobiographical recall (Harrison & Fowler, 2004). Finally, Berna et al. (2011) showed that an impaired ability to give meaning to memories that have a strong influence on one's development of self-identity is associated with higher levels of negative symptoms.

Agency can be broadly understood as the basic recognition of the experience of owning and generating one's own thoughts, feelings and behaviours (Lysaker & Leonhardt, 2012). This is a fundamental starting point for experiencing more complex thoughts and is therefore a foundation capacity underpinning metacognition/mentalisation. It is likely that self-regulatory processes associated with impairments of autobiographical memory interact with both the capacity for mentalisation and cognitive variables such as self-efficacy (i.e. appraisals of one's ability to act successfully in the face of challenges). Negative symptoms are associated with reduced self-efficacy (Bentall et al., 2010; Hill & Startup, 2013) as well as the endorsement of attitudes that undermine functioning (e.g. "If you cannot do something well, there is no point in doing it at all") (Ventura et al., 2014). Recent research also suggests that negative symptoms develop in response to self-defeatist beliefs, and these beliefs may affect social functioning because they undermine the ability to see oneself as competent and able (Vaskinn et al., 2015). It seems likely that relationships between self-efficacy, dysfunctional attitudes and negative symptoms are mutually reinforcing. As an individual's experience and sense of autonomy become ever more restricted, negative symptoms become more entrenched, further restricting opportunities for rich life experience. Given that the sharing of personal stories is fundamental to the development of meaningful human relationships, restricted life narratives may foster increasing isolation. Beliefs about loss, humiliation and entrapment (Iqbal et al., 2000) may then further limit an individual's ability to build an assertive identity as an agentive self who is capable of participation in interpersonal domains.

The costs of these self-regulatory processes are evident in those individuals whose recovery style following the trauma of an acute episode of psychosis has been characterised as 'sealing over'. These individuals tend not to try to integrate or make sense of their psychotic experience in the context of their overall life experience (McGlashan, 1987). Such avoidant coping styles are associated with negative early childhood experience, insecure attachment, negative self-evaluation and insecure identity (Tait et al., 2004). Sealing over is associated with higher levels of negative symptoms (Modestin et al., 2004, 2009; Thompson et al., 2003), poorer social functioning and lower quality of life (McGlashan, 1987; Drayton et al., 1998).

To summarise, it is known that attachment states of mind and the associated capacity for mentalisation are significant determinants of the production of self narratives, the evolution of a personal sense of meaning to life experience and the generation of personal identity. Psychological adjustment to life experience that is underpinned by the restriction of attention to personal memory gives priority to the preservation of a coherent personal identity whilst compromising the self's ability to drive future activity. Such self-regulation may therefore constitute significant risk not only for the emergence of diminished expressivity but also for avolition and motivational difficulties, and impinge significantly on the ongoing evolution of personal identity.

Limitations of pure deficit models – critique of contemporary models

Negative symptoms have typically not been a main treatment target in psychological treatment trials for psychosis over the past two decades (Velthorst et al., 2015). This lack of therapeutic attention is unfortunate given that there is convincing evidence that addressing negative symptoms such as apathy and lack of initiative is a top treatment priority for many people with psychosis (Sterk et al., 2013). Recently, more studies have specifically addressed the psychological understanding and treatment of negative symptoms in psychosis with four trials published between 2006–14 where allocation to treatment of a comparison condition was determined at random (see McLeod et al., 2014 for further discussion). The description of the intervention in three of these trials was based on a form of the standard CBT model that proposes that low expectations of success in social and functional spheres undermine role engagement and effort expenditure (Grant & Beck, 2009; Rector et al., 2005). This model leads to the use of treatment strategies such as challenging defeatist cognitions, supporting goal setting, testing out beliefs and expectations in real world situations, and making deliberate plans and schedules of activities (Grant et al., 2012). However, the data arising from these trials suggest the need for refinement of the standard CBT model. One indicator of this is that the standard approach may require a large number of treatment sessions to get quite modest symptom improvements (e.g. Grant et al.'s 2012 trial delivered an average of 51 sessions). Also, the standard CBT approach does not seem to be superior to strategies such as Cognitive Remediation Therapy that do not explicitly focus on changing thoughts and beliefs (Klingberg et al., 2011). These results do suggest that it is possible to make some progress in helping with negative symptoms via psychological methods. We suggest that viewing negative symptoms from the perspective of attachment theory has implications for understanding the delivery of psychological treatments, which may be improved if we develop techniques that more directly target relational factors and the attachment concerns already described. The following case example points to many of these issues.

A case example

In the following example, we examine how applying attachment principles to case formulation could lead to useful adaptations of a commonly used therapy, CBT. Andreas is a 38-year-old man who lives at home with his elderly mother. His first episode of psychosis at 18 years of age resulted in a hospital admission. At that time he was experiencing distressing hallucinations and paranoia, he was socially withdrawn, had given up attending college and was isolating himself in his bedroom. He was originally encouraged to see his GP by his mother who was increasingly concerned that he was neglecting his self-care and losing weight. When first assessed, he was reluctant to discuss any sources of distress and he denied any need for help or support. The clinical team found it very difficult to engage Andreas in treatment activities. Even gentle encouragement would sometimes result in an agitated and hostile response. This discouraged the clinicians from continuing to push for engagement. A pattern of minimal interaction developed, with the focus of intervention mainly limited to safety monitoring and medication support.

Andreas was eventually referred for psychological treatment. The main areas of concern at that time were his arrested recovery and pervasive failure to engage with social and occupational activities. The assessment and engagement phase of therapy took eight sessions of gradual titration of contact. Andreas' therapeutic goals were to improve his motivation and to understand what was going on in his life, but he was reluctant to set himself any targets in terms of increased activity and was unable to identify potential sources of pleasure. In view of the fact that people with a diagnosis of schizophrenia may experience a form of anhedonia that arises from a fundamental impoverishment of internal experience such that they have substantial difficulty reflecting on and being fully aware of their likes, preferences, wishes and goals (Buck et al., 2014), the therapist was aware that trying to set goals and engage in activity scheduling in the standard CBT approach may be experienced as stressful rather than therapeutic.

It was therefore agreed to spend the next sessions improving his self-understanding. Although he repeatedly downplayed the severity of his current difficulties, Andreas did slowly open up about early difficulties attributable to his mother's alcoholism. He had been repeatedly sent to live with relatives at times when his mother was unable to cope. During many of these episodes he was sexually and physically abused. Although he made these disclosures, Andreas continued to describe many of these experiences in a dispassionate and unemotional way during this early phase of therapy. Although slow exploration of early memories and perceptions of key experiences were summarised by the therapist into a time-line, Andreas found it extremely difficult to reflect on how his early experiences might have had an impact on his current situation. Throughout therapy, the therapist maintained an awareness that people exhibiting an avoidant attachment style will likely experience the therapeutic relationship to be a source of stress and threat which may elicit deactivating emotion regulation strategies such as social withdrawal and down-regulation of metacognition (Gumley et al., 2014; Lysaker et al., 2015). This prompted the therapist to be particularly sensitive to relational patterns during sessions, attending to pacing and timing of sessions, continuously assessing the client's tolerance for addressing previously avoided emotional material, and actively working to strengthen the security of the therapeutic relationship. The experienced therapist required regular supervision to support this kind of work. Such strategies facilitated the development of a therapeutic relationship that the therapist believed was able to provide a helpful emotional experience (Daly & Mallinckrodt, 2009; Mallinckrodt & Jeong, 2015).

Adding these attachment dimensions to Andreas' therapeutic formulation also guided the matching of therapeutic strategies to the level of metacognitive capacity exhibited by him. The formulation that emerged over time was that Andreas had coped with repeated episodes of abusive behaviour from caregivers through social and emotional withdrawal. His aim was to become as inconspicuous as possible. Andreas' mental model of others became dominated by the view that people were at best unreliable as sources of support and at worst, dangerous and abusive. Unsurprisingly, he also seemed to have an impoverished capacity to think about the reasons why others act in the way that they do. Having had little opportunity to learn effective self-regulation, attempts to consider his own mental states were similarly experienced as overwhelmingly painful.

In this case we can see how there were barriers to implementing a standard CBT approach. Andreas' difficulties with engagement with professional carers and the limited emotional connectedness to his mother both reflect a fundamental disruption of the ability to use relationships to meet challenges, soothe negative affect or provide a source of encouragement and drive to engage with life challenges. Goals that involved any level of social connectedness and interpersonal relating activated distress, confusion and withdrawal behaviours. The goal setting process was further impeded by Andreas' diminished ability to reflect on his autobiographical memories and lack of access to previous sources of reward and meaning. Engaging in standard CBT techniques of exploring thoughts and feelings about others (e.g. expectations of low social acceptance) was difficult for Andreas because he experienced them as highly aversive.

Instead, Andreas' therapist used the formulation to guide treatment in the following ways. First, the carefully titrated engagement and assessment process created an opportunity to decrease the threat associated with interpersonal contact. The next therapeutic task was to help Andreas explore and differentiate his thoughts, feelings, goals, aspirations and wishes (e.g. see Lysaker et al., 2011 for a description of principles underpinning this approach). This then led to the therapist providing a model of her mind by describing in transparent terms some of the thoughts and understandings that occurred as therapy progressed. At a more subtle level, the therapy interaction also provided opportunities to shape up expressive behaviours that facilitated social interactions (e.g. the therapist explicitly provided feedback when she noticed an expression of affect passing across Andreas' face). This provided an opportunity for Andreas to practise noticing and reflecting on mental states in a way that minimised threat, ambiguity and misinterpretation. He was gradually encouraged to communicate to the therapist when he was experiencing high levels of affect during the session. The therapist then prompted the use of strategies such as grounding and soothing techniques. Once the basic ability to engage in conversations about thoughts, feelings, goals and aspirations had been re-established, therapy could move on to more conventional CBT strategies such as setting between session behavioural tasks, examining the accuracy of thoughts and beliefs that undermine behaviour change (e.g. engaging socially with others will always be unrewarding), and gradually expanding the range of behaviours that Andreas was willing to attempt (e.g. scheduling an achievable array of master and pleasure focused tasks).

This approach uses an understanding of attachment states of mind and the associated problems with mentalisation to reach people who are less responsive to standard CBT for negative symptom strategies. Our suggestions share commonalities with other variants of mentalisation-based therapy which have recently been adapted for individuals diagnosed with psychotic disorder to facilitate therapeutic alliance (Brent, 2015) and social functioning (Weijers et al., 2016). Most importantly, these approaches all identify the need to specifically target disturbances in thinking capacities related to awareness of self and others. Sensitively titrated therapy adapted along mentalisation-based therapy principles provides an opportunity to learn the interpersonal thinking and relating skills needed to re-engage with more traditional goal and task focused CBT.

Conclusions

There is increasing recognition that interventions for negative symptoms of schizophrenia require more attention. In fact, data collected from people diagnosed with psychoses suggest that improving motivation and self-understanding are highly ranked treatment targets (Byrne & Morrison, 2015; Sterk et al., 2013). In this chapter, we have tried to articulate an important but often overlooked issue for psychological treatments: there is a need to tailor the treatment strategies not just to address cognitive maintenance factors (e.g. self-defeating cognitions), but also to take account of relevant sources of resilience (Dudley et al., 2011) and interactions between distal risk factors such as abuse, neglect and disrupted attachment (Nolen-Hoeksema & Watkins, 2011). For some people exhibiting negative symptoms, attempts at standard approaches (e.g. CBT, social skills training) may not be possible until the impact of disrupted attachment has been assessed, understood and incorporated into the formulation and treatment plan. As our case study portrays, without attention being paid to these issues the likelihood of successful recovery is greatly reduced.

References

Aleman, A., Hijman, R., de Haan, E. H., & Kahn, R. S. (1999). Memory impairment in schizophrenia: a meta-analysis. *American Journal of Psychiatry*, *156*(9), 1358–1366.

Aleman, A., Lincoln, T. M., Bruggeman, R., Melle, I., Arends, J., Arango, C., & Knegtering, H. (2016). Treatment of negative symptoms: Where do we stand, and where do we go? *Schizophrenia Research*. http://doi.org/10.1016/j.schres.2016.05.015

Amminger, G. P., Schäfer, M. R., Papageorgiou, K., Klier, C. M., Schlögelhofer, M., Mossaheb, N., ... & McGorry, P. D. (2012). Emotion recognition in individuals at clinical high-risk for schizophrenia. *Schizophrenia Bulletin*, *38*(5), 1030–1039.

Barrowclough, C., Tarrier, N., Humphreys, L., Ward, J., Gregg, L., & Andrews, B. (2003). Self-esteem in schizophrenia: relationships between self-evaluation, family attitudes, and symptomatology. *Journal of Abnormal Psychology*, *112*(1), 92.

Bentall, R. P., Simpson, P. W., Lee, D. A., Williams, S., Elves, S., Brabbins, C., & Morrison, A. P. (2010). Motivation and avolition in schizophrenia patients: The role of self-efficacy. *Psychosis*, *2*(1), 12–22.

Berna, F., Potheegadoo, J., Aouadi, I., Ricarte, J. J., Allé, M. C., Coutelle, R., ... & Danion, J. M. (2015). A meta-analysis of autobiographical memory studies in schizophrenia spectrum disorder. *Schizophrenia Bulletin*, sbv099.

Berna, F., Bennouna-Greene, M., Potheegadoo, J., Verry, P., Conway, M. A., & Danion, J. M. (2011). Impaired ability to give a meaning to personally significant events in patients with schizophrenia. *Consciousness and Cognition*, *20*(3), 703–711.

Berry, K., Band, R., Corcoran, R., Barrowclough, C., & Wearden, A. (2007). Attachment styles, earlier interpersonal relationships and schizotypy in a non-clinical sample. *Psychology and Psychotherapy: Theory, Research and Practice*, *80*(4), 563–576.

Berry, K., Barrowclough, C., & Wearden, A. (2008). Attachment theory: A framework for understanding symptoms and interpersonal relationships in psychosis. *Behaviour Research and Therapy*, 46, 1275–1282.

Berry, K., Wearden, A., Barrowclough, C., & Liversidge, T. (2006). Attachment styles, interpersonal relationships and psychotic phenomena in a non-clinical student sample. *Personality and Individual Differences*, *41*(4), 707–718.

Bora, E., Yucel, M., & Pantelis, C.. (2009). Theory of mind impairment in schizophrenia: Meta-analysis. *Schizophrenia Research*, *109*(1), 1–9.

Brent, B. K. (2015). A Mentalization-Based approach to the development of the therapeutic alliance in the treatment of Schizophrenia. *Journal of Clinical Psychology*, *71*(2), 146–156.

Briere, J. (2002). Treating Adult Survivors of Severe Childhood Abuse. *The APSAC Handbook on Child Maltreatment*, 175.

Buck, K. D., McLeod, H. J., Gumley, A., Dimaggio, G., Buck, B. E., Minor, K. S., ... & Lysaker, P. H. (2014). Anhedonia in prolonged schizophrenia spectrum patients with relatively lower vs. higher levels of depression disorders: Associations with deficits in social cognition and metacognition. *Consciousness and Cognition, 29*, 68–75.

Byrne, R., & Morrison, A. P. (2014). Service users' priorities and preferences for treatment of psychosis: a user-led Delphi study. *Psychiatric Services.*

Choi-Kain, L. W., & Gunderson, J. G. (2008). Mentalization: ontogeny, assessment, and application in the treatment of borderline personality disorder. *American Journal of Psychiatry, 165*(9), 1127–1135.

Cole, P. M., & Putnam, F. W. (1992). Effect of incest on self and social functioning: A developmental psychopathology perspective. *Journal of Consulting and Clinical Psychology, 60*(2), 174.

Conway, M. A., & Pleydell-Pearce, C. W. (2000). The construction of autobiographical memories in the self-memory system. *Psychological Review, 107*(2), 261.

Conway, M. A., Singer, J. A. & Tagini, A. (2004) The Self and Autobiographical Memory: Correspondence and Coherence. *Social Cognition, 22*(5), 491–529.

Conway, M. A. (2005). Memory and the self. *Journal of Memory and Language, 53*(4), 594–628.

Cuervo-Lombard, C., Jovenin, N., Hedelin, G., Rizzo-Peter, L., Conway, M., & Danion, J. (2007). Autobiographical memory of adolescence and early adulthood events: An investigation in schizophrenia. *Journal of the International Neuropsychological Society, 13*(2), 335–343.

Daly, K. D., & Mallinckrodt, B. (2009). Experienced therapists' approach to psychotherapy for adults with attachment avoidance or attachment anxiety. *Journal of Counseling Psychology, 56*(4), 549–563. http://doi.org/10.1037/a0016695

Devylder, J. E., Ben-David, S., Schobel, S. A., Kimhy, D., Malaspina, D., & Corcoran, C. M. (2013). Temporal association of stress sensitivity and symptoms in individuals at clinical high risk for psychosis. *Psychological Medicine, 43*(2), 259–268.

Demjaha, A., Valmaggia, L., Stahl, D., Byrne, M., & McGuire, P. (2012). Disorganization/cognitive and negative symptom dimensions in the at-risk mental state predict subsequent transition to psychosis. *Schizophrenia Bulletin, 38*(2), 351–359.

Drayton, M., Birchwood, M., & Trower, P. (1998). Early attachment experience and recovery from psychosis. *British Journal of Clinical Psychology, 37*(3), 269–284.

Drukker, M., Krabbendam, L., Driessen, G., & Van Os, J. (2006) Social disadvantage and schizophrenia. A combined neighbourhood and individual-level analysis. *Social Psychiatry and Psychiatric Epidemiology, 41*, 595–604.

Dudley, R., Kuyken, W., & Padesky, C. A. (2011). Disorder specific and trans-diagnostic case conceptualisation. *Clinical Psychology Review, 31*(2), 213–224.

Evensen, J., Røssberg, J. I., Barder, H., Haahr, U., ten Velden Hegelstad, W., Joa, I., ... & Friis, S. (2012). Flat affect and social functioning: a 10year follow-up study of first episode psychosis patients. *Schizophrenia Research, 139*(1), 99–104.

Fenton, W. S., & McGlashan, T. H. (1991). Natural history of schizophrenia subtypes: II. Positive and negative symptoms and long-term course. *Archives of General Psychiatry, 48*(11), 978–986.

Fett, A-K. J., Viechtbauer, W., Dominguez, M-de-G., Penn, D. L., Van Os, J., & Krabbendam, L. (2010). The relationship between neurocognition and social cognition with functional outcomes in schizophrenia: A meta-analysis. *Neuroscience and Biobehavioral Reviews, 35*(3), 573–588.

Fonagy, P., Gergely, G., Jurist, E., *et al* (2002) *Affect Regulation, Mentalization and the Development of the Self.* New York: Other Press.

Fonagy, P., & Target, M. (1997). Attachment and reflective function: Their role in self-organization. *Development and Psychopathology, 9*(4), 679–700.

Frith, C. (1992). *The Cognitive Neuropsychology of Schizophrenia* (Essays in cognitive psychology). Hove: L. Erlbaum.

Fusar-Poli, P., Papanastasiou, E., Stahl, D., Rocchetti, M., Carpenter, W., Shergill, S., & McGuire, P. (2014). Treatments of negative symptoms in schizophrenia: meta-analysis of 168 randomized placebo-controlled trials. *Schizophrenia Bulletin,* sbu170.

Gard, D. E., Kring, A. M., Gard, M. G., Horan, W. P., & Green, M. F. (2007). Anhedonia in schizophrenia: distinctions between anticipatory and consummatory pleasure. *Schizophrenia Research, 93*(1), 253–260.

Grant, P. M., & Beck, A. T. (2009). Defeatist beliefs as a mediator of cognitive impairment, negative symptoms, and functioning in schizophrenia. *Schizophrenia Bulletin, 35*(4), 798–806.

Grant, P. M., Huh, G. A., Perivoliotis, D., Stolar, N. M., & Beck, A. T. (2012). Randomized trial to evaluate the efficacy of cognitive therapy for low-functioning patients with schizophrenia. *Archives of General Psychiatry, 69*(2), 121–127.

Gumley, A. (2011). Metacognition, affect regulation and symptom expression: A transdiagnostic perspective. *Psychiatry Research, 190*(1), 72–78.

Gumley, A. I., Schwannauer, M., MacBeth, A., Fisher, R., Clark, S., Rattrie, L., ... & Birchwood, M. (2014). Insight, duration of untreated psychosis and attachment in first-episode psychosis: prospective study of psychiatric recovery over 12-month follow-up. *British Journal of Psychiatry, 205*(1), 60–67.

Gumley, A. I., Taylor, H. E. F., Schwannauer, M., & MacBeth, A. (2014). A systematic review of attachment and psychosis: measurement, construct validity and outcomes. *Acta Psychiatrica Scandinavica, 129*(4), 257–274.

Hamm, J. A., Renard, S. B., Fogley, R. L., Leonhardt, B. L., Dimaggio, G., Buck, K. D., & Lysaker, P. H. (2012). Metacognition and social cognition in schizophrenia: stability and relationship to concurrent and prospective symptom assessments. *Journal of Clinical Psychology, 68*(12), 1303–1312.

Harder, S. (2014). Attachment in schizophrenia—implications for research, prevention, and Treatment. *Schizophrenia Bulletin, 40*(6), 1189–1193.

Harrison, C. L., & Fowler, D. (2004). Negative symptoms, trauma, and autobiographical memory: an investigation of individuals recovering from psychosis. *Journal of Nervous and Mental Disease, 192*(11), 745–753.

Hill, K., & Startup, M. (2013). The relationship between internalized stigma, negative symptoms and social functioning in schizophrenia: The mediating role of self-efficacy. *Psychiatry Research. 206*(2–3), 151–153.

Ho, B. C., Nopoulos, P., Flaum, M., Arndt, S., & Andreasen, N. C. (1998). Two-year outcome in first-episode schizophrenia: predictive value of symptoms for quality of life. *American Journal of Psychiatry, 155*(9), 1196–1201.

Hunter, R., & Barry, S. (2012). Negative symptoms and psychosocial functioning in schizophrenia: neglected but important targets for treatment. *European Psychiatry, 27*(6), 432–436.

Iqbal, Z., Birchwood, M., Chadwick, P., & Trower, P. (2000). Cognitive approach to depression and suicidal thinking in psychosis. 2. Testing the validity of a social ranking model. *British Journal of Psychiatry: Journal of Mental Science, 177*, 522–528.

Janssen, I., Hanssen, M., Bak, M., Bijl, R. V., De Graaf, R., Vollebergh, W., ... & Van Os, J. (2003). Discrimination and delusional ideation. *British Journal of Psychiatry, 182*(1), 71–76.

Kimhy, D., Vakhrusheva, J., Jobson-Ahmed, L., Tarrier, N., Malaspina, D., & Gross, J. J. (2012). Emotion awareness and regulation in individuals with schizophrenia: Implications for social functioning. *Psychiatry Research, 200*(2), 193–201.

Kimhy, D., Vakhrusheva, J., Khan, S., Chang, R. W., Hansen, M. C., Ballon, J. S., ... & Gross, J. J. (2014). Emotional granularity and social functioning in individuals with schizophrenia: An experience sampling study. *Journal of Psychiatric Research, 53*, 141–148.

Klingberg, S., Wölwer, W., Engel, C., Wittorf, A., Herrlich, J., Meisner, C., ... & Wiedemann, G. (2011). Negative symptoms of schizophrenia as primary target of cognitive behavioral therapy: results of the randomized clinical TONES study. *Schizophrenia Bulletin, 37*(suppl 2), S98-S110.

Korver-Nieberg, N., Berry, K., Meijer, C., De Haan, L., & Ponizovsky, A. M. (2015). Associations between attachment and psychopathology dimensions in a large sample of patients with psychosis. *Psychiatry Research, 228*(1), 83–88.

Kvrgic, S., Beck, E., Cavelti, M., Kossowsky, J., Stieglitz, R., & Vauth, R. (2011). Focusing on the adult attachment style in schizophrenia in community mental health centres: Validation of the Psychosis Attachment Measure (PAM) in a German speaking sample. *International Journal of Social Psychiatry, 58*, 362–373.

Lincoln, T., Mehl, S., Kesting, M., & Rief, W. (2011). Negative Symptoms and Social Cognition: Identifying Targets for Psychological Interventions. *Schizophrenia Bulletin, 37*(Suppl2), S23-S32.

Lincoln, T. M., Hartmann, M., Köther, U., & Moritz, S. (2015). Dealing with feeling: Specific emotion regulation skills predict responses to stress in psychosis. *Psychiatry Research, 228*(2), 216–222.

Livingstone, K., Harper, S., & Gillanders, D. (2009). An exploration of emotion regulation in psychosis. *Clinical Psychology and Psychotherapy, 16*(5), 418–430.

Liu, X., Li, L., Xiao, J., Yang, J., & Jiang, X. (2013), Abnormalities of autobiographical memory of patients with depressive disorders: A meta-analysis. *Psychology and Psychotherapy: Theory, Research and Practice, 86*, 353–373. doi: 10.1111/j.2044-8341.2012.02077.x

Lyne, J., O'Donoghue, B., Owens, E., Renwick, L., Madigan, K., Kinsella, A., ... & O'Callaghan, E. (2012). Prevalence of item level negative symptoms in first episode psychosis diagnoses. *Schizophrenia Research, 135*(1), 128–133.

Lysaker, P. H., & Leonhardt, B. L. (2012). Agency: its nature and role in recovery from severe mental illness. *World Psychiatry, 11*(3), 165–166.

Lysaker, P. H., Buck, K. D., Carcione, A., Procacci, M., Salvatore, G., Nicolò, G., & Dimaggio, G. (2011). Addressing metacognitive capacity for self reflection in the psychotherapy for schizophrenia: A conceptual model of the key tasks and processes. *Psychology and Psychotherapy: Theory, Research and Practice, 84*, 58–69. http://doi.org/10.1348/147608310X520436

Lysaker, P. H., Carcione, A., Dimaggio, G., Johannesen, J. K., Nicolò, G., Procacci, M., & Semerari, A. (2005). Metacognition amidst narratives of self and illness in schizophrenia: associations with neurocognition, symptoms, insight and quality of life. *Acta Psychiatrica Scandinavica, 112*(1), 64–71.

Lysaker, P. H., Gumley, A., Brüne, M., Vanheule, S., Buck, K. D., & Dimaggio, G. (2011). Deficits in the ability to recognize one's own affects and those of others: associations with neurocognition, symptoms and sexual trauma among persons with schizophrenia spectrum disorders. *Consciousness and Cognition, 20*(4), 1183–1192.

Lysaker, P. H., Kukla, M., Belanger, E., White, D. A., Buck, K. D., Luther, L. et al. (2016). Individual psychotherapy and changes in self-experience in schizophrenia: A qualitative comparison of patients in metacognitively focused and supportive psychotherapy. *Psychiatry: Interpersonal and Biological Processes, 78*(4), 305–316. http://doi.org/10.1080/00332747.2015.1063916

Lysaker, P. H., Kukla, M., Dubreucq, J., Gumley, A., McLeod, H., Vohs, J. L. et al. (2015). Metacognitive deficits predict future levels of negative symptoms in schizophrenia controlling for neurocognition, affect recognition, and self-expectation of goal attainment. *Schizophrenia Research, 168*(1–2), 267–72. http://doi.org/10.1016/j.schres.2015.06.015

Lysaker, P. H., Shea, A. M., Buck, K. D., Dimaggio, G., Nicolò, G., Procacci, M., ... & Rand, K. L. (2010). Metacognition as a mediator of the effects of impairments in neurocognition on social function in schizophrenia spectrum disorders. *Acta Psychiatrica Scandinavica, 122*(5), 405–413.

MacBeth, A., & Gumley, A. (2008). Premorbid adjustment, symptom development and quality of life in first episode psychosis: a systematic review and critical reappraisal. *Acta Psychiatrica Scandinavica, 117*(2), 85–99.

MacBeth, A., Gumley, A., Schwannauer, M., Carcione, A., Fisher, R., McLeod, H. J., & Dimaggio, G. (2014). Metacognition, symptoms and premorbid functioning in a First Episode Psychosis sample. *Comprehensive Psychiatry, 55*(2), 268–273.

MacBeth, A., Gumley, A., Schwannauer, M., Carcione, A., McLeod, H. J., & Dimaggio, G. (2016). Metacognition in first episode psychosis: item level analysis of associations with symptoms and engagement. *Clinical Psychology and Psychotherapy, 23*(4), 329–39.

MacBeth, A., Gumley, A., Schwannauer, M., & Fisher, R. (2011). Attachment states of mind, mentalization, and their correlates in a first-episode psychosis sample. *Psychology and Psychotherapy: Theory, Research and Practice, 84*(1), 42–57.

Malla, A., & Payne, J. (2005). First-episode psychosis: psychopathology, quality of life, and functional outcome. *Schizophrenia Bulletin, 31*(3), 650–671.

Mallinckrodt, B., & Jeong, J. (2015). Meta-analysis of client attachment to therapist: Associations with working alliance and client pretherapy attachment. *Psychotherapy, 52*(1), 134–139.

Mcglashan, T. H. (1987). Recovery style from mental illness and long-term outcome. *Journal of Nervous and Mental Disease, 175*(11), 681–685.

McLeod, H. J., Wood, N., & Brewin, C. R. (2006). Autobiographical memory deficits in schizophrenia. *Cognition and Emotion, 20*(3–4), 536–547.

McLeod, H. J., Gumley, A. I., MacBeth, A., Schwannauer, M., & Lysaker, P. H. (2014). Metacognitive functioning predicts positive and negative symptoms over 12 months in first episode psychosis. *Journal of Psychiatric Research, 54*, 109–115.

McLeod, H. J., Gumley, A., & Schwannauer, M. (2014). The impact of metacognition on the development and maintenance of negative symptoms. *Social Cognition and Metacognition in Schizophrenia: Psychopathology and Treatment Approaches*, 115.

Milev, P., Ho, B. C., Arndt, S., & Andreasen, N. C. (2005). Predictive values of neurocognition and negative symptoms on functional outcome in schizophrenia: a longitudinal first-episode study with 7-year follow-up. *American Journal of Psychiatry, 162*(3), 495–506.

Minor, K. S., & Lysaker, P. H. (2014). Necessary, but not sufficient: Links between neurocognition, social cognition, and metacognition in schizophrenia are moderated by disorganized symptoms. *Schizophrenia Research, 159*(1), 198–204.

Mitchell, L. J., Gumley, A., Reilly, E. S., MacBeth, A., Lysaker, P., Carcione, A., & Dimaggio, G. (2012). Metacognition in forensic patients with schizophrenia and a past history of interpersonal violence: an exploratory study. *Psychosis, 4*(1), 42–51.

Modestin, J., Caveng, I., Wehrli, M., & Malti, T. (2009). Correlates of coping styles in psychotic illness – an extension study. *Psychiatry Research, 168*, 50–56.

Moore, S. A., & Zoellner, L. A. (2007). Overgeneral autobiographical memory and traumatic events: an evaluative review. *Psychological Bulletin, 133*(3), 419.

Myin-Germeys, I., & van Os, J. (2007). Stress-reactivity in psychosis: evidence for an affective pathway to psychosis. *Clinical Psychology Review, 27*(4), 409–424.

Nicolo, G., Dimaggio, G., Popolo, R., Carcione, A., Procacci, M., Hamm, J., ... & Lysaker, P. H. (2012). Associations of metacognition with symptoms, insight, and neurocognition in clinically stable outpatients with schizophrenia. *Journal of Nervous and Mental Disease, 200*(7), 644–647.

Nolen-Hoeksema, S., & Watkins, E. R. (2011). A heuristic for developing transdiagnostic models of psychopathology explaining multifinality and divergent trajectories. *Perspectives on Psychological Science, 6*(6), 589–609.

O'Driscoll, C., Laing, J., & Mason, O. (2014). Cognitive emotion regulation strategies, alexithymia and dissociation in schizophrenia, a review and meta-analysis. *Clinical Psychology Review, 34*(6), 482–495.

Piskulic, D., Addington, J., Cadenhead, K. S., Cannon, T. D., Cornblatt, B. A., Heinssen, R., ... & McGlashan, T. H. (2012). Negative symptoms in individuals at clinical high risk of psychosis. *Psychiatry Research, 196*(2), 220–224.

Ponizovsky, A. M., Nechamkin, Y., & Rosca, P. (2007). Attachment patterns are associated with symptomatology and course of schizophrenia in male inpatients. *American Journal of Orthopsychiatry, 77*(2), 324.

Rabin, S., Hasson-Ohayon, I., Avidan, M., Rozencwaig, S., Shalev, H., & Kravetz, S. (2014). Metacognition in schizophrenia and schizotypy: relation to symptoms of schizophrenia, traits of schizotypy and social quality of life. *Journal of Psychiatry and Related Sciences, 51*(1), 44–53.

Read, J., Perry, B. D., Moskowitz, A., & Connolly, J. (2001). The contribution of early traumatic events to schizophrenia in some patients: a traumagenic neurodevelopmental model. *Psychiatry, 64*(4), 319–345.

Rector, N. A., Beck, A. T., & Stolar, N. (2005). The negative symptoms of schizophrenia: a cognitive perspective. *Canadian Journal of Psychiatry, 50*(5), 247–257.

Savill, M., Banks, C., Khanom, H., & Priebe, S. (2015). Do negative symptoms of schizophrenia change over time? A meta-analysis of longitudinal data. *Psychological Medicine, 45*(08), 1613–1627.

Schmid, L. A., Lässer, M. M., Herold, C. J., Seidl, U., & Schröder, J. (2010). Autobiographical memory deficits and their relationship with symptom dimensions in older patients with chronic schizophrenia. *Schizophrenia Research, 117*(2), 216.

Shannon, C., Douse, K., McCusker, C., Feeney, L., Barrett, S., & Mulholland, C. (2011). The association between childhood trauma and memory functioning in schizophrenia. *Schizophrenia Bulletin, 37*(3), 531–537.

Sprong, M., Schothorst, P., Vos, E., Hox, J., & Van Engeland, H. (2007). Theory of mind in schizophrenia: Meta-analysis. *British Journal of Psychiatry: The Journal of Mental Science, 191*, 5–13.

Stampfer, H. G. (1990). "Negative Symptoms": A Cu Mu Latlve Trauma Stress Disorder? *Australian and New Zealand Journal of Psychiatry, 24*(4), 516–528.

Sterk, B., Winter, R. I., Muis, M., & de Haan, L. (2013). Priorities, satisfaction and treatment goals in psychosis patients: an online consumer's survey. *Pharmacopsychiatry.* http://doi.org/10.1055/s-0032-1

Tait, L., Birchwood, M., & Trower, P. (2003). Predicting engagement with services for psychosis: insight, symptoms and recovery style. *British Journal of Psychiatry, 182*(2), 123–128.

Tait, L., Birchwood, M., & Trower, P. (2004). Adapting to the challenge of psychosis: Personal resilience and the use of sealing-over (avoidant) coping strategies. *British Journal of Psychiatry, 185*, 410–5.

Taylor, P. J. et al. (2010). "Memory specificity as a risk factor for suicidality in non-affective psychosis: The ability to recall specific autobiographical memories is related to greater suicidality." *Behaviour Research and Therapy, 48*(10), 1047–1052.

Thomas, N. (2015). What's really wrong with cognitive behavioral therapy for psychosis? *Frontiers in Psychology, 6.* http://doi.org/10.3389/fpsyg.2015.00323

Thompson, K. N., McGorry, P. D., & Harrigan, S. M. (2003). Recovery style and outcome in first-episode psychosis. *Schizophrenia Research, 62*(1), 31–36.

Varese, F., Smeets, F., Drukker, M., Lieverse, R., Lataster, T., Viechtbauer, W., … & Bentall, R. P. (2012). Childhood adversities increase the risk of psychosis: a meta-analysis of patient-control, prospective-and cross-sectional cohort studies. *Schizophrenia Bulletin, 38*(4), 661–671.

Vaskinn, A., Ventura, J., Andreassen, O. A., Melle, I., & Sundet, K. (2015). A social path to functioning in schizophrenia: From social self-efficacy through negative symptoms to social functional capacity. *Psychiatry Research, 228*(3), 803–807.

Velthorst, E., Koeter, M., van der Gaag, M., Nieman, D. H., Fett, A. K., Smit, F., … & de Haan, L. (2015). Adapted cognitive–behavioural therapy required for targeting negative symptoms in schizophrenia: meta-analysis and meta-regression. *Psychological Medicine, 45*(3), 453–465.

Ventura, J., Nuechterlein, K. H., Green, M. F., Horan, W. P., Subotnik, K. L., & Mintz, J. (2004). The timing of negative symptom exacerbations in relationship to positive symptom exacerbations in the early course of schizophrenia. *Schizophrenia Research, 69*(2), 333–342.

Ventura, J., Wood, R., & Hellemann, G. (2013). Symptom domains and neurocognitive functioning can help differentiate social cognitive processes in schizophrenia: A meta-analysis. *Schizophrenia Bulletin, 39*(1), 102–111.

Ventura, J., Subotnik, K. L., Ered, A., Gretchen-Doorly, D., Hellemann, G. S., Vaskinn, A., & Nuechterlein, K. H. (2014). The relationship of attitudinal beliefs to negative symptoms, neurocognition, and daily functioning in recent-onset schizophrenia. *Schizophrenia Bulletin, 40*(6), 1308–1318.

Weijers, J., ten Kate, C., Eurelings-Bontekoe, E., Viechtbauer, W., Rampaart, R., Bateman, A., & Selten, J. P. (2016). Mentalization-based treatment for psychotic disorder: protocol of a randomized controlled trial. *BMC Psychiatry*, *16*(1), 191.

Williams, J., Stiles, M., & Shapiro, G. (1999). Cognitive Mechanisms in the Avoidance of Painful and Dangerous Thoughts: Elaborating the Assimilation Model. *Cognitive Therapy and Research*, *23*(3), 285–306.

Wilson, J. S., & Costanzo, P. R. (1996). A preliminary study of attachment, attention, and schizotypy in early adulthood. *Journal of Social and Clinical Psychology*, *15*(2), 231–260.

5

ATTACHMENT AND SOCIAL FUNCTIONING IN PSYCHOSIS

Jasper E. Palmier-Claus, Nikie Korver-Nieberg, Anne-Kathrin Fett and Shannon Couture

Introduction

Service user accounts have highlighted the importance of improving social functioning in recovery from psychosis (Pitt et al., 2007; Wood et al., 2010). This includes improving occupational opportunities in terms of activities of daily living and employment, but also improving relationships and social interactions with other people. Impaired social functioning is common in individuals who experience psychosis, where it is related to other adverse outcomes, including relapse (Robinson et al., 1999) and hospitalisation (Perlick et al., 1992). It is therefore imperative to better understand the factors leading to problems in social function. In this chapter, we discuss the relationship between attachment style and social functioning in psychosis; a potentially important, but seldom investigated, area of research.

What is attachment?

Previous chapters in this book have discussed the definitions and theoretical bases of attachment. To summarise, attachment theory suggests that early experiences of significant others determine individuals' subsequent interpretations and expectations of relationships. These so-called 'internal working models' of relationships continue into later life, where they shape individuals' social interactions and engagement with others. In other words, attachment style is a set of emotional and cognitive representations or heuristics, which influences a person's appraisals of future social encounters (Bowlby, 1969).

In psychosis research, attachment has been conceptualised and measured in a variety of ways. As a result, the research literature is relatively heterogeneous with little methodological consistency or overlap. The number of terms or labels used to distinguish forms of attachment further complicates the area with the same constructs often taking different names (e.g. dismissive and avoidant attachment are often used interchangeably). The most commonly employed self-report measure of attachment in the psychosis literature is the Psychosis Attachment Measure (PAM; Berry et al., 2008), which explores the separate, but related, concepts of attachment avoidance and attachment anxiety.

Attachment and social functioning

It is tempting to predict that insecure attachment style, by its very definition, will have a significant bearing on an individual's ability to function in social situations. The person who believes that they will derive little gain from interaction with others and therefore avoids close and meaningful relationships may find him or herself isolated and without regular social contact. Conversely, the person who is overly fearful of rejection from others may create conflict by being overly involved in relationships. These relational styles in turn could have wide-reaching implications for functioning in employment, education and other social activities. Attachment style is particularly pertinent to individuals with psychosis where social contact might already be limited by symptoms, discrimination, loss of opportunity and stigma (Repper & Perkin, 2003). Thus, insecure attachment may be one of a multitude of barriers interacting to increase the likelihood of isolation and social withdrawal.

As detailed elsewhere in the book, there is evidence that people with psychosis are more likely to have insecure attachment styles than in the general population However, the research exploring the relationship between attachment and social functioning in psychosis to date is somewhat limited. The majority of studies of this nature have explored the association between attachment and interpersonal exchanges specifically between individuals with psychosis and their health care team. The studies have used a range of attachment measures, and measures of therapeutic relationships, making it somewhat difficult to make comparisons across studies and integrate findings. However, on the whole, there is stronger evidence for the role of avoidant attachment in predicting relationship difficulties. For example, an earlier study by Dozier and colleagues (2001) found that individuals with a more dismissive attachment style on the Adult Attachment Interview spent less time on task with their case managers, and were more confused after meeting with them. Later studies by Kvrgic and colleagues (2011) and Berry et al. (2008) also found a significant association between self-reported attachment avoidance and difficult client-clinician interactions and poorer client-rated measures of therapeutic alliance, respectively. Anxious attachment appears to be a less consistent predictor of the quality of therapeutic relationship, with relatively few studies finding evidence of any associations between the concepts. Arguably, people with an anxious attachment style may be more dependent on others for support and may therefore be more willing to engage in health care relationships. Nonetheless, their dependence on others and hypersensitivity to rejection may result in more ruptures in therapeutic alliance over time, which will not be captured in the studies that only measure therapeutic relationships at one point in time (Shattock et al., 2017).

Research has also explored the impact of attachment on social outcomes and interpersonal relationships outside of health care settings. Couture and colleagues (2007) found that attachment avoidance was associated with worse social and independent living skills in individuals with first episode psychosis. Berry and colleagues' (2008) study observed that attachment anxiety was associated with greater clinician-rated 'neediness' in relationships, whereas attachment avoidance was associated with greater outward hostility. This research suggests that different types of insecure attachment styles can lead to different types of problems in social behaviour in people with psychosis.

In addition to the above studies, a recent study explored the impact of attachment on real-time social interactions in individuals with early psychosis and healthy controls during a social experiment involving trust games with unfair and co-operative partners (Fett et al. 2016). The authors found that attachment anxiety was associated with higher trust towards others even when they were behaving in ways that might be considered unfair. Worries about acceptance by others and low self-esteem were associated with psychosis and attachment anxiety and might explain social behaviour that is focused on conciliation, rather than self-protection. Finally, Palmier-Claus and colleagues (2016) explored whether childhood adversity acts on social functioning by influencing a person's attachment style. In this study, the authors recruited a large sample of individuals at varying stages (e.g. from first episode to many years post diagnosis) and severities of symptoms. Contrary to their initial hypotheses, the authors found that although adversity predicted greater attachment avoidance and attachment anxiety, neither attachment style was associated with social functioning after accounting for levels of depression.

In summary, there is evidence from some, but not all, studies that both anxious and avoidant attachment styles are associated with difficulties in social behaviour in people with psychosis. However, other factors such as depression may partly explain the association between attachment and social functioning, suggesting that future studies need to control for such potentially confounding variables. In addition, a lack of longitudinal research which measures attachment and social functioning over time hampers inferences about a causal relationship. For example, it is possible that attachment anxiety leads to impaired social functioning, but also that impaired social functioning generates a more anxious or avoidant attachment style. Further research is also needed to explore the differential impact of attachment avoidance and attachment anxiety on social functioning within different contexts (e.g. when with strangers, partners, colleagues etc.) and the role of disorganised attachment in social difficulties given the association between disorganised attachment pattern and more problematic social behaviours in childhood. Based on the promising early research in this area, these avenues for future studies could provide useful insights into the determinants of social difficulties often experienced by those with psychosis.

Attachment and social functioning: a role for social cognition?

In addition to further research exploring the relationship between attachment and social functioning, it is important to identify potential mediators of any such relationship in order to understand how attachment may influence social functioning. This in turn could help to identify suitable intervention targets. The question here is whether attachment acts on social functioning through a third variable. In this sense, it might be possible to map out the pathway by which early life experiences lead to impaired social relationships later in life. One such mediator might be social cognition. Social cognition refers to the mental processes that underlie perceiving, interpreting and responding appropriately to social stimuli, such as the intentions and actions of others (Fiske & Taylor, 1991). Typically, social cognition is subdivided into four categories (Green et al., 2005). Emotion perception is the ability to perceive and use emotions (Green et al., 2008); Theory of Mind, or the conceptually related mentalisation or reflective functioning, is the ability to understand and make accurate inferences about the intentions and thoughts of others, and to see things from their perspective (Corcoran, 2001; Couture et al., 2006); social perception is the ability to decode and interpret social cues; and attribution style represents how a person interprets the causes of particular social events (Pinkham et al., 2013).

Social cognition enables individuals to act appropriately in response to their social environment. For example, the ability to take others' perspectives may allow for smooth social interactions and enable individuals to form long lasting relationships and to function in the social community (Frith, 2007). A reduced social cognitive ability may lead to difficulties in social communication, including misunderstandings, conflicts and increased interpersonal distress. Alternatively, a biased attributional style, whereby an individual attributes particularly negative events to other people may lead to greater levels of hostility or conflict (Martin & Penn, 2002). Taken together, these difficulties in social cognition and communication may ultimately lead to social exclusion and withdrawal (Cotter et al., 2015; Couture et al., 2006; Fett et al., 2012).

It has been suggested that the development of an insecure attachment style in childhood, may cause problems in the development of social cognitive skills throughout childhood and adolescence. That is, since insecure attachment style is characterised by negative views about the likelihood of acceptance, reassurance and safety in interpersonal relationships, it may promote greater withdrawal from social relationships (thereby decreasing the opportunities for learning), or produce a cognitive bias in which the developing child interprets social interactions through a distorted lens. The continued presence of an insecure internal working model of relationships could therefore lead to poor social cognitive skills and result in the pronounced social difficulties observed in people with psychosis, including small social networks (Berry et al., 2007), hostile or aggressive behaviour (Bartells et al., 1991; Darrell-Berry et al., 2017), and problems establishing therapeutic alliance with providers and services (Berry et al., 2008; Kvrgic et al., 2011).Tentative evidence from non-clinical samples supports an association between attachment style and impaired social cognition. Two studies have suggested that insecurely attached individuals are less effective in identifying emotional expressions when asked to rate pictures of people's faces (Kafetsios, 2004; Magai et al., 1995). These findings fit with the theory that attachment style influences an individual's ability to attend to and encode emotional information from his other environment (Feeney, Noller, & Callan, 1994; Tucker & Anders, 1999). Conversely and contrary to expectations, Searle and Meara (1999) showed that dismissing-avoidant participants demonstrated *intact* performance on emotion perception. In order to explain this unexpected finding, the authors suggest that dismissing-avoidant individuals do not experience greater emotional arousal when confronted with social stimuli, so they are perhaps better able to encode and process social information (Searle & Meara, 1999). However, this hypothesis requires further exploration through future research.

As well as exploring the impact of different attachment styles on social cognition, researchers have also begun to study the neurological models of the impact of attachment and social cognition. An innovative neuroimaging study by Nolte and colleagues (2013) required participants to complete an adapted Reading the Mind in the Eyes Theory of Mind task. Participants were asked to complete the task under normal conditions and in an "attachment stress induction" condition, which involved creating an imagery script from a participant's report of a stressful event from the past year with a significant other. Participants were asked to rate the level of stress they experienced. Attachment stress induction was associated with reduced activation of the mentalising related brain system, supporting the link between the attachment system and social cognition.

Research findings on the association between attachment and social cognition in clinical samples are mixed. For example, Pos and colleagues (2014) found that Theory of Mind abilities are reduced in adults with a diagnosis of schizophrenia, who showed insecure attachment patterns. MacBeth and colleagues (2011) also found that mentalising abilities were associated with both insecure attachment and poorer social functioning in daily life. In particular, people with higher levels of attachment avoidance had lower mentalisation skills as assessed by a measure of the ability to reflect on mental states compared to people with an anxious or secure attachment style. Conversely, Aydin et al. (2016) reported that attachment anxiety, but not attachment avoidance, was related to metacognitive abilities assessed on a measure of metacogitive capacity. In terms of attributional style, Donohoe and colleagues (2008) found that in a sample of outpatients with non-affective psychosis, secure attachment style was associated with lower levels of personalising attribution bias (i.e. a lower tendency to blame others for negative events). However, in contrast to the above evidence of associations between social cognition and attachment, Korver-Nieberg and colleagues (2013) showed that perspective taking, as a basic cognitive Theory of Mind component, was unrelated to attachment in adolescents with an early onset of psychosis and a control sample. The authors point out that unlike previous studies which focus on the emotional component of Theory of Mind, the 'Director Condition' in their study that was used to measure perspective taking focuses on cognitive or thinking components of Theory of Mind only. They argue that attachment styles may therefore be more likely to be associated with the emotional measures of Theory of Mind, which were the focus of other studies. Further research is therefore required to investigate these specific components of Theory of Mind and the association with attachment styles.

In the future, researchers should also directly explore whether social cognition mediates the relationship between attachment and social functioning in psychosis, as although studies have looked at associations between attachment, social cognition and social functioning, there is a paucity of evidence testing casual (or mediation) models. Alternatively, it may be possible that social cognitive ability represents a separate pathway to social dysfunction that, nevertheless, sensitises an individual to the negative effects of insecure attachment. For example, the individual with an avoidant attachment style who, due to social cognitive deficits, might misread social cues as signs of rejection may be particularly prone to social withdrawal. Conversely, a lack of social awareness may also make the individual less aware of and distressed by their 'outsider' status, which, in turn, could reduce the impact that it has on their behaviour. (Researchers will sometimes refer to these relationships as moderation, rather than mediation, effects; see Mackinnon, 2008, for a discussion of these concepts).

Clinical implications

Assessing and formulating clients' attachment styles may provide useful insights into the underlying motives of their social behaviour. This could aid the identification of appropriate interventions and barriers to recovery. Sensitively sharing these predictions with clients may help them to understand their own ways of responding within relationships, allowing them to recognise and address any unhelpful patterns of behaviour.

Attachment theory may also be useful in understanding clients' relationships with their clinicians. Formulating relational processes in terms of attachment mechanisms can identify barriers to engagement, rapport building and social recovery. For example, knowledge of an avoidant attachment style may help clinicians to take early precautions against a client disengaging from services. This potential for disengagement could be prevented by greater emphasis on rapport building, requesting and responding to regular feedback, or therapeutic contracting. Increasing staff insight into their clients' attachment styles may allow them to better assume the perspective of their clients, which could generate greater levels of compassion and empathy (Berry et al. 2016). Clinicians may also use their knowledge of their own attachment styles to prevent themselves from being drawn into interpersonal patterns which might maintain clients' own attachment difficulties, and help them to create a safe base for clients by sensitively responding to clients needs' (Gumley et al., 2014).

There are some interventions for improving social cognition, which are relatively in their infancy, but might be one way in which clinicians could mitigate against the impact of insecure attachment on social functioning (should a mediation effect be supported in the literature). There are now cognitive rehabilitation packages designed for improving Theory of Mind ability (Bechi et al., 2012; Combs et al., 2007; Roncone et al., 2004). These generally involve role-plays, video exercises and group discussions. Although pilot studies have produced promising findings, these interventions require further validation through randomised controlled trials before integration into clinical settings (Couture et al., 2006).

Case example

In order to illustrate how clients and clinicians might use attachment theory to formulate social difficulties in psychosis we present the case example of Jane. Jane is a 23-year-old woman who is a client of an early intervention service. Jane presents with an avoidant attachment style. Growing up, Jane's parents were largely absent. She notes that they were more concerned with her grades, than spending time with her. She has one particularly vivid memory of trying to telephone her parents on her birthday, but getting no response. Jane reports that her parents were both professional and aloof. At school, she was the victim of bullying by her schoolmates. When her mental health deteriorates she experiences voices, which mirror her earlier experiences of being bullied, and she worries that other people are laughing at her.

A hypothesised result of her earlier experience and consequent avoidant attachment style is that Jane rejects intimate, or even superficial, relationships and spends much of her time alone. She reports having few friends with whom she is not close and a number of failed relationships. Although Jane is typically high achieving, she reports finding it difficult to fit in. She describes herself as a loner and will often turn down opportunities to socialise with others, saying that "it's a waste of time". Her interpersonal style influences the care that she receives; she is dismissive of the support available to her and as a result does not access social help at times of elevated risk. In the past, Jane has taken two overdoses with the intention of taking her own life. At these times, she does not access support and will often refuse to pick up her phone or answer her door. She will attend appointments with her care coordinator, but tends to be highly critical of the service's input. She also takes steps to ensure that conversations remain on a very intellectual level and that she does not "give too much away". This sometimes makes it difficult for her care coordinator to get a sense of how things are going for her.

Introducing Jane to an attachment formulation may help her to understand how her early social experiences affect her current relationships. We believe that her clinical team should be careful to facilitate this in a sensitive and normalising manner, particularly given her already limited engagement with services. They may wish to outline how attachment avoidance is an understandable reaction to past events; one that was previously, but is no longer, adaptive given her current difficulties. By helping Jane to become more aware of her own interpersonal style and automatic reactions to others, it might be possible for her to monitor and change them in the future. Collaboratively developing a person-focused attachment formulation could help to guide future integration of therapeutic work such as verbal reattribution strategies (e.g. exploring the evidence for and against relationships being pointless) and behavioural experiments (e.g. exploring possible rewards from engaging with others). It is possible that Jane's care team is feeling pushed out and rejected. Sharing Jane's attachment formulation with them may also aid perspective taking, which could build empathy and ultimately allow them to persist in engaging her.

Conclusion

To summarise, attachment theory might provide a useful framework for understanding interpersonal behaviour and interpersonal difficulties in psychosis. Research in this area generally supports an association between attachment and social functioning in this population, although future studies should endeavour to control for key factors such as depression whilst establishing whether attachment style plays a causal role in social dysfunction. Investigation of potential mediating pathways (e.g. through social cognition) could also help to identify suitable targets for intervention. Although further research in these areas is essential to drive the field forward, there is enough evidence available to suggest that clinicians could benefit from using attachment theory to understand interpersonal processes and client behaviours in their everyday practice.

References

Abu-Akel, A., & Shamay-Tsoory, S. (2011). Neuroanatomical and neurochemical bases of theory of mind. *Neuropsychologia, 49*(11), 2971–2984.

Adolphs, R. (1999). Social cognition and the human brain. *Trends in Cognitive Sciences, 3*(12), 469–479.

Aydin, O., Balikci, K., Tas, C., Aydin, P. U., Danaci, A. E., Brunce, M., & Lysaker, P. H. (2016). The development origins of metacognitive deficits in schizophrenia. *Psychiatry Research, 245*, 15–21.

Bartels, S. J., Drake, R. E., Wallach, M. A., & Freeman, D. (1991). Characteristic hostility in schizophrenic outpatients. *Schizophrenia Bulletin, 17*(1), 163–171.

Bartholomew, K., & Horowitz, L. M. (1991). Attachment styles among young adults: a test of a four-category model. *Journal of Personality and Social Psychology, 61*(2), 226–244.

Bateman, A. W., & Fonagy, P. (2012). *Handbook of Mentalizing in mental health practice.* Washington, DC: American Psychiatric Publishing, Inc.

Berry, K., Wearden, A., & Barrowclough, C. (2007). Adult attachment styles and psychosis: an investigation of associations between general attachment styles and attachment relationships with specific others. *Social Psychiatry and Psychiatric Epidemiology, 42*(12), 972–976.

Berry, K., Band, R., Corcoran, R., Barrowclough, C., & Wearden, A. (2007). Attachment styles, earlier interpersonal relationships and schizotypy in a non-clinical sample. *Psychology and Psychotherapy-Theory Research and Practice, 80*, 563–576.

Berry, K., Barrowclough, C., & Wearden, A. (2007). A review of the role of adult attachment style in psychosis: Unexplored issues and questions for further research. *Clinical Psychology Review, 27*, 458–475.

Berry, K., Barrowclough, C., & Wearden, A. (2008). Attachment theory: A framework for understanding symptoms and interpersonal relationships in psychosis. *Behaviour Research and Therapy, 46*, 1275–1282.

Berry, K., Haddock, G., Kellett, S., Roberts, C., Drake, R., & Barrowclough, C. (2016). Feasibility of ward-based psychological intervention to improve staff and patient relationships in psychiatric rehabilitation settings. *British Journal of Clinical Psychology, 55*, 236–352.

Bora, E., & Pantelis, C. (2013). Theory of mind impairments in first-episode psychosis, individuals at ultra-high risk for psychosis and in first-degree relatives for schizophrenia: Systematic review and meta-analysis. *Schizophrenia Research, 144*, 31–36.

Brent, B. K., Holt, D. J., Keshavan, M. S., Seidman, L. J., & Fonagy, P. (2014). Mentalization-based treatment for psychosis: Linking an attachment-based model to the psychotherapy for impaired mental state understanding in people with psychotic disorders. *Journal of Psychiatry and Related Sciences, 51*(1), 17–24.

Collins, N. L. (1996). Working models of attachment: Implications for explanation, emotion, and behaviour. *Journal of Personality and Social Psychology, 71*(4), 810–832.

Cornblatt, B. A., Carrion, R. E., Addington, J., & Seidman, L. et al. (2012). Risk factors for psychosis: Impaired social and role functioning. *Schizophrenia Bulletin, 38*, 1247–1257.

Cotter, J., Kaess, M., & Yung, A. R. (2015). Childhood trauma and functional disability in psychosis, bipolar disorder and borderline personality disorder: A review of the literature. *Irish Journal of Psychological Medicine, 32*, 21–30.

Couture, S. M., Penn, D. L., & Roberts, D. L. (2006). The functional significance of social cognition in schizophrenia: a review. *Schizophrenia Bulletin, 32*, 44–63.

Darrell-Berry, Bucci, S., Palmier-Claus, J., Emsley, R., Drake, R., & Berry, K. (2017). Predictors and Mediators of Trait Anger across the Psychosis Continuum: the role of attachment style, paranoia and social cognition. *Psychiatry Research, 249*, 132–138.

DeWall, C. N., Masten, C. L., Powell, C., Combs, D., Schurtz, D.R., & Eisenberger, N.I. (2012). Do neural responses to rejection depend on attachment style? An fMRI study. *Social Cognitive and Affect Neuroscience, 7*(2), 184–192.

Donohoe, G., Spoletini, I., McGlade, N., Behan, C. et al. (2008). Are relational style and neuropsychological performance predictors of social attributions in chronic schizophrenia? *Psychiatry Research, 161*, 19–27.

Dozier, M., Lomax, L., Tyrrell, C. L., & Lee, S. W. (2001). The challenge of treatment for clients with dismissing states of mind. *Attachment & Human Development, 3*(1), 62–76.

Dumontheil, I., Apperly, I. A. & Blakemore, S. J. (2010). Online usage of theory of mind continues to develop in late adolescence. *Developmental Science, 13*(2), 331–338.

Dumontheil, I., Kuster, O., Apperly, I. A., & Blakemore, S. J. (2010). Taking perspective into account in a communicative task. *NeuroImage, 52*, 1574–1583.

Feeney, J. A., Noller, P., & Callan, V. J. (1994). Attachment style, communication and satisfaction in the early years of marriage. *Personal Relationships, 1*, 333–334.

Fett, A. K. J. et al. (2012). To trust or not to trust: the dynamics of social interaction in psychosis. *Brain, 135*(3), 976–984.

Fett, A. J., Shergill, S. S., Korver-Nieberg, N., Yakub, F., Gromann, P. M., & Krabbendam, L. (2016). Learning to trust: trust and attachment in early psychosis. *Psychological Medicine, 46*(7), 1437.

Fett, A. K. J. et al. (2011). The relationship between neurocognition and social cognition with functional outcomes in schizophrenia: A meta-analysis. *Neuroscience and Biobehavioral Reviews, 35*(3), 573–588.

Fett, A. K. J., Shergill, S. & Krabbendam, L. (2015). Social neuroscience in psychiatry: unravelling the neural mechanisms of social dysfunction. *Psychological Medicine, 45*(6), 1145–1165.

Fonagy, P., Gergely, G., & Target, M. (2007). The parent-infant dyad and the construction of the subjective self. *Journal of Child Psychology and Psychiatry, 48*(3–4), 288–328.

Fonagy, P., & Luyten, P. A. (2009). Developmental, mentalization-based approach to the understanding and treatment of borderline personality disorder. *Development and Psychopathology, 21*, 1355–1381.

Frith, C. D., & Frith, U. (2006). How we predict what other people are going to do. *Brain Research, 1079*(1), 36–46.

Frith, C. D. (2007). The social brain? *Philosophical Transactions: Biological Sciences, 362*(1480), 671–678.

Green, M. F., Olivier, B., Crawley, J. N., Penn, D. L., & Silverstein, S. (2005). Social cognition in schizophrenia: recommendations from the MATRICS New Approaches Conference. *Schizophrenia Bulletin, 31*, 882–887.

Harris, S. T., Oakley, C., & Picchioni, M. M. (2014). A systematic review of the association between attributional bias/interpersonal style and violence in schizophrenia/psychosis. *Aggression and Violent Behaviour, 19*, 235–241.

Hall-Lande, J. A., Eisenberg, M. E., Christenson, S. L., & Neumark-Sztainer, D. (2007). Social isolation, psychological health, and protective factors in adolescence. *Adolescence, 42*(166), 265–286.

Hughes, C., & Leekam, S. (2004). What are the links between theory of mind and social relations? Review, reflections and new directions for studies of typical and atypical development. *Social Development*, *13*(4), 590–619.

Llerena, K., Park, S. G., Couture, S. M., & Blanchard, J. J. (2012). Social anhedonia and affiliation: examining behavior and subjective reactions within a social interaction. *Psychiatry Research*, *200*(2), 679–686.

Kafetsios, K. (2004). Attachment and emotional intelligence abilities across the life course. *Personality and Individual Differences*, *37*(1), 129–145.

Kalbe, E., Grabenhorst, F., Brand, M., Kessler, J., Hilker, R., & Markowitsch, H. J. (2007). Elevated emotional reactivity in affective but not cognitive components of theory of mind: a psychophysiological study. *Journal of Neuropsychology*, *1*(1), 27–38.

Kvrgic, S., Beck, E. M., Cavelti, M., Kossowsky, J., Stieglitz, R. D., & Vauth, R. (2012). Focusing on the adult attachment style in schizophrenia in community mental health centres: validation of the Psychosis Attachment Measure (PAM) in a German-speaking sample. *International Journal of Social Psychiatry*, *58*(4), 362–373.

Korver-Nieberg, N., Fett, A. K. J., Meijer, C. J., Koeter, M. W., Shergill, S. S., de Haan, L., & Krabbendam, L. (2013). Theory of mind, insecure attachment and paranoia in adolescents with early psychosis and healthy controls. *Australian and New Zealand Journal of Psychiatry*, *47*(8), 737–745.

Mayer, J. D., Salovey, P., Caruso, D. R., & Sitarenios, G. (2003). Measuring emotional intelligence with the MSCEIT V2. 0. *Emotion*, *3*(1), 97.

Martin, J. A., & Penn, D. L. (2002). Attributional style in schizophrenia: an investigation in outpatients with and without persecutory delusions. *Schizophrenia Bulletin*, *28*(1), 131–141.

MacBeth, A., Gumley, A., Schwannauer, M., & Fisher, R. (2011). Attachment states of mind, mentalization, and their correlates in a first-episode psychosis sample. *Psychology and Psychotherapy: Theory, Research and Practice*, *84*(1), 42–57.

Magai, C., Distel, N., & Liker, R. (1995). Emotion socialisation, attachment, and patterns of adult emotional traits. *Cognition and Emotion*, *9*(5), 461–481.

Michail, M., & Birchwood, M. (2014). Social anxiety in first-episode psychosis: the role of childhood trauma and adult attachment. *Journal of Affective Disorders*, *163*, 102–109.

Mikulincer, M., & Shaver, P. R. (2007). *Attachment in Adulthood: Structure, Dynamics, and Change*. Guilford Press.

Nolte, T., Bolling, D. Z., Hudac, C., Fonagy, P., Mayes, L. C., & Pelphrey, K. A. (2013). Brain mechanisms underlying the impact of attachment-related stress on social cognition. *Frontiers in Human Neuroscience*, *7*, 816.

Perkins, R. (2001). What constitutes success?. *The British Journal of Psychiatry*, *179*(1), 9–10.

Pos, K., Bartels-Velthuis, A. A., Simons, C. J., Korver-Nieberg, N., Meijer, C. J., de Haan, L., ... & van Os, J. (2015). Theory of Mind and attachment styles in people with psychotic disorders, their siblings, and controls. *Australian and New Zealand Journal of Psychiatry*, *49*, 171–180.

Quijada, Y., Kwapil, T. R., Tizón, J., Sheinbaum, T., & Barrantes-Vidal, N. (2015). Impact of attachment style on the 1-year outcome of persons with an at-risk mental state for psychosis. *Psychiatry Research*, *228*(3), 849–856.

Repper, J. and Perkins, R. (2003). *Social Inclusion and Recovery. A Model for Mental Health Practice*. Edinburgh: Baillière Tindall.

Sabbagh, M. A. (2004). Understanding orbitofrontal contributions to theory-of-mind reasoning: Implications for autism. *Brain and Cognition*, *55*(1), 209–219.

Savla, G. N., Vella, L., Armstrong, C. C., Penn, D. L., & Twamley, E. W. (2013). Deficits in domains of social cognition in schizophrenia: a meta-analysis of the empirical evidence. *Schizophrenia Bulletin*, *39*, 979–992.

Schiffman, J., Walker, E., Ekstrom, M., Schulsinger, F., Sorensen, H., & Mednick, S. (2004). Childhood videotaped social and neuromotor precursors of schizophrenia: a prospective investigation. *American Journal of Psychiatry*, *161*(11), 2021–2027.

Shaw, P., Lawrence, E. J., Radbourne, C., Bramham, J., Polkey, C. E., & David, A. S. (2004). The impact of early and late damage to the human amygdala on 'theory of mind'reasoning. *Brain*, *127*(7), 1535–1548.

Simons, K. J., Paternite, C. E., & Shore, C. (2001). Quality of parent/adolescent attachment and aggression in young adolescents. *The Journal of Early Adolescence*, *21*(2), 182–203.

Searle, B., & Meara, N. M. (1999). Affective dimensions of attachment styles: Exploring self-reported attachment style, gender, and emotional experience among college students. *Journal of Counseling Psychology*, *46*(2), 147–158.

Sharp, C., & Fonagy, P. (2008). Social *Cognition and Attachment-Related Disorders*. Oxford: Oxford University Press.

Sharp, C., Monterosso, J., & Montague, P. R. (2012). Neuroeconomics: a bridge for translational research. *Biological Psychiatry*, *72*(2), 87–92.

Simpson, J. A., Rholes, W. S., & Phillips, D. (1996). Conflict in close relationships: an attachment perspective. *Journal of Personality and Social Psychology*, *71*(5), 899.

Steptoe, A., Shankar, A., Demakakos, P., & Wardle, J. (2013). Social isolation, loneliness, and all-cause mortality in older men and women. *Proceedings of the National Academy of Sciences*, *110*(15), 5797–5801.

Stoffers, J. M., Völlm, B. A., Rücker, G., Timmer, A., Huband, N., & Lieb, K. (2012). Psychological therapies for people with borderline personality disorder. *The Cochrane Library*.

Tucker, J. S., & Anders, S. L. (1999). Attachment style, interpersonal perception accuracy, and relationship satisfaction in dating couples. *Personality and Social Psychology Bulletin*, *25*(4), 403–412.

Van Lange, P. A., De Bruin, E., Otten, W., & Joireman, J. A. (1997). Development of prosocial, individualistic, and competitive orientations: theory and preliminary evidence. *Journal of Personality and Social Psychology*, *73*(4), 733.

6

PARENTING IN PSYCHOSIS FROM AN ATTACHMENT PERSPECTIVE

Susanne Harder and Kirstine Davidsen

Parenting in psychosis

Although the fertility rate for people with psychosis, including people diagnosed with schizophrenia and bipolar disorder, is lower than in the general population (Laursen & Munk-Olsen, 2010), surveys suggest that more than half of women and a quarter of men do become parents (Cambell et al., 2012; Howard et al., 2001). There is also evidence that fertility rates have increased over time (Vigod et al., 2012). Possible explanations for an increase in fertility rates might be a greater focus on early intervention in first episode psychosis and more community-based treatment, which might have given women with psychosis more opportunities to establish relationships and become pregnant (Solari et al., 2008). Fertility rates may also have increased due to a shift from traditional to atypical antipsychotic medication with different side effect profiles, which do not affect menstruation patterns (Currier & Simpson, 1998), or possibly even due to an increased tendency amongst clinicians to consider people's desire for fertility when making decisions about which type, and doses of, medication to prescribe. Despite increases in fertility, little is known about how severe the mental health problems are for those individuals who choose to become parents compared to the broader population of people with psychosis.

The majority of parents with psychosis live with and raise their children. They are, however, at high risk of losing custody of their children. In Denmark, 20 per cent of mothers with a diagnosis of schizophrenia have lost custody periodically or permanently at the end of the infant's first year, and another 20 per cent lose custody after the first year, mostly during the child's adolescence. For fathers with a diagnosis of schizophrenia, the cumulative risk is much lower: 5 per cent after the first year and 15 per cent by the time the child is aged 18 (Ranning et al., 2015). A survey from the United Kindgom of 58 mothers in contact with rehabilitation services and experiencing severe mental health problems (88% with psychosis) found that 68 per cent had had a child taken into custody (Dipple et al., 2002). In an American study of 379 mothers diagnosed with severe mental health problems, 36 per cent had lost custody of a child (Hollingsworth, 2004).

In spite of a dawning interest in the role of paternal mental health problems and its impact on parenting capacities and child outcomes, the current knowledge about parenting in psychosis is based on studies about maternal psychosis. Fathers play a significant role in childcare in most Western countries, and studies show that paternal mental health problems like depression and anxiety have an adverse effect on child outcome (Ramchandani & Psychogiou, 2009). It is most probable that paternal psychosis also affects child outcome, both directly by undermining the father's ability to provide sensitive care for the children, and indirectly by, for example, influencing maternal psychological wellbeing and the socio-economic condition of the family. However, studies specifically investigating the role of paternal psychosis are still needed. Most of the following chapter will therefore focus on maternal psychosis.

Child development

A child of a parent with psychosis can be at increased risk of experiencing a range of developmental difficulties, reflecting a non-optimal developmental trajectory. Between 50 and 70 per cent of offspring of parents with a psychosis exhibit socioemotional, cognitive or neuromotor problems, some of which start in early childhood (Liu et al., 2015). These problems are suggested to be risk factors for later mental health problems (Liu et al., 2015). Accordingly, the risk of developing a mental health problem for children with a parent with a diagnosis of schizophrenia is relatively high compared to the general population. Research has suggested that 55 per cent of people with a parent with a diagnosis of schizophrenia receive a mental health diagnosis (Rasic et al., 2013), and the risk for receiving a diagnosis of schizophrenia is 7 per cent (Gottesman et al., 2010) compared to the respective rates of 18 per cent and 1 per cent in the general population (NIMH, 2016). Genetic and perinatal biological risks are not sufficient to account for the development of schizophrenia in children of parents with psychosis. Psychosocial factors such as growing up with a parent with a severe mental health problem can also put children at developmental risk (Tienari et al., 2004). However, it is important to note that even though a heightened developmental risk is present in children of parents with psychosis, half of them do not develop a mental health problem. This reflects the importance of resilience factors and the ability of a large number of families with a parent with psychosis to provide a sufficiently good psychosocial environment.

How does psychosis influence parenting?

How a person develops as a parent and meets the needs of his or her child is influenced by personal characteristics and previous caregiving experiences. In addition, contextual sources of stress and support as well as characteristics of the child are found to have implications for parental development (Belsky,

1984). Contextual stress such as financial and social challenges and social stigma are found to be higher in families where a parent has a psychosis (Liu et al., 2015). In addition, contextual and partner support may be lower and there may be more household instability (Liu et al., 2015). Regarding child characteristics, a meta-analysis by Sacker et al. (1996) found increased risk of low birthweight and consequent poor neonatal condition in samples of women diagnosed with schizophrenia. Taken together, these factors are likely to increase parental stress and impede parental functioning to a larger extent in psychosis than in non-clinical populations.

Having taken these moderating factors into account, a main concern is how the psychological wellbeing of the parents can affect their caretaking behaviour and the development of the child. One possible aspect is the direct impact of psychotic experiences, such as hallucinations and delusions, and related behaviour on caregiving. Another aspect concerns the impact of more persistent emotional, relational and cognitive difficulties, which are often apparent in addition to more overt psychotic symptoms. A further aspect, which is beyond the scope of this chapter but which warrants mention, is the effect of medication. Arguably, medication may have a positive effect on parenting by ameliorating symptoms, but conversely the side effects associated with it, namely drowsiness, motor retardation and emotional numbing, may also adversely affect the capacity to parent.

Severity of maternal psychosis symptoms has been found to make a unique contribution to maternal reported child internalising and externalising problems (Mowbray et al., 2005). Using qualitative methods, Diaz-Caneja and Johnson (2004) explored the impact of psychotic experiences on parenting as experienced by mothers with a diagnosis of schizophrenia. While most of the mothers described motherhood in positive terms (e.g. giving them a purpose in life), they also expressed serious concerns. Several described how they might function well for long periods, but how, at times of relapse and the return of depressive and psychotic symptoms, their ability to care for their child was severely impeded. Mothers also felt socially stigmatised and expressed fear of disclosing their difficulties for fear of losing custody of the child. In one study of adult children of mothers with psychosis, participants reported strong memories of frightening episodes of intrusive paranoid delusional behaviours of the mother and life-threatening behaviour directly affecting them as a child. Examples include being forced to leave home and hide under a bridge in a swamp with the parent for several days or experiencing a parent threatening to drive off the road in the car in order to kill them all (Duncan & Browning, 2009).

While behaviour related to psychotic symptoms may severely impede caregiving capacities, psychotic symptoms might only be present periodically in connection to relapse of psychosis. The impact on parenting of more persistent emotional, relational and cognitive difficulties might be more subtle than the impact of positive psychotic symptoms and overt psychotic behaviour. However, these might potentially have a larger impact on child development due to their more persistent and subtle presence, which might go more or less undetected and thus not lead to sufficient support from the family's network or to interventions from social services. In the study noted above, for some children, the most disturbing or sad memories from their childhood were the psychological absence of the parent, such as the experience of lack or loss of a caring mother even when she was physically present (Duncan & Browning, 2009).

In the following section, we will discuss possible emotional, relational and socio-cognitive difficulties in psychosis affecting parenting and child developmental outcome. We will approach this from an attachment perspective as attachment theory provides a framework for conceptualising psychosocial development, affect regulation and social cognition. Before presenting this literature, it is important to note that on the basis of current studies investigating the impact of psychotic symptoms or the impact of related emotional, relational and cognitive difficulties on parenting and child outcomes, it is difficult to determine the extent to which parental wellbeing plays a causal role. First, many of the studies that have explored the impact of schizophrenia and other psychoses on parenting and childhood outcomes do not specify the degree to which mothers are currently symptomatic or whether they just have a history of psychosis, meaning it is difficult to say whether it is symptoms per se or the sequelea of the diagnosis that has the impact. Second, most studies fail to control for the full range of confounding variables that may influence both parental mental health and parenting capacity or developmental outcomes. Third, the majority of studies are cross-sectional, meaning that it is not possible to tease out whether parental mental health leads to poor child outcomes or poor child outcomes lead to poorer parental mental health. In fact the relationships between parental mental health and child outcomes are most likely bi-directional and influenced by a range of complex factors that are likely to differ from family to family, highlighting the need for idiosyncratic formulations to help understand each family's needs on a case-by-case basis.

Attachment theory and parenting

Infants' attachment behaviours reflect their expectations regarding their caregivers' response to attachment-related needs and cues. Infants in secure attachment relationships have learnt from previous experiences that they can count on their caregiver when distressed. This enables them to use the attachment figure as a secure base for exploration and to use the relationship to regulate emotions when distress emerges. In contrast, children with insecure attachment patterns adopt one of two defensive strategies for dealing with non-optimal caregiving. They can restrain the expression of needs in the anxious-avoidant type of attachment. Conceptually, this is explained as a strategy to secure the best available protection from a caregiver, who is unresponsive or who tends to minimise or reject the infant's needs. In the second strategy, termed anxious-ambivalent (or -resistant), infants amplify their expression of needs in order to optimise attention to needs from an inconsistent caregiver (Ainsworth et al., 1978). Main and Solomon (1986) introduced an additional, fourth category: disorganied attachment. Disorganied attachment is said to develop when children are emotionally and physically dependent on a caregiver, but the caregiver is also a source of fear due to disruptive forms of parental behaviour (Lyons-Ruth et al., 1999). The behaviour of these infants reflects a breakdown in an organised strategy to deal with stress and they exhibit disturbed behaviour such as sudden loss of tonus, freezing and stereotyped movements.

Bowlby assumed that attachment experiences would be carried forward into later life through the impact of internal working models on our behaviour in new relationships (Bowlby, 1969). In accordance with this idea, a mother's attachment experiences would have an impact on her caregiving behaviours, which would in turn affect the infant's attachment patterns. This hypothesis has been supported empirically as research has consistently shown that the security of an infant's attachment relationship with their primary caregiver can be reliably predicted from the caregiver's own attachment classification (autonomous, dismissing, pre-occupied and unresolved) based on the Adult Attachment Interview, AAI (Hesse, 2008). This process has been named the "intergenerational transmission of attachment" (van Ijzendoorn, 1995).

In addition to the regulation of distress and negative emotions, the attachment relationship allows the infant to learn from the caregiver in various ways. In a secure attachment relationship, the parent can stimulate exploration (Bernier, 2014) and support the infant's cognitive development by promoting self-esteem, mastery motivation, attention control and persistence in problem solving tasks (De Ruiter & van Ijzendoorn, 1993). Furthermore, Fonagy and colleagues have proposed that an important function of the attachment relationship is to promote reflective functioning skills, which comprise the ability to understand mental states in self and other (Fonagy et al., 2002). In an insecure attachment relationship, development of these capacities may not be stimulated to the same extent and empirical evidence suggests that infants with insecure patterns of attachment are at increased risk of later childhood difficulties and mental health problems (Fearon et al., 2010; Madigan et al., 2013).

Attachment and parenting in psychosis

There is increasing interest in attachment theory as a promising framework for understanding social and emotional functioning in psychosis (Berry et al., 2007; Harder, 2014). There is a high frequency of insecure attachment in people with psychosis. For example, studies report rates of insecure attachment between 68–78 per cent (Bucci et al., 2017; Gumley et al., 2014;

MacBeth et al., 2011). Most insecurely attached people with psychosis have a dismissing-avoidant attachment pattern (48–62%); only a small proportion shows a preoccupied pattern (the adult 'equivalent' to ambivalent/resistant, 12–20%; Gumley et al., 2014; MacBeth et al., 2011). This distinguishes psychosis from most other mental health problems where insecure-preoccupied attachment is the most common attachment pattern. In addition, 32 per cent of individuals with psychosis are found to have an unresolved attachment pattern (a pattern related to attachment disorganisation) (Gumley et al., 2014). For comparison, a recent meta-analysis showed that the non-clinical distribution of attachment patterns is 56 per cent secure, 16 per cent dismissing, 9 per cent preoccupied and 18 per cent unresolved/cannot classify (Bakermans-Kranenburg & van Ijzendoorn, 2009). Unfortunately, to our knowledge, there are no studies that have assessed attachment classification in parents with psychosis and it is therefore unclear whether the distribution of attachment patterns differs between those with psychosis who become parents and those who do not.

In a recent meta-analysis, Verhage et al. (2016) studied intergenerational transmission of attachment patterns in general community samples, at risk samples (e.g. teenage mothers) and samples with diagnosed various mental health problems. Overall, 58 per cent of infants had the corresponding attachment pattern to their parent's (autonomous – secure, dismissing – avoidant, preoccupied – resistant). Whereas 46 per cent of the general community sample of parents had an insecure attachment pattern, the proportion was as high as 62 per cent for parents from at-risk or mental health samples. Similarly, 44 per cent of infants of parents in the general community sample had an insecure attachment pattern compared with 54 per cent of infants from at risk or mental health samples. Thus, across both samples and in the at-risk sample in particular, the infants had a slightly higher probability of having secure attachment than the parents. This difference might be explained by protective factors such as the presence of a partner with a secure attachment, as both parents are known to contribute to the attachment pattern of the child (Verhage et al., 2015). Another protective factor might be characteristics of the child, as some children seem to be more resilient to negative influences from their environment than others (Belsky & Pluess, 2009).

Transgenerational transmission of attachment has not yet been studied in psychosis and studies of attachment in infants of mothers with psychosis are sparse. Only one small study was identified, which used the strange situation procedure following the standardised approach to classifying infant attachment (D'Angelo, 1986). In this study, infants of mothers diagnosed with schizophrenia had more avoidant attachment styles compared to infants of mothers with depression and without diagnosed mental health conditions. Infants of mothers with depression had more ambivalent/resistant attachment styles compared to those with mothers diagnosed with schizophrenia and or those without mental health problems. Thus, both in infants of mothers diagnosed with schizophrenia and in adults with schizophrenia, avoidant/ dismissing attachment patterns are more common compared to people with depression and or without mental health problems, indicating that a possible transmission of dismissing/avoidant attachment from parent to infant could be hypothesised.

Transmission mechanisms

In this section, we will present various possible mechanisms for how a specific pattern of attachment can be carried forward from a parent to a child. This will be followed by a discussion of their relevance and empirical support in relation to parenting in psychosis. We will present three behavioural concepts: caregiver sensitivity, caregiver support of autonomy and exploration, and patterns of dyadic caregiver-infant interaction; and three representational concepts: parental mind-mindedness, parental reflective functioning and caregiver representation.

Caregiver sensitivity

A child's attachment pattern is formed during interactions within the attachment relationship between a parent and a child. The concept of caregiver sensitivity was originally proposed by Mary Ainsworth (1978) as the mechanism through which maternal attachment patterns are transmitted to the infant. A sensitive parent is defined as able to notice the infant's cues, interpret these signals correctly and respond to them promptly and appropriately. Ainsworth regarded these basic elements of parental behaviour as universal aspects of caregiving both in meeting the infant's basic needs and regulating negative emotions, as well as in promoting social development and exploration in playful interactions. Following Ainsworth's proposal, there has been considerable effort to explore maternal sensitivity as a core element in providing emotional care for the infant and as a mechanism for transmission of attachment. A recent meta-analysis supports the role of sensitivity as a mediator for transmission of attachment; sensitivity was found to explain 25 per cent to 50 per cent of the variance in transmission (Verhage et al., 2015).

As attachment patterns in parents with psychosis have not yet been explored, we lack knowledge about the association between the parents' attachment patterns and parental sensitivity in psychosis. However, there is some knowledge of maternal sensitivity in psychosis and its association with infant attachment. In a recent review, we identified 27 studies of mother-infant interaction in schizophrenia from 10 cohorts including three longitudinal cohorts (Davidsen et al., 2015). Our review found that during the early neonatal period, mothers with psychosis showed less social interaction with their infants and higher maternal tension and uncertainty compared to mothers without mental health problems. Similar patterns were identified with infants aged 1–12 months, where mothers diagnosed with schizophrenia showed reduced spontaneity, reduced social and physical contact with their infants and increased tension during feeding. This pattern continued for infants aged 13–36 months, where mothers diagnosed with schizophrenia showed reduced responsiveness to, and stimulation of, infants compared to mothers without mental health problems. Across these findings there is some evidence to suggest that maternal behaviour could be characterised by a lack of engagement and a withdrawn behavioural style concordant with a dismissing/avoidant attachment pattern. One study (Persson-Blennow et al., 1986) found that insensitive behaviour, in the form of greater maternal tension and uncertainty in mothers diagnosed with a history of non-organic psychosis-related disorders, was associated with insecure attachment amongst their infants. However, after reviewing the literature, Davidsen et al. (2015) concluded that the degree of non-optimal parenting was less marked than expected in mothers with severe mental health problems compared to mothers without a psychiatric diagnosis. No differences were found on several of the measures at various ages, including social and bodily contact at 3 weeks and 3 ½ months (Naslund et al., 1985) and smiling, vocalising and cuddling at 12 months (Sameroff et al., 1982). However, the results must be interpreted with caution because of the presence of considerable methodological problems within the studies. For example, only one of the scales used for measuring maternal sensitivity, Murrays Global Rating Scale, used in only two out of the 27 studies reviewed, could be considered valid according to Mesman and Emmen's (2013) criteria.

Caregiver support of autonomy and exploration

Sensitivity only partially explains the transmission of attachment, leaving a so-called "transmission gap" (van Ijzendoorn, 1995). In a recent paper, Bernier et al. (2014) made the point that even though Ainsworth underscored sensitivity as a multidimensional construct, empirical studies often used a more narrow definition of sensitivity focusing on sensitivity towards meeting the child's emotional needs and less towards parental support of child autonomy. In a longitudinal study of 130 mother-infant dyads, Bernier et al. (2014) explored the role of both sensitivity to the infant's need for comfort and sensitivity to the infant's need for autonomy, the latter expressed by scaffolding and supporting the infant's exploratory behaviour. The authors were able to show that both aspects of sensitivity independently contributed to transmission of attachment with equal magnitude. Together, maternal sensitivity to infants' needs and maternal autonomy fully accounted for the relationship between maternal and child attachment on a secure-insecure dimension. The qualitatively different insecure attachment patterns and the disorganised dimension were not explored in the study. To understand how maternal as well as infant behaviour contributes to these dimensions, a more detailed intersubjective approach seems warranted.

In terms of mothers diagnosed with schizophrenia, one study was identified that explored both maternal sensitivity to emotional needs and maternal support of exploration. Goodman and Brumley (1990) found that mothers with a diagnosis of schizophrenia scored significantly more poorly than mothers without mental health problems on scales measuring sensitivity to emotional needs and sensitivity to the infant's need for automony, whereas mothers diagnosed with depression scored between mothers diagnosed with schizophrenia and non-clinical mothers on both of these aspects of sensitivity. Thus, sensitivity, both in relation to meeting the infant's emotional needs and in relation to supporting autonomy and exploration, may be diminished in mothers with psychosis. The study also found that in mothers with a diagnosis of schizophrenia, maternal support of exploration, such as provision of appropriate play materials, emotional and verbal responsiveness and play stimulation, had a significant positive effect on infant development with regard to social behaviour.

Patterns of dyadic caregiver-infant interaction

Attachment theory has traditionally focused on the behaviour of the mother, whereas research combining attachment and intersubjective approaches focuses on patterns of dyadic interaction between parent and infant. The intersubjective approach underlines the infant's role as an active partner in the interaction with a parent right from birth. Trevarthen (1979) proposed the concept of "primary intersubjectivity" to describe the early affective interactive exchange observable between parents and infants. This approach assumes that the infant is able to share subjective emotional states with a caregiver from very early on. Findings using this approach indicate that patterns of dyadic interaction are important for infant social emotional development, including attachment and affect regulation capacity. Tronick and Beeghly (2011) highlight the importance of reparation of ruptures in the dyadic interaction. The experience that relationship ruptures can be repaired fosters resilience and helps the infant to cope with the stress of building new relationships and exploring the environment. Infants are highly sensitive to contingent responses of the parent; that is, responses that occur so promptly after the infant's actions that they experience them as a direct response to their own actions. Early mother-infant interactive patterns characterised by more responsive infants and more contingent responsive mothers predict later secure infant attachment classification, whereas early mother-infant interactive patterns exhibiting complex forms of dysregulation including conflicting affect in the dyad and lack of repair of interactive ruptures predict later insecure disorganised attachment (Beebe & Steele, 2013). Furthermore, latency in interactive repair has been shown to be related to increased cortisol reactivity in infants during the Still Face Paradigm (Mueller et al.,

2015). In the Still Face Procedure, the mother exhibits a "still face" and stops responding to the child for two minutes in the middle of a play session.

Studies of dyadic parent-infant patterns in psychosis have found less mutual harmony in feeding compared to other dyads during the neonatal period and continuing at three and six months, with infants showing less social contact during feeding (Davidsen et al., 2015). Mutual anger and hostility were also evident in the interaction. More disturbances in reciprocity of behaviour at three weeks and at six months predicted insecure attachment. These findings are in line with the research in people without psychosis, as highlighted above (Beebe & Steele, 2013).

Parental reflective functioning and parental mind-mindedness

Not only parental behaviour, but also parental mental representations and the capacity to understand the infant's mental states, have gathered considerable interest as possible mechanisms for transmission of attachment. Based on the concept of reflective functioning (Fonagy et al., 2002), Slade and colleagues (2005) defined parental reflective functioning as the parent's capacity to reflect upon the internal experience of the child and their own experience as a parent. The authors showed that parental reflective functioning contributed to intergenerational transmission of attachment in a general community sample.

Having a diagnosis of schizophrenia has been shown to be associated with impaired reflective functioning (MacBeth et al., 2011) and theory of mind ability (Brüne, 2005), which makes these aspects of parenting of specific interest in the context of psychosis. Our review (Davidsen et al., 2015) did not identify any studies exploring parental reflective functioning in psychosis. There are, however, studies of the related concept of mind-mindedness, which is from the theory of mind tradition, and focuses more on social cognition; specifically, the caregiver's ability to read their infant's internal states with regard to thought, desires, intention and memories. High levels of parental mind-mindedness during the infant's first year have been found to predict secure infant-mother attachment and infant theory of mind capacity at four years in general population samples (Meins et al., 2002). Pawlby et al. (2010) studied mind-mindedness in mothers who were inpatients at a mother-infant unit, compared to mothers without mental health problems. Contrary to expectations, they did not find any significant differences in mind-mindedness between mothers with a diagnosis of schizophrenia and mothers without mental health problems. The findings in this study challenge the view that mothers with a diagnosis of schizophrenia are less sensitive to their infants' needs and intentions. However, the findings might also be explained by the fact that there were only 15 participants in the study and consequent lack of power to identify significant group differences.

Caregiving representation

Parental reflective functioning and mind-mindedness are dimensions of caregiving theoretically linked to secure attachment. In addition, George and Solomon (2008) have conceptualised dimensions of caregiving related to insecure forms of attachment. Based on Bowlby's original formulations, they have described the caregiving system as the reciprocal parental system to the infant's attachment system (George & Solomon, 2008). They proposed four types of caregiving representations mirroring the four infant attachment classifications: (i) flexible integration (infant secure); (ii) deactivation and diminishing the importance of attachment (infant insecure avoidant); (iii) cognitive disconnection leading to close protection and diminished autonomy support (infant ambivalent resistant) and (iv) segregated systems leading to abdication of care and helplessness as caregiver (infant disorganised). Becoming a parent means a shift from an attachment position of receiving care and having one's own needs met to a caregiving position providing care and protection to meet the emotional needs of a child. The difficulty in making this shift can be a product of being overwhelmed by one's own emotional distress. This can, for example, be due to trauma or as a consequence of having a mental health problem, resulting in disorganised forms of caregiving. Indeed, George and Solomon (2008) describe disorganised types of caregiving representation as a result of exposure to trauma. This has not yet been studied in psychosis, but the high prevalence of childhood trauma and disorganised patterns of attachment in psychosis indicates that this could be important to explore.

Intervention

The finding that children of parents with psychosis may be at risk of poorer developmental outcomes suggests the need for preventive interventions. Services during pregnancy and in the perinatal period are relatively widespread (Seeman, 2013). During the post-natal period for infants up to one year of age, the most common intervention occurs in mother-baby-units (MBU) for mothers experiencing postpartum psychosis (Gearing et al., 2012). Descriptive studies of MBU treatment report favourable outcomes, with reduced level of stress, improved ability to fulfill the infant's developmental needs and enhanced mother-infant bonding. However, there is a lack of trial-based evidence for the effectiveness of MBU units (Irving & Saylan, 2007). There are few specialised outpatient treatment programmes for parents experiencing psychosis and their infants described in the literature and a scarcity of studies reporting effectiveness of these programmes (Gearing et al., 2012; Schrank et al., 2015). Intensive home visits focusing on the mother's relationship to her youngest child after the mother's discharge from hospitalisation for severe mental disorder were found to improve adaptive functioning and capacity for closeness in the mothers (Cohler &

Grunebaum, 1983). A complex community programme offering either social learning based group counseling or CBT-based parenting education for mothers with psychotic symptoms was tested in a study comparing two types of treatment in an experimental cohort design. Social relations improved for the education group, whereas family relations improved for the counselling group (Lucas et al., 1984). Finally, an online parenting programme for mothers diagnosed with a mood disorder or schizophrenia was tested in a randomised control trial study and found improvement in the parents' experience of parental skills and parental stress (Kaplan et al., 2014). The available studies support the view that interventions can be helpful for parents with psychosis in improving their parenting skills and their ability to fulfill the infant's developmental needs. In the field of post-partum depression it has been shown that treating maternal symptoms is not enough to improve the early mother-child relationship and child outcome (Forman et al., 2007). In line with this finding, complex interventions covering several areas and intervention components are recommended for parents with psychosis (Schrank et al. 2015). This includes provision of practical parenting support, skills training and focus on improving the relationship between parent and infant. As there is a high risk of residual symptoms and relapse, and since the child's developmental needs change with age, ongoing availability of services and long term intervention models are likely to be important. In the majority of instances, with adequate and timely supports for those who are in need, it is highly likely that people with severe mental health problems such as schizophrenia will be able to successfully parent their children. In our experience, many breakdowns in family functioning and suboptimal experiences of parenting could be prevented by the provision of support early on. Whilst this support is clearly essential for some and should be routinely available, in the same way that it should be available for all families who are struggling for whatever reason, as highlighted at various points throughout this chapter, it is important to note that many parents diagnosed with schizophrenia are able to successfully parent their children and many children of parents diagnosed with schizophrenia do not have adverse developmental outcomes.

References

Ainsworth, M., Blehar, M., Waters, E., & Wall, S. (1978). *Patterns of Attachment: A Psychological Study of the Strange Situation*. Hillsdale, NJ: Erlbaum.

Bakermans-Kranenburg, M. J., & van Ijzendoorn, M. H. (2009). The first 10,000 Adult Attachment Interviews: Distributions of adult attachment representations in clinical and non-clinical groups. *Attachment & Human Development, 11*(3), 223–263.

Beebe, B., & Steele, M. (2013). How does microanalysis of mother–infant communication inform maternal sensitivity and infant attachment? *Attachment & Human Development, 15*(5–6), 583–602. doi: http://dx.doi.org/10.1080/14616734.2013.841050

Belsky, J. (1984). The determinants of parenting: A process model. *Child Development*, 83–96.

Belsky, J., & Pluess, M. (2009). Beyond diathesis stress: differential susceptibility to environmental influences. *Psychological Bulletin, 135*(6), 885.

Bernier, A., Matte-Gagné, C., Bélanger, M. È., & Whipple, N. (2014). Taking stock of two decades of attachment transmission gap: broadening the assessment of maternal behavior. *Child Development, 85*(5), 1852–1865.

Berry, K., Wearden, A., & Barrowclough, C. (2007). Adult attachment styles and psychosis: an investigation of associations between general attachment styles and attachment relationships with specific others. *Social Psychiatry and Psychiatric Epidemiology, 42*(12), 972–976.

Bowlby, J. (1969). *Attachment and Loss: Vol. 1. Attachment.* New York: Basic Books.

Brüne, M. (2005). "Theory of mind" in schizophrenia: a review of the literature. *Schizophrenia Bulletin, 31*(1), 21–42.

Bucci, S., Emsley, R., & Berry, K. (2017). Attachment in psychosis: A latent profile analysis of attachment styles and association with symptoms in a large psychosis cohort. *Psychiatry Research, 247*, 243–249.

Cohler, B. J., & Grunebaum, H. (1983). Children of parents hospitalized for mental illness: II. The evaluation of an Intervention Program for Mentally 111 Mothers of Young Children. *Journal of Children in Contemporary Society, 15*(1), 57–66.

Currier, G. W., & Simpson, G. M. (1998). Psychopharmacology: antipsychotic medications and fertility. *Psychiatric Services, 49*(2), 175–176.

D'Angelo, E. J. (1986). Security of attachment in infants with schizophrenic, depressed, and unaffected mothers. *The Journal of Genetic Psychology, 147*(3), 421–422. doi: http://dx.doi.org/10.1080/00221325.1986.9914517

Davidsen, K. A., Harder, S., MacBeth, A., Lundy, J., & Gumley, A. (2015). Mother-infant interaction in schizophrenia: transmitting risk or resilience? A systematic review of literature. *Social Psychiatry and Psychiatric Epidemiology.* doi: http://dx.doi.org/10.1007/s00127-015-1127-x

De Ruiter, C., & van Ijzendoorn, M. H. (1993). Attachment and cognition. *International Journal of Educational Research, 19*(6), 521–599.

Dipple, H., Smith, S., Andrews, H., & Evans, B. (2002). The experience of mother-hood in women with severe and enduring mental illness. *Social Psychiatry and Psychiatric Epidemiology, 37*(7), 336–340.

Duncan, G., & Browning, J. (2009). Adult attachment in children raised by parents with schizophrenia. *Journal of Adult Development, 16*(2), 76–86.

Fearon, R., Bakermans-Kranenburg, M. J., van Ijzendoorn, M. H., Lapsley, A. M., & Roisman, G. I. (2010). The significance of insecure attachment and dis-organization in the development of children's externalizing behavior: a meta-analytic study. *Child Development, 81*(2), 435–456. doi: http://dx.doi.org/10.1111/j.1467-8624.2009.01405.x

Fonagy, P., Gergely, G., & Jurist, E. L. (2002). *Affect Regulation, Mentalization and the Development of the Self.* New York: Other Press.

Gearing, R., Alonzo, D., & Marinelli, C. (2012). Maternal schizophrenia: psycho-social treatment for mothers and their children. *Clinical Schizophrenia & Related Psychoses, 6*(1), 27–33B.

George, C., & Solomon, J. (2008). The caregiving system: a behavioral systems approach to parenting. In J. Cassidy & P. Shaver (Eds.), *Handbook of Attachment: Theory, research, and clinical applications* (Vol. 2, pp. 833–856).

Goodman, S. H., & Brumley, H. E. (1990). Schizophrenic and depressed mothers: Relational deficits in parenting. *Developmental Psychology, 26*(1), 31–39.

Gottesman, I. I., Laursen, T. M., Bertelsen, A., & Mortensen, P. B. (2010). Severe mental disorders in offspring with 2 psychiatrically ill parents. *Archives of General Psychiatry, 67*(3), 252–257. doi: http://dx.doi.org/10.1001/archgenpsychiatry.2010.1

Gumley, A., Schwannauer, M., MacBeth, A., Fisher, R., Clark, S., Wilcox, L., ... Birchwood, M. (2014). Insight, Duration of untreated psychosis and attachment in first episode psychosis: a prospective study of psychiatric recovery over 12-months follow-up. *British Journal of Psychiatry, 205*, 60–67.

Harder, S. (2014). Attachment in Schizophrenia—implications for research, prevention, and treatment. *Schizophrenia Bulletin, 40*(6), 1189–1193. doi: http://dx.doi.org/10.1093/schbul/sbu133

Hesse, E. (2008). The Adult Attachment Interview: Protocol, method of analysis, and empirical studies. In J. Cassidy & P. R. Shaver (Eds.), *Handbook of Attachment: Theory, research, and clinical applications* (pp. 552–5598). New York, NY, US: The Guilford Press.

Hollingsworth, L. D. (2004). Child custody loss among women with persistent severe mental illness. *Social Work Research, 28*(4), 199–209.

Irving, C. B., & Saylan, M. (2007). Mother and baby units for schizophrenia. *Cochrane Database of Systematic Reviews* (1). doi: 10.1002/14651858.CD006333

Kaplan, K., Solomon, P., Salzer, M. S., & Brusilovskiy, E. (2014). Assessing an Internet-based parenting intervention for mothers with a serious mental illness: A randomized controlled trial. *Psychiatric Rehabilitation Journal, 37*(3), 222.

Laursen, T. M., & Munk-Olsen, T. (2010). Reproductive patterns in psychotic patients. *Schizophrenia Research, 121*, 234–240.

Liu, C. H., Keshavan, M. S., Tronick, E., & Seidman, L. J. (2015). Perinatal risks and childhood premorbid indicators of later psychosis: next steps for early psychosocial interventions. *Schizophrenia Bulletin*, sbv047. doi: http://dx.doi.org/10.1093/schbul/sbv047

Lucas, L. E., Montgomery, S. H., Richardson, D. A., & Rivers, P. A. (1984). Impact project: reducing the risk of mental illness to children of distressed mothers. *New Directions for Mental Health Services, 1984*(24), 79–94.

Lyons-Ruth, K., Bronfman, E., & Parsons, E. (1999). Maternal frightened, frightening, or atypical behavior and disorganized infant attachment patterns. *Monographs of the Society for Research in Child Development*, 67–96. doi: http://dx.doi.org/10.1111/1540–5834.00034

MacBeth, A., Gumley, A., Schwannauer, M., & Fisher, R. (2011). Attachment states of mind, mentalization, and their correlates in a first-episode psychosis sample. *Psychology and Psychotherapy-Theory Research and Practice, 84*(1), 42–57. doi: 10.1348/147608310x530246

Madigan, S., Atkinson, L., Laurin, K., & Benoit, D. (2013). Attachment and internalizing behavior in early childhood: A meta-analysis. *Developmental Psychology, 49*(4), 672. doi: http://dx.doi.org/10.1037/a0028793

Main, M., & Solomon, J. (1986). Discovery of an insecure-disorganized/disoriented attachment pattern. In T. B. Brazelton & M. W. Yogman (Eds.), *Affective Development in Infancy* (pp. 95–124). Norwood, NJ: Ablex Publishing Corporation.

Meins, E., Fernyhough, C., Wainwright, R., Das Gupta, M., Fradley, E., & Tuckey, M. (2002). Maternal mind–mindedness and attachment security as predictors of theory of mind understanding. *Child Development, 73*(6), 1715–1726.

Mesman, J., & Emmen, R. A. (2013). Mary Ainsworth's legacy: a systematic review of observational instruments measuring parental sensitivity. *Attachment & Human Development, 15*(5–6), 485–506.

Mowbray, C. T., Lewandowski, L., Bybee, D., & Oyserman, D. (2005). Relationship between maternal clinical factors and mother-reported child problems. *Community Mental Health Journal, 41*(6), 687–704.

Mueller, M., Zietlow, A.-L., Tronick, E., & Reck, C. (2015). What dyadic reparation is meant to do: an association with infant cortisol reactivity. *Psychopathology, 48*(6), 386–399.

Naslund, B., Persson-Blennow, I., McNeil, T. F., & Kaij, L. (1985). Offspring of women with nonorganic psychosis: mother-infant interaction at three and six weeks of age. *Acta Psychiatrica Scandinavica, 71*(5), 441–450.

NIMH. (2016). Any Mental Illness (AMI) among U.S. Adults. Retrieved 26-06, 2016, from www.nimh.nih.gov/health/statistics/prevalence/any-mental-illness-ami-among-us-adults.shtml

Pawlby, S., Fernyhough, C., Meins, E., Pariante, C., Seneviratne, G., & Bentall, R. (2010). Mind-mindedness and maternal responsiveness in infant–mother interactions in mothers with severe mental illness. *Psychological Medicine, 40*(11), 1861–1869.

Persson-Blennow, I., Naslund, B., McNeil, T., & Kaij, L. (1986). Offspring of women with nonorganic psychosis: mother-infant interaction at one year of age. *Acta Psychiatrica Scandinavica, 73*(2), 207–213.

Ranning, A., Laursen, T. M., Thorup, A., Hjorthøj, C., & Nordentoft, M. (2015). Serious Mental Illness and Disrupted Caregiving for Children: A Nationwide, Register-Based Cohort Study. *The Journal of Clinical Psychiatry, 76*(8), 478–1014.

Rasic, D., Hajek, T., Alda, M., & Uher, R. (2013). Risk of mental illness in offspring of parents with schizophrenia, bipolar disorder, and major depressive disorder: a meta-analysis of family high-risk studies. *Schizophrenia Bulletin*, sbt114. doi: http://dx.doi:10.1093/schbul/sbt114

Sacker, A., Done, D., & Crow, T. (1996). Obstetric complications in children born to parents with schizophrenia: a meta-analysis of case–control studies. *Psychological Medicine, 26*(2), 279–287.

Sameroff, A. J., Seifer, R., Zax, M., & Garmezy, N. (1982). Early development of children at risk for emotional disorder. *Monographs of the Society for Research in Child Development*, 1–82. doi: http://dx.doi.org/10.2307/1165903

Schrank, B., Moran, K., Borghi, C., & Priebe, S. (2015). How to support patients with severe mental illness in their parenting role with children aged over 1 year? A systematic review of interventions. *Social Psychiatry and Psychiatric Epidemiology, 50*(12), 1765–1783.

Seeman, M. V. (2013). Clinical interventions for women with schizophrenia: pregnancy. *Acta Psychiatrica Scandinavica, 127*(1), 12–22.

Slade, A., Grienenberger, J., Bernbach, E., Levy, D., & Locker, A. (2005). Maternal reflective functioning, attachment, and the transmission gap: A preliminary study. *Attachment & Human Development*, 7(3), 283–298.

Solari, H., Dickson, K., & Miller, L. (2008). Understanding and treating women with schizophrenia during pregnancy and postpartum–Motherisk Update 2008. *The Canadian Journal of Clinical Pharmacology= Journal Canadien De Pharmacologie Clinique*, 16(1), e23–32.

Tienari, P., Wynne, L. C., Sorri, A., Lahti, I., Läksy, K., Moring, J., ... Wahlberg, K.-E. (2004). Genotype-environment interaction in schizophrenia-spectrum disorder Long-term follow-up study of Finnish adoptees. *The British Journal of Psychiatry*, 184(3), 216–222.

Trevarthen, C. (1979). Communication and cooperation in early infancy: A description of primary intersubjectivity. In M. Bullowa (Ed.), *Before Speech: The beginning of interpersonal communication* (pp. 321–347). Cambridge: Cambridge University Press.

Tronick, E., & Beeghly, M. (2011). Infants' meaning-making and the development of mental health problems. *American Psychologist*, 66(2), 107.

van Ijzendoorn, M. (1995). Adult attachment representations, parental responsiveness, and infant attachment: a meta-analysis on the predictive validity of the Adult Attachment Interview. *Psychological Bulletin*, 117(3), 387.

Verhage, M. L., Schuengel, C., Madigan, S., Fearon, R., Oosterman, M., Cassibba, R., ... van Ijzendoorn, M. H. (2016). Narrowing the Transmission Gap: A Synthesis of Three Decades of Research on Intergenerational Transmission of Attachment. *Psychological Bulletin*, 142(4), 337–366.

Vigod, S. N., Seeman, M. V., Ray, J. G., Anderson, G. M., Dennis, C. L., Grigoriadis, S., ... Rochon, P. A. (2012). Temporal trends in general and age-specific fertility rates among women with schizophrenia (1996–2009): a population-based study in Ontario, Canada. *Schizophrenia Research*, 139(1), 169–175.

7

THE NEUROBIOLOGY OF ATTACHMENT AND PSYCHOSIS RISK

A theoretical integration

Benjamin K. Brent, Martin Debbané, and Peter Fonagy

Introduction

The last decade has witnessed a significant growth of research and clinical interest in understanding how the vicissitudes of attachment relationships may play a part in the development and course of psychotic-spectrum disorders (Berry, Barrowclough, & Wearden, 2007; B. K. Brent, Holt, Keshavan, Seidman, & Fonagy, 2014). This has been motivated by several considerations. First, there is a large body of evidence suggesting that childhood adversity broadly speaking (i.e., exposure to stressors such as living in an urban environment, or minority group status) is an indicator of psychosis risk (van Os, Kenis, & Rutten, 2010). Second, several studies have shown that dysfunction in the childhood caregiving environment (e.g., aberrant relationships with caregivers and trauma) confers greater vulnerability to psychosis (Cannon et al., 2002; Jones, Rodgers, Murray, & Marmot, 1994; Wahlberg et al., 1997). Third, recent studies have linked attachment insecurity with increased symptom levels and poorer social functioning in people with a diagnosis of schizophrenia (Berry, Barrowclough, & Wearden, 2008; Gumley, Taylor, Schwannauer, & MacBeth, 2014).

Importantly, we view attachment insecurity not as a causal variable in the etiology of psychotic-spectrum disorder, but rather as an environmental risk factor that likely interacts with an underlying genetic predisposition to potentiate psychosis risk (B. K. Brent & Fonagy, 2014). The hypothesis that attachment could modulate the expression of the genetic vulnerability to psychosis is consistent with evidence from animal research showing that the quality of the caregiving environment can influence gene expression and, as a result, the development of behavioural patterns and biological systems (Sullivan, 2012). The goal of this chapter is to discuss possible interactions between disruptions in the neurobiology of attachment and psychosis. Determining the biological mechanisms linking attachment disturbances to psychosis may be critical for refining predictions about the effects of the attachment environment on the development of young people who go on to develop psychosis. It may also contribute to the development of treatment interventions that could help prevent, or delay psychosis onset in at-risk youth, and/or to improve clinical outcomes among people with established psychotic-spectrum diagnoses. We begin by reviewing the neural underpinnings of the attachment system. This is followed by a discussion of how disruptions within the neural circuitry mediating attachment might interact with the neurobiology of the symptoms and social cognitive deficits associated with a psychotic-spectrum diagnosis. Finally, we consider some of the therapeutic implications of the neurobiological interconnections between disturbances of the attachment system and the symptoms of psychotic disorders.

Neurobiology of attachment

An extensive body of animal research has provided considerable insight into the neural basis of attachment-related behaviour (e.g., social bonding, affiliation, or caregiving). A comprehensive review of the neural circuitry implicated in attachment is beyond the scope of this chapter. Here, we highlight evidence supporting the involvement of three key neural systems in attachment-related behaviour: the oxytocinergic/arginine vasopressinergic, dopaminergic and hypothalamic-pituitary-adrenal (HPA) stress-response systems.

Oxytocinergic/arginine vasopressinergic system

Oxytocin and arginine vasopressin (AVP) are neuropeptide hormones/neurotransmitters synthesised primarily in the paraventricular and supraoptic nuclei of the hypothalamus and stored in the pituitary. Animal studies suggest that the oxytocinergic/AVP neural circuitry comprises several central brain areas, including the ventral striatum (nucleus accumbens [NAcc]), ventral tegmental area (VTA), medial preoptic area and the bed nucleus of the stria terminalis (Strathearn, 2011). The role of oxytocin and AVP in the attachment-related behaviour of rodents (e.g., the formation of adult attachment [pair bonding] and caregiving behaviour) has been particularly well studied. Experiments in prairie voles (small rodents indigenous to North America), for example, have shown that intracerebral oxytocin and/or AVP infusion can induce partner preference in the absence of prior mating (a key facilitator in partner bonding in voles) (Young, Liu, & Wang, 2008).

Consistent with these findings, studies in humans link peripheral measures of oxytocin to a wide range of mental processes that foster social affiliation (e.g., social perception, social cognition, social memory) (Sobrian & Holson, 2011), as well as to maternal and paternal bonding behaviours (e.g., greater closeness and warmth during parent-infant interactions) (Gordon, Martin, Feldman, & Leckman, 2011). For example, Gordon and colleagues have shown

that increased levels of peripheral oxytocin predicted greater physical proximity and affectionate touch between parents and their first child at six month
of age (Gordon, Zagoory-Sharon, Leckman, & Feldman, 2010). The role of
AVP in caregiving and other social behaviour has been less studied, but initial
research in humans also parallels findings in the animal literature (Sobrian &
Holson, 2011). Intranasal AVP administration, for example, has been linked
with increased social cooperation in men (Rilling et al., 2012), and variance
in the AVP receptor is associated with the likelihood of monogamy and
marital satisfaction in males (Walum et al., 2008). Additionally, as reviewed by
Strathearn (Strathearn, 2011), neuroimaging studies have shown: 1) engagement of oxytocin-associated neural circuitry during attachment-related processing (e.g., mothers' responses to hearing their infant's cries); 2) reduced
levels of oxytocin in adulthood in association with deficits in the childhood
caregiving environment (e.g., emotional neglect and maltreatment); and
3) aberrant activation of oxytocinergic-related brain regions in response to
infantile attachment-seeking behaviour in insecurely attached mothers.

Dopaminergic system

Animal research has also provided a strong empirical basis for linking
attachment-related behaviour to the dopamine (DA) mesocorticolimbic
reward system – a neural system that includes the VTA, NAcc and prefrontal
cortex (PFC). In particular, it has been suggested that mesocorticolimbic DA
may mediate the motivational drive necessary for the initiation and maintenance of caregiving and affiliative behaviours (Insel, 2003). For example,
activation of DA receptors in the NAcc has been implicated in the facilitation
of maternal behaviours in rats, while infusion of DA antagonists in the NAcc
of postpartum rats has been linked with the disruption of pup retrieval (i.e.,
maternal rodent behaviour that involves locating and bringing back newborn
pups who have strayed from the litter) (Stoesz, Hare, & Snow, 2013). Notably,
disruption of the early caregiving environment in rodents (e.g., maternal separation) is also associated with long-term, chronic dysfunction of the DA
system; such as, increased DA levels and greater DA release in response to
stress in adulthood (Strathearn, 2011).

Consistent with research in animals, fMRI studies in humans have
demonstrated the engagement of DA reward circuitry during maternal
responses to infant stimuli (e.g, viewing photographs of one's own baby),
suggesting its role in caregiving behaviour (Strathearn, 2011). Further, several fMRI studies have linked neural activity in the mesolimbic DA reward
circuitry with love between romantic partners (for review see: Strathearn,
2011). Bartels and Zeki, as well as Aron and colleagues, have shown in separate studies that people who are in love demonstrate increased activation of
DA-rich brain areas (e.g., VTA and anterior cingulate gryus) when viewing
pictures of their beloved (Aron et al., 2005; Bartels & Zeki, 2004). Taken

together with the evidence from animal studies, these findings are thought to support the role of the dopaminergic reward system in human attachment (Gordon et al., 2011).

HPA stress-response system

Animal research has identified the HPA stress-response system as a third key contributor to the neurobiology of attachment. Psychological, or physiological stress triggers the release of stress hormones (corticotrophic-releasing hormone [CRH] and AVP) from the paraventricular nucleus of the hypothalamus into the hypophyseal portal system where they then stimulate the anterior pituitary gland to release adrenocorticotrophin hormone (ACTH) into the bloodstream. ACTH travels to the adrenal cortex, initiating the release of glucocorticoids (cortisol, in humans). Under normal conditions, cortisol facilitates adaptive responses to stress while also exerting an inhibitory effect on the stress-response system via a negative feedback mechanism.

Several lines of evidence implicate HPA axis activity in the development and maintenance of attachment bonds. For example, in male prairie voles, the enhancement of partner bond formation has been associated with stimulation of CRH receptors in the NAcc (a central brain area in the mesolimbic DA reward circuitry as described above) (Lim et al., 2007). Further, HPA axis activation in response to stress in rodents may mediate the association between depressive-like behavioural symptoms and attachment loss (Burkett & Young, 2012). By pairing an aversive state with the disruption of attachment relationships, HPA axis activity may provide an important neurobiological basis for the motivation to re-establish attachment bonds after separation and, thus, to maintain attachment bonds over time. Additionally, studies in rats have shown that while rat pups' exposure to prolonged maternal separation is associated with elevation of corticosterone (the rodent equivalent of cortisol), the presence of the mother suppresses corticosterone levels in rat pups during social stress ("social buffering") (Johnson & Young, 2015). Conversely, disturbances of the early care environment of rodents have been linked with long-term HPA axis system dysfunction and chronically elevated corticosterone levels (Sullivan, 2012).

In humans, a growing number of studies have shown associations between HPA axis activity and attachment-related behaviour (e.g., romantic love, development of adult attachment and maternal caregiving) (Gordon et al., 2011). For example, maternal behaviour and infant responsiveness (Fleming, Steiner, & Corter, 1997) have been linked with increased levels of HPA-associated cortisol release, as has the initial phase of pair bonding (falling in love) (Marazziti & Canale, 2004). Additionally, reviews of the literature suggest that while a sensitive caregiving environment is associated with adaptive responses to stress and may help protect the HPA axis during early development, childhood maltreatment is consistently correlated with HPA axis dysfunction (Nemeroff, 2004; Toth, Gravener-Davis, Guild, & Cicchetti, 2013).

Disruptions of the attachment system and the neurobiology of psychotic disorders

Clearly, alterations of the neurobiology of attachment cannot be sufficient to cause psychosis, as disturbances of the attachment system are implicated in many other psychiatric disorders, particularly borderline personality disorder (Fonagy & Luyten, 2009). Nevertheless, growing evidence supports several plausible interactions between disturbances of the neural systems mediating attachment and positive symptoms (e.g., delusions, hallucinations), negative symptoms (e.g., asociality, affective blunting) and social cognitive impairments (e.g., theory of mind [ToM]) in people who meet diagnostic criteria for schizophrenia. Below, we highlight some of these putative interactions.

Positive symptoms

The notion that dysregulation of striatal DA plays a central role in the positive symptoms of schizophrenia and related psychotic disorders is broadly supported by over four decades of research (Howes & Kapur, 2009). According to contemporary neurodevelopmental models, the abnormal function of striatal DA gives rise to a vulnerability to positive symptoms that is initially held in check, or modulated, because of relatively intact PFC inhibitory control over subcortical (striatal) DA (Keshavan, 1999). During adolescence, however, aberrant synaptic pruning may lead to excessive cortical (PFC) grey matter loss and, consequently, to subcortical disinhibition (Keshavan, 1999). In conjunction with heightened social stress, the erosion of PFC inhibitory control over striatal DA could then lead to the emergence of positive symptoms.

How might disturbances of the neurobiology of attachment contribute to the emergence of positive symptoms? As described above, animal studies have shown that disruption of the early attachment environment (e.g., maternal separation) is associated with persistently elevated DA levels and heightened DA release during stress (Strathearn, 2011). Dysregulation of striatal DA, however, could be additionally affected by depletion of available oxytocin and over-activation of the HPA axis system, which both have been associated with a dysfunctional early care environment. Oxytocin, for example, has been shown to have a modulatory effect on excessive mesolimbic DA in rodents receiving psychostimulants, leading to the suggestion that oxytocin may have intrinsic antipsychotic properties (Rich & Caldwell, 2015). Additionally, over-activation of the HPA axis has been associated with elevated DA synthesis and alterations of striatal DA receptors (Walker & Diforio, 1997). We suggest that, taken together, early neurobiological alterations of the attachment system could increase the likelihood of a premorbid susceptibility to striatal DA dysregulation and, therefore, increase the risk of psychosis during later adolescent/early adult development.

Negative symptoms

Alterations of a number of different brain areas involved in social and emotional processing, such as the PFC and amygdala, have been implicated in the neurobiology of negative symptoms (i.e., asociality, anhedonia, avolition, alogia and blunted affect) (Millan, Fone, Steckler, & Horan, 2014). For example, it is thought that elevated striatal DA may induce reductions in PFC function and, thus, social deficits, as a result of indirect communications from the striatum to the PFC by way of the thalamus (Fusar-Poli et al., 2011). This view is in part based on animal studies showing that excessive striatal DA can lead to deficits of PFC DA activity in conjunction with behavioural inflexibility (Kellendonk et al., 2006). Evidence that the level of striatal DA is negatively correlated with PFC activation in prodromal individuals (Fusar-Poli et al., 2011) further supports the possibility that the neurobiology of positive symptoms (excessive striatal DA) and negative symptoms (reduced PFC DA; "hypofrontality") may be inter-related.

An alternative (though not mutually exclusive) model, however, suggests that overactivity of the amygdala may generate inappropriate responses (e.g., heightened fear and anxiety) to neutral, or benign social stimuli and, thus, mediate the asocial dimension of negative symptoms in schizophrenia (Sobota, Mihara, Forrest, Featherstone, & Siegel, 2015). Consistent with this model, animal studies in rats have shown that phencyclidine (PCP)-induced amygdylar hyperactivity is associated with significant disruptions of socially interactive behaviour (Katayama et al., 2009). Further, neuroimaging studies in people with a schizophrenia diagnosis have demonstrated that increased amygdylar activity is associated with aberrant responses to social and emotional stimuli (Holt et al., 2006; Satterthwaite et al., 2010).

Based on these findings, alterations of the neural system mediating attachment could contribute to both hypofrontal and hyperamygdylar pathways to negative symptoms. First, as previously discussed, disturbances of the early attachment environment may lead to chronic dysfunction of striatal DA, and, thus, indirectly, to impairments of social functioning, given the potential contribution of elevated striatal DA to reductions in PFC DA function. Rodent research, for example, has showed that adult rats exposed to disruptions in their early maternal care environment exhibit aberrant social behaviour and increased anxiety that is similar to negative symptoms (Rich & Caldwell, 2015).

Additionally, however, the oxytocinergic system is densely interconnected with the amygdala and is thought to exert much of its "prosocial" effects by way of dampening down amygdylar activity (Sobota et al., 2015).

Attachment-related alterations of the oxytocinergic system (oxytocin depletion) could, therefore, lead to a greater likelihood of amygdylar overactivation
during social interactions and, consequently, greater social inhibition and
anxiety. Suggestive evidence along these lines comes from a study of rats, in
which PCP-induced negative-symptom-like social deficits were reversed by
injection of oxytocin into the central nucleus of the amygdala (Lee, Brady,
Shapiro, Dorsa, & Koenig, 2005). Implicitly, therefore, attachment-related
alterations of oxytocinergic regulation over amygdalar activity could contribute to an increased vulnerability to negative symptoms.

Social cognition

Impaired social cognition – i.e., the capacity to perceive, interpret and
respond to the behaviour of other people – is recognised as a distinct component of the phenomenology of schizophrenia and related psychotic-spectrum
disorders (Mehta et al., 2013). Here, we focus on one aspect of social cognitive dysfunction associated with psychosis that may be closely tied to the
quality of attachment relationships; namely, mentalisation – i.e., the ability to
think about states of mind in the self and others. Mounting evidence suggests
that mentalisation deficits (most commonly measured via ToM tasks) confer
vulnerability to psychosis and may be among the earliest indicators of the
risk for developing a psychotic disorder (for review see (B. K. Brent, Seidman,
Thermenos, Holt, & Keshavan, 2014).

Numerous functional neuroimaging studies in healthy subjects have shown
that the retrieval of information about the self and/or other people engages
a neural system that includes cortical midline structures ([CMS]; i.e., medial
PFC (MPFC) and posterior cingulate cortex [PCC]), as well as parts of the lat-
eral temporal cortex ([LTC]; e.g., superior temporal gyrus [STG]) (for review
see: (B. K. Brent, Seidman, Coombs et al., 2014). These same brain areas
show increased activity when people are not engaged in any goal-directed
tasks – i.e., during the so-called resting state. In people with a schizophrenia
diagnosis, fMRI studies have shown aberrant engagement of CMS and/or
LTC structures during mentalising tasks, as well as abnormal functional connectivity of CMS during the resting state (Bosia, Riccaboni, & Poletti, 2012).
These findings suggest that mentalisation deficits associated with psychosis
may be mediated by an overall change in the coordinated function of this network of CMS and LTC brain areas.

A significant body of evidence links the development of self and other
understanding with the quality of attachment relationships (Dykas &
Cassidy, 2011). Evidence exists for the link between attachment security and
mentalising in infants (Laranjo, Bernier, Meins, & Carlson, 2014) and pre-
adolescent children (Harris, de Rosnay, & Pons, 2005). Further, many studies
support the suggestion that secure children are better than insecure children
at mentalisation tasks (see, e.g., de Rosnay & Harris, 2002). Additionally,

maltreated children have shown delays in the successful acquisition of basic ToM abilities (Cicchetti, Rogosch, Maughan, Toth, & Bruce, 2003; Pears & Fisher, 2005a), and studies suggest that the capacity to discern complex and emotionally charged representations of the parent and of the self may even deteriorate with development (Toth, Cicchetti, Macfie, Maughan, & VanMeenen, 2000).

A growing body of evidence indicates that childhood maltreatment can have a negative impact on several aspects of developing social-cognitive capacities, including: less ability to use object or actions to stand for other objects or actions as play (Valentino, Cicchetti, Toth, & Rogosch, 2011), failing to show empathy when witnessing distress in other children (Klimes-Dougan & Kistner, 1990), and fewer references to internal states (Shipman & Zeman, 1999). Findings concerning significant developmental delay in the emotional understanding of maltreated young children are quite consistent (Pears & Fisher, 2005b), if somewhat reduced when controlling for IQ and socioeconomic status (Smith & Walden, 1999). Further, a comprehensive, systematic review (Macintosh, 2013) lends support to the assumption that mentalising mediates the relationship between attachment and/or adversity and adult functioning. However, more research is clearly needed in this area, as we do not fully understand the nature of mentalising deficits associated with childhood maltreatment. Regardless of the specific mechanism, if the maltreatment is perpetrated by a family member, it can contribute to an acquired partial "mind-blindness" (i.e., the inability to understand mental states in the self and/or others) by compromising open, reflective communication between parent and child. Maltreatment may also undermine the benefit derived from learning about the links between internal states and actions in attachment relationships (e.g., the child is told that he/she "deserves", "wants", or even "enjoys" the abuse). In such a situation the child finds that reflective discourse does not correspond to his/her feelings, a consistent misunderstanding that could reduce the child's ability to understand and mentalise verbal explanations of other people's actions.

Somewhat paradoxically, activation of the attachment system (e.g., during exposure to physical or psychological threat) is thought to have an inhibitory, deactivating effect on the mentalising network, as heightened emotional arousal associated with the engagement of the attachment system could disrupt the function of the higher cortical brain areas (MPFC, PCC, STG) within the mentalising network (Fonagy & Luyten, 2009). The functioning of the oxytocin system, however, provides an obvious possible mechanism for the replicated association between attachment security and the development of mentalisation competencies (Heinrichs, von Dawans, & Domes, 2009). Oxytocin facilitates empathic facial recognition and in-group trust (Bakermans-Kranenburg & van Ijzendoorn, 2013); it also increases perceived salience of social cues (Shamay-Tsoory et al., 2009) and improves empathic accuracy in less socially skilled individuals (Bartz et al., 2010).

Further, by enhancing activity in the insula and inferior frontal gyrus, oxy-tocin improves understanding of others' emotions, and it reduces anxiety by decreasing amygdalar activity, facilitating contingent responses of help and compassion (Bakermans-Kranenburg & van, 2013). A secure attachment, therefore, may function to optimise the balance between engagement of the attachment and mentalising neural systems, leading to the eventual ability to keep mentalising online during relational stress and to integrate attachment needs with appropriate social judgement and socio-emotional understanding.

Alternatively, in the setting of attachment insecurity, underlying dis-ruption of regulatory controls over stress and/or emotional arousal may lead to imbalance, or dyscoordination of the attachment and mentalising systems (Fonagy & Luyten, 2009). Attachment history may moderate the effects of oxytocin as well as the setting of the "switch" that turns the mentalising system from planned, controlled and organised cogni-tion to automatic processing with narrowed, poorly sustained attention, and increased vigilance for attachment disruptions such as rejection and abandonment (Cullen et al., 2011). This is in line with our previous suggestion that secure attachment requires the simultaneous (and paradox-ical) activation of components that are normally reciprocally activated – mentalising and reward-salience associated regions of the brain (Fonagy & Bateman, 2006). These observations are also in line with the assumption that secure attachment consists of a combination of low anxiety and low avoidance. Avoidant attachment may reflect a maladaptive attempt to regu-late attachment-related anxiety through prolonged deactivation of the attachment system in conjunction with hyperactivation of the mentalising network. Anxious resistant attachment, in which anxiety may be regulated through repeated efforts to maintain physical proximity to an attachment figure, could involve repeated hyperactivation of the attachment system together with hypoactivation of the mentalising network.

These proposed interactions between the functioning of the neural systems mediating attachment and mentalisation remain to be empirically tested in children. However, neuroimaging studies have shown that post-traumatic stress disorder (PTSD) in adults is associated with altered resting-state func-tional connectivity of key nodes within the mentalising network (e.g., MPFC and PCC) (Bluhm et al., 2009; Sripada et al., 2012). These findings in PTSD, though indirect and correlational, support the possibility that stress exposure could link dysfunction of the mentalising network with dysregulation of anxiety and emotional distress (as is thought also to occur in an insecure attachment). In the context of an underlying genetic vulnerability to psych-osis, attachment-related stress could be predictive of dysfunction of the mentalising system and heightened vulnerability to impairments of self and other understanding during early development.

Therapeutic implications

Several therapeutic implications follow from the foregoing considerations. First, as discussed above, attachment-related alterations in the oxytocinergic system could contribute to dysregulation of striatal DA and amygdalar activity, both of which are implicated in the symptoms and social cognitive impairments associated with psychotic disorders. Pharmacotherapy with oxytocin, therefore, may offer a promising approach to reducing the symptoms and social disability in people with psychosis. Indeed, over the last decade a growing number of clinical trials of intranasal oxytocin administration in schizophrenia have shown reductions in positive and negative symptoms, and improvements in socio-emotional processing (K. Macdonald & Feifel, 2012).

Second, there is mounting case-report evidence that psychotherapeutic treatments that target mentalising deficits within attachment-related contexts could contribute to improvements in social functioning in people diagnosed with schizophrenia (e.g., mentalisation-based treatment for psychosis (B. Brent, 2009), metacognitive psychotherapy (Lysaker et al., 2010) and compassion focused psychotherapy (Braehler & Schwannauer, 2012). The neural mechanisms that might be facilitated by these psychotherapeutic approaches are not known. However, one recent study has shown that people with a diagnosis of schizophrenia who completed a six-month-long cognitive training programme that included mentalising exercises exhibited significant recovery of social function in conjunction with improvement in MPFC activation during a reality monitoring task (Subramaniam et al., 2012). One possibility is that psychotherapies that focus on engaging the mentalising system during relational stress could enhance PFC function and (eventually) the capacity to manage anxiety/negative social stimuli, given the role of the PFC in modulating subcortical (e.g., amygdalar) activity. These psychotherapeutic interventions, therefore, may provide a valuable additional approach to the improvement of interpersonal relatedness among people with a diagnosis of schizophrenia.

Third, although we focused on the possible negative effects of insecure attachment, it is equally possible that attachment security could have a protective effect with respect to psychosis risk. By facilitating the regulation of striatal DA, HPA axis and amygdalar activity, and fostering mentalisation, secure attachment could attenuate the likelihood that an underlying vulnerability for psychosis will become expressed. A large body of evidence suggests that secure attachment is an important resilience factor in childhood mental health, protecting the developing brain against the potentially adverse effects of psychological stress and negative social experience (Schore, 2001). Young people at familial high-risk (FHR) for schizophrenia (i.e., offspring of a parent with a schizophrenia diagnosis) may be particularly likely to benefit from early interventions that foster sensitive caregiving. Research suggests, for example, that mothers with a diagnosis of schizophrenia frequently struggle with the demands of parenting and that FHR youth are at increased risk not only for receiving a schizophrenia diagnosis, but also for a wide range of poor developmental outcomes (Gearing, Alonzo, & Marinelli, 2012). However, there is also evidence that a healthy parent-child relationship, social support during adolescence, or the presence of a positive relationship with a highly-involved non-patient parent can help prevent the risk of a poor developmental course (Gearing et al., 2012). Home-based interventions to foster attachment security in mothers-infant dyads (e.g., Minding the Baby®) have shown promising initial results in young, first-time mothers in terms of the development of more sensitive parenting and fewer externalising behaviours in children during the first three years of life (Ordway et al., 2014; Sadler et al., 2013). Whether similar interventions could be successfully adapted to aid mothers (or other primary caregivers) with a diagnosis of schizophrenia with the challenges of parenting, however, remains to be tested.

Conclusion

In this chapter, we reviewed the evidence supporting interactions between alterations of the neural system mediating attachment and the neurobiology of psychosis-spectrum disorders. Preclinical and human studies linking attachment insecurity with dysfunction of the mesocorticolimbic DA, oxytocinergic and HPA axis systems suggest that attachment-related disturbances in childhood could potentiate the vulnerability to positive symptoms, negative symptoms and social cognitive impairments in the context of a psychosis diathesis. Several valuable clinical interventions could follow from the potential interconnections between disturbances of the neural systems mediating attachment and psychosis, such as: 1) pharmacotherapy with oxytocin to reduce symptoms and social deficits among people diagnosed with a psychotic disorder; 2) psychotherapies that target deficits of mentalisation within attachment contexts to bolster resilience to social stress and foster the recovery of interpersonal relatedness and 3) family-based interventions to address disturbances in parent-child interactions in genetic high-risk youth that could facilitate greater caregiver sensitivity and attenuate the risk of poor developmental outcomes.

Significant evidence implicates genetic factors in the etiology of developing a schizophrenia diagnosis (approximately 40–60% of the liability to a schizophrenia diagnosis is estimated to be owing to genes (A. W. MacDonald & Schulz, 2009)). Further, structural and functional alterations of the same brain areas involved in attachment-related behaviour are commonly found in people with psychosis (B. K. Brent, Thermenos, Keshavan, & Seidman, 2013). Thus, the possibility cannot be excluded that the relationship between attachment disturbances and schizophrenia could be epiphenomenal – i.e., a byproduct of genetically-mediated dysmaturational processes that are

THE NEUROBIOLOGY OF ATTACHMENT

thought to be part of the pathoetiology of schizophrenia. Nevertheless, there is increasing recognition that environmental risk factors (particularly those related to the early social environment, such as childhood adversity (Varese et al., 2012), while not sufficient to cause the symptoms of schizophrenia, may interact with susceptibility genes to heighten psychosis risk (van Os et al., 2010). Future longitudinal research in high-risk youth, however, is needed to determine the extent to which the attachment environment is associated with the structural/functional development of brain areas mediating the key symptoms and social dysfunction associated with psychotic disorders and to examine interactive effects of attachment on the trajectory of psychosis risk.

References

Aron, A., Fisher, H., Mashek, D. J., Strong, G., Li, H., & Brown, L. L. (2005). Reward, motivation, and emotion systems associated with early-stage intense romantic love. *Journal of Neurophysiology, 94*(1), 327–337. doi: 10.1152/jn.00838.2004

Bakermans-Kranenburg, M. J., & van, Ijzendoorn, M. H. (2013). Sniffing around oxytocin: review and meta-analyses of trials in healthy and clinical groups with implications for pharmacotherapy. *Transl Psychiatry, 3*, e258. doi: 10.1038/tp.2013.34

Bartels, A., & Zeki, S. (2004). The neural correlates of maternal and romantic love. *Neuroimage, 21*(3), 1155–1166. doi: 10.1016/j.neuroimage.2003.11.003

Bartz, J. A., Zaki, J., Bolger, N., Hollander, E., Ludwig, N. N., Kolevzon, A., & Ochsner, K. N. (2010). Oxytocin selectively improves empathic accuracy. *Psychological Science, 21*(10), 1426–1428. doi: 10.1177/0956797610383439

Berry, K., Barrowclough, C., & Wearden, A. (2007). A review of the role of adult attachment style in psychosis: unexplored issues and questions for further research. *Clinical Psychology Review, 27*(4), 458–475. doi: 10.1016/j.cpr.2006.09.006

Berry, K., Barrowclough, C., & Wearden, A. (2008). Attachment theory: a framework for understanding symptoms and interpersonal relationships in psychosis. *Behavourial Research Therapy, 46*(12), 1275–1282. doi: 10.1016/j.brat.2008.08.009

Bluhm, R. L., Williamson, P. C., Osuch, E. A., Frewen, P. A., Stevens, T. K., Boksman, K., ... Lanius, R. A. (2009). Alterations in default network connectivity in post-traumatic stress disorder related to early-life trauma. *J Psychiatry Neuroscience, 34*(3), 187–194.

Bosia, M., Riccaboni, R., & Poletti, S. (2012). Neurofunctional correlates of theory of mind deficits in schizophrenia. *Current Top Medical Chemistry, 12*(21), 2284–2302.

Braehler, C., & Schwannauer, M. (2012). Recovering an emerging self: exploring reflective function in recovery from adolescent-onset psychosis. *Psychology Psychotherapy, 85*(1), 48–67. doi: 10.1111/j.2044-8341.2011.02018.x

Brent, B. (2009). Mentalization-based psychodynamic psychotherapy for psychosis. *Journal of Clinical Psychology, 65*(8), 803–814. doi: 10.1002/jclp.20615

Brent, B. K., & Fonagy, P. (2014). *A Mentalization-Based Treatment Approach to Disturbances of Social Understanding in Schizophrenia* (P. H. Lysaker & G. Dimaggio Eds.). Oxford: Elsevier Press.

Brent, B. K., Holt, D. J., Keshavan, M. S., Seidman, L. J., & Fonagy, P. (2014). Mentalization-based Treatment for Psychosis: Linking an Attachment-based Model to the Psychotherapy for Impaired Mental State Understanding in People with Psychotic Disorders. *Israel Journal of Psychiatry Related Sciences*, *51*(1), 17–23.

Brent, B. K., Seidman, L. J., Coombs, G., 3rd, Keshavan, M. S., Moran, J. M., & Holt, D. J. (2014). Neural responses during social reflection in relatives of schizophrenia patients: relationship to subclinical delusions. *Schizophrenia Research*, *157*(1–3), 292–298. doi: 10.1016/j.schres.2014.05.033

Brent, B. K., Seidman, L. J., Thermenos, H. W., Holt, D. J., & Keshavan, M. S. (2014). Self-disturbances as a possible premorbid indicator of schizophrenia risk: a neurodevelopmental perspective. *Schizophrenia Research*, *152*(1), 73–80.

Brent, B. K., Thermenos, H. W., Keshavan, M. S., & Seidman, L. J. (2013). Gray matter alterations in schizophrenia high-risk youth and early-onset schizophrenia: a review of structural MRI findings. *Child Adolescent Psychiatry Clinics of North America*, *22*(4), 689–714. doi: 10.1016/j.chc.2013.06.003

Burkett, J. P., & Young, L. J. (2012). The behavioral, anatomical and pharmacological parallels between social attachment, love and addiction. *Psychopharmacology (Berl)*, *224*(1), 1–26. doi: 10.1007/s00213-012-2794-x

Cannon, M., Caspi, A., Moffitt, T. E., Harrington, H., Taylor, A., Murray, R. M., & Poulton, R. (2002). Evidence for early-childhood, pan-developmental impairment specific to schizophreniform disorder: results from a longitudinal birth cohort. *Archives of General Psychiatry*, *59*(5), 449–456.

Cicchetti, D., Rogosch, F. A., Maughan, A., Toth, S. L., & Bruce, J. (2003). False belief understanding in maltreated children. *Developmental Psychopathology*, *15*(4), 1067–1091.

Cullen, K. R., Vizueta, N., Thomas, K. M., Han, G. J., Lim, K. O., Camchong, J., … Schulz, S. C. (2011). Amygdala functional connectivity in young women with borderline personality disorder. *Brain Connectivity*, *1*(1), 61–71. doi: 10.1089/brain.2010.0001

de Rosnay, M., & Harris, P. L. (2002). Individual differences in children's understanding of emotion: The roles of attachment and language. *Attachment and Human Development*, *4*(1), 39–54. doi: 10.1080/14616730210123139

Dykas, M. J., & Cassidy, J. (2011). Attachment and the processing of social information across the life span: theory and evidence. *Psychology Bulletin*, *137*(1), 19–46. doi: 10.1037/a0021367

Fleming, A. S., Steiner, M., & Corter, C. (1997). Cortisol, hedonics, and maternal responsiveness in human mothers. *Hormone Behaviour*, *32*(2), 85–98. doi: 10.1006/hbeh.1997.1407

Fonagy, P., & Bateman, A. W. (2006). Mechanisms of change in mentalization-based treatment of BPD. *Journal of Clinical Psychology*, *62*(4), 411–430. doi: 10.1002/jclp.20241

Fonagy, P., & Luyten, P. (2009). A developmental, mentalization-based approach to the understanding and treatment of borderline personality disorder. *Development Psychopathology*, *21*(4), 1355–1381. doi: 10.1017/s0954579409990198

Fusar-Poli, P., Howes, O. D., Allen, P., Broome, M., Valli, I., Asselin, M. C., … McGuire, P. (2011). Abnormal prefrontal activation directly related to pre-synaptic striatal dopamine dysfunction in people at clinical high risk for psychosis. *Molecular Psychiatry, 16*(1), 67–75. doi: 10.1038/mp.2009.108

Gearing, R. E., Alonzo, D., & Marinelli, C. (2012). Maternal schizophrenia: psychosocial treatment for mothers and their children. *Clinical Schizophrenic Related Psychoses, 6*(1), 27–33. doi: 10.3371/csrp.6.1.4

Gordon, I., Martin, C., Feldman, R., & Leckman, J. F. (2011). Oxytocin and social motivation. *Developmental Cognitive Neuroscience, 1*(4), 471–493. doi: 10.1016/j.dcn.2011.07.007

Gordon, I., Zagoory-Sharon, O., Leckman, J. F., & Feldman, R. (2010). Oxytocin, cortisol, and triadic family interactions. *Physiological Behaviour, 101*(5), 679–684. doi: 10.1016/j.physbeh.2010.08.008

Gumley, A. I., Taylor, H. E., Schwannauer, M., & MacBeth, A. (2014). A systematic review of attachment and psychosis: measurement, construct validity and outcomes. *Acta Psychiatrica Scandinavica, 129*(4), 257–274. doi: 10.1111/acps.12172

Harris, P.L., de Rosnay, M., & Pons, F. (2005). Language and children's understanding of mental states. *Current Directory of Psychological Science, 14*(2), 69–73.

Heinrichs, M., von Dawans, B., & Domes, G. (2009). Oxytocin, vasopressin, and human social behavior. *Frontiers in Neuroendocrinology, 30*(4), 548–557. doi: 10.1016/j.yfrne.2009.05.005

Holt, D. J., Kunkel, L., Weiss, A. P., Goff, D. C., Wright, C. I., Shin, L. M., … Heckers, S. (2006). Increased medial temporal lobe activation during the passive viewing of emotional and neutral facial expressions in schizophrenia. *Schizophrenia Research, 82*(2–3), 153–162. doi: 10.1016/j.schres.2005.09.021

Howes, O. D., & Kapur, S. (2009). The dopamine hypothesis of schizophrenia: version III–the final common pathway. *Schizophrenia Bulletin, 35*(3), 549–562. doi: 10.1093/schbul/sbp006

Insel, T. R. (2003). Is social attachment an addictive disorder? *Physiological Behaviour, 79*(3), 351–357.

Johnson, Z. V., & Young, L. J. (2015). Neurobiological mechanisms of social attachment and pair bonding. *Current Opinion in Behavioural Science, 3*, 38–44. doi: 10.1016/j.cobeha.2015.01.009

Jones, P., Rodgers, B., Murray, R., & Marmot, M. (1994). Child development risk factors for adult schizophrenia in the British 1946 birth cohort. *Lancet, 344*(8934), 1398–1402.

Katayama, T., Jodo, E., Suzuki, Y., Hoshino, K. Y., Takeuchi, S., & Kayama, Y. (2009). Phencyclidine affects firing activity of basolateral amygdala neurons related to social behavior in rats. *Neuroscience, 159*(1), 335–343. doi: 10.1016/j.neuroscience.2009.01.002

Kellendonk, C., Simpson, E. H., Polan, H. J., Malleret, G., Vronskaya, S., Winiger, V., … Kandel, E. R. (2006). Transient and selective overexpression of dopamine D2 receptors in the striatum causes persistent abnormalities in prefrontal cortex functioning. *Neuron, 49*(4), 603–615. doi: 10.1016/j.neuron.2006.01.023

Keshavan, M. S. (1999). Development, disease and degeneration in schizophrenia: a unitary pathophysiological model. *Journal of Psychiatric Research, 33*(6), 513–521.

Klimes-Dougan, B., & Kistner, J. (1990). Physically abused preschoolers' responses to peers' distress. *Developmental Psychology, 25*, 516–524.

Laranjo, J., Bernier, A., Meins, E., & Carlson, S. M. (2014). The roles of maternal mind-mindedness and infant security of attachment in predicting preschoolers' understanding of visual perspective taking and false belief. *Journal of Experimental Child Psychology, 125*, 48–62. doi: 10.1016/j.jecp.2014.02.005

Lee, P. R., Brady, D. L., Shapiro, R. A., Dorsa, D. M., & Koenig, J. I. (2005). Social interaction deficits caused by chronic phencyclidine administration are reversed by oxytocin. *Neuropsychopharmacology, 30*(10), 1883–1894. doi: 10.1038/sj.npp.1300722

Lim, M. M., Liu, Y., Ryabinin, A. E., Bai, Y., Wang, Z., & Young, L. J. (2007). CRF receptors in the nucleus accumbens modulate partner preference in prairie voles. *Hormone Behaviour, 51*(4), 508–515. doi: 10.1016/j.yhbeh.2007.01.006

Lysaker, P. H., Buck, K. D., Carcione, A., Procacci, M., Salvatore, G., Nicolo, G., & Dimaggio, G. (2010). Addressing metacognitive capacity for self-reflection in the psychotherapy for schizophrenia: a conceptual model of the key tasks and processes. *Psychology and Psychotherapy: Theory, Research, and Practice, 84*, 58–69.

MacDonald, A. W., & Schulz, S. C. (2009). What we know: findings that every theory of schizophrenia should explain. *Schizophrenia Bulletin, 35*(3), 493–508. doi: 10.1093/schbul/sbp017

Macdonald, K., & Feifel, D. (2012). Oxytocin in schizophrenia: a review of evidence for its therapeutic effects. *Acta Neuropsychiatrica, 24*(3), 130–146. doi: 10.1111/j.1601-5215.2011.00634.x

Macintosh, H. (2013). Mentalizing and its role as a mediator in the relationship between childhood experiences and adult functioning: exploring the empirical evidence. *Psihologija, 46*(2), 193–212.

Marazziti, D., & Canale, D. (2004). Hormonal changes when falling in love. *Psychoneuroendocrinology, 29*(7), 931–936. doi: 10.1016/j.psyneuen.2003.08.006

Mehta, U. M., Thirthalli, J., Subbakrishna, D. K., Gangadhar, B. N., Eack, S. M., & Keshavan, M. S. (2013). Social and neuro-cognition as distinct cognitive factors in schizophrenia: a systematic review. *Schizophrenia Research, 148*(1–3), 3–11. doi: 10.1016/j.schres.2013.05.009

Millan, M. J., Fone, K., Steckler, T., & Horan, W. P. (2014). Negative symptoms of schizophrenia: clinical characteristics, pathophysiological substrates, experimental models and prospects for improved treatment. *European Neuropsychopharmacology, 24*(5), 645–692. doi: 10.1016/j.euroneuro.2014.03.008

Nemeroff, C. B. (2004). Neurobiological consequences of childhood trauma. *Journal of Clinical Psychiatry, 65 Suppl 1*, 18–28.

Ordway, M. R., Sadler, L. S., Dixon, J., Close, N., Mayes, L., & Slade, A. (2014). Lasting effects of an interdisciplinary home visiting program on child behavior: preliminary follow-up results of a randomized trial. *Journal of Pediatric Nursing, 29*(1), 3–13. doi: 10.1016/j.pedn.2013.04.006

Pears, K. C., & Fisher, P. A. (2005a). Emotion understanding and theory of mind among maltreated children in foster care. *Development and Psychopathology, 17*(1), 47–65. doi: 10.1017/S0954579405050030

Pears, K. C., & Fisher, P. A. (2005b). Emotion understanding and theory of mind among maltreated children in foster care: evidence of deficits. *Developmental Psychopathology, 17*(1), 47–65.

Rich, M. E., & Caldwell, H. K. (2015). A Role for Oxytocin in the Etiology and Treatment of Schizophrenia. *Front Endocrinol (Lausanne)*, 6, 90. doi: 10.3389/ fendo.2015.00090

Rilling, J. K., DeMarco, A. C., Hackett, P. D., Thompson, R., Ditzen, B., Patel, R., & Pagnoni, G. (2012). Effects of intranasal oxytocin and vasopressin on cooperative behavior and associated brain activity in men. *Psychoneuroendocrinology*, *37*(4), 447–461. doi: 10.1016/j.psyneuen.2011.07.013

Sadler, L. S., Slade, A., Close, N., Webb, D. L., Simpson, T., Fennie, K., & Mayes, L. C. (2013). Minding the baby: Enhancing reflectiveness to improve early health and relationship outcomes in an interdisciplinary home visiting program. *Infant Mental Health Journal*, *34*(5), 391–405. doi: 10.1002/imhj.21406

Satterthwaite, T. D., Wolf, D. H., Loughead, J., Ruparel, K., Valdez, J. N., Siegel, S. J., … Gur, R. C. (2010). Association of enhanced limbic response to threat with decreased cortical facial recognition memory response in schizophrenia. *American Journal of Psychiatry*, *167*(4), 418–426. doi: 10.1176/appi. ajp.2009.09060808

Schore, A. N. (2001). Effects of a secure attachment relationship on right brain development, affect regulation, and infant mental health. *Infant Mental Health Journal*, *22*(1–2), 7–66.

Shamay-Tsoory, S. G., Fischer, M., Dvash, J., Harari, H., Perach-Bloom, N., & Levkovitz, Y. (2009). Intranasal administration of oxytocin increases envy and schadenfreude (gloating). *Biological Psychiatry*, *66*(9), 864–870. doi: 10.1016/ j.biopsych.2009.06.009

Shipman, K. L., & Zeman, J. (1999). Emotional understanding: a comparison of physically maltreating and nonmaltreating mother-child dyads. *Journal of Clinical Child Psychology*, *28*(3), 407–417. doi: 10.1207/S15374424jccp280313

Smith, M., & Walden, T. (1999). Understanding feelings and coping with emotional situations: a comparision of maltreated and nonmaltreated preschoolers. *Social Development*, *8*(1), 93–116.

Sobota, R., Mihara, T., Forrest, A., Featherstone, R. E., & Siegel, S. J. (2015). Oxytocin reduces amygdala activity, increases social interactions, and reduces anxiety-like behavior irrespective of NMDAR antagonism. *Behavioural Neuroscience*, *129*(4), 389–398. doi: 10.1037/bne0000074

Sobrian, S. K., & Holson, R. R. (2011). Social behavior of offspring following prenatal cocaine exposure in rodents: a comparison with prenatal alcohol. *Front Psychiatry*, *2*, 66. doi: 10.3389/fpsyt.2011.00066

Sripada, R. K., King, A. P., Welsh, R. C., Garfinkel, S. N., Wang, X., Sripada, C. S., & Liberzon, I. (2012). Neural dysregulation in posttraumatic stress disorder: evidence for disrupted equilibrium between salience and default mode brain networks. *Psychosomatic Medcine*, *74*(9), 904–911. doi: 10.1097/PSY.0b013e318273bf33

Stoesz, B. M., Hare, J. F., & Snow, W. M. (2013). Neurophysiological mechanisms underlying affiliative social behavior: insights from comparative research. *Neuroscience and Biobehavioural Review*, *37*(2), 123–132. doi: 10.1016/j.neubiorev. 2012.11.007

Strathearn, L. (2011). Maternal neglect: oxytocin, dopamine and the neurobiology of attachment. *Journal of Neuroendocrinology*, *23*(11), 1054–1065. doi: 10.1111/ j.1365-2826.2011.02228.x

Subramaniam, K., Luks, T. L., Fisher, M., Simpson, G. V., Nagarajan, S., & Vinogradov, S. (2012). Computerized cognitive training restores neural activity within the reality monitoring network in schizophrenia. *Neuron, 73*, 842–853.

Sullivan, R. M. (2012). The neurobiology of attachment to nurturing and abusive caregivers. *Hastings Law Journal, 63*(6), 1553–1570.

Toth, S. L., Cicchetti, D., Macfie, J., Maughan, A., & VanMeenen, K. (2000). Narrative representations of caregivers and self in maltreated pre-schoolers. *Attachment and Human Development, 2*(3), 271–305. doi: 10.1080/14616730010000849

Toth, S. L., Gravener-Davis, J. A., Guild, D. J., & Cicchetti, D. (2013). Relational interventions for child maltreatment: past, present, and future perspectives. *Developmental Psychopathology, 25*(4 Pt 2), 1601–1617. doi: 10.1017/s0954579413000795

Valentino, K., Cicchetti, D., Toth, S. L., & Rogosch, F. A. (2011). Mother-child play and maltreatment: a longitudinal analysis of emerging social behavior from infancy to toddlerhood. *Developmental Psychology, 47*(5), 1280–1294. doi: 10.1037/a0024459

van Os, J., Kenis, G., & Rutten, B. P. (2010). The environment and schizophrenia. *Nature, 468*(7321), 203–212. doi: 10.1038/nature09563

Varese, F., Smeets, F., Drukker, M., Lieverse, R., Lataster, T., Viechtbauer, W., ... Bentall, R. P. (2012). Childhood adversities increase the risk of psychosis: a meta-analysis of patient-control, prospective- and cross-sectional cohort studies. *Schizophrenic Bulletin, 38*(4), 661–671. doi: 10. 1093/schbul/sbs050

Wahlberg, K. E., Wynne, L. C., Oja, H., Keskitalo, P., Pykalainen, L., Lahti, I., ... Tienari, P. (1997). Gene-environment interaction in vulnerability to schizophrenia: findings from the Finnish Adoptive Family Study of Schizophrenia. *American Journal of Psychiatry, 154*(3), 355–362.

Walker, E. F., & Diforio, D. (1997). Schizophrenia: a neural diathesis-stress model. *Psychological Review, 104*(4), 667–685.

Walum, H., Westberg, L., Henningsson, S., Neiderhiser, J. M., Reiss, D., Igl, W., ... Lichtenstein, P. (2008). Genetic variation in the vasopressin receptor 1a gene (AVPR1A) associates with pair-bonding behavior in humans. *Proc Natl Acad Sci U S A, 105*(37), 14153–14156. doi: 10.1073/pnas.0803081105

Young, K. A., Liu, Y., & Wang, Z. (2008). The neurobiology of social attachment: A comparative approach to behavioral, neuroanatomical, and neurochemical studies. *Comp Biochem Physiol C Toxicol Pharmacol, 148*(4), 401–410. doi: 10.1016/j.cbpc.2008.02.004

Part II

THERAPEUTIC APPROACHES

8

BRINGING TOGETHER PSYCHODYNAMIC AND ATTACHMENT PERSPECTIVES ON PSYCHOSIS

Alison Summers and Gwen Adshead

Introduction

Attachment theory developed from the object relations school of psychoanalysis, which assumes that humans have an instinctual drive to relate to others (Holmes, 1993). Bowlby, who initially developed attachment theory, was an active and influential member of the Institute of Psychoanalysis, but was seen by some psychoanalysts as unacceptably unorthodox for his emphasis on the importance of environmental experience in the development of the mind.

As attachment theory was increasingly used as a basis for hypothesis testing in ethology, developmental psychology and psychopathology, so it diverged from psychoanalytic thinking and practice. However, in the 1990s, a dialogue began between attachment researchers and psychoanalysts, which recognised the important contribution that attachment-based research could make to the confirmation of many psychoanalytic concepts and hypotheses and explored the commonalities and differences between the two theoretical models (Fonagy, 2001). Developments in neuroscience and neuroimaging also fostered dialogue between these two groups. In relation to psychosis, developments within the attachment field have been considerable, yet dialogue between attachment and psychodynamic perspectives has been somewhat limited.

One challenge for those interested in such dialogue is that there is no single psychodynamic model of psychosis and no single approach to psychodynamic therapy. The ideas discussed in this chapter are broadly in line with a branch of psychodynamic theory and practice known as British Independent Object Relations (Lemma, 2016). We have chosen this as an approach because it is one that is widely used among contemporary UK psychotherapists and one which, like attachment theory, is rooted in the idea that human beings have an instinctive motivation to relate to each other. There are other major schools of psychotherapy, for example Freudian and Lacanian approaches (Leader 2012), which have less in common with attachment theory, and others, particularly self psychology (Steinmann & Garfield, 2015), where the overlap may be considerable.

We believe that another obstacle to the dialogue between attachment and psychodynamic perspectives may have been the persistence of discouraging myths. One such myth is that psychodynamic therapy is, as Freud believed, not applicable in psychosis. This view is not supported by later analysts or by research evidence (Summers & Rosenbaum, 2013). As we will describe below, there is increasing evidence that psychodynamic thinking is relevant and helpful to understanding how psychosis develops and persists and to the development of clinical frameworks for therapy.

Theory

A brief psychodynamic account of psychosis

Object relations theory (Lemma, 2016) holds that in our earliest relationships we develop 'internal object relationships' or templates of ourselves in relation to others. These shape our later experience of ourselves and our relationships and the emotional character of these. A key psychodynamic concept is that important aspects of mental life are not conscious, and that we develop a range of psychological mechanisms ('defences'), which help to keep disturbing emotions, such as fear, guilt and rage, from full consciousness. Our unconscious mental lives, especially our defences, are often revealed in repetitive patterns of dysfunctional relationships, fixed narratives of self-experience, language patterns, persistent dreams or physical or mental symptoms.

According to a psychodynamic view, psychotic states can arise as a response to unbearable aspects of internal or external reality. The content of psychotic experiences is seen as expressing aspects of the person's inner world. It may express intolerable aspects such as fear or rage, or reconstructions of reality, such as hallucinations or beliefs that protect against these (Martindale & Summers, 2013).

Psychodynamic theory offers models for understanding how life experiences may combine with biological factors and psychological processes to shape a person's internal world and their vulnerability to developing psychosis under particular circumstances. For example, childhood trauma, long recognised as a risk factor for psychosis (Freud, 1923; Freud, 1960), is considered to interact with other factors such as early failures in the containment of an infant's distress and rage. These, in turn, might occur through temperamental intensity of the infant's emotions or caregiver difficulties in accepting and metabolising these. Such failures of containment are conceived as leading to limitations in the infant's capacity to tolerate and symbolise painful feelings and to distinguish internal and external reality (Bion, 1959).

Psychotic thinking (especially paranoid thinking) is viewed as occurring both as a normal stage in development and as a response to distress in adulthood (Klein, 1935; Bion, 1959). With this perspective, everyone can be seen as somewhere on a spectrum of psychotic thinking, with psychotic thinking dominating to varying degrees and with varying persistence, and psychotic and non-psychotic thinking able to co-exist at the same time in the same person. Whether a particular experience provokes psychotic thinking depends on its conscious and unconscious meaning for that individual and thus whether it can be tolerated and thought about (Martindale & Summers, 2013). For example, an individual who has no difficulty speaking in an ordinary manner on most topics may struggle to talk coherently about recent events which reinforce underlying feelings of inadequacy and may return at this point to a grandiose account of possessing superhuman abilities.

Some past psychodynamic theories are not supported by evidence and have been discarded. These include Freud's theory of paranoia as a response to same-sex erotic orientation, and his assertion that people in psychotic states could not make attachments to therapists (Lysaker & Silverstein, 2009). Research from non-psychoanalytic domains, however, increasingly supports psychoanalytic accounts of the development and nature of psychosis. For example, it is now generally accepted that 'psychosis' is a dimensional condition in that there is a continuum of different degrees of severity (van Os et al., 2009), that psychotic symptoms such as paranoia and voice hearing are frequent in non-clinical populations (Freeman, Pugh & Garety, 2008), and that people with psychotic beliefs have specific problems in thinking, such as an external attribution style and difficulties with social understanding (Garety et al., 2001).

Comparing psychodynamic and attachment perspectives on psychosis

Psychodynamic and attachment perspectives share the view that adversity in early relationships contributes to vulnerability to psychosis. This view is increasingly evidenced by epidemiological studies of psychosis that do not use an attachment paradigm (Varese et al., 2012). An extensive programme of attachment research over the last 50 years has clearly established that failure to make secure attachment bonds in early childhood (before the second decade) leads to deficits in specific psychological capacities including capacities to: (a) monitor reality, discerning what is thought, and what is external experience, including bodily experience (Waller & Scheidt, 2006); (b) reflect on one's own thoughts and feelings and on the reality of other people's minds (called *mentalising* or metacognition) (MacBeth et al., 2011); (c) trust others sufficiently to consider what is learned from them as trustworthy and personally relevant (called *epistemic trust* (Fonagy, Luyten & Allison, 2014); (d) regulate affect and arousal (Waller & Scheidt, 2006); and (e) develop a coherent narrative of self-experience, including capacity for organising thought, and experiencing agency (Liotti & Gumley, 2008). Insecure and disorganised attachment patterns (and hence limitations in the above capacities) are over-represented amongst people experiencing psychosis (Bucci, Emsley & Berry, 2016; Gumley et al., 2014).

From both psychodynamic and attachment perspectives, psychosis is precipitated when negative affects are unmanageable and uncontainable. Attachment theory elaborates this idea in terms of impairments in the capacities outlined above, suggesting that there may be different pathways to psychosis for those with different attachment strategies (Harder, 2014).

Both psychodynamic and attachment theory offer models for linking developmental history with later experience and behaviour. There is a sense in which attachment theory is to psychoanalysis as quantum theory is to classical physics: attachment theory explains and provides evidence for some of the phenomena that have been observed by psychodynamic theorists for nearly a century. The attachment field can also be seen as offering more accessible language and theory, with useful attention to emotion regulation and to conscious experience of close relationships. Psychodynamic approaches offer additional attention to unconscious emotion and defences and to motivational states other than those that involve care seeking or care giving. They also draw on a wider range of information, attending to clues to unconscious dynamic mental processes that emerge in language, dreams, psychotic associations, and, as we discuss below, in practitioners' responses to their clients.

Practice

Formulation: using psychodynamic theory to understand individual experience

One way in which psychodynamic approaches may be helpful in practice is in developing an understanding ('formulation') of what may be contributing to an individual's difficulties and strengths. This may generate ideas about paths to recovery and a more coherent and sustaining self-narrative. Psychodynamic approaches to formulation pay particular attention to patterns in the person's relationships, including with practitioners, and to practitioners' own responses or countertransference (Summers & Martindale, 2013). In considering countertransference, a useful psychodynamic contribution is the concept of projective identification, the idea that a person's feelings and behaviour may unconsciously change to meet the expectations ('projections') of another and that in this change may be a communication which cannot be expressed in words (Lemma, 2016). This is something that may be particularly important in psychosis. Projective identification might manifest, for example, in a therapist noticing that she feels little empathy for her client when he describes something very upsetting to him and recognising that this is an unusual situation for her, particularly troubling as this client often talks angrily about other people's indifference to his suffering. The therapist's experience here could be understood as an expression of the client's internal world, that is, of his internal template of feeling neglected by an uncaring, uninterested internal figure. In this situation the therapist's loss of empathy can be seen as a 'projection' of this figure into her, which she has then identified with.

Using psychodynamic theory, several possible psychological routes to recovery from psychosis can be identified. Firstly, the need for a psychotic state as a defence against mental pain may grow less. This might happen either through external changes, e.g. less stressful relationships, or through internal changes, e.g. strengthening non-psychotic defences through new relationships or therapy. With new relational experiences, over time, a person may grow less prone to psychotic states under stress, developing a more robust sense of self, more adaptive internal working models, stronger alternative defences, and more capacity to manage anxiety. Secondly, better understanding of what triggers psychotic experiences may allow triggers to be more often avoided or better managed. Thirdly, an individual may develop more adaptive responses to their psychosis and treatment. This might happen through better conscious understanding of what is helpful, or through changes in the person's internal world. For example, people may change the way they respond to hallucinatory figures and other psychotic experiences, to stigma and social effects of psychosis, to family and others offering support, to opportunities for participation in ordinary life and to professional help of all kinds, including medication. This may result in their being able to develop more supportive relationships and make more use of social, leisure and occupational opportunities as well as of professional help.

Psychodynamic therapy for psychosis

Just as there is no single psychodynamic model of psychosis, there is no single psychodynamic therapy for psychosis. Nevertheless, therapies using a broadly object relations approach will share some common features listed below:

(a) Adherence to boundaries of time, setting and task as an integral part of therapy;
(b) Sessions without fixed agenda, which aim to create space for reflection;
(c) A focus in the therapist's mind on the 'here and now' of the moment, considering the way in which this may be distorted by the client's internal world (transference), and considering the therapist's own countertransference as a means to understanding this;
(d) Use of the moment-to-moment experience to continually refine a formulation in terms of hypotheses about the client's internal world and unconscious processes;
(e) Therapist interventions guided by the formulation and their perception of the client's immediate state of mind;
(f) Measures aimed at enhancing the therapist's capacity to be aware of, tolerate and mentalise their own mental states. These would in turn be

135

expected to enhance their receptiveness to clients' emotional states in therapy, and their ability to avoid intervening on the basis of their own rather than the client's needs. This is particularly important with challenging feelings such as hostility and erotic attraction.

Psychodynamic therapies include a balance of exploratory and supportive elements. Exploration aims to help clients gain insight into their difficulties, while supportive elements are concerned with developing or restoring aspects of functioning, such as adaptive defences, sense of self, or capacity to mentalise. A recent Delphi study (Kongara et al., 2017) found that therapists experienced in working with psychosis hold many views in common and see a need for support and exploration to be balanced according to an individual's need at any particular time. There were differences, however, in views about just how far therapy needs to incorporate supportive techniques.

A contemporary example of psychodynamic therapy for psychosis is Supportive Psychodynamic Psychotherapy (SPP; Rosenbaum, 2015; Rosenbaum et al., 2013; Rosenbaum & Thorgaard, 1998), which draws on decades of psychoanalytic work. This model explicitly encourages development of capacities for integration of emotion and thinking. It uses interpretation, that is, comments on possible underlying meaning, only when an individual is judged to be in a state of mind where they are able to use this, and maybe not at all. SPP has been studied in a multi-centre controlled trial (Rosenbaum et al., 2012), which showed that 119 first episode psychosis patients who received 12–24 months SPP plus treatment as usual (TAU) after two years had significantly better symptom and functional improvement than 150 similar patients treated with TAU only. SPP is designed to be used as soon as possible after psychosis is diagnosed. The example later in this chapter describes using the SPP approach but at a later stage of treatment.

Psychodynamic therapy as an attachment based therapy

The relationship between psychodynamic and attachment approaches to therapy has been extensively discussed (Holmes, 2015). Therapies based on attachment theory and research aim to use approaches designed to enhance the security of the client's attachment to the therapist. We will argue that psychodynamic therapies like SPP may do exactly this, and are thus attachment-based, though without using the particular language of attachment security. Therapies which do not explicitly and primarily seek to increase security of attachment have been categorised as 'attachment-informed' rather than 'attachment-based' (Burke et al., 2016) but in our view, using the term 'attachment-informed' for psychodynamic therapies such as SPP would conceal that attachment may be at the core of these therapies, and not an add-on.

Daniel (2014) suggests that psychodynamic therapies are likely to enhance attachment security; various features are likely to contribute to this. Firstly, attachment security is likely to be supported by the predictability of time and setting, especially where difficulty in mentalising leads to increased risk of misinterpretation of therapist actions and intentions, and thus to therapeutic ruptures. Secondly, the focus on clients' moment-to-moment experience and use of certain supportive techniques, means that skilled therapists are likely to behave in various ways likely to enhance attachment security, for example, with sensitively attuned responses, curiosity, tentativeness, willingness to acknowledge errors, mentalising responses to affect, and attention to alliance ruptures (Gumley & Clark, 2012; Holmes, 2015). Thirdly, a skilled therapist will adapt their style of interaction to the client, only shifting towards being less restricted by the client's expectations when the client can cope with this without undue anxiety. Attachment research suggests that adapting to the client's predominant attachment style may help insecure clients engage in therapy and start to experience the therapist as a secure base (Daly & Malinckrodt, 2009), particularly important in psychosis, when dismissive and unresolved styles are common (Bucci, Emsley & Berry, 2016; Gumley, 2014). Fourthly, if therapists' capacities to manage their own emotional states are enhanced as intended through personal therapy and psychodynamic supervision, this may enable therapists to be better able to help clients mentalise difficult states and to avoid reinforcing clients' insecure attachment patterns (Rubino et al., 2000).

In addition, the longer duration of psychodynamic therapies, compared with many therapies currently offered to people with psychosis, offers correspondingly more possibility of procedural learning, with lasting changes in the client's relational models and emotional capacities. Therapists using SPP report better results with longer therapies, with benefits continuing beyond two years (Rosenbaum, personal communication) and there is empirical evidence that longer therapies may have greater benefit in more severe problems generally (Rabung & Leichsenring, 2014).

Taking the example of SPP, there are additional features specific to this model that may further support attachment security. The therapist's flexibility and the cognitive focus in initial sessions may allow easier engagement for clients with dismissive or unresolved attachment styles. The discussion of the client's life story and shared formulation may support a cognitive pathway to managing attachment insecurity (and other difficulties). The SPP approach may also include some interventions that help mentalising, though they are likely to have scope to do more of this through more systematic adoption of specific techniques.

New developments in psychodynamic therapy for psychosis

Combining ideas from psychodynamic and attachment fields can lead to development of new therapeutic approaches. It has led for example to the development of Mentalising Based Therapy (MBT), a therapy for borderline personality disorder which has psychodynamic roots, but uses techniques designed specifically to enhance mentalising capacities. Such techniques include the therapist thinking aloud, or encouraging the client to stop and consider what they or others might be thinking or feeling. As discussed earlier, mentalising is commonly an area of difficulty for people who experience psychotic states and one which may underlie the difficulties in social functioning commonly associated with psychosis. MBT has been adapted for people with psychotic diagnoses (Brent et al., 2014) and studies of its efficacy are currently underway (Weijers et al., 2016).

An example of psychodynamic therapy

Daniel was 25 and living with his father and stepmother following a hospital admission two years earlier where he was given a diagnosis of schizophrenia. Cognitive behavioural therapy had helped him feel less dominated by voices, which he believed to be transmitted to him from unknown authorities monitoring him, but despite medication and help from a support worker he had not managed to resume work or social life. Daniel's psychiatrist discussed with him what psychodynamic therapy might involve, and how it might help and Daniel agreed he would like to try this.

The therapist, Mary, used an approach based on SPP and was able to offer up to 18 months of 50-minute sessions, at the same time and location each week. In the first few sessions, Mary spent time talking with Daniel about the process and purpose of therapy and learning more about him so that she could begin to develop a psychodynamic formulation. Thus, she sought information about his life, his experience of himself and his relationships, his psychotic experiences and their precursors, his suicidal and violent thoughts, his attitudes to treatment and areas of his life that were not problematic. Throughout, she paid careful attention to Daniel's interaction with herself and the moment-to-moment patterns in this.

Mary noticed that Daniel seemed happy to talk about his background in information technology, about the surveillance systems he believed to be targeting him, and his recently acquired knowledge of psychoanalysis. However, when speaking about more personal issues he spoke more briefly, less coherently and with little eye contact. In line with the SPP approach, Mary was keen to avoid therapy being excessively anxiety provoking and to develop a therapeutic relationship that would continue to function even in the presence of a difficult transference. Rather than remaining emotionally neutral, she empathised with Daniel's struggles, used an ordinary conversational style and avoided lengthy silences. She demonstrated her interest in the issues Daniel wanted to talk about and only as she felt he was more at ease with her did she gently encourage him to say more about the topics he found less comfortable. Mary noted that although she wanted to be sympathetic, she often felt emotionally 'disconnected' when Daniel talked about painful things that had happened to him.

After a few weeks, Mary started to discuss with Daniel what seemed to be key events and patterns in his life that might form a focus for therapy. They considered his tendency since infant school to feel that people looked down on him (including his father, and his hallucinatory figures), his sense of his father as not really interested in him, and his difficulty coping with relationships ending. Daniel and Mary both felt that the onset of his voices and beliefs might be linked to his girlfriend leaving him some months before. Unlike Mary, however, Daniel felt that his mother's death when he was eight was something that was no longer relevant.

In the following months Daniel tended to use the sessions to talk about day-to-day events, for example, his annoyance with his psychiatrist, who he felt looked down on him, his occasional half-hearted attempts to contact friends via social media, and the feedback he received from his hallucinatory voices, such as suggestions that other people found him tedious and uninteresting.

The formulation continuing to develop in Mary's mind included the themes discussed after the initial sessions, but with additional elements. She felt that in Daniel's internal world he often experienced himself as under attack from figures that disapproved of him, with potential caregiver figures uninterested or unreliable. She saw Daniel as projecting some of these expectations on to people in his external life. He seemed to treat Mary as helpful, interested and sympathetic to him in a way others were not and she saw this as a somewhat distorted view, i.e. a positive transference. However, she felt that underlying this he might also fear that she was uninterested and looking down on him (negative transference).

In talking with Daniel, Mary continued to seek a balance between encouraging exploration and maintaining security. She generally avoided interpreting the positive transference, but she did discuss the negative transference, choosing points when she felt there were cues that Daniel might be able to make use of her comments. On one occasion, for example, Daniel had been talking about how his father and his psychiatrist didn't care that he found things difficult. Mary was aware that she herself felt disconnected from his distress, and also that Daniel had just noticed her glancing at the time. She told him she thought that if this feeling of others not being there for him emotionally was happening to him in so many places, it seemed likely it must happen with her too, and she wondered if her looking at the clock made him feel she wasn't interested. Daniel seemed relieved at being able to admit this. He said for the first time that he believed she saw him as too stuck, and not worth working with, and that she would welcome an opportunity to end the therapy early. His response seemed to Mary to confirm that her formulation was useful and her comment helpful.

In the middle months of therapy, both Mary and Daniel were feeling there had been little progress, but Mary knew that this was not an indication to consider ending, but rather an experience to reflect on together. Several months before the planned ending, she began to look for openings to bring this into the conversation, encouraging Daniel to discuss his achievements and disappointments in therapy, and his feelings about it ending.

Daniel was adamant that therapy had been very important for him, helping him to make sense of his life, and feel more hopeful. Mary was aware that he still did not feel ready to apply for part-time work and that his voices were as frequent as ever, and she wondered if his positive view of ending might still be partly attributable to positive transference. However, she felt there was some clear evidence of potentially valuable changes. In the therapy sessions, Daniel had grown much more able to stay with uncomfortable topics, speaking reflectively, with emotion and eye contact and without Mary feeling disconnected. His conviction that his voices originated from an external source was now only strong when he felt very anxious and at other times he considered it just his particular way of responding to stress. He had managed to talk to his father about some of his long held grievances and felt their relationship had deepened considerably, and he was now gradually rebuilding contact with old friends, and making some new ones.

Conclusions

In summary, we have focused on psychodynamic approaches derived from object relations theory and have considered these in relation to attachment perspectives on theory and practice. Important questions remain unanswered about how psychotic experiences develop, how attachment-based therapies may help and what psychodynamic approaches may or may not contribute. It would be helpful to understand, for example, to what extent therapy may change internal working models and reduce vulnerability to relapse, in what ways the length of therapy may matter, and whether and how therapists might make things worse. Some questions are specific to psychodynamic therapies, for example, whether personal therapy and attention to countertransference in therapy are necessary, or even relevant, to psychological change and whether psychodynamic therapies for psychosis could be more effective through embracing additional techniques based on attachment theory and research. The mechanisms by which psychodynamic therapies work remain unclear, and one question is whether attachment security may be enhanced not only through supportive aspects of therapy but through classical techniques of interpretation of defences and working through of transference.

It seems clear that attachment and psychodynamic perspectives have much in common as well as areas of complementary difference. To psychodynamic therapists, achievements in the attachment field suggest possibilities for integrating research findings into psychodynamic theory and practice, for recognising the value of an accessible language, and of specific therapy techniques. To those starting from an attachment perspective, we believe that psychodynamic literature and experience might offer new directions for development of theory, research and therapy.

We have argued that supportive psychodynamic therapies may be considered attachment-based therapies, and that their particular and added value lies in features such as attention to the minutiae of interactions in therapy, to countertransference and to motivational states other than attachment, along with training and supervision intended to enhance therapists' capacities to tolerate affect. In conclusion, we believe that increasing dialogue between attachment and psychodynamic perspectives could contribute to research, training and development of new therapeutic approaches, and could thus have much to offer to people who experience psychosis.

References

Bion, W. R. (1959). Attacks on linking. *International Journal of Psycho-Analysis*, *40*(308), 8.

Burke, E., Danquah, A. N., & Berry, K. (2016). Clinical psychology and psychotherapy a qualitative exploration of the use of attachment theory in adult psychological therapy. *Clinical Psychology and Psychotherapy*, *23*(2), 142–150.

Brent, B. K., Holt, D. J., Keshavan, M. S., Seidman, L. J., & Fonagy, P. (2014). Mentalization based treatment for psychosis: Linking an attachment-based model to the psychotherapy for impaired mental state understanding in people with psychotic disorders. *Israel's Journal of Psychiatry Related Science*, *51*(1), 17–24.

Bucci, S., Emsley, R., & Berry, K. (2017). Attachment in psychosis: a latent profile analysis of attachment styles and association with symptoms in a large psychosis cohort. *Psychiatry Research*, *247*, 243–249. DOI: 10.1016/j.psychres.2016.11.036

Daly, K. D., & Mallinckrodt, B. (2009). Experienced therapists' approach to psychotherapy for adults with attachment avoidance or attachment anxiety. *Journal of Counseling Psychology*, *56*(4), 549.

Daniel, S. (2014). *Adult Attachment Patterns in a Treatment Context: Relationship and Narrative*. London: Routledge.

Fonagy, P. (2001). *Attachment Theory and Psychoanalysis*. New York: Other Press.

Fonagy, P., & Adshead, G. (2012). How mentalisation changes the mind. *Advances in Psychiatric Treatment*, *18*(5), 353–362.

Freeman, D., Pugh, K., & Garety, P. (2008). Jumping to conclusions and paranoid ideation in the general population. *Schizophrenia Research*, *102*(1), 254–260.

Freud, A. (1960). *The Ego and the Mechanisms of Defence*. London: Karnac Books., 1992.

Freud, S. (1923). Neurosis and psychosis. In *The Standard Edition of the Complete Psychological Works of Sigmund Freud, Volume XIX (1923–1925): The Ego and the Id and Other Works* (pp. 147–154). London: Hogarth. 1961.

Garety, P. A., Kuipers, E., Fowler, D., Freeman, D., & Bebbington, P. E. (2001). A cognitive model of the positive symptoms of psychosis. *Psychological Medicine*, *31*(2), 189–195.

Garfield, D. & Steinman, I. (2015). *Self Psychology and Psychosis: The Development of the Self During Intensive Psychotherapy of Schizophrenia and Other Psychoses*. London: Karnac.

Gumley, A. & Clark, S. (2012). Risk of arrested recovery following first episode psychosis: an integrative approach to psychotherapy. *Journal of Psychotherapy Integration*, *22*(4), 298–313.

Gumley, A. I., Taylor, H. E. F., Schwannauer, M., & MacBeth, A. (2014). A systematic review of attachment and psychosis: measurement, construct validity and outcomes. *Acta Psychiatrica Scandinavica*, *129*(4), 257–274.

Harder, S. (2014). Attachment in schizophrenia: implications for research, prevention and treatment. Schizophrenia Bulletin, *40*(6), 1189–1193.

Holmes, J. (1993). *John Bowlby and Attachment Theory*. London: Routledge.

Holmes, J. (2015). Attachment theory in clinical practice: a personal account. *British Journal of Psychotherapy*, *31*(2), 208–228.

Klein, M. (1935). A contribution to the psychogenesis of manic-depressive states. *The International Journal of Psychoanalysis*, *16*, 145–174.

Kongara, S., Douglas, C., Martindale, B. & Summers, A. (2017). Individual psychodynamic therapy for psychosis: a Delphi study. *Psychosis: Psychological, Social and Integrative Approaches*, *9*(3), 216–224. Published on line March 17, 2017: http://dx.doi.org/10.1080/17522439.2017.1300185.

Leader, D. (2012). *What is Madness?* London: Penguin Books Ltd.

Lemma, A. (2016). Introduction *to the Practice of Psychoanalytic Psychotherapy*. Chichester: John Wiley & Sons.

Liotti, G., & Gumley, A. (2008). An attachment perspective on schizophrenia: The role of disorganized attachment, dissociation and mentalization. In A. Moskowitz, I. Schafer, & M. J. Dorahy (Eds.), *Psychosis, Trauma And Dissociation: Emerging perspectives on severe psychopathology* (pp. 117–133). Chichester: John Wiley & Sons.

Lysaker, P. H., & Silverstein, S. M. (2009). Psychotherapy of schizophrenia: A brief history and the potential to promote recovery. *Clinical Case Studies*. First published November 24, 2009 Research article doi.org/10.1177/1534650109351930

MacBeth, A., Gumley, A., Schwannauer, M., & Fisher, R. (2011). Attachment states of mind, mentalization, and their correlates in a first-episode psychosis sample. *Psychology and Psychotherapy: Theory, Research and Practice*, *84*(1), 42–57.

Martindale, B. & Summers, A. (2013). The psychodynamics of psychosis. *Advances in Psychiatric Treatment*, *19*: 124–131.

Rabung, S., & Leichsenring, F. (2012). Effectiveness of long-term psychodynamic psychotherapy: First meta-analytic evidence and its discussion. In *Psychodynamic Psychotherapy Research* (pp. 27–49). Humana Press.

Rosenbaum, B. & Thorgaard, L. (1998). *Early and sustained dynamic intervention in schizophrenia*. A short version of the Danish National Schizophrenia project (DNS) manual for psychodynamic individual psychotherapy with persons in states of psychosis.

Rosenbaum, B., Harder, S., Knudsen, P. et al. (2012). Supportive psychodynamic therapy versus treatment as usual for first episode psychosis: two year outcome. *Psychiatry: Interpersonal and Biological Approaches*, *75*, 331–341.

Rosenbaum, B., Martindale, B. & Summers, A. (2013). Supportive psychodynamic therapy for psychosis. *Advances in Psychiatric Treatment, 19*, 310–318.

Rosenbaum, B. (2015). Psychodynamic psychotherapy for persons in states of psychosis: some research perspectives. *British Journal of Psychotherapy, 31*(4), 476–491.

Rubino, G., Barker, C., Roth, T., & Fearon, P. (2000). Therapist empathy and depth of interpretation in response to potential alliance ruptures: The role of therapist and patient attachment styles. *Psychotherapy Research, 10*(4), 408–420.

Steinmann, I. & Garfield, D. (2015) *Self Psychology and Psychosis: The development of the self during intensive psychotherapy of schizophrenia and other psychoses.* London: Karnac.

Summers, A. & Martindale, B. (2013). Using psychodynamic principles in formulation in. everyday practice. *Advances in Psychiatric Treatment, 19*, 203–211.

Summers, A. & Rosenbaum, B. (2013). Psychodynamic therapy for psychosis: empirical evidence. In Read, J., & Dillon, J. (Eds) *Models of Madness: Psychological, social and biological approaches to psychosis.* Hove: Routledge, 336–344.

Van Os, J., Linscott, R. J., Myin-Germeys, I., Delespaul, P., & Krabbendam, L. (2009). A systematic review and meta-analysis of the psychosis continuum: evidence for a psychosis proneness–persistence–impairment model of psychotic disorder. *Psychological Medicine, 39*(02), 179–195.

Varese, F., Smeets, F., Drukker, M., Lieverse, R., Lataster, T., Viechtbauer, W., Read, R., van Os, J., Bentall, P. (2012). Childhood adversities increase the risk of psychosis: a meta-analysis of patient-control, prospective- and cross-sectional cohort studies. *Schizophrenia Bulletin, 38*(4), 661–671.

Waller, E., & Scheidt, C. E. (2006). Somatoform disorders as disorders of affect regulation: a development perspective. *International Review of Psychiatry, 18*(1), 13–24.

Weijers, J., ten Kate, C., Eurelings-Bontekoe, E., Viechtbauer, W., Rampaart, R., Bateman, A., & Selten, J-P. (2016). Mentalization-based treatment for psychotic disorder: protocol of a randomized controlled trial, v16 and p. 191. *BMC Psychiatry, 16*(4) (June 8, 2016). doi:1186/s12888-016-0902-x.

9

COGNITIVE INTERPERSONAL THERAPY FOR RECOVERY IN PSYCHOSIS

Angus MacBeth, Andrew Gumley and Matthias Schwannauer

Introduction

Cognitive Interpersonal Therapy for psychosis (CIT-P; Gumley & Schwannauer, 2006) emerged from our work in understanding staying well after psychosis. It is an approach that applies cognitive behavioural and interpersonal techniques to support individuals recovering from the experience of psychosis. Its focus is on using psychological therapies to delay or prevent exacerbation of psychotic symptoms, otherwise known as relapse. From a theoretical perspective, our model is based on the idea that cognitive, emotional interpersonal factors, viewed alongside the developmental context in which individuals come to understand themselves and others, can act together to speed up or slow down recovery.

Initially, CIT-P was mainly concerned with relapse prevention. In proposing CIT-P, we argued that relapse needs to be understood in relation to: (1) the experiences of the person, their beliefs and appraisals of relapse and psychosis (e.g. experiences of traumatic and frightening hospital admissions giving rise to fear of recurrence); (2) the individual's interpersonal context (e.g. social networks including family and friends as a source of support or stress); and (3) the manner in which service systems respond to the challenge of relapse prevention for individuals who are prone to recurrent psychotic experiences (e.g. lack of attuned responses to help seeking, use of coercive measures that leads to further fear of help seeking). We viewed relapse prevention strategies (such as early warning signs monitoring) as necessary, but not sufficient, in promoting recovery from psychosis. So we therefore expanded our conceptualisation of CIT-P to capture both a broader range of presenting problems (e.g. difficulties in help-seeking and adaptation in both first and multi-episode presentations of psychosis, emotional dysfunction and negative symptoms) and to unpack the mechanisms of change in CIT-P drawing on concepts such as emotional recovery, compassion, attachment and metacognitive understanding. This chapter gives an overview of our current understanding of CIT-P and outlines the next steps for development of the intervention. We will also present a fictionalised vignette illustrating the application of CIT-P.

Recovery in psychosis

Data on relapse rates from the first episode of psychosis to five-year follow-up show a steady increase in relapse rates from 20 per cent at one year to 80 per cent at five years (Robinson et al., 1999). The recurrence of psychosis can lead to feelings of demoralisation and entrapment, and has been linked to poorer emotional adaptation following psychosis (Gumley, O'Grady, Power, & Schwannauer, 2004). Individuals who feel they are unable to prevent a relapse are more likely to develop depression and anxiety (Karatzias, Gumley, Power, & O'Grady, 2007).

Approaches to the prediction of relapse have moved from monitoring behavioural signs of relapse (Birchwood et al., 1989) or assessment of idiosyncratic changes in perception, cognition, emotion or interpersonal experiences (Docherty, Van Kammen, Siris, & Marder, 1978; McGHIE & Chapman, 1961); through to more contemporary approaches, which emphasise cognitive appraisals (i.e. how an individual understands a given situation as it impacts on them e.g. "I'm hopeless at this"), or interpretation of low-level psychotic-like experiences, including cognitive perceptual anomalies, hearing voices, suspiciousness and heightened interpersonal sensitivity (Gumley, White, & Power, 1999).

There is also considerable evidence that the experience of psychosis is traumatic and is often associated with the development of psychosis-related post-traumatic stress disorder, characterised by intrusive memories linked to the experience of psychosis, hypervigilance and fear, and sealing over (reflecting active attempts to minimise, avoid or isolate the experience of psychosis; Shaw, McFarlane, Bookless, & Air, 2002; White & Gumley, 2009). The threat of recurrence of psychosis can therefore generate competing and disorganising reactions, such as catastrophic appraisals of relapse, fear, vigilance and interpersonal threat sensitivity on the one hand, and cognitive, emotional and behavioural avoidance and delayed help seeking on the other (Gumley & MacBeth, 2006). For CIT-P, the threat-driven response of 'fear of relapse' (Herz & Melville, 1980) in response to low-level psychotic experiences is important in increasing the risk of making the transition to full relapse, fuelled by increasing emotional distress (Birchwood, 2003; Gumley et al., 1999).

We developed the Fear of Recurrence Scale (ForSe; Gumley et al., 2015) to measure the cognitive appraisals of psychotic phenomena and fear of recurrence. The scale includes items focused on awareness of psychotic phenomena ("My thoughts have been more interesting", "My thinking has been clearer than usual"), the intrusiveness of these phenomena ("My thoughts have been uncontrollable", "My thoughts have been distressing") and the fear of recurrence ("The thought of becoming unwell has frightened me", "I have felt unable to control my illness"). The scale does not include traditional early monitoring items, such as low mood, suspiciousness, voice hearing or anxiety.

145

When testing the FoRSE over a period of six months in a sample of 169 individuals with a diagnosis of psychosis and a recent relapse, we found no difference between the FoRSe and the Early Signs Scale (the existing gold standard relapse detection scale; Birchwood et al., 1989), in terms of their sensitivity (a measure's ability to correctly identify relapse) and specificity (a measure's ability to correctly identify when someone is not going to relapse). Both measures showed good sensitivity (FoRSe: 72% and ESS: 79%) and poor specificity (FoRSe: 46% and ESS: 35%). We also identified the Fear of Relapse subscale of the FoRSe as a significant predictor of time to relapse. In this respect, the FoRSe measure may help facilitate psychological interventions by helping clinicians and patients identify idiosyncratic experiences that give rise to increased fear of recurrence, and thus support clinicians in targeting psychological techniques to prevent relapse and promote emotional recovery (Braehler et al., 2013; Gleeson, Alvarez-Jimenez, Cotton, Parker, & Hetrick, 2010; Gleeson et al., 2013; Gumley et al., 2003; White et al., 2011).

Although our focus on early signs has highlighted the role of appraisals and the emotional-interpersonal context of relapse and recovery, the authors were also struck by the observation that people's ways of help-seeking and ways of relating in times of crisis potentially have their roots in developmental models of relating. This led us to incorporate attachment theory into our thinking as a key theory of help-seeking (Bowlby, 1973, 1980). In this respect, secure attachment facilitates active, optimal help-seeking, whereas insecure attachment (be it avoidance or preoccupation) inhibits an individual's capacity and ability to actively make use of supports in a crisis. In addition, we noted the close similarity between unresolved or disorganised attachment (the breakdown of an organised attachment pattern – either secure or insecure; see discussion below) and the disconnect of affect and cognitive appraisal in acute psychotic experiences (Bleuler, 1950).

In reviewing the literature, we identified that attachment theory in psychosis is a valid construct, with small to moderate associations between attachment and a range of outcomes, including positive and negative symptoms, depression and quality of life (Gumley, Taylor, Schwannauer, & MacBeth, 2014). Of particular relevance to CIT-P, the review suggested that insecure (dismissing or avoidant) attachment may be an important risk factor for problematic recovery following psychosis (MacBeth, Gumley, Schwannauer, & Fisher, 2011; Tait, Birchwood, & Trower, 2004). This was apparent from the first episode of psychosis onwards. In a cross-sectional sample of people in an Early Intervention Service receiving treatment after experiencing a first episode of psychosis (MacBeth et al., 2011), we identified a predominance of insecure (dismissing and preoccupied) attachment classifications and a significantly different distribution of these insecure classifications in comparison with non-clinical samples or samples with longer histories of psychosis (Dozier & Tyrrell, 1997; van Ijzendoorn & Bakermans-Kranenburg, 1996). Specifically, we identified higher rates of dismissing attachment classifications in our

146

first episode sample compared to non-clinical comparisons, but lower rates of dismissing attachment than in samples of individuals with long-standing psychosis. However, we also reported that more than a quarter of our sample coded as secure with regard to attachment on the Adult Attachment Interview (AAI). Moreover, although we did not find associations with symptoms, secure attachment was significantly associated with better engagement with clinical services. Secure attachment may, therefore, confer an advantage in facilitating adaptation to the experience of psychosis – these individuals being perceived by key workers to be better engaged with the process of treatment. In a broader longitudinal cohort of 79 individuals in their first episode of psychosis (Gumley, Schwannauer et al., 2014), we reported similar distributions of attachment to our earlier study, and a similar lack of association between attachment and positive symptoms. However, in terms of recovery from negative symptoms, insecure avoidant attachment and baseline insight predicted recovery from negative symptoms at both six and 12 months. We suggest that attachment processes may have a role in the unfolding of negative symptoms and that deactivation strategies (involving the dampening down of emotional processes) linked to insecure dismissing attachment may be linked to the deactivation of positive and negative affect in psychosis. Our findings in relation to positive symptom outcomes are consistent with formulating attachment as an affect-regulation strategy (Bowlby, 1973; 1980), whereby attachment security exerts an influence on positive symptom recovery via shorter duration of untreated psychosis (DUP) and higher insight. Attachment security is a marker for resilience and is characterised by openness to seeking help (shorter DUP) when distressed and greater awareness of thoughts, feelings and memories (improved insight). Furthermore, we identified an overlap between dismissing attachment and an associated diminished capacity to understand and reflect on one's own thoughts and those of others (metacognition).

Mechanisms of change

In parallel to the development of the evidence base for CIT-P, we have also begun to unpack the mechanisms of change in our approach. In doing so, we have expanded our understanding of CIT-P from being focused mainly on attachment in recovery to incorporate consideration of a broader affect regulation approach. In common with contemporary models of psychotherapy for complex mental health difficulties in Borderline Personality Disorder (BPD; Fonagy & Luyten 2009) and in non-borderline mixed Personality Disorders (Dimaggio et al., 2013), we consider attachment within a broader psychological framework that encompasses mentalisation or metacognition (i.e. the ability to think about one's own and others' mental states and use this information to determine an interpersonal or behavioural course of action) and broader emotion regulation approaches. However, this approach introduces a number of practical and theoretical questions, which we consider below.

Measuring attachment and implications for treatment

With regard to measurement, there are a number of challenges in measuring attachment and mentalisation in people seeking psychological intervention. Addressing this is important to CIT-P as measurement of attachment can give an indicator of underlying affect regulation strategies. The attachment literature in general has long been divided by the use of self-report versus interview measures of attachment. The former approach gives a quick, easy to measure approach to attachment, and can rapidly derive meaningful factors. However, self-reports may not tap into attachment representations, instead taking the form of a measure of beliefs about attachment-relevant relationships. There has been criticism of the factor structure (subscales) of attachment self-reports, with most measures reducing to two attachment anxiety and attachment avoidance factors. Finally, the concept of attachment disorganisation has, to date, been poorly operationalised in self-report approaches (Granqvist et al., 2017). In contrast, the adult attachment representation literature (linked to developmental psychology) focuses on using transcript coding of interview material to categorise people in terms of attachment representations (e.g. Adult Attachment Interview (Main, Hesse & Goldwyn, 2002) and Adult Attachment Projective (George & West, 2012). These measures tend to have good comparative validity to infant categorisations, and give detailed attachment-related material. However, they are time-consuming to administer, transcribe and code, and require reliability in the coding frameworks. This makes them too resource intensive for most clinical settings.

We suggest that a compromise can be achieved by using the measures heuristically, rather than seeking to categorise people into attachment types. Therefore, the value of both self- and interview reports lies in the use of the raw 'data' i.e. the items endorsed on a questionnaire or the interview narrative, to develop an attachment-informed formulation. For example, does the material suggest a pattern of coping in interpersonal situations that links to under- or over-activation of affect? Does the individual keep others at arm's length, or are there selective situations or relationships where they can achieve a sense of security in relationships? We propose that the measure gives an insight into where and when the individual feels safety and security in close relationships. In this sense, we suggest that attachment gives CIT-P a window onto an individual's sense of relational safety and security, which is the antithesis of relational fears and anxieties. Attachment also taps into key goals of CIT-P regarding increasing psychological flexibility and promoting more active help-seeking in the individual.

However, these measures can only tap into the attachment system either by a prompt to reflect on attachment-related concerns, or in the case of the AAI by 'surprising the unconscious' in activating the (adult) attachment system (Steele & Steele, 2008). Therefore, the impact of attachment on social, emotional and interpersonal functioning at other 'offline' times remains difficult to establish. The developmental literature highlights the impact in particular of infant disorganised attachment as reflective of the adult's experience of unresolved trauma and loss, which itself overlaps with adult attachment disorganisation, dissociation and frightened or helpless mental states (Granqvist et al., 2017). From a CIT-P perspective, we can extrapolate that these risks may manifest in the breakdown of appropriate affect regulation or help-seeking strategies in the context of increased stress. This may in turn lead to coercive cycles of suboptimal responding from services and the individual – the 'relapse dance' (Gumley & Read, 2008). In this regard, CIT-P serves as a therapeutic secure base from which to model adaptive responding under stress. Importantly, although we view the presence of mental state disorganisation as a meaningful signal for complexity, we follow the contemporary attachment literature and do not conflate disorganisation with the experience of childhood trauma. Disorganisation may occur as a sequelae of trauma, and trauma may be associated with disorganisation, but there is not a one-to-one mapping.

Mentalisation and the attachment switch

A further mechanism at play in CIT-P is mentalisation or metacognition. We use mentalisation and metacognition interchangeably to refer to how an individual uses mental state information to integrate psychological knowledge about the self and the others into complex psychological representations (Fonagy & Luyten, 2009; Carcione et al., 2010; Dimaggio & Lysaker, 2010; Lysaker et al., 2013). To an extent this overlaps with social cognition approaches to metacognition such as Theory of Mind. These approaches refer to an individual's capacity to make judgements regarding one aspect of a given social situation – e.g. the presence or absence of sadness. In our work with first episode psychosis, we have identified that lower scores for metacognitive understanding of *others'* minds were significantly correlated with more severe negative symptoms, poorer early adolescent social adjustment and poorer clinician-rated help-seeking (MacBeth et al., 2014; 2016). This is consistent with our earlier findings for mentalisation, suggesting that people experiencing a first episode of psychosis with difficulties in understanding others' minds experience more difficulties in social relationships and may be less able to make effective use of treatment (MacBeth et al., 2011). Longitudinal data from our group also indicated that problems with mental state processing may be important determinants of negative symptom expression from the very early stages of psychosis (McLeod et al., 2014).

Our data (MacBeth et al., 2014) suggest that, when we unpack metacognition, higher understanding of one's own and others' mental states may represent increased capacity to appreciate one's own need for help and confidence in the capacity of the treatment team to provide help. In contrast, our data have not yet identified a strong effect of the emotional component of metacognition. From a treatment perspective, this has implications for session-by-session progress in CIT-P, whereby the therapist works with the individual to foster attention and recognition of mental states in a nuanced way, drawing on the individual's subjective experience and the mental states of the others during everyday life interactions. This is similar to the focus on the 'here-and-now' of both classic CBT and of the other contemporary metacognitive or mentalisation-based psychological therapies (e.g. Fonagy & Bateman, 2006; Bargenquast & Schweitzer, 2014; Harder & Folke, 2012; Gumley & Schwannauer, 2006; Lysaker et al., 2011; Moritz et al., 2014; Salvatore et al., 2012).

We also support the notion of an attachment and metacognition 'switch' whereby, under increased stress or emotional activation, mentalisation goes 'offline', and attachment or more primitive 'fight or flight' strategies are activated. There is substantial evidence from the BPD literature supporting the concept of a neurobiological and neurochemical substrates from flexible, mental-state supported, conscious processing, to automatic, arousal driven implicit processing (Fonagy & Luyten, 2009). In the BPD literature, it has been proposed that hyperactivating affect regulation is a predominant strategy, where the trigger for mentalisation going offline is at a low threshold, frequently triggered by more subjective interpretations of interpersonal stressors. Therefore, therapy seeks to move individuals more towards secure (keeping mentalisation online for longer) strategies. In this model, it was suggested that dismissing or deactivating attachment has the benefit of keeping mentalisation skills available for longer, but at the cost of a breakdown on mentalisation at higher stress. We suggest a different conceptualisation in psychosis – in that the dismissing or deactivating approach predominates as a reflection of a combined deactivation of affect in order to manage social situations, but that this is achieved at the cost of attending to one's own and others' mental states. Therefore, as subjective social stress increases mentalisation can be easily overwhelmed, leading to either emotionally laden intrusions or overload (perhaps experienced as positive psychotic symptoms); or instead a retreat into social avoidance and inhibition (as seen in negative symptom presentations). In addition, the dampening effect of antipsychotic medication may serve to compound these patterns. In CIT-P, therefore, the goal becomes to gradually increase emotional awareness in interpersonal situations, accompanied by the development of cognitive and behavioural strategies to manage affect.

An attachment and affect regulation-informed approach further links to the notion of the therapist as both secure base and safe-haven. We have used these terms interchangeably to reflect the role of the therapist both as able to model emotion regulation and preserved mentalisation in the discussion of emotionally-laden topics or situations; and as a non-judgemental figure able to reduce distress in times of crisis. We note that these two functions have differing implications. In a successful treatment outcome we would anticipate that over time the individual develop their own sense of 'felt security' and in doing so is better able to regulate affect and use mental state information to plot a course through social situations. Alongside this, the safe-haven function requires, over time, a movement from either over-reliance on one safe haven figure, or lack of reliance on any figure, towards the creation of a distributed network of potential safe haven figures including, but not limited to, family, close partners and friends, the treatment team and the therapist. From an attachment perspective, the individual is not immune to stress or crisis, but is better able to draw on and expect to draw on, the prompt, emotionally avail-able and compassionate responses of others at these times. Following from this CIT-P can therefore sit alongside either family-based interventions or team-formulation approaches, depending on the person's needs and the need of others within their social networks.

CIT-P in practice: case vignette

We will now illustrate the use of CIT-P using a case vignette. The person concerned had no previous experience of psychological interventions for psychosis. In this example, we highlight the value of CIT-P approach in a scenario where the staying well rationale was less clear – in this case with the focus initially being on the treatment-resistant nature of the person's problems. The vignette highlights the key processes in CIT-P namely: engage-ment and assessment; attachment or developmentally influenced formulation; focus on affect regulation and self and other understanding as vehicles for change; stabilisation and recovery phase.

"Alec"

Background and assessment

Alec's referral to clinical psychology was triggered by his psychiatrist's concern that the community team had exhausted all pharmacological and social options for Alec's care. With regard to his own goals, Alec stated that he wanted to 'keep getting better every day'. We agreed that developing an understanding of Alec's triggers for relapse, and developing skills for man-aging these triggers would contribute to this goal.

On point of referral to clinical psychology "Alec" was a 29-year-old male with a diagnosis of chronic, treatment-resistant schizophrenia. Alec was on a complex medication regime of Clozapine, additional antipsychotics and mood stabilisers. At initial assessment, Alec presented with chronic positive symptoms of psychosis. In particular, he described a complex and entrenched system of delusions fluctuating between religious delusions (that his symptoms were a test from God and that his recovery would occur at a time

151

of God's choosing), delusions of grandeur (that he was particularly attractive to women and that female celebrities wished to have intimate relations with him) and more frank paranoid delusions regarding family members. In addition, Alec experienced delusions of reference with regard to the TV communicating messages to him consistent with the themes above. Importantly for treatment, Alec reported a frequent "black" feeling visited upon him by one of his persecutors, which he construed as an indicator of a future negative event. It became apparent in assessment that this was a misinterpretation of somatic anxiety. Alec had been with adult mental health services for approximately 10 years, with frequent admissions to hospital when his symptoms became more pronounced. The deterioration in Alec's symptoms was usually indicated by increased disinhibition and accompanying risky behaviour. This behaviour predominantly took the form of frequenting local bars and becoming overly familiar with women; or he would become verbally or physically aggressive towards his family. This decline in function would generate a heightened response from mental health services, and was frequently accelerated by Alec making a spontaneous decision to discontinue his medication. Relapse would culminate in admission to the inpatient ward and a period of time would ensue where Alec would be recommenced on medication before discharge back into the community. At the time of assessment, he resided with his parents, having vacated his own accommodation. In addition, Alec's family were often angry and critical towards services. In the context of a potential crisis his mother would often signal to services that Alec required immediate hospitalisation. Alec himself found the prospect of hospitalisation very stressful so his mother's response therefore had the unintended effects of exacerbating his symptoms.

During assessment it became apparent that Alec had experienced difficulties in social functioning since childhood. Alec said he had been something of a 'dreamer' at school, although he stated that his school performance would have been above average had he applied himself to his studies. Alec reported trying cannabis once or twice in his teens, but felt that it didn't agree with him. His family owned a successful local business, and he described his father as a 'good dad' who was hard working, but distant, consistent with the cultural norm for males in the area in which Alec had grown up. After leaving school he briefly joined the armed forces, and at this point Alec's mental health began to suffer. During his training he became increasingly paranoid and disinhibited. Ultimately, he was assessed by a military doctor who discharged him from the Forces due to mental health issues. During assessment Alec acknowledged that although he described really enjoying military life, he was verbally and physically bullied by several of his superiors during his training.

After he moved back home, Alec entered treatment with the local mental health team, being prescribed low dose antipsychotic medication (Risperidone) and being treated on an outpatient basis. Over the course of a year Alec appeared to recover functioning, and he entered into a supported employment post. Around this point Alec opted to spontaneously discontinue his medication, and in conjunction with the change in circumstances brought about by the return to work, he experienced an acute relapse of his psychosis, precipitating an inpatient admission. Alec acknowledged that at the time he felt he was back to his premorbid level of function, and on reflection reported that the decision to discontinue medication may have been influenced by psychotic delusions. Over the next eight years Alec became increasingly functionally disabled by his psychotic symptoms – with repeated crisis admissions to the inpatient ward and numerous changes of dosage, number and type of medications. In parallel his family became increasingly hypervigilant to potential signs of relapse, evidenced by Alec's behaviour. As noted above, the emergence of this so-called high expressed emotion dynamic served to lower both Alec's mother's and mental health services' threshold for moving into crisis mode, precipitating a 'relapse dance' (Gumley & Park 2010). As a consequence of this increasingly coercive pattern of responding, Alec also became increasingly wary of mental health services, tending to under-report symptoms and passively disengage from any additional opportunities offered, consistent with a deactivating or dismissing pattern of attachment. Although Alec had moved into a flat of his own, he subsequently returned to his parents' house after a few months, due to being unable to manage living on his own.

Formulation (see Figure 9.1)

From assessment, it became apparent that although Alec continued to experience residual positive symptoms, particularly paranoid delusions, these were relatively low level. More damaging to Alec's recovery was his fear of relapse. It quickly became apparent that understanding this anxiety required an appreciation of Alec's experience of mental health services to date. He had become unwell as a young adult and been given standard medical management. Alec had learned to 'seal over' with regard to disclosing his positive symptoms, compounding the impact of a deactivating attachment strategy, and also limiting his opportunity to engage in mentalisation due to his increased social isolation. Relapse had thus only been detected when Alec was no longer able to adequately conceal his symptoms. This had invariably led to hospital admission and often compulsory treatment, thus strengthening the association between experience of positive symptoms and coercive treatment. We also note that Alec was viewed by clinicians as having a chronic illness with a poor prognosis. Accordingly, with each relapse a degree of therapeutic pessimism became apparent. This was compounded by numerous unsuccessful trials of various combinations of antipsychotic medication and Alec's own disengagement from multi-professional input when it was offered. This left Alec in a situation whereby his own reluctance to disclose changes in his mental state left him with limited resources to monitor his own symptoms, whilst also being unable or unwilling to seek help from clinical services.

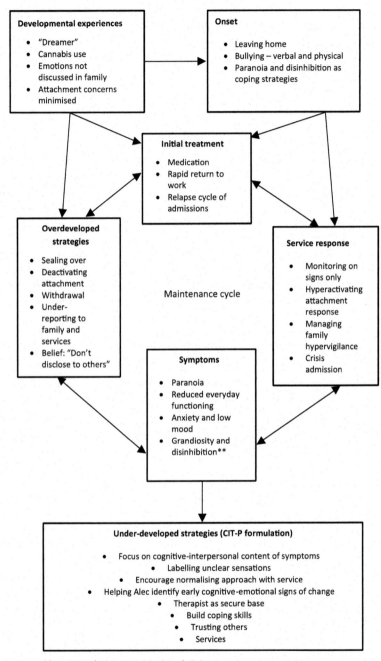

Figure 9.1 Formulation for Alec

Equally, clinical services had little information with regard to Alec's own day-to-day mental state, and were left waiting for very overt, 'alarm bell' signs of relapse. These indicators would inevitably be behavioural in form, and probably occurred late in the evolution of Alec's relapse trajectory. Therefore services were caught between a 'boy cried wolf' approach and a very low threshold for intervention, which served to compound Alec's antipathy towards treatment. Finally, this situation also disempowered Alec by leaving him without robust coping strategies for managing his mental state, instead remaining reliant on steadily more complex medication regimes.

Consequently, our formulation proceeded from the basis that developing a cognitive-interpersonal formulation of the idiosyncratic meaning of relapse would both enable Alec to take a degree of ownership over changes in his mental state, whilst also enabling him to develop an appreciation of when changes in his appraisals were indicative of heightened risk, as opposed to representing 'normal' fluctuation in his mental state. To do this we adopted a normalising approach to psychotic phenomena, consistent with existing best practice in CBT approaches for psychosis (Morrison, 2014). Furthermore, we hypothesised that a normalising, cognitive-interpersonal approach to early signs would also enable mental health services to support Alec via a more engaged and reflexive model of service engagement, rather than being limited to a crisis-driven mode of response. By sharing this formulation with the mental health team we also introduced the option that services could model positive risk taking with regard to tolerating changes in Alec's day-to-day symptoms. Finally, we identified that Alec's relatively impoverished range of coping skills required addressing in order to bolster his capacity to manage changes in his mental state. In particular, we surmised that this would be beneficial by reducing his anxiety and low mood, which both served to compound his sense of therapeutic 'stuckness.'

Progress in treatment

Due to Alec's historical reluctance to engage, and the frequent disruption caused by his positive psychotic symptoms, we trimmed back the agreed goals to focusing on Alec's stated aim of "getting better every day". We used a developmental formulation to map out the shared understanding of Alec's path into his psychosis, identify strengths and the current risks to his recovery. An unexpected effect of this approach was that Alec became far more curious in sessions regarding the links between his thoughts, feelings and physiology (particularly the 'black feeling'). This would be theoretically consistent with the role of clinician as a secure base, and with a compassionate pattern of responding; if Alec felt that sessions were a 'safe space' and the therapist was sufficiently containing, he could begin to explore his idiosyncratic interpretations of his experiences. However, on reflection, it could also be the case that this curiosity was consistent with a sense of psychological

155

exploration, analogous to the developmental psychology principle that when attachment needs have been met, the child is then free to explore their social world. We therefore began to present psychology sessions to Alec as a way of exploring his thoughts and feelings in a new way. To enhance engagement, we agreed that there would be no fixed agenda between sessions, with the focus of our work being on exploring what had been stressful for Alec in the periods between sessions. We agreed a schedule of fortnightly sessions, with the option to bring these into weekly sessions if Alec reported, or it was felt by the treatment team that he was in crisis. Importantly, for treatment, we encouraged a sense of openness to discussing moving forward in a supportive manner, incorporating tolerance of psychotic intrusions when they occurred.

Around halfway through treatment we introduced regular early signs monitoring using the Early Signs Scale (ESS; Birchwood et al., 1989) and Fear of Recurrence Scale (FoRSe; Gumley et al., 2014) – initially to enable us to identify which scale would give greater scope to model early predictors of relapse. Interestingly, on the ESS Alec had very low scores for all subscales – anxiety, depression, disinhibition and incipient psychosis. In contrast, when we used the FoRSe we identified a relatively high baseline for Awareness of psychotic phenomena, and moderate levels of Fear of Relapse and Intrusions.

Over the course of two years Alec attended more than 20 sessions of psychological therapy. We varied the length of appointment time from 30–60 minutes as a function of Alec's engagement, motivation and level of positive symptoms. As Alec's condition improved appointments were spaced out to monthly, then bimonthly.

Outcome

Alec found the process of completing regular early signs monitoring helpful, and over time he accepted this as a normalising way of taking forward the management of his symptoms. On several occasions, he spontaneously asked to complete the questionnaires as he wished to monitor his progress since the last session. The FoRSe was sensitive to Alec's heightened risk of relapse, and also enabled us to track his relative stability as treatment progressed. There are several points to note from the repeated measurement of early signs. Firstly, positive psychotic symptoms lacked sensitivity as markers of relapse for Alec, due to the high baseline awareness of psychotic experiences. However, at times of increased vulnerability to relapse the intrusive quality of his symptoms increased markedly, as did the fear of relapse. At times of stability his symptoms and awareness remaining heightened, but fear of relapse had reduced. Secondly, Alec's symptoms fluctuated across the duration of treatment; whereas as Alec became better able to manage his affect and behaviour, fear of recurrence followed a steady downward trajectory. Over the course of the second year of therapy it became apparent that Alec's presentation was at its most stable for over ten years. Accordingly, his sessions were further reduced. The use of monitoring provided a focal point to open up discussion within sessions – using the responses on the monitoring items to trigger discussion – e.g. "I notice that since I last saw you, you've noted that you've been thinking more about when you were unwell – can we talk a bit more about that?" By opening up the dialogue around recent events (often interpersonal and related to the family) we were able to scaffold a growing awareness of self and others, including the capacity to mentalise about others' responses e.g. "Why do you think they phoned the mental health team? Perhaps they were worried about you?". These exchanges built up over sessions to enable Alec to more openly discuss his emotions and foster an awareness of the impact of psychosis on his early adulthood. Although difficult, over the second year of treatment Alec developed a perspective on psychosis whereby although he considered it a significant facet of his life, it no longer defined him.

At our final appointment Alec reported that he had continued to maintain the gains he had made. His medication adherence remained excellent and he had remained out of hospital. He was engaging in competitive sports, and had recently played in a local tournament. Although disappointed by his placing, he was continuing to play sports at least once a week. Alec was also spending more time with his extended family and once a week had begun helping in the family business. Reports from his family indicated that they were delighted with Alec's progress and the family's ad-hoc contacts with the mental health service had ceased.

Reflection on the use of CIT-P

The above vignette illustrates the key components of CIT-P in action. In presenting this we wish to emphasise that CIT-P provides a framework that can be adapted to different presentations and stages of psychosis, from FEP to chronic presentations. The key driver is the intention to forestall relapse and promote recovery and staying well. Within the vignette we have noted the importance of a thorough, but gently paced assessment. Through this, autobiographical memories are used to build up an understanding of key developmental events, pre- and post-onset use of affect regulation strategies, signals for potential attachment representations, and the understanding of one's own and others' mental states, particularly in the context of interpersonal stress. Attachment measures can be used, although they were not in Alec's case, to scaffold the development of narrative.

We view the use of early signs monitoring as crucial to the treatment phase of CIT-P. At cognitive, emotional and interpersonal levels the use of the FoRSe gives a rich understanding of fluctuations in mental states, but also the role of intrusions and fear of relapse as accelerants in the relapse dance. In addition, we underline that CIT-P draws on attachment principles to develop flexibility both in terms of the therapeutic relationship, and for the individual.

From a therapist stance the strategy is to pull back to a monitoring phase when the individual is stable (although we do not suggest that therapists disengage entirely or promote early discharge), but increase involvement when the individual shows potential early signs of relapse or symptom exacerbation. At the individual level, we see this flexibility as reflecting the development in the individual of a more reflexive and curious stance towards their own capacity to monitor their own mental states and to use more adaptive coping strategies. From an attachment perspective, this requires the therapeutic discourse to either focus on enhancing awareness of affect in situations where deactivating attachment predominates, and where attachment preoccupation is an issue, to focus on moving towards a more cognitive, detached stance, decoupled form affect. We also emphasise that CIT-P relies on the therapist working together with the broader treatment team and family supports, again with the aim of achieving consistency and coherence within a broader recovery-focused approach. Finally, and perhaps most importantly, we strongly suggest that CIT-P addresses therapeutic pessimism regarding the capacity for individuals with psychosis to engage in psychological therapies, regardless of initial presentation. This hopeful stance echoes that of Bowlby, in emphasising the value of an attachment framework in psychotherapy. Appropriately, we therefore leave the last words in this chapter with him.

"...change continues throughout the life cycle so that changes for better or for worse are always possible. It is this continuing potential for change that means that at no time of life is a person invulnerable to every possible adversity and also at no time of life is a person impermeable to favourable influence. It is this persisting potential for change that gives opportunity for effective therapy (Bowlby 1988a, p.154)".

References

Birchwood, M. (2003). Pathways to emotional dysfunction in first-episode psychosis: *British Journal of Psychiatry, 182,* 373–375.

Birchwood, M., Smith, J., Macmillan, F., Hogg, B., Prasad, R., Harvey, C., & Bering, S. (1989). Predicting relapse in schizophrenia: the development and implementation of an early signs monitoring system using patients and families as observers, a preliminary investigation. *Psychological Medicine, 19*(3), 649–656.

Bowlby, J. (1973). *Attachment and Loss: Separation* (vol. 2): New York: Basic Books.

Bowlby, J. (1980). *Attachment and Loss: Volume 3. Loss.* New York: Basic Books.

Braehler, C., Gumley, A., Harper, J., Wallace, S., Norrie, J., & Gilbert, P. (2013). Exploring change processes in compassion focused therapy in psychosis: Results of a feasibility randomized controlled trial. *British Journal of Clinical Psychology, 52*(2), 199–214.

Dozier, M., & Tyrrell, C. (1997). Attachment and communication among persons with serious psychopathological disorders. *Attachment Theory and Close Relationships.* New York: Guilford Press.

George, C. & West, M. L. (2012). *The Adult Attachment Projective Picture System: Attachment Theory and Assessment in Adults.* New York: Guilford Press.

Gleeson, J. F., Alvarez-Jimenez, M., Cotton, S. M., Parker, A. G., & Hetrick, S. (2010). A systematic review of relapse measurement in randomized controlled trials of relapse prevention in first-episode psychosis. *Schizophrenia Research, 119*(1–3), 79–88. doi:10.1016/j.schres.2010.02.1073

Gleeson, J. F., Cotton, S. M., Alvarez-Jimenez, M., Wade, D., Gee, D., Crisp, K., ... McGorry, P. D. (2013). A randomized controlled trial of relapse prevention therapy for first-episode psychosis patients: outcome at 30-month follow-up. *Schizophria Bulletin, 39*(2), 436–448. doi:10.1093/schbul/sbr165

Granqvist, P., Sroufe, L. A., Dozier, M., Hesse, E., Steele, M., van Ijzendoorn, M., ... Bakermans-Kranenburg, M. (2017). Disorganized attachment in infancy: a review of the phenomenon and its implications for clinicians and policy-makers. *Attachment and Human Development, 19*(6), 534–558.

Gumley, A., O'Grady, M., McNay, L., Reilly, J., Power, K., & Norrie, J. (2003). Early intervention for relapse in schizophrenia: results of a 12-month randomized controlled trial of cognitive behavioural therapy. *Psychological Medicine, 33*(3), 419–431.

Gumley, A., O'Grady, M., Power, K., & Schwannauer, M. (2004). Negative beliefs about self and illness: a comparison of individuals with psychosis with or without comorbid social anxiety disorder. *Australian & New Zealand Journal of Psychiatry, 38*(11–12), 960–964.

Gumley, A., & Schwannauer, M. (2006). *Staying Well After Psychosis: A cognitive interpersonal approach to recovery and relapse prevention.* Chichester: John Wiley & Sons.

Gumley, A., White, C. A., & Power, K. (1999). An interacting cognitive subsystems model of relapse and the course of psychosis. *Clinical Psychology & Psychotherapy, 6*(4), 261–278.

Gumley, A. I., & MacBeth, A. (2006). A trauma-based model of relapse in psychosis. In W. Larkin, & A. Morrison (Eds.), *Trauma and Psychosis: New directions for theory and therapy* (pp.259–304), Abingdon: Routledge.

Gumley, A. I., MacBeth, A., Reilly, J. D., O'Grady, M., White, R. G., McLeod, H., ... Power, K. G. (2015). Fear of recurrence: results of a randomized trial of relapse detection in schizophrenia. *British Journal of Clinical Psychology, 54*(1), 49–62. doi:10.1111/bjc.12060

Gumley, A. I., Schwannauer, M., MacBeth, A., Fisher, R., Clark, S., Rattrie, L., ... Birchwood, M. (2014). Insight, duration of untreated psychosis and attachment in first-episode psychosis: prospective study of psychiatric recovery over 12-month follow-up. *British Journal of Psychiatry, 205*(1), 60–67. doi:10.1192/bjp.bp.113.126722

Gumley, A. I., Taylor, H. E., Schwannauer, M., & MacBeth, A. (2014). A systematic review of attachment and psychosis: measurement, construct validity and outcomes. *Acta Psychiatrica Scandinavica, 129*(4), 257–274. doi:10.1111/acps.12172

Herz, M. I., & Melville, C. (1980). Relapse in schizophrenia. *The American Journal of Psychiatry, 137*(7), 801–805.

Jorgensen, P. (1998). Early signs of psychotic relapse in schizophrenia. *The British Journal of Psychiatry, 172*(4), 327–330. doi:10.1192/bjp.172.4.327

Karatzias, T., Gumley, A., Power, K., & O'Grady, M. (2007). Illness appraisals and self-esteem as correlates of anxiety and affective comorbid disorders in schizophrenia. *Comprehensive Psychiatry, 48*(4), 371–375.

MacBeth, A., Gumley, A., Schwannauer, M., & Fisher, R. (2011). Attachment states of mind, mentalization, and their correlates in a first-episode psychosis sample. *Psychology & Psychological Therapy: Theory, Research and Practice, 84*(1), 42–57; discussion 98–110. doi:10.1348/147608310X530246

Main, M., Goldwyn, R., & Hesse, E. (2002). *Classification and Scoring Systems for the Adult Attachment Interview*. Berkeley, CA: University of California.

McGhie, A., & Chapman, J. (1961). Disorders of attention and perception in early schizophrenia. *Psychology and Psychotherapy: Theory, Research and Practice, 34*(2), 103–116.

Morrison, A. P. (2014). *A Casebook of Cognitive Therapy for Psychosis*. London: Routledge.

Robinson, D., Woerner, M. G., Alvir, J. M. J., Bilder, R., Goldman, R., Geisler, S., ... Mayerhoff, D. (1999). Predictors of relapse following response from a first episode of schizophrenia or schizoaffective disorder. *Archives of General Psychiatry, 56*(3), 241–247.

Shaw, K., McFarlane, A. C., Bookless, C., & Air, T. (2002). The aetiology of postpsychotic posttraumatic stress disorder following a psychotic episode. *Journal of Traumatic Stress, 15*(1), 39–47.

Steele, H., & Steele, M. (2008). *Clinical Applications of the Adult Attachment Interview*. New York: Guilford Press.

Tait, L., Birchwood, M., & Trower, P. (2004). Adapting to the challenge of psychosis: personal resilience and the use of sealing-over (avoidant) coping strategies. *The British Journal of Psychiatry, 185*(5), 410–415.

van Ijzendoorn, M. H., & Bakermans-Kranenburg, M. J. (1996). *Attachment Representations in Mothers, Fathers, Adolescents, and Clinical Groups: A meta-analytic search for normative data:* American Psychological Association.

White, R., Gumley, A., McTaggart, J., Rattrie, L., McConville, D., Cleare, S., & Mitchell, G. (2011). A feasibility study of Acceptance and Commitment Therapy for emotional dysfunction following psychosis. *Behavioural Research Therapy, 49*(12), 901–907.

White, R. G., & Gumley, A. I. (2009). Postpsychotic posttraumatic stress disorder: Associations with fear of recurrence and intolerance of uncertainty. *Journal of Nervous Mental Disorders, 197*(11), 841–849.

10

COGNITIVE ANALYTIC THERAPY (CAT) FOR PSYCHOSIS

Contrasts and parallels with attachment theory
and implications for practice

Peter James Taylor and Claire Seddon

Introduction

Cognitive Analytic Therapy (CAT) is a widely used, integrative model of psychotherapy which draws upon psychoanalytic (particularly object relations) theory, social developmental theory, cognitive approaches and personal construct theory (Ryle, 2004; Ryle & Kerr, 2002). Key characteristics of the CAT approach, which differentiate it from other therapeutic models in common use such as Cognitive Behavioural Therapy, includes its focus on a dialogical construction of the self and how patterns of relating to the self and others come to be repeated over time (Ryle, 2001, 2012; Ryle & Kerr, 2002). These two characteristics may also sound familiar to anyone with an understanding of attachment theory. The CAT model therefore seems to have many similarities with the principles of attachment theory, but important differences also exist. The preceding chapters have already made a strong case for the importance of attachment theory in psychosis. Whilst the use of CAT has often been in the context of neurotic and personality disorders (Calvert & Kellett, in 2014), there is a growing consideration of CAT as an intervention for individuals with experiences of psychosis, both within the UK (Kerr, Birkett, & Chanen, 2003; Kerr, Crowley, & Beard, 2006; Perry, 2012; Taylor et al., 2015) and elsewhere (Gleeson et al., 2012). Consequently, it is timely to consider the CAT approach to psychosis and how this contrasts with a purely attachment theory perspective. The aim of the current chapter is to explore some of the parallels and differences between CAT and attachment theory within the context of psychosis. We will: a) outline the key similarities and differences between CAT and attachment theory in explaining the difficulties associated with psychosis, b) consider areas of integration in working with psychosis, and c) provide a clinical case example of using CAT with an individual with experiences of psychosis.

A brief overview of CAT

CAT is a psychotherapy model developed within the UK by Anthony Ryle in the 1980s (Ryle & Kerr, 2002). The model was in part influenced by Ryle's experiences as a general practitioner and the commonalities in the difficulties experienced by his clients. The model was further informed through Ryle's later research and work as a psychotherapist. CAT was developed with the aim of fitting into the context of the National Health Service (NHS) in the UK and for this reason was designed to be time-limited (typically 16 sessions).

The model underlying CAT is essentially developmental, focusing on how patterns of relating to others and oneself develop and become internalised over the course of an individual's life (Denman, 2001; Ryle & Kerr, 2002). These internalised structures, called Reciprocal Roles (RRs), are believed to play an important role in guiding how individuals perceive and respond to the world around them, including how they interact with others. As an example, imagine a child with a critical parent. Through the child's early life there is an ongoing interaction or dialogue with this parent, characterised by the message that they have let the parent down, are not good enough and should try harder. The child on their part reacts with submissiveness and feelings of failure. Two inter-linked roles can be delineated here; a criticising, judging parent and a submissive, criticised child. Over time the child internalises this on-going dialogue, as this conversation continues within their mind. This RR will influence how this individual acts as an adult. A romantic partner highlights a concern (e.g., a missed anniversary), and the Criticising/judging to Criticised/submissive RR is reactivated. The partner comes to be seen as criticising and judging (even though the partner's remarks were not meant this way) and the individual experiences the same feelings of failure (even though they may not seem proportional to this current scenario by others), and the same submissiveness emerges. Thus, the first implication of RRs is that they inform the way individuals interpret and respond to others. A second implication, though, is that RRs can also shape the reactions of others. Notably, in this example the strong reaction and submissiveness are likely to frustrate the partner, who expects a proactive attempt to rectify the issues. Over time we can imagine a difficult dynamic emerging between individual and partner, with the partner becoming increasingly frustrated with the way this individual responds to criticism. Ultimately, the partner's responses may become more punitive and critical, and thus the individual in essence recreates the earlier relationship with his parent.

RRs can be understood as representing specific aspects of the self or states, a particular way of feeling, thinking and acting, each capturing a particular relational dynamic. For example, an RR of 'Abused and powerless' in relation to 'Abusive and controlling' may be apparent for someone with a history of abuse. It is assumed that healthy individuals move fluidly between a wide variety of RRs. However, in the context of psychological and emotional difficulties, one or more dominant and unhelpful RRs (possibly tied to particular adverse relationships) may exert an undue influence. A person may experience either pole of an RR at different times, for example sometimes feeling powerless but at other times becoming controlling. Different RRs become embedded in particular patterns of aim-directed action referred to as 'procedures' (Reciprocal Role Procedures or RRPs). These are chains of thoughts, feelings and behaviours. For example, in response to an RR of 'Not good enough' in relation to 'Superior and judging', an individual may feel that to talk with others at a social event would risk evaluation, and so react by avoiding eye contact or others' company. This could lead to different reactions from others, including further 'Superior and judging' behaviour, illustrating the cyclical nature of RRPs.

CAT is a fundamentally dialogical model. This 'dialogical' stance essentially refers to the way in which people are continually engaged in dialogue not only with others, but also an ongoing inner dialogue with themselves (Ryle, 2001). CAT therefore emphasises how RRs may feature in a number of different forms of relating, both interpersonally (self to other; other to self) and intrapersonally (self to self). This latter phenomenon includes self-critical or punishing dialogues with oneself. Not all RRs are maladaptive or negative; for example, 'Supportive' in relation to 'Supported and understood' may reflect an exchange between friends or even an intrapersonal process of comforting oneself after a difficult day. The goal of CAT is often to work towards creating and making use of these 'healthier' RRs. A further goal of CAT is to develop the client's awareness of the problematic patterns that occur in their lives, developing what is known in CAT as the "observing 'I'" (Denman, 2001).

CAT is a collaborative, relational therapy carried out within a predetermined time limit (typically 16 sessions). It involves weekly sessions that progress through three broad phases, *Reformulation, Recognition* and *Revision*. The reformulation phase follows a process of working with the client to help them identify and understand dysfunctional patterns of relating to others and self. This involves the identification of key RRs and an understanding of the processes that maintain these relational patterns (RRPs). The focus is specifically on developing the narrative for understanding how relational experiences (particularly early relationships) continue to influence current patterns of relating. The structure of CAT therapy supports this process with the creation of a pictorial representation of these key patterns (known as a Sequential Diagrammatic Reformulation; SDR) and a letter, which offers a narrative description. The Recognition phase works on developing recognition of the key patterns before the Revision phase, which involves working towards revision of a healthier pattern of relating. Through the therapist's countertransference CAT explicitly uses the therapy relationship to identify and understand enactments of key RRPs within the sessions. Within CAT countertransference is understood as individuals experiencing one pole of an

RR then inducing feelings associated with the opposite pole of this RR in others (Ryle & Kerr, 2002). An example would be the hostility and criticism felt by the partner in our example of an RR, above. The therapist aims to avoid reinforcing and colluding with dysfunctional RRPs.

CAT and psychosis

The literature on the application of CAT to psychosis is currently relatively limited, although developing. A number of case studies illustrate how CAT can be applied to individuals with experiences of psychosis (Kerr, 2001; Kerr et al., 2003; Kerr et al., 2006; Margison, 2005; Perry, 2012). Further evidence of the acceptability and feasibility of this model comes from a pilot randomised trial of CAT for bipolar disorder (Evans & Kellett, 2014), and a pilot randomised trial of a multi-component intervention based around CAT for individuals with co-morbid early psychosis and personality disorder difficulties (Gleeson et al., 2012).

A CAT-based model of psychosis has emerged (Kerr et al., 2003). The model proposes that psychotic phenomena, even when seemingly incomprehensible, relate to "disordered or distorted enactments" of underlying RRPs and a lack of integration between aspects of the self (Kerr et al., 2006). In this sense there is a shared understanding of psychosis with other non-psychotic mental health difficulties, whereby the internalisation of a repertoire of maladaptive RRPs is used as a framework to understand the individual's experiences and difficulties. Within CAT, internalised voices are viewed as normal phenomena from a dialogic perspective with psychosis-like-experiences seen as an extreme version of being 'out of dialogue' both internally and externally for the individual with these otherwise normal phenomena (Falchi, 2007). An example of this would be someone misattributing internal dialogue to an external source. The consequences of these enactments of RRPs may be a form of 'internal expressed emotion' that can be highly distressing to the individual (e.g., a critical or controlling voice) and may mirror experiences of external expressed emotion in the outside world (Kerr et al., 2003).

Comparing and contrasting CAT and attachment theory

Parallels

In terms of their historical influences, both CAT and attachment theory (Bowlby, 1969, 1973, 1980) have their origins to some extent in object relations theory. Attachment theory originated with Bowlby bringing together the ideas of object relations theory and evolutionary theory with the methodological insights of ethology (Holmes, 1993). Likewise the central concept of RRs in CAT was heavily influenced by object relations theory (Ryle, 1991, 2004). CAT also makes reference to evolutionary drives, recognising that infants are predisposed to seeking social and emotional engagement with others (Ryle, 2004; Ryle & Kerr, 2002). This suggestion clearly mirrors the idea in attachment theory that humans carry an evolved drive for proximity seeking, which manifests from a young age (Ainsworth, 1979).

Attachment theory and CAT both provide an explanation of psychotic experiences that emphasises the impact of social and interpersonal factors. Interpersonal trauma appears to be a major influence in the development of psychosis for many individuals (Read, van Os, Morrison, & Ross, 2005; Varese et al., 2012). Attachment theory has provided one framework for understanding how early interpersonal experiences may become internalised and subsequently contribute to an individual's risk of difficulties such as psychosis (e.g., Sitko et al., 2014). Likewise, CAT emphasises how the formation of disordered RRs is a socially mediated process, where early neglectful, hostile or abusive relationships are likely to be a major influence.

Both CAT and attachment theory emphasise the role of mediating internalised relational structures in determining how individuals relate to others and the self. Attachment theory has Internal Working Models (IWM; Bretherton & Munholland, 1999) whilst CAT refers to RRs. The similarity between CAT and attachment theory can be illustrated by considering how certain attachment patterns could also be understood as specific sets of RRs and associated procedures. Figure 10.1, for example, provides a hypothetical, simplified SDR for a client with a dismissing attachment style who experiences voices. In this example the individual adopts a dismissing strategy

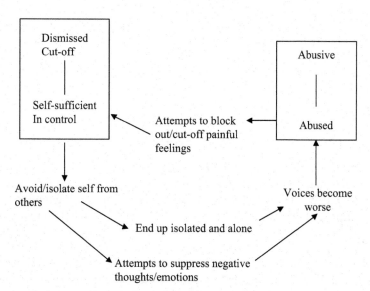

Figure 10.1 A hypothetical Sequential Diagrammatic Reformulation of a client with a dismissing attachment

(characterised by the 'Self-sufficient/in control' in relation to 'Dismissed/cut-off' RR) as a means of avoiding an intolerably painful RR of 'Abused' to 'Abusive'. This dismissing strategy has the unfortunate consequence of leaving the individual isolated and cut-off from others, which exacerbates his voices. Attempts to suppress painful feelings, also associated with the dismissing RR, exacerbate the voices. These voices reflect the avoided, painful RR, and so further maintain the dismissing strategy.

The putative interpersonal nature of the internalised structures in both CAT and attachment theory is consistent with the observation that many psychotic symptoms tend to be interpersonal in nature. Relationships with voices (or auditory hallucinations), for example, carry many of the characteristics of interpersonal relationships, including elements of reciprocity (Hayward, Berry, & Ashton, 2011; Hayward, Berry, McCarthy-Jones, Strauss, & Thomas, 2014). Similarly, paranoia may relate to interpersonal attribution processes (Bentall et al.,1994). Collerton and Dudley (2004) describe the case of a woman experiencing visual hallucinations of her deceased husband, who was abusive towards her, and imbuing the hallucination with the same relational qualities of fear and hostility.

Both models also provide a framework for making sense of difficult interpersonal relationships. Research has identified preliminary evidence of a negative association between attachment security and the level of expressed emotion engaged in by relatives (see review by Berry et al.,2007). Within CAT prominent, dysfunctional interpersonal dynamics may reflect in part the enactment of dominant RRPs. For example, the 'Self-sufficient/in control' in relation to 'Dismissed/cut-off' RR from the example above (see Figure 10.1) may lead to attempts to avoid support or input from relatives (or clinical services) who may become frustrated when their efforts to help are rejected and themselves feel dismissed or disregarded. It is also worth noting that where relatives are a client's parents or caregivers, they will have had a major role in shaping the client's RRPs and so inter-generational patterns of interpersonal difficulties would be expected.

Points of difference

Whilst some have emphasised the overlap between CAT and attachment theory (Jellema, 1999, 2000, 2002), others have notably challenged this position (Ryle, 1995, 2000b; Ryle & Kerr, 2002). An important difference has been the attempt to classify internalised structures. Within attachment theory there is an emphasis on delineating distinct patterns or categories of attachment style. Traditionally a categorical approach has been adopted, as reflected in instruments such as the Adult Attachment Interview (AAI) whereby an individual may be classified as being secure, preoccupied, dismissing or unresolved (George et al., 1996). The validity of this categorical model of attachment has been questioned (Fraley & Spieker, 2003), and more flexible dimensional approaches have been developed such as Brennan and colleagues identification of underlying avoidant and anxious adult attachment continua (Brennan et al.,1998), or similarly, Crittenden's (2006) specification of a continuum of increasingly severe avoidant and anxious/dismissing strategies. In contrast, within CAT the repertoire of reciprocal roles an individual has may vary substantially from client to client, and the therapist will often seek to develop idiosyncratic labels for particular reciprocal roles with a client. These differences are understandable in context of the different aims of CAT and attachment theory (a psychotherapy versus a research endeavour) and so criticisms that attachment theory lacks a 'coherent clinical method' are perhaps unfair considering this has not been the primary aim of attachment theory (Jellema, 2001; Ryle, 2000a). CAT may actually provide a fruitful clinical framework through which the conclusions of attachment theory can be applied, as we discuss further in the next section.

Ryle (1995) has argued that IWMs fundamentally differ to RRs. He states that IWM rely on cognitivist assumptions, where a child carries a mental representation (akin to software on a computer) of their attachment figure and the way their attachment figure sees them. In contrast, Ryle argues that RRs derive more from Vygotskian and Bakhtinian ideas, and capture the ongoing dialogue between the attachment figure and child, which begins as an external process but continues within the child through a process of internalisation. One related criticism of attachment theory levelled by Ryle (1995) was that it understates the importance of ongoing, *joint* (dialogic) interaction between infant and caregiver, and the formation and use of shared signs (e.g., language) in an individual's development. CAT assumes that the meanings an individual places upon the world are elaborated through interpersonal interaction, but also through the influence of the wider social and cultural context. This issue has relevance for psychosis, as the way we define many psychotic symptoms is heavily culturally bounded. Delusions, in particular, are often defined as being in some way bizarre, unusual or inconsistent with normal cultural expectations (Morrison, 2001). It has been suggested that Ryle's (1995) earlier criticisms of attachment theory are less relevant to newer variants of attachment theory where, for example, the ongoing, bi-directional nature of child-caregiver interactions is more recognised (Jellema, 1999, 2002). Similarly, theorists have more recently applied a cultural lens when considering attachment (see Chapter 12 in this book).

CAT and attachment theory have increasingly converged as they have developed (Jellema, 1999, 2002). CAT initially focused on the common patterns of relating to others that clients often became stuck in, but the idea that social experiences could be internalised and inform later relational behaviour through the formation of RRs developed later and became an increasing focus of the model. Similarly, as attachment theory has developed there has been an increasing focus on the internalisation of attachment patterns and the recognition that different patterns of attachment may form with different individuals. In the context of psychosis, where biomedical explanations have historically been dominant, attachment theory and CAT, with their emphasis on socially-mediated formation of psychological difficulties, appear to have more points of commonality than difference.

How CAT offers an attachment based therapy for psychosis

Schwannauer and Gumley (2014) argue that five elements are essential in therapeutic work with people experiencing psychosis to re-orientate attachment-related behaviours (collaboration, reflective dialogue, repair, coherent narratives, emotional communication). These five elements originated from the work of Siegel (2001) who was concerned with identifying how caregivers can foster a secure attachment in children within their care. We will present the argument that CAT offers these essential elements.

Collaboration

Siegel (2001) describes collaboration as an attuned communication between two individuals, with each individual being directly responsive to the other in quality and timing. He emphasises the importance of non-verbal communication to allow the joining of two minds at a basic level of 'primary' emotions. The strong relational focus within the therapy dialogue (on both inter and intrapersonal communication) ensures CAT therapy is a collaborative venture between the client and therapist. The therapist remains alert to shifts in the therapy relationship, and dynamics within this relationship are actively reflected upon both developing the reformulation (e.g., identifying RRs) and in working to revise it (e.g., therapist avoiding collusion with RRs that are playing out in therapy). The therapy relationship therefore plays a major role in assisting change.

Reflective dialogue

This process involves the verbal sharing of internal experiences, which can promote the development of an internal representation of the mind of self and others (Siegel, 2001). In CAT therapy this would involve the therapist recognising signals (e.g., changes in emotion or behaviour, such as a client suddenly becoming more distressed) from the client and attempting to build an understanding of these signals to allow the client to develop new meanings. This could lead to enhanced recognition of previously dismissed affect or cognitive understandings, depending on the individual's attachment style. The former more likely with a dismissing attachment style, the letter with a pre-occupied attachment style (Crittenden, 2006). Within CAT the use of RRs, the sharing of transference and countertransference observations within the therapy dialogue and the emphasis on the development of an 'observing I' supports the notion of building this reflective capacity.

Repair

At times there will be inevitable disconnections in attuned communication. The process of repair allows for healing, and learning that connections can be recreated and that rejection is not inevitable following a disconnection. CAT is a relational therapy, which actively uses the therapeutic relationship to further the client's awareness of his or her relational patterns. Within CAT the therapist would be active in identifying ruptures within the therapy relationship that could threaten the therapeutic alliance. These ruptures are viewed as enactments of the dysfunctional patterns, in which both therapist and client are active participants. The aim for the therapist within CAT is to avoid colluding with the familiar RRPs and instead to respond from a different position, thus working with the client to provide opportunities to revise the RRP, by experiencing a different relational response.

Coherent narratives

Autobiographical self-awareness is created through a narrative that connects past, present and future. This constructs a meaningful reality from which to understand the self and world (Siegel, 2001). Within CAT the process of reformulation links historical experiences to current difficulties. The client has an opportunity to develop a narrative that through the therapy identifies relational patterns that began in childhood and continue in the present. CAT intervention may focus on building awareness of previously neglected aspects of the client's experiences. For clients with insecure attachment patterns this can expand their understanding of the links between past and present to add greater meaning and develop a more coherent narrative. Tools such as the reformulation letter help strengthen this new narrative.

The experience of psychosis can be very frightening and at times feel incomprehensible. Therefore, building an understanding of why an individual has experienced psychosis seems essential. A key aim of a CAT intervention for psychosis would be to support a client to get back into dialogue with themselves, with particular focus on the 'self-stressful' RRPs, which create 'internal expressed emotion' (Kerr et al., 2003).

Emotional communication

Siegel (2001) argues that remaining interpersonally connected at times of heightened emotions is important to the development of a positive sense of self. The experience of abandonment (or indeed other problematic emotional responses such as anger) at times of emotional distress when growing up can prevent opportunities for soothing, which provide a template for self-soothing in later life (Cassidy, 1994). Individuals with a dismissing insecure attachment style may have had to learn to ignore emotional distress, resulting in unresolved feelings. Equally individuals with a preoccupied attachment style may feel consumed by unresolved feelings.

Within CAT the therapist would support the client through the expression of difficult emotions, allowing space for clients to express these feelings but also working at a level that is tolerable to the client. Depending on the individual's attachment style this could guide interventions to focus on the area they have previously been defended against. Individuals with a preoccupied attachment strategy may have learnt to exaggerate (though not necessarily in a conscious way) their feelings to get their needs met (Mikulincer et al.,2009). Interventions for this group may focus on developing their cognitive understanding, such as understanding the actions that lead to movements between RRs. Individuals with a dismissing attachment style may have learnt to feel safe by distorting or falsifying affect (as a means of inhibiting affect) and becoming more self-reliant. Interventions for these individuals may need to work on re-connecting with unresolved feelings (Crittenden, 2006; Jellema, 1999).

Clinical case example

The application of CAT for psychosis-type experiences can vary, so that whilst the focus may sometimes be on specific psychotic experiences at other times the focus may be more around self-worth or acceptance. In all cases the understanding of clients' difficulties in terms of underlying relational patterns or RRs and RRPs is central. Whilst terminology may differ, this focus on a relational understanding of clients' difficulties coincides with the way attachment-based therapies would seek to understand clients.

Lisa[1] had a long history of hearing two tormenting, critical voices. She also believed that she was being tracked by people in her local area via mobile phones, although her levels of conviction varied considerably. Generally, she found it difficult to trust others. She was a single mother and maintained her home but struggled to ensure that her son attended school consistently, relying on family support to care for her son at times. Lisa received the support of an early intervention service following admission to a psychiatric hospital. She identified wanting to trust and connect more with others and improving her self-esteem as areas she would like to work on in therapy.

CAT began with the reformulation phase, whereby the focus was on identifying those relational patterns underlying Lisa's difficulties. Lisa reported that her parents had a volatile relationship, separating when she was aged seven years. Lisa described her mother as dominating and controlling, leaving her feeling powerless and not listened to or valued. In contrast, Lisa felt doted upon by her father, but with the expectation that she had to be perfect. In both

170

instances Lisa felt unable to be herself. She learned to manage her parents' expectations by trying to please them through being compliant and hiding her true feelings, striving to be 'good' and 'keep the peace'. This bottling up of feelings and memories led to a great deal of stress, which Lisa likened to having a grenade inside her.

Subsequent experiences of sexual abuse occurring outside the family contributed to Lisa's strong need to feel safe and her distrust of others. As a result of this, Lisa was very wary of people and would scrutinise their actions for any evidence that they were dishonest or had the potential to be abusive. This became pervasive, leading Lisa to believe that all mobile phone use was related to others tracking her, although she did not know why. Lisa's distrust of others further reinforced her tendency to hide her real feelings.

Lisa's assessment led to her difficulties being understood in terms of a negative IWM of both her self (not good enough) and others (abusive or controlling), consistent with a fearful avoidant attachment (Bartholomew & Horowitz, 1991). Linked to this were particular behavioural strategies including compliance and emotional suppression or avoidance. The CAT reformulation captured these IWMs and associated strategies, but also allowed a more nuanced representation of these interpersonal patterns. For example, the reformulation was able to distinguish between Lisa's Controlling to Powerless RR and her Doting to Special Perfect RR. The SDR for Lisa is presented in Figure 10.2. Lisa was fearful of her voices and did not wish to discuss them in therapy. This could be seen as a further manifestation of Lisa's emotional avoidance, again consistent with a fearful avoidant attachment.

The next stage of therapy focused on the recognition of those patterns that were hypothesised to underlie Lisa's difficulties. Through this practice, Lisa became increasingly able to identify when she was becoming suspicious of others, and why (though at times Lisa's suspiciousness was so intense it became difficult for her to reflect on her experiences). Lisa also became more aware of her inner dialogue, particularly the interplay of thoughts and feelings, which reinforced her suspiciousness and the sense of feeling 'not good enough', which led to her hiding her true feelings.

The revision stage of therapy focuses on the identification of exits orstrategies for revising the problematic relational patters that exist. Within both CAT and attachment theory, the relevance of Lisa's unresolved or avoided emotions, described metaphorically by Lisa as a grenade, would be emphasised (e.g., Jellema, 1999). Reconnecting with memories and feelings from childhood was thus a focus of the work with Lisa. Attachment theory supports the suggestion in the formulation that reconnecting with unresolved or avoided emotions would be emotionally challenging for Lisa. As expected, reconnecting with these childhood memories and feelings was an extremely difficult period within the therapy for Lisa. Given that Lisa expected to be ignored, punished and crushed for being herself and talking about her

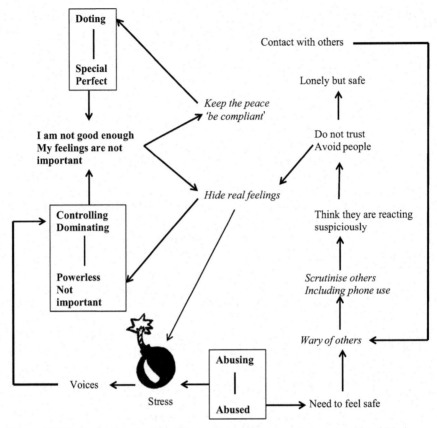

Figure 10.2 Simplified SDR for Lisa. Text in bold could be viewed as components of Lisa's IWM, whilst text in italics could be understood as attachment-related strategies.

feelings, the therapy and support of the wider team at this time focused on emotionally supporting Lisa to feel safe. This was achieved by listening, and explicitly providing positive reinforcement for disclosure of personal information and feelings. This could be likened to the therapist and team providing a secure base for Lisa, during this difficult time. Lisa's attachment to the therapist was important to the success of the therapy (e.g., Taylor et al., 2015b), and this could also be further conceptualised as the adaptive RR Lisa was developing with the therapist (e.g., Supported/heard to Supportive/listening). However the transition to developing more adaptive RRs is a process and it is to be expected that the client will on occasion fall back into relating to the therapist from the familiar RR positions (e.g., experiencing the therapist as controlling). The potential for this will have been highlighted in the therapy letter and when it happens it will be named and discussed in the therapy as it provides a further learning opportunity.

The therapy appeared helpful in reducing Lisa's suspiciousness. Whilst Lisa remained wary of others, she became better able to recognise and manage her fearful inner dialogue. Over time, Lisa was able to see her suspiciousness as a product of her own difficulties around trust. This in turn meant Lisa was able to become less preoccupied with other people's motives and would instead draw on her new strategies for keeping herself safe, such as accepting care from others and learning to self-soothe. Lisa also began to relate differently to her parents, speaking her mind and not falling into her old pattern of compliance with their wishes. Whilst Lisa's mother remained critical, Lisa learned that the world did not end when she asserted herself. The process of understanding why and how she related to her parents and others in the way she did, and the focus on developing alternative ways of relating helped Lisa to achieve this.

Although Lisa's voices were not the focus of therapy, Lisa experienced a change here, with one voice changing from critical to supportive. Overall, Lisa's relationship with her voices changed. CAT would understand this as suggesting a shift in an underlying RR towards becoming less dominant, but it may also be helpful to think about Lisa's voices as a manifestation of her attachment patterns (e.g., an expectation of being criticised or controlled). Lisa became less fearful and avoidant of her voices, and found ways for them to be functional for her. Lisa began to explore whether the voices represented her own unspoken feelings. This new understanding of her voices was highly normalising for Lisa.

Conclusions

Within this chapter argued that attachment theory and CAT carry many similarities, and that CAT provides one vehicle by which the ideas contained within attachment theory can be implemented and built upon within therapeutic work in psychosis. It is possible to consider RRs as more specific, idiographic descriptions of broader attachment patterns. However, there are also ways in which a better understanding of attachment theory, and integration of attachment theory into practice, can help inform the CAT approach to psychosis (Jellema, 1999, 2000B, 2002). The particular patterns delineated within attachment theory can provide a useful framework for understanding a client's difficulties and so help facilitate the process of reformulation within CAT. Moreover, the extensive research around attachment theory can, in turn, provide insights into the possible links these patterns have with particular early experiences and subsequent psychotic experiences (e.g., Sitko et al., 2014). Research also helps inform the therapist how the client's way of relating may affect therapy (e.g., impact upon working alliance; Taylor, Rietzschel, Danquah, & Berry, 2015a) and be affected by therapy (e.g., likelihood of therapy changing an attachment pattern; (Taylor et al., 2015b). Attachment theory also provides a number of validated tools and instruments that can further inform therapeutic work (Jellema, 1999). In summary, we believe CAT and attachment theory have much to learn and gain from each other in understanding the difficulties faced by those with psychosis.

Acknowledgement

We would like to acknowledge Dr Anna Jellema for her helpful feedback on an earlier draft of this chapter.

Note

1 Lisa is an amalgamation of two real word cases, combined to help maintain the anonymity of the individuals involved.

References

Ainsworth, M. S. (1979). Infant–mother attachment. *American Psychologist, 34*(10), 932–937. doi: 10.1037/0003-066X.34.10.932

Bartholomew, K., & Horowitz. L. M. (1991). Attachment styles among young adults: A test of a four-category model. *Journal of Personality and Social Psychology, 61,* 226–244. doi: 10.1017/S0033291714002633

Bentall, R. P., Kinderman, P., & Kaney, S. (1994). The self, attributional processes and abnormal beliefs: Towards a model of persecutory delusions. *Behaviour Research and Therapy, 32*(3), 331–341. doi: http://dx.doi.org/10.1016/0005-7967(94)90131-7

Berry, K., Barrowclough, C., & Wearden, A. (2007). A review of the role of adult attachment style in psychosis: Unexplored issues and questions for further research. *Clinical Psychology Review, 27*(4), 458–475. doi: http://dx.doi.org/10.1016/j.cpr.2006.09.006

Brennan, K. A., Clark, C. L., & Shaver, P. R. (1998). Self-report measurement of adult attachment: An integrative overview. In J. A. Simpson & W. S. Rholes (Eds.), *Attachment Theory and Close Relationships* (pp. 46–76). New York: Guilford Press.

Bretherton, I., & Munholland, K. A. (1999). Internal working models in attachment relationships: Elaborating a central construct in attachment theory. In J. Cassidy & P. R. Shaver (Eds.), *Handbook of Attachment: Theory, research, and clinical applications* (pp. 89–114). New York: The Guilford Press.

Bowlby J. (1969). *Attachment and Loss, Volume 1: Attachment.* New York: Basic Books.

Bowlby J. (1973). *Attachment and Loss, Volume 2: Separation: Anxiety and Anger.* New York: Basic Books.

Bowlby J. (1980). *Attachment and Loss, Volume 3: Loss: Sadness and Depression.* New York: Basic Books.

Calvert, R., & Kellett, S. (2014). Cognitive analytic therapy: A review of the outcome evidence base for treatment. *Psychology & Psychotherapy: Theory, research & practice, 87,* 253–277. doi: 10.1111/papt.12020

Cassidy, J. (1994). Emotion regulation: Influence of attachment relationships. *Monographs of the Society for Research in Child Development, 59*(2–3), 228–249. doi: 10.1111/j.1540–5834.1994.tb01287.x

Collerton, D., Perry, E., & McKeith, I. (2005). Why people see things that are not there: A novel perception and attention deficit model for recurrent complex visual hallucinations. *Behavioral and Brain Sciences, 28*(06), 737–757. doi: 10.1017/S0140525X05000130

Crittenden, P. M. (2006). A dynamic-maturational model of attachment. *Australian and New Zealand Journal of Family Therapy, 27*(2), 105–115. doi: 10.1002/j.1467-8438.2006.tb00704.x

Denman, C. (2001). Cognitive–analytic therapy. *Advances in Psychiatric Treatment, 7*(4), 243–252. doi: 10.1192/apt.7.4.243

Evans, M., & Kellett, S. (2014). *RCT in CAT and bipolar disorder.* Paper presented at the ACAT Annual National Conference Liverpool.

Falchi, V. (2007). Using CAT in an assertive outreach team: A reflection on current issues. *Reformulation, summer,* 11–17. Retrieved from www.acat.me.uk/reformulation.php?issue_id=9&article_id=153

Fraley, R. C., & Spieker, S. J. (2003). Are infant attachment patterns continuously or categorically distributed? A taxometric analysis of strange situation behavior. *Developmental Psychology, 39,* 387–404. doi: 10.1037/0012-1649.39.3.387

George, C., Kaplan, N., & Main, M. (1996). *Adult Attachment Interview protocol* (3rd ed.). University of California at Berkeley: Unpublished manuscript.

Gleeson, J. F. M., Chanen, A., Cotton, S. M., Pearce, T., Newman, B., & McCutcheon, L. (2012). Treating co-occurring first-episode psychosis and borderline personality: A pilot randomized controlled trial. *Early Intervention in Psychiatry, 6*(1), 21–29. doi: 10.1111/j.1751-7893.2011.00306.x

Hayward, M., Berry, K., & Ashton, A. (2011). Applying interpersonal theories to the understanding of and therapy for auditory hallucinations: A review of the literature and directions for further research. *Clinical Psychology Review, 31*(8), 1313–1323. doi: 10.1016/j.cpr.2011.09.001

Hayward, M., Berry, K., McCarthy-Jones, S., Strauss, C., & Thomas, N. (2014). Beyond the omnipotence of voices: Further developing a relational approach to auditory hallucinations. *Psychosis, 6*(3), 242–252. doi: 10.1080/17522439.2013.839735

Holmes, J. (1993). Attachment theory: A biological basis for psychotherapy? *The British Journal of Psychiatry, 163*(4), 430–438. doi: 10.1192/bjp.163.4.430

Jellema, A. (1999). Cognitive analytic therapy: Developing its theory and practice via attachment theory. *Clinical Psychology & Psychotherapy, 6*(1), 16–28. doi: 10.1002/(SICI)1099-0879(199902)6:1<16::AID-CPP182>3.0.CO;2-N

Jellema, A. (2000). Insecure attachment states: Their relationship to borderline and narcissistic personality disorders and treatment process in cognitive analytic therapy. *Clinical Psychology & Psychotherapy, 7*(2), 138–154. doi: 10.1002/(SICI)1099-0879(200005)7:2<138::AID-CPP231>3.0.CO;2-9

Jellema, A. (2001). CAT and attachment theory: A reply to Tony Ryle. *Reformulation, ACAT News Autumn.*

Jellema, A. (2002). Dismissing and preoccupied insecure attachment and procedures in CAT: Some implications for CAT practice. *Clinical Psychology & Psychotherapy, 9*(4), 225–241. doi: 10.1002/cpp.310

Kerr, I. B. (2001). Brief cognitive analytic therapy for post-acute manic psychosis on a psychiatric intensive care unit. *Clinical Psychology & Psychotherapy, 8*(2), 117–129. doi: 10.1002/cpp.251

Kerr, I. B., Birkett, P. B., & Chanen, A. (2003). Clinical and service implications of a cognitive analytic therapy model of psychosis. *Australia & New Zealand Journal of Psychiatry, 37*(5), 515–523.

Kerr, I. B., Crowley, V., & Beard, H. (2006). A cognitive analytic therapy-based approach to psychotic disorder. In J. O. Johannessen, B. V. Martindale & J. Cullberg (Eds.), *Evolving Psychosis* (pp. 172–184). London: ISPS.

Margison, F. (2005). Integrating approaches to psychotherapy in psychosis. *Australian and New Zealand Journal of Psychiatry, 39*, 972–981. doi: 10.1111/j.1440-1614.2005.01715.x

Mikulincer, M., Shaver, P. R., Cassidy, J., & Berant, E. (2009). Attachment-related defensive processes. In J. H. Obegi & E. Berant (Eds.), *Attachment Theory and Research in Clinical Work with Adults.* New York: The Guilford Press.

Morrison, A. P. (2001). The interpertation of intrusions in psychosis: An integrative cognitive approach to hallucination and delusions. *Behavioural and Cognitive Psychotherapy, 29*(03), 257–276. doi: doi:10.1017/S1352465801003010

Perry, A. (2012). CAT with people who hear distressing voices. *Reformulation, Summer,* 16–22.

Read, J., van Os, J., Morrison, A. P., & Ross, C. A. (2005). Childhood trauma, psychosis and schizophrenia: A literature review with theoretical and clinical implications. *Acta Psychiatrica Scandinavica, 112*(5), 330–350. doi: 10.1111/j.1600-0447.2005.00634.x

Ryle, A. (1991). Object relations theory and activity theory: A proposed link by way of the procedural sequence model. *British Journal of Medical Psychology, 64,* 307–316.

Ryle, A. (1995). Holmes on Bowlby and the future of psychotherapy: A response. *British Journal of Psychotherapy, 170,* 82–87.

Ryle, A. (2000a). Attachment theory and cognitivism. *Reformulation, ACAT News Autumn.*

Ryle, A. (2000b). CAT, attachment theory and cognitivism. *Reformulation, 8.*

Ryle, A. (2001). CAT's dialogic perspective on the self. *Reformulation, Autumn.*

Ryle, A. (2004). The contribution of cognitive analytic therapy to the treatment of borderline personality disorder. *Journal of Personality Disorders, 18*(1), 3–35.

Ryle, A. (2012). Critique of CBT and CAT by Dr Anthony Ryle. In E. W. McCormick (Ed.), *Change for the Better: Self-help through practical psychotherapy* (4th ed.). London: SAGE publications.

Ryle, A., & Kerr, I. B. (2002). *Introducing Cognitive Analytic Therapy: Principles and practice.* Oxford: Wiley-Blackwell.

Schwannauer, M., & Gumley, A. I. (2014). Attachment theory and psychosis. In A. N. Danquah & K. Berry (Eds.), *Attachment Theory in Adult Mental Health: A guide to clinical practice* (pp. 63–77). Abingdon: Routledge.

Siegel, D. J. (2001). Toward an interpersonal neurobiology of the developing mind: Attachment relationships, "mindsight," and neural integration. *Infant Mental Health Journal, 22,* 67–94. doi: 10.1002/1097-0355(200101/04)22:1 <67::AID-IMHJ3>3.0.CO;2-G

Sitko, K., Bentall, R. P., Shevlin, M., O'Sullivan, N., & Sellwood, W. (2014). Associations between specific psychotic symptoms and specific childhood adversities are mediated by attachment styles: an analysis of the National Comorbidity Survey. *Psychiatry Research, 217*(3), 202–209. doi: 10.1016/j.psychres.2014.03.019

Taylor, P. J., Perry, A., Hutton, P., Seddon, C., & Tan, R. (2015). Curiosity and the CAT: Considering cognitive analytic therapy as an intervention for psychosis. *Psychosis, 7*, 276–278. doi: 10.1080/17522439.2014.956785

Taylor, P. J., Rietzschel, J., Danquah, A. N., & Berry, K. (2015b). Changes in attachment representations during psychological therapy. *Psychotherapy Research, 25*, 222–238. doi: 10.1080/10503307.2014.886791

Taylor, P. J., Rietzschel, J., Danquah, A. N., & Berry, K. (2015a). The role of attachment style, attachment to therapist and working alliance in response to psychological therapy *Psychology and Psychotherapy: Theory, research and practice, 88*, 240–253. doi: 10.1111/papt.12045.

Varese, F., Smeets, F., Drukker, M., Lieverse, R., Lataster, T., Viechtbauer, W., ... Bentall, R. P. (2012). Childhood adversities increase the risk of psychosis: a meta-analysis of patient-control, prospective- and cross-sectional cohort studies. *Schizophrenia Bulletin, 38*(4), 661–671. doi: 10.1093/schbul/sbs050

11

ATTACHMENT THEMES IN COMPASSION-FOCUSED THERAPY (CFT) FOR PSYCHOSIS

Charles Heriot-Maitland and Angela Kennedy

Background to CFT

CFT was originally developed for people with high levels of shame and self-criticism (Gilbert, 2000; Gilbert & Irons, 2005). Such people can find it very difficult to be self-supporting or compassionate, often because they do not have experience of compassionate caregiving from which to draw and learn. CFT helps people develop the capacity for close, affiliative, relationships and to become orientated towards self-reassurance and self-compassion. The theory underpinning CFT suggests that there are three major emotion regulation systems, each with distinct evolutionary functions: threat-protection, drive-excitement and soothing-contentment. The threat system evolved to detect and respond to threats in the world, and the other two are 'positive' affect regulation systems, with one focused on achieving and doing and the other focused on contentment and social soothing. This latter system is believed to play an important role in regulating the threat system. In early attachment relationships, affiliative experiences of parental (or other caregiver) calming will stimulate, develop and integrate the soothing system as a natural regulator of threat. Aversive or inadequate early experiences with caregivers may disrupt this process, making it difficult in adulthood to access any attachment-based resources in the self as a source of integration and regulation.

CFT and psychosis: trauma, attachment and dissociation

In psychosis, people can experience both their external and internal worlds as sources of threat. In terms of the external world, it is well established that experiences of threatening or shaming interpersonal traumas, such as physical, sexual and emotional abuse, can play a causal role in the development of psychosis (Arseneault et al., 2011; Shevlin et al., 2007). Also, criticism and hostility from others is found to be a key predictor of relapse in psychosis (Butzlaff & Hooley, 1998). Unfortunately, traumatic experiences can often become intertwined with attachment relationships (referred to as attachment trauma), where caregivers themselves are either the sources of threat and shaming, or unable to provide protection or nurturing in the context of threat from others. In terms of the internal world, hostile and malevolent voices are often threatening, critical or shaming, whilst paranoia is associated with perceived threat from others. Experiences of voices and paranoia are often compounded by self-criticism and associated feelings of shame.

The empirical and theoretical overlap between trauma, attachment and psychosis has, in recent times, been informed by the dissociation literature. Dell and O'Neil (2009) define dissociation as a partial or complete disruption of the normal integration of a person's psychological functioning. Nijenhuis and van der Hart (2011) use the term 'dissociation' to refer to divisions in the experience of self, with relationships between aspects of self dominated by phobic avoidance of each other and what each represents. Such *structural* accounts of dissociation essentially describe the emergence of dissociated aspects of self when the mind's integrative capacities are overwhelmed by attachment trauma, due to the degree of uncontained and disregulated affect. Hence, a key mechanism underpinning this theory is the suggested breakdown of integrative processes as a result of trauma-related over-arousal of the evolutionary threat system. With reduced integrative capacity, these confusing and contradictory personal experiences can lead to splits in internal representations of self and others.

In structural dissociation terms, voices can be understood as intrusions from split-off components of self (Moskowitz & Corstens, 2008), and, in particular, may often represent some disowned part of self or experience related to a trauma within an attachment relationship (Longden, 2010). Support for this theory comes from findings that voices often share characteristics with a person's abusers (Read, Agar, Argyle, & Aderhold, 2003) and that the kind of internal relationship a person has with their voices often reflects subordination in external attachments with dominating or controlling others (Birchwood, Meaden, Trower, Gilbert, & Plaistow, 2000).

The literature on psychosis and dissociation has focused predominantly on voice-hearing. However, dissociative processes may be equally important in understanding delusions and paranoia. Delusions or paranoia may often be maintained in spite of evidence to the contrary because they can either represent fears that are dissociated from their origins or meaning or attempts to make sense of unusual experiences (Maher, 1974). Paranoia can be understood as a functional response to chronic threat or interpersonal adversity. For example, when Campbell and Morrison (2007) used Interpretative Phenomenology Analysis (IPA; Smith 1996), a qualitative research method which seeks to explore and understand each person's lived experience of phenomena, to analyse 12 interviews about experiences of paranoia, all participants linked their anxiety with negative life experiences. In addition to experiences of persecution or danger, shaming and humiliating experiences are also found to be highly associated with paranoia (Matos, Pinto-Gouveia

& Gilbert, 2013). Shame experiences, which can similarly be understood in terms of threat, i.e. the threat of social rejection and devaluation, can themselves be recorded in the brain as traumatic and can impact on later sense of trust and safety with others. The difference between paranoia and social anxiety is hypothesised to relate to the assumptions the person makes about the intention of the person threatening, shaming or hurting them. If the victim believes that the intention of the other is malevolent, then paranoia can result. In social anxiety, however, the focus is on whether the self is likeable enough to gain social acceptance and not be rejected (Matos, Pinto-Gouveia & Gilbert, 2013).

In psychosis, shame-based threat from internal and external sources can maintain dissociative processes, through the phobic avoidance of aspects of self that shame sets up. This in turn prevents rebuilding of integrative capacities. Recent evidence for the traumatic-like qualities of shame comes from Dorahy et al. (2016), who showed that both external and internal shame can activate dissociative processes. We can therefore see how shame, like other threat experiences in psychosis, will orientate, through evolutionary processes, an individual's information processing and behaviour towards the motive of self-protection, activating automatic safety responses such as avoidance and dissociation.

In CFT terms, Gumley et al. (2010) suggest that threat system sensitisation in psychosis may be related to an underdeveloped soothing system. Soothing is the capacity to self-regulate threat-based emotions such as fear or shame, and is learnt through healthy attachment experiences. In the same way that a threat system will have become vigilant and sensitised through experiences of threatening environments, the development of a soothing system will have been determined by experiences of nurturing and affection. Evidence for self-soothing capacity as a protective factor in psychosis comes from Connor and Birchwood (2013), who studied both self-critical thoughts (a form of internal threat) and self-reassuring capacities (linked to internal soothing) in a sample of voice-hearers. As well as finding that self-critical thoughts of self-hatred and inadequacy were related to appraisals of voice power, which they suggest reflects an underlying perception of low social rank in relation to others; their findings also suggest that capacity to self-reassure, which was linked to less shaming voice content, may be a protective factor for voice-hearers. These findings complement evidence for self-compassion being protective against psychotic symptoms (Eicher, Davis, & Lysaker, 2013); however, since both studies are based on correlational designs, neither can directly imply causation. Nonetheless, as we have seen, there is still a strong theoretical basis for employing interventions that aim to build up capacity in the soothing system. The building of internal resources is a key part of the stabilisation phase of treatment for dissociation (Boon, Steele, & van der Hart, 2011).

CFT for psychosis: key elements

CFT was developed for helping individuals with high levels of shame and internal self-criticism, and one of its core interventions is to help people move out of mentalities or mindsets that focus attention and cognition on the (potentially harmful) power of others (which in CFT are referred to as 'social ranking' mentalities), towards activating cooperative, caring and affiliative processes to self and others. The evolution of attachment in mammals is crucial for understanding our capacity for compassion as attachment and compassion are each linked to evolved motives for care-giving, and each are mutually supportive; just as affiliative and secure attachment experiences will support the types of mental states that are conducive to compassion, compassionate intentions and actions will also foster experiences of affiliation and attachment. CFT aims to engage this broader caring motivational system at each of the biological, psychological and social levels. Generally speaking, a CFT intervention aims to provide contexts, practices and insights that facilitate the development of compassion in self-other, other-self and self-self relationships as has been detailed elsewhere (Gilbert, 2009, 2013, 2014). This section will outline the key elements of a CFT intervention, as applied to working with psychosis. Three of the five main elements (*establish safeness and connection; psycho-education; cultivate / deepen the compassionate self*) will be described generically, but the remaining elements (*formulation; direct compassion to others, self, dissociated parts/voices*) are more individually tailored and will therefore be illustrated by a clinical case, Stuart. Stuart is a fictional character but is based on a number of different people that the authors have worked with.

1. Establish safeness and connection

The establishment of safeness involves engaging the brain's soothing system as a natural threat regulator, as well as creating environments and relationships that will support experiences of safeness and connection. CFT attends to issues of social safeness first, with its associated physiology, because of the resilience this facilitates towards engaging more directly with the frightening aspects of psychotic experiences. Social safeness also creates the conditions from which compassionate intentions and mentalities arise, harnessing the person's commitment to engaging with their own experience. It creates a context for living that aims to develop a self that can care for itself and keep itself safe, engage with some meaningful activity and social networks, set small goals and learn new regulation skills. The focus is on developing a mindful curiosity about the experience of psychosis, strengths and survival mechanisms. The aim is to decrease the disintegration experienced as a result of stress-related arousal (Siegel, 2010).

An important way of increasing the bodily experience of safeness is through the practice of soothing rhythm breathing, which seeks to establish a gentle pace to the breath and so activate the parasympathetic system. This can be accompanied by learning to recognise what postures and activities ground and centre the person. Imagery work in CFT also facilities experiences of safeness and connection with others by using images of safe places and compassionate beings/objects. This harnesses both memories of positive external attachment experiences and also the potential ideal attachment to oneself. Research has shown that such imagery can help develop soothing capacities (Rockliff, Gilbert, McEwan, Lightman, & Glover, 2008). Scripts for compassionate image work are documented in the CFT literature (Gilbert, 2013). Such images create a *safe haven* and *secure base* for exploration and the resilience to turn towards one's psychotic experiences to consider how to cope differently or address the underlying traumas. Through these exercises, the person with psychosis can generate courage, well-being and capacity to mentalise and be mindful; skills that are needed to reduce dissociative avoidance of aspects of self and experience.

2. Psycho-education about evolved brains, emotion systems and multiple selves

Psycho-education has a key role in CFT in that it establishes a de-shaming, evolutionary understanding about the human brain. Clients are educated about the brain's evolution alongside the development of social groups and about attachment as an improved reproductive strategy. They are guided through understanding the problems and benefits naturally arising from a brain's evolutionary design, with the aim of recognising that their problematic thoughts, emotions and behavioural reactions are not their fault, but rather understandable and biologically typical reactions to difficult experiences. Psycho-education in CFT also helps to build a sense of common humanity; e.g. an understanding *what we all share* as human beings, and what we're all up against in the flow of life. This can be particularly important for people with psychosis, who often experience stigma and shame in relation to their experiences, which can leave them feeling lonely and alienated from others.

A helpful way to normalise experiential divisions within the self as functional is through psycho-education on the concept of multiple selves (Gilbert, 2014). What we call the 'self' is really our personal experience of continuity, whilst consisting of various different mindsets, mentalities or emotional states. For instance, we have an 'angry self', an 'anxious self and a 'sad self', each of which shape our attention/thinking in very different ways, and set up different responses. Pathological dissociation is where a division occurs between selves that would otherwise be integrated were it not for the overwhelming stress or trauma associated with this. Education about the functionality of such divisions, the unique function of each dissociated state,

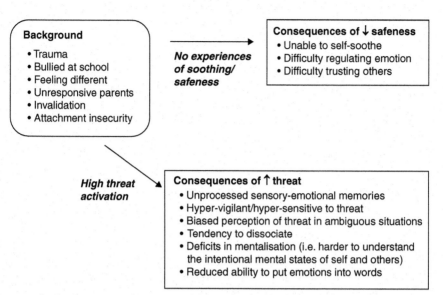

Figure 11.1a CFT formulation (development) – *combination of ↑ threat and ↓ safeness*

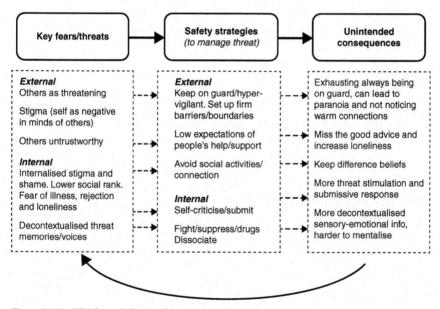

Figure 11.1b CFT formulation (maintenance)

and also of voice-hearing as a common human experience, can be shared through both personal accounts (Romme, Escher, Dillon, Corstens, & Morris, 2009) and studies of anomalous experiences in non-clinical populations (Heriot-Maitland, Knight, & Peters, 2012). Dissociative experiences have been described as a 'logical way of being', given the extreme nature of abuse occurring within attachments (First Person Plural, 2011). Dissociation protects the person from the full force of awareness or emotion in order to enable the person to function in day-to-day life. However, when people get bombarded by the dissociated parts, it can be confusing and frightening.

3. Formulation not diagnosis

A formulation aims to help people understand how early interpersonal and attachment experiences have contributed, alongside other experiences, to the development of both external and internal safety strategies to manage key threats and fears. Again, the de-shaming narrative is crucial here, meaning that clients will be helped to respect the function of these strategies as completely understandable coping responses. To illustrate, consider the case of Stuart, who came to therapy with difficulties relating to critical, threatening voices. Stuart reported a history of bullying at school and experiences of feeling different from other children. He also described unresponsive and invalidating parents, and a distinct lack of places to turn to for comfort, security and nurturing. Stuart and his therapist decided not to try and formulate the presence of external voices to begin with. Instead, they identified an inner critic, which seemed to relate to Stuart in a similar way as the voices. This critic targeted his insecurities, and directed similar emotions towards him. Stuart's inner critic, or 'self-critic', was formulated as an understandable internal strategy aimed at self-protection. The self-critic was linked to Stuart's fear of social rejection, protecting him from humiliating himself in front of others by self-correction, keeping his attention focused on his own weaknesses, and ensuring that he avoids social situations. Later in the therapy, Stuart assigned a similar role to his critical voices. The dissociative voice-hearing experience was understood in the context of disorganised early attachment relationships, and an underdeveloped soothing system, which prevented him being able to deal with his anxieties in ways other than phobic divisions and submission to his inner critic. Figure 1 includes illustrative examples of Stuart's formulation for both the (a) development and (b) maintenance of his difficulties.

4. Cultivate/deepen the compassionate self

In CFT, the client is helped to cultivate a compassionate self, which provides an inner 'secure base' from which to explore their fears and dissociated emotional parts. While continuing to build up the client's capacity for safeness, soothing and affiliative emotion, the focus here is on cultivating a part of the client that has the required qualities and attributes to slowly engage with dissociated aspects of self and intrusions. Key compassionate capacities, such as wisdom, strength and caring-commitment, are built around this sense of identity, using behavioural practices, and practices with posture, voice tone, facial expression and imagery. This often begins with the client imagining themselves in a compassionate role. The image can be oneself at one's best (perhaps a memory of being kind to another), another archetypal being (such as a character from literature) or a perceptual representation (maybe a colour). The compassionate self can then be used to understand and moderate the bodily responses of threatened states of mind. It is a place of safeness and strength within the self to both come from, and go to. In the language of attachment, an inner *secure base* and *safe haven*. This parallels the work of a lot of therapy for dissociative disorders, where the 'functional adult' self is encouraged to liaise with and moderate the responses of 'emotional' or 'child' parts (Van der Hart, Nijenhuis, & Steele, 2006). There is emerging evidence of the value of such deliberate image work in creating good internal attachments (e.g. between the self and an imagined compassionate self or other) and the regulation associated with this (Lincoln, Hohenhaus, & Hartmann, 2012).

For many people with psychosis, particularly those who have experienced trauma, this process of cultivating compassionate qualities may be met with resistance. This means that in CFT, a major aspect of the therapy becomes identifying and navigating these blocks to compassion. For instance, safeness and connection are sometimes too frightening for traumatised people, because such compassion is contrary to the perceived value of threat protection strategies. As dissociation can be understood as a phobia of aspects of experience (Van der Hart et al., 2006), gently addressing this avoidance becomes the main route to recovery. For example, witnessing domestic violence could lead to a fear of experiencing anger, but also lead to internalising the representation of an abusive 'other'. Both the client's own disowned rage and the imagined rage of another could emerge as an abusive voice that is not experienced as part of the self. CFT can initially help the client to focus on small changes in bodily state with the intention to be aware of such changes as dissociative triggers and desensitise the client to them. Boon et al. (2011) describe other useful ways of addressing such fear that is applicable to people who hear voices. The person may need to have a variety of safe places that meet the needs of different dissociated elements. Some angry elements may be able to tolerate safeness only once they realise that their style of protection is ultimately counterproductive now that the person is no longer being abused. All this may require negotiation and experimentation. For some clients, a dissociative framework can be useful, and formulating their symptoms as linked to traumatic events and adaptive responses can more closely mirror the client's own experience of themselves.

5. *Direct compassion to others, self, dissociated parts/voices*

Once the person can access a compassionate self, with compassionate qualities of wisdom, strength and caring-commitment, they can begin to use this in a deliberate way to address their issues and goals, asking 'what do I need this aspect of myself to do in order to …?' This uses the compassionate self both as a safe, secure base and also as a wise, internal attachment figure that can advise and regulate. The benefit of enhancing the compassionate self-qualities, and that of the whole system of mind, is that it facilitates a harmonious but firm acceptance of unwanted aspects of self. It can resource the person with the qualities needed to manage internal conflicts, and paves the way for supportive internal dialogue between parts. Identifying where to direct the compassionate self will be a collaborative process with the client. Some examples of where the person with psychosis may decide to direct their compassionate self are:

• Compassionate dialogue between voices that would aim to harmonise the relationships a person has between themselves and their voices;
• Compassion to multiple experiences of themselves that may react to voices in different ways and set up internal conflicts, e.g. avoidant self, submissive self, self-critic (whether dissociated from their own sense of self, or simply different self-states);
• Compassion to the part that fears he or she will be rejected, neglected, abandoned, abused, attacked, and developing wisdom and empathy about causation of such attachment based fears and how they link to adapting to previous relationships (e.g. inner critic, focused threat attention);
• Compassion to the dissociated part that still lives exclusively in 'trauma time' and will intrude its terror, horror, images and pain into consciousness in ways that may or may not be contextualised (PTSD, somatisation, paranoia);
• Compassion to other emotions (e.g. anger, sadness) that may be blocked because they have been learned or conditioned to be associated with threat, so that they can be accessed and expressed in a safe way;
• Compassion to other people in order to facilitate a more rewarding social world.

In Stuart's case, it did not feel safe, initially, to dialogue with his voices. What felt safer was to create internal characters representing the two main emotional parts of him that he wished to work with. Billy and David were the characters' names; essentially parts of Stuart that organised the way he thinks, feels, and acts. Billy was Stuart's compassionate self – wise, kind, strong and committed to caring for self and others. David was Stuart's self-critic – suspicious, untrusting, critical and always erring on 'better safe than sorry'. Stuart engaged with dialogues between David and Billy. He was able to develop empathy and compassion for David; for example, understanding where this part of him originated. He recognised that David had probably developed earlier in his life at a time when he was scared about what other people thought and how other people acted towards him. He recognised that David might have orginally been his mind's way of trying to protect him from the things he was afraid of. He thought the reason why David, the self-critic, had always been so suspicious of people is that he'd always been trying to protect him from what he feared would be the worst outcome. David remembered that people were not very accepting of Stuart at school, made him feel different and that sometimes he was treated badly at home. Stuart could empathise with why David kept warning him to be suspicious of people. Stuart discovered that David was very quick to criticise him because he wanted to try and stop him from doing things in his life; from taking risks. Again, this is protective. The process of identifying the function of voices is done by the client; the therapist simply facilitates this process using guided discovery.

In CFT, the internal relationships between the compassionate self and other parts or voices can be facilitated using a variety of techniques common to other therapeutic approaches, such as imagery, chair work (using different chairs to represent different self-states or voices), and letter writing (composing a kind and wise letter to self that is based on the understanding of how the voices developed). In the case of voice dialoguing, a CFT therapist would use similar techniques to those described in Chapter 13 in this book and also Kennedy and Dillon (submitted), but with the addition of a compassionate self as a moderator of the dialogue. For instance, in the compassionate approach to voice dialogue using chairs, one example would be to designate one chair for a critical voice, one chair for the part of self that receives this criticism, and then a third chair for the compassionate self. The compassionate self can then draw on qualities of wisdom, authority and warmth to engage with the emotions and functions of the parts in the other chairs. The compassionate self can either address voices and parts directly from their compassionate stance, or take more of a reflective overview of the conflicts between different parts, moving towards resolution and integration. Importantly, whenever the client takes the chair of compassionate self, it is helpful to stop and create space to bring the soothing system online. This may be through, for example, soothing breathing, posture, imagery of compassionate qualities, as outlined previously.

Making peace with voices

Based on 50 narratives of recovery, Romme et al. (2009) suggest a number of factors relating to internal relationships with dissociated elements that are critical to well-being: having a framework to normalise the experience as a response to life events, being curious about the voices, making one's own choices, changing the power relationship to voices, and recognising which emotions are difficult to learn better ways of dealing with them. A mindful, compassionate self can greatly facilitate these relational processes. As time went on for Stuart, with further cultivation of his compassionate self, and further compassionate relating with his self-critic, there was an important shift in the relationship between Stuart and his voices. The main shift was the voices becoming less critical and threatening and more supportive and caring. Towards the end of therapy, Stuart decided that he now felt safe, confident and ready to start a dialogue with the voices themselves.

One month after this therapy (of 25 weekly sessions) had ended, Stuart reflected that it had been an incredibly helpful experience. He felt that his mood and self-confidence had improved, which had allowed him to start paid work, which he was enjoying. Stuart reported that he still heard two voices, and that the content of these voices was half negative and half positive. The negative voices were critical, while the positive voices tried to boost his self-esteem by saying things like 'You're in control' and 'You're eating well'. Stuart acknowledged a link between his relationship with himself and his relation-ship with the voices, especially around self-care; for example, he noticed that if he didn't look after himself (in terms of going to the gym or eating healthily), the voices would be more critical. Stuart said that he found the negative voices slightly distressing but he had learnt to manage them. He said that he didn't feel the voices disrupted his life anymore and his concentration and focus had improved. Stuart felt that with the help of the techniques he had learnt in therapy he was more at peace with the voices. He said that now, when he felt stressed, he would use breathing exercises and this would help him feel more calm and peaceful. Stuart reported to have not experienced any distressing beliefs at all in the month following therapy.

Previous studies of CFT with people with experiences of psychosis

In a small case series of compassionate mind training involving three people who heard malevolent voices, Mayhew and Gilbert (2008) helped participants to visualise the compassionate part of themselves, with associated feelings of warmth, and to develop empathic understanding for their distress and self-criticism. Interestingly, they found that working with self-critical thoughts (as opposed to with critical voices directly) led to a reduction in the malevolence of voices. There is also evidence that group-based CFT is potentially bene-ficial for people recovering from psychosis, Braehler et al. (2013) studied 22 participants in CFT groups, which involved applying compassionate prac-tice and skills in relation to internal and external threats, such as shame, stigma, paranoia, self-attacking and hostile voices. Their main finding was that the CFT group participants reported significant reductions in depres-sion associated with psychosis, compared to treatment as usual. Braehler et al. (2013) also analysed the recovery narratives of CFT participants and showed that more than half felt the therapy group had helped them in their recovery journey, whilst very few of the control group had made much progress. Compassion was increased in participants and this was associated with less fear of relapse, less depression and fewer negative beliefs about their psychosis. To complement these preliminary studies a series of first person account papers has recently been published by an individual with psychosis receiving CFT, who has been in services for 20 years (Ellerby, 2014; Kennedy & Ellerby, 2016). This includes an account of engaging with voices from the compassion perspective (Ellerby, 2017).

Summary

This chapter has highlighted how attachment traumas can lead to problems in regulating responses to threat, which cultivates the conditions for dissociation. It has outlined the rationale for CFT for psychosis by highlighting how delusions and hallucinations can be understood in terms of dissociation, and also by highlighting the role of attachment in both CFT formulations and interventions. In addition to attachment theory, CFT also draws on evolutionary psychology and neuroscience. CFT aims to help people regulate threat processing by building internal feelings of safeness and affiliation, and by providing contexts, practices and insights that facilitate the development of compassion to self, others and dissociated parts. The focus is on helping people feel safe in relation to their experiences and their social worlds. The outline of a (non-linear) five-stage approach to applying CFT to psychosis is provided. Although there is currently very little in the way of published evaluations of this relatively new approach to helping people with psychosis, the strong theoretical rationale outlined in this chapter has recently attracted funding to conduct a programme of research, led by the first author. This research may not only inform the design of future therapies for people with psychosis, but may also inform service-level approaches to reducing stigma and shame by, for example, developing a culture of acceptance and empathic connection, as opposed to the still sadly not uncommon culture aimed at increasing insight into an 'illness' narrative about delusions and hallucinations as being the meaningless manifestations of an abnormal brain. In our view, the more that therapies and systems can promote external and internal experiences of social safeness, the greater the chance of dissociative integration and recovery from psychosis.

References

Arseneault, L., Cannon, M., Fisher, H. L., Polanczyk, G., Moffitt, T. E., & Caspi, A. (2011). Childhood trauma and children's emerging psychotic symptoms: A genetically sensitive longitudinal cohort study. *American Journal of Psychiatry, 168*(1), 65–72. doi: 10.1176/appi.ajp.2010.10040567

Birchwood, M., Meaden, A., Trower, P., Gilbert, P., & Plaistow, J. (2000). The power and omnipotence of voices: subordination and entrapment by voices and significant others. *Psychological Medicine, 30*(2), 337–344.

Boon, S., Steele, K., & van der Hart, O. (2011). *Coping with Trauma-Related Dissociation: Skills training for patients and therapists*. New York, NY: W W Norton & Co; US.

Braehler, C., Gumley, A., Harper, J., Wallace, S., Norrie, J., & Gilbert, P. (2013). Exploring change processes in compassion focused therapy in psychosis: results of a feasibility randomized controlled trial. *British Journal of Clinical Psychology*, *52*(2), 199–214. doi: 10.1111/bjc.12009

Butzlaff, R. L. & Hooley, J. M. (1998). Expressed emotion and psychiatric relapse: A meta-analysis. *Archives General Psychiatry*, *55*(6), 547–552.

Campbell, M. L., & Morrison, A. P. (2007). The subjective experience of paranoia: Comparing the experiences of patients with psychosis and individuals with no psychiatric history. *Clinical Psychology and Psychotherapy*, *14*(1), 63–77.

Connor, C., & Birchwood, M. (2013). Through the looking glass: self-reassuring meta-cognitive capacity and its relationship with the thematic content of voices. *Frontiers in Human Neuroscience*, *7*, 213. doi: 10.3389/fnhum.2013.00213

Dell, P. F., & O'Neil, J. A. (2009). *Dissociation and the Dissociative Disorders: DSM-V and beyond*. New York: Routledge.

Dorahy, M. J., McKendry, H., Scott, A., Yogeeswaran, K., Martens, A., & Hanna, D. (2016). Reactive dissociative experiences in response to acute increases in shame feelings. *Behaviour Research and Therapy*, *89*, 75–85. doi:10.1016/j.brat.2016.11.007

Eicher, A. C., Davis, L. W., & Lysaker, P. H. (2013). Self-compassion: a novel link with symptoms in schizophrenia? *Journal of Nervous and Mental Disease*, *201*(5), 389–393. doi: 10.1097/NMD.0b013e31828e10fa

Ellerby, M. (2014). How compassion may help me. *Psychosis*, 6(3), 266–270. doi: 10.1080/17522439.2013.816338

Ellerby, M. (2017). Resisting voices through finding our own compassionate voice. *Schizophrenia Bulletin*, *43*(2), 230–232 doi: 10.1093/schbul/sbu035

First Person Plural (2011). *A Logical Way of Being: The Reality of Dissociative Identity Disorder and Other Complex Dissociative Conditions (DVD)*. FPP (http://firstpersonplural.org.uk)

Gilbert, P. (2009). Introducing compassion-focused therapy. *Advances in Psychiatric Treatment*, *15*(3), 199–208.

Gilbert, P. (2013). *Mindful Compassion: Using the power of mindfulness and compassion to transform our lives*. Hachette UK.

Gilbert, P. (2014). The origins and nature of compassion focused therapy. *British Journal of Clinical Psychology*, *53*(1), 6–41. doi: 10.1111/bjc.12043

Gilbert, P., & Irons, C. (2005). *Focused therapies and compassionate mind training for shame and self-attracking. Compassion: Conceptualisations, research and use in psychotherapy* (pp.263–325). New York: Routledge.

Gumley, A., Braehler, C., Laithwaite, H., MacBeth, A., & Gilbert, P. (2010). A compassion focused model of recovery after psychosis. *International Journal of Cognitive Therapy*, *3*(2), 186–201.

Heriot-Maitland, C., Knight, M., & Peters, E. (2012). A qualitative comparison of psychotic-like phenomena in clinical and non-clinical populations. *British Journal of Clinical Psychology*, *51*(1), 37–53. doi: 10.1111/j.2044-8260.2011.02011.x

Kennedy, A. & Ellerby, M. (2016). A compassion focused approach to working with someone diagnosed with schizophrenia. *Journal of Clinical Psychology: In Session*. *72*(2), 123–131.

Kennedy, A. & Dillon, J. (submitted) Engaging voices in a compassionate dialogue. *Psychology and Psychotherapy, Research theory and Practice.*

Lincoln, T. M., Hohenhaus, F., & Hartmann, M. (2012). Can paranoid thoughts be reduced by targeting negative emotions and self-esteem? An experimental investigation of a brief compassion-focused intervention. *Cognitive Therapy and Research, 37*(2), 390–402. doi: 10.1007/s10608-012-9470-7

Longden, E. (2010). Making sense of voices: A personal story of recovery. *Psychosis-Psychological Social and Integrative Approaches, 2*(3), 255–259. doi:10.1080/17522439.2010.512667

Maher, B. A. (1974). Delusional thinking and perceptual disorder. *Journal of Individual Psychology, 30*(1), 98–113.

Matos, M., Pinto-Gouveia, J., & Gilbert, P. (2013). The effect of shame and shame memories on paranoid ideation and social anxiety. *Clinical Psychology and Psychotherapy, 20*(4), 334–349. doi: 10.1002/cpp.1766

Mayhew, S. L., & Gilbert, P. (2008). Compassionate mind training with people who hear malevolent voices: a case series report. *Clinical Psychology and Psychotherapy, 15*(2), 113–138. doi: 10.1002/cpp.566

Morrison, A. P., Frame, L., & Larkin, W. (2003). Relationships between trauma and psychosis: A review and integration. *British Journal of Clinical Psychology, 42,* 331–353. Doi 10.1348/0144665503322528892

Moskowitz, A., & Corstens, D. (2008). Auditory hallucinations: psychotic symptom or dissociative experience? *Journal of Psychological Trauma, 6*(2–3), 35–63. doi: 10.1300/J513v06n02_04

Nijenhuis, E. R., & van der Hart, O. (2011). Dissociation in trauma: a new definition and comparison with previous formulations. *Journal of Trauma and Dissociation, 12*(4), 416–445. doi: 10.1080/15299732.2011.570592

Read, J., Agar, K., Argyle, N., & Aderhold, V. (2003). Sexual and physical abuse during childhood and adulthood as predictors of hallucinations, delusions and thought disorder. *Psychology and Psychotherapy, 76*(Pt 1), 1–22. doi: 10.1348/14760830260569210

Rockliff, H., Gilbert, P., McEwan, K., Lightman, S., & Glover, D. (2008). A pilot exploration of heart rate variability and salivary cortisol responses to compassion-focused imagery. *Journal of Clinical Neuropsychiatry, 5,* 132–139.

Romme, M., Escher, S., Dillon, J., Corstens, D., & Morris, M. (2009). *Living with Voices: 50 Stories of Recovery.* Living with voices: 50 stories of recovery ii, 350 pp Ross-on-Wye, England: PCCS Books; England.

Shevlin, M., Dorahy, M., & Adamson, G. (2007). Childhood traumas and hallucinations: an analysis of the National Comorbidity Survey. *Journal of Psychiatric Research, 41*(3–4), 222–228. doi: 10.1016/j.jpsychires.2006.03.004

Siegel, D. J. (2010). *Mindsight: The new science of personal transformation.* London: Random House LLC.

Smith, J. A. (1996). Beyond the divide between cognitive and discourse: using interpretative phenomenological analysis in health psychology. *Psychology and Health, 11,* 261–271.

Van der Hart, O., Nijenhuis, E. R., & Steele, K. (2006). *The Haunted Self: Structural dissociation and the treatment of chronic traumatization.* New York: WW Norton & Company.

12

CULTURAL VARIATIONS IN ATTACHMENT AND PSYCHOSIS

The application of attachment theory to inform therapeutic work with Black Caribbean families

Amy Degnan, Lucy Shattock and Dawn Edge

Introduction

Attachment theory is one of the few social psychological theories that is considered to be culturally universal (Agishtein & Brumbaugh, 2013; van Ijzendoorn & Sagi-Schwartz, 2008). According to Bowlby (1982), the *attachment system* is an evolved biological-behavioural system experienced by all humans and influenced by interpersonal relations, and the social norms and values of the caregiver's culture. Early infant-caregiver attachment research was carried out in Uganda and Baltimore (Ainsworth, 1967), nonetheless most of the empirical studies in child and adult attachment since then have been based on Western populations. The cultural applicability of attachment theory has previously been debated based on the idea that there are fundamental differences in maternal sensitivity and child security across Western and non-Western cultures[1] (Rothbaum, Weisz, Pott, Miyake, & Morelli, 2000). It is now widely accepted that it is the *expression* of attachment that has a strong cultural component (Cowan & Cowan, 2007). This is supported by cross-cultural attachment research suggesting that although the attachment system is present across all cultures, there are variations in definitions and patterns of attachment and what constitutes a 'secure' or healthy attachment (Agishtein & Brumbaugh, 2013).

Mary Ainsworth and colleagues (Ainsworth, Blehar, Water, & Wall, 1978) initially identified three specific attachment styles in childhood: *secure, insecure anxious-avoidant* and *insecure anxious-ambivalent*. Since then, many conceptualisations of attachment have been proposed by attachment theorists. As outlined in earlier chapters, one of the most widely used conceptualisations in adult attachment is the two-dimensional model of *avoidance* (dismissive and defensive) and *anxiety* (fearful and dependent), with low levels on both dimensions indicating secure attachment (Bartholomew & Horowitz, 1991; Brennan, Clark, & Shaver, 1998). Some have argued that these adult attachment styles may not be applicable across cultures as they are based on

Western values relating to interpersonal and emotional expression, such as those related to autonomy and individualism (Wang & Mallinckrodt, 2006b). There is thus a need to consider cultural variation in the conceptualisation and measurement of attachment and to steer away from pathologising diverse attachment responses across cultures.

There has been limited research examining cultural differences in attachment expression among diverse ethnic and cultural groups in the UK. This chapter builds on previous chapters in its application of attachment theory to understand interpersonal processes and experiences of psychosis specifically in the UK's Black Caribbean[2] population. This group is the focus of this chapter because members are particularly vulnerable to experiencing trauma-related disrupted attachments and difficult relationships with mental health services. There has been growing interest in adapting psychological interventions to meet the cultural needs of individuals with psychosis (Degnan et al., 2018) and family intervention is one area where efforts have been made to culturally-adapt therapy for Black Caribbean people with psychosis in the UK (Edge et al., 2018). The aim of the current chapter is to: i) provide an overview of the literature on ethnic disparities in psychosis and relationships with mental health services among the UK Black Caribbean population; ii) draw on attachment theory as a framework for understanding the interpersonal experiences (trauma, separation and loss) of Black Caribbean people with psychosis in the UK and their relationships with services; and iii) consider family intervention for Black Caribbean people in the UK as an example of how such a framework may be useful, drawing on a particular case example of culturally-adapted family therapy.

Psychosis in the Black Caribbean population

The increased risk of being diagnosed with schizophrenia and other psychoses among migrant and minority ethnic groups is well established (Cantor-Graae & Selten, 2005; Fearon et al., 2006; Kirkbride et al., 2012; Tortelli et al., 2015). Most research in the UK has focused on Black Caribbean people as the increased risk is considered to have the largest impact in terms of the mental health burden in England (Kirkbride et al., 2010; Morgan & Hutchinson, 2010). Meta-analyses of incidence rates [pooled risk ratio (RR)] in England over a 60-year period suggest that, compared to the White British population, diagnostic rates of schizophrenia are 5.6 times higher in people of Black Caribbean origin (95% CI: 3.4–9.2, N=5), 4.7 in Black African-descended groups (95% CI: 3.3–6.8, N=5) and 2.4 in people from the Indian Sub-Continent, commonly referred to as 'South Asians' (95% CI: 1.3–4.5, N=3) (Kirkbride et al., 2012). There is limited evidence to suggest that rates are slightly higher among Black Caribbean women than men (Tortelli et al., 2015). There is no consistent evidence for differences in migration status, with few studies examining separate effects for people born in the UK versus migrants (Kirkbride et al., 2012; Tortelli et al., 2015).

Numerous hypotheses have been put forward to explain the higher rates of psychosis in Black populations in the UK, with current literature favouring psychosocial explanations (for reviews, see Bhugra & Bhui, 2001; Fung, Bhugra, & Jones, 2009; Morgan, Charalambides, Hutchinson, & Murray, 2010; Pinto, Ashworth, & Jones, 2008; Sharpley, Hutchinson, Murray, & McKenzie, 2001; Tortelli et al., 2015). Perhaps the most robust evidence to date comes from the Aetiology and Ethnicity in Schizophrenia and Other Psychoses (AESOP) study, a large incidence and case-control study in first episode psychosis covering three UK catchment areas (London, Bristol and Nottingham; Morgan & Fearon, 2007). Taken together, findings from AESOP suggest that childhood adversity, including early separation from parents (Morgan et al., 2007), cumulative social disadvantage (Morgan et al., 2008), and living in socially fragmented communities (i.e. being a minority within one's own neighbourhood) (Kirkbride et al., 2007) contribute to explaining the increased risk of psychosis in Black ethnic groups in the UK (Morgan et al., 2017). Recent ten-year follow up findings of the AESOP study showed that the enhanced risk extends to poorer social and service use outcomes (i.e. social disadvantage, social isolation and compulsory hospital admissions) in Black Caribbean and African people, and poorer clinical outcomes (i.e. persistent symptoms and low recovery rates) in Black Caribbeans (but not Black Africans), when compared to their White British counterparts (Morgan et al., 2017).

Relationships with services in Black Caribbean people with psychosis

Interactions between people of Black Caribbean origin and mainstream mental health services are arguably the most difficult relationships of all ethnic groups in the UK. Empirical research (Bhui et al., 2003; Morgan et al., 2017; Morgan et al., 2005a, 2005b; Morgan, Mallett, Hutchinson, & Leff, 2004) has repeatedly highlighted that Black Caribbean people in the UK experience marked ethnic inequalities in access, experiences and outcomes of mental health services. Black Caribbean people are more likely to access services via adverse and coercive care pathways, including high rates of compulsory admissions and police arrest (Morgan et al., 2017; Morgan et al., 2005a; The Schizophrenia Commission, 2012). They also experience longer hospital stays, more seclusion and restraint, higher doses of medication, and are less likely to be offered psychological therapy (Bhui et al., 2003; Morgan et al., 2004; The Schizophrenia Commission, 2012). In response, UK health-related reports and policies have consistently reported that mental health services for Black Caribbean people are inadequate (Mental Health Taskforce, 2016; National Institute for Health and Care Excellence, 2009; The Schizophrenia Commission, 2012).

Black Caribbean people have historically been labelled as 'hard-to-reach' in the UK, but this narrative has been challenged based on literature suggesting that they often make multiple help-seeking attempts (Morgan et al., 2004) and are less likely to be referred to specialist mental health services by primary care providers (Islam, Rabiee, & Singh, 2015). Previous adverse experiences of services have been argued to increase fear, mistrust and perceived stigma in Black Caribbean communities, reducing subsequent help-seeking for psychosis (Keating, Roberson, McCulloch, & Francis, 2002; Keating & Robertson, 2004; Morgan et al., 2004). There have been a number of UK policy initiatives to reduce ethnic disparities and discrimination in UK mental health services (Care Quality Commission, 2011; Commission for Healthcare Audit and Inspection, 2005; Department of Health, 2005; Keating et al., 2002; National Institute for Mental Health, 2003). The Delivering Race Equality (DRE) Framework (National Institute for Mental Health, 2003) included strategies to enable more appropriate and responsive services, including the employment of community development workers (CDWs) to strengthen engagement with marginalised communities. However, despite these efforts, ethnic inequalities persist, and unfair treatment and mistrust is still reported among people of Black ethnic backgrounds (Henderson et al., 2015).

Attachment theory as a framework for understanding the interpersonal experiences of Black Caribbean people with psychosis

African-descended cultures, including Caribbean cultures, are traditionally collectivist and families are extended rather than nuclear (i.e. wider family versus two parents and their children; Arnold, 2012). During slavery, which entailed forced separation from family members, people transported to the Caribbean recreated traditional African family structures by developing extended kinship and community network ties (Arnold, 2012). These extended social ties and support networks were called upon to provide care for children of parents who migrated to the UK between the post-war period and the 1960s. It has been suggested that the migration process weakened family structures and access to social ties and supportive relationships (Mallett, Leff, Bhugra, Pang, & Zhao, 2002; Murphy, 1996). Large scale migration to the UK, predominantly in the 1950s and 1960s, left behind extended families and tight-knit communities and replaced them with smaller family units or single adult households in the UK (Arnold, 2012; Murphy, 1996). For those children that eventually migrated from the Caribbean to join their parents in the UK, lack of knowledge of the UK education and welfare systems meant that families were often unaware both of their rights and where or how to seek help when experiencing family difficulties. Hypervigilance by the authorities was fuelled by a lack of understanding of the role of extended networks and by common stereotypes of Caribbean culture, such as marital instability, illegitimacy and matriarchal single parent households (Arnold, 2012). This led to large numbers of Black Caribbean children being taken into the care of Local Authority, resulting in breakdowns in parental-child

195

attachments and negative attitudes towards, and mistrust of, health and social care professionals, which have persisted into current times (Henderson et al., 2015). It is now understood that broken attachments, separation and loss through the process of migration from the Caribbean to the UK also had adverse psychological effects on both the children and the parents (Arnold, 2012). The experiences of broken attachments and their impact on family structure and dynamics are crucial to understanding Caribbean histories of multiple and repeated separations, during periods of enslavement and migration (Thomas, 2013).

The majority of Black Caribbean-descended people in the UK today are not immigrants but British born (Office for National Statistics, 2011). Black Caribbean people are one of the ethnic groups in the UK most likely to experience current and long-standing social disadvantage, such as unemployment, having poor education and limited social networks, increasing their risk for psychosis (Morgan et al., 2008). A discontinuity of attachment styles from infancy into adulthood (transition from secure to insecure) has been found to be predicted by more difficult and chaotic life experiences, including child maltreatment, maternal depression and family functioning in early adolescence (Weinfield, Sroufe, & Egeland, 2000). Separation from parents (resulting from family breakdown including parental separation, divorce or abandonment) is associated with increased risk of psychosis across ethnic groups (Morgan et al., 2007). There is evidence to show that Black Caribbean people in the UK are more likely to experience long-term separation from parents when compared to their White British counterparts, due at least in part to patterns of migration, which may contribute to the high rates of psychosis found in this population (Mallett et al., 2002; Morgan et al., 2007). Morgan and colleagues (2007) highlight that early family breakdown, separation and loss may disrupt the attachment system and have long-lasting negative effects in terms of the formation of secure and stable relationships in adulthood. Separation from parents, particularly fathers, has historically been reported as commonplace in the Caribbean but is often cited without the contextual understanding of collectivist approaches to child-rearing (Littlewood & Lipsedge, 1981). It is hypothesised that the negative effects of separation from primary caregivers may be buffered in the Caribbean (Foster & Involvement, 2013), to a greater extent compared with separation due to migration, as children move on to live with extended family where secure attachment relationships can develop. Research suggests that early social deprivation (i.e. institutionalised, adoptive or foster care) can negatively influence attachment formation and security, but this is partly dependent on the stability and quality of subsequent caregiving (Carlson, Hostinar, Mliner, & Gunnar, 2014; Fox, Nelson, & Zeanah, 2017).

As discussed in previous chapters, there is now robust evidence for the relationship between childhood adversity (sexual abuse, physical abuse, emotional/psychological abuse, neglect, parental death, and bullying) and psychosis onset (Varese et al., 2012). Traumatic experiences in childhood may result in insecure early attachment relationships (Bentall, Wickham, Shevlin, & Varese, 2012), and lead to difficulties managing subsequent trauma. Early interpersonal trauma has been associated with insecure attachment in people with psychosis (Berry, Barrowclough, & Wearden, 2009), and has been argued to increase vulnerability, via disturbances in the attachment system, to specific psychotic experiences such as voice-hearing (Berry & Bucci, 2016; Longden, Madill, & Waterman, 2012) and paranoia (Berry, Barrowclough, & Wearden, 2008). Most of this literature has been based on predominantly White samples with a lack of research in ethnically or culturally diverse populations in the UK. Given that people of Black Caribbean descent in the UK are more likely to experience multiple traumas related to separation, social disadvantage, social exclusion and discrimination (Morgan et al., 2017) it could be hypothesised that they are more likely to experience (insecure) attachment related difficulties. There is some evidence that negative life events (e.g. loss of a parent or family member, parental divorce and abuse) and deprivation (i.e. living in poverty) are important predictors of stability and change in secure attachment during infancy and childhood, as they directly impact caregiving behaviour and the quality of the parent-child relationship (McConnell, Moss, & Psychology, 2011). However, lack of research into intersections between ethnicity and social class means there is limited understanding of the extent to which these observations apply to Black Caribbean families with higher socio-economic status. There is also currently a lack of research assessing attachment expression across different cultural or ethnic groups who experience psychosis. Additionally, there is limited empirical research examining the influence of psychosocial factors such as social deprivation and marginalisation on attachment in clinical and non-clinical samples. Nonetheless, it is possible that these interpersonal stressors may render an individual more vulnerable to attachment insecurity in childhood via negative influence on the quality or availability of caregiver relationships (e.g. increased caregiver stress leading to neglect). The positive relationship between maternal insensitivity and attachment insecurity in both has been found to be mediated by lower income, suggesting that poverty may hamper the quality of the infant-mother relationship (Bakermans-Kranenburg, van Ijzendoom, & Kroonenberg, 2004). Difficulties with affect regulation related to insecure attachment styles may also increase sensitivity to stress in the social environment (Mikulincer, Shaver, & Pereg, 2003), perhaps triggering negative responses from others and interpersonal difficulties. Moreover, stressful interpersonal experiences that are pertinent for Black Caribbean people in the UK, such as social exclusion and discrimination, may trigger individuals' insecure attachment systems and negative beliefs about the self and others in adulthood. These relationships have not been empirically tested and require further investigation.

There is a growing body of research to suggest attachment styles vary across cultures in general population samples, with differences existing across countries, geographical regions and ethnic origin (Agishtein & Brumbaugh, 2013). Based on meta-analytic evidence, it is generally agreed that the three core adult attachment styles (Brennan et al., 1998) exist worldwide with global norms suggesting the majority of people are securely attached, a larger minority are avoidant and a smaller minority are anxious (van Ijzendoorn & Sagi-Schwartz, 2008). A relatively consistent finding is that African Americans tend to be rated higher on avoidant attachment compared to European Americans (e.g. Magai et al., 2001; Wei, Russell, Mallinckrodt, & Zakalik, 2004), which has been explained by a more punitive parenting style and social deprivation leading to lower maternal sensitivity (Agishtein & Brumbaugh, 2013). Additionally, higher levels of attachment anxiety tend to be reported in collectivist cultures and East Asian countries (Agishtein & Brumbaugh, 2013; Cheng & Kwan, 2008; Cowan & Cowan, 2007; Wang & Mallinckrodt, 2006b). Western cultures that originate in Europe and include non-indigenous cultures in North America and Australasia, generally value individualism and independence, with individuals acting as separate units and in self-interest (Markus & Kitayama, 1991). This contrasts with non-Western cultures that tend to be collectivist (such as Asia and Africa), whose values emphasise interdependency, mutual obligation and connectedness among individuals and families (Wang & Mallinckrodt, 2006a). People from collectivist and interdependent cultures are more likely to sacrifice their own needs and goals for their social reference group (Markus & Kitayama, 1991). It has been argued that the greater value placed on family connections, interdependent social ties and shared responsibility in non-Western cultures may be misinterpreted as 'insecure' attachment anxiety on current attachment measures (Wang & Mallinckrodt, 2006b). Similarly, emotional restraint and limited self-disclosure, which are valued in some non-Western cultures, could be misconceived as higher 'insecure' attachment avoidance from the Western perspective (Wang & Mallinckrodt, 2006b). The definition of 'secure' adult attachment may therefore be based on culturally-specific norms and attitudes relating to how to act and communicate in interpersonal relationships (Agishtein & Brumbaugh, 2013; Cheng & Kwan, 2008; Wang & Mallinckrodt, 2006b). However, the social and psychological mechanisms by which culture influences attachment patterns and outcomes have been largely untested and may involve a number of interrelated variables such as country of origin, ethnicity, religion, individualism-collectivism and acculturation (Agishtein & Brumbaugh, 2013).

There has been some research to suggest that attachment styles may influence level of acculturation and ethnic identity among minority communities in the UK. Strong ethnic identity (i.e. affinity to one's own ethnic group) is argued to play a central role in interpersonal networks of Black Caribbeans, low levels of community integration has been linked to experiences of social exclusion and marginalisation (Campbell, Cornish, & McLean, 2004; Eliacin, 2013). A study carried out by the present authors in a small sample (n=51) of Black African and Caribbean people with psychosis showed that Black service users tended to form social relationships with people of similar ethnic background to their own rather than people from different ethnic backgrounds (Degnan, 2017); consistent with previous qualitative research in Black Caribbean community members (Mclean, Campbell, & Cornish, 2003). Black Caribbean people have reported forming community ties with people of the same ethnicity to facilitate trust and cooperation in the face of inequalities and social exclusion (Mclean et al., 2003). Higher levels of identification with the dominant culture have been related to lower attachment anxiety and higher levels of identification with any (native or adopted) culture have been related to lower attachment avoidance (Agishtein & Brumbaugh, 2013). The secure base provided by attachment figures may act as a platform, enabling individuals to explore novel environments and to integrate into dominant cultures (Wang & Mallinckrodt, 2006a). Individuals from minority groups that are socially excluded from the dominant culture may feel less accepted and more anxious or, alternatively, those who are less anxious may be less preoccupied with social concerns and be more able to immerse themselves in the dominant culture (Agishtein & Brumbaugh, 2013). Individuals that are lower in avoidance groups may be more likely to feel closely connected to their primary caregivers and hence with their native culture and ethnic identity (Agishtein & Brumbaugh, 2013). Additionally, individuals low in avoidance may be more likely to accept, explore and identify with the values and beliefs of any culture (Agishtein & Brumbaugh, 2013).

Evidence suggests that negative ethnic identity may render minority groups more vulnerable to psychosis via the negative impact of social adversity and discrimination (Veling, Hoek, Wiersma, & Mackenbach, 2010). Strong ethnic identification with a Black and minority ethnic group subject to perceived social disadvantage has been associated with increased risk of psychosis in the UK (Reininghaus et al., 2010). Epidemiological studies have found an 'ethnic density effect' where members of ethnic minority groups have better mental health when living in areas with higher proportions of people of the same ethnicity (Becares, Nazroo, & Stafford, 2009; Das-Munshi et al., 2012), an effect that has been observed in Black ethnic communities in the UK (Kirkbride, Jones, Ullrich, & Coid, 2014; Schofield, Ashworth, & Jones, 2011). It has been suggested that the beneficial effects of ethnic density may be explained by greater levels of social capital and support that buffer the negative impact of social adversity and discrimination on psychological distress (Broome et al., 2005; Brugha, 2010; Das-Munshi et al., 2012). Though not directly tested, attachment theory could be useful in explaining these effects. Being surrounded by people of similar ethnic background may reduce distress through increased positive beliefs about the self and others, improving self-esteem and ethnic identity, and the ability to develop secure and trusting attachment relationships.

To summarise, attachment is a universal construct and its expression is largely influenced by cultural factors such as caregiving practices, norms related to interpersonal roles and dynamics, collectivism, and ethnic identification and acculturation. It is worth noting that much of the cross-cultural attachment research is based on correlational data and self-report measures of attachment in adulthood which means one cannot infer causality, there is a risk of reporting bias, and the findings may not be generalisable to attachment experiences in childhood. There has been limited empirical study of attachment in Black Caribbean people in general and among those with psychosis living in the UK more specifically. Most research examining cultural differences in adult attachment has compared majority ethnic groups (i.e. country of origin), rather than minority groups. Though not directly tested, it is theorised that Black Caribbean people may be more likely to experience insecure attachment and related interpersonal difficulties than other ethnic groups in the UK because of their enhanced risk of early and continued adversity related to separation and loss, racial discrimination and social segregation. Attachment theory may provide a useful framework to help understand and formulate variations in interpersonal processes and difficulties for Black Caribbean people with psychosis.

Attachment theory as a framework for understanding relationships between mental health services and Black Caribbean people diagnosed with psychosis

As discussed in Chapter 14, attachment theory offers a framework to conceptualise engagement with services and therapeutic alliance development (Barber et al., 2006; Goodwin, Holmes, Cochrane, & Mason, 2003). The attachment system is designed to be a help-seeking system (Bowlby, 1982), and may therefore help us to understand how individuals seek help from mental health services (Bucci, Roberts, Danquah, & Berry, 2015). Attachment theory may also be useful in helping to understand difficult intepersonal dynamics with staff and relationships with mental health services among Black Caribbean people with psychosis in the UK. Greater attachment difficulties have been associated with poorer service engagement, poorer alliance and more severe symptoms in psychosis (Gumley, Taylor, Schwannauer, & MacBeth, 2014). Key considerations for an attachment-informed service include establishing and maintaining stable and consistent relationships with staff and providing a 'secure base' to support recovery (Bucci et al., 2015).

Attachment avoidance, but not attachment anxiety, has previously been associated with staff- and client-rated alliance in a predominately White sample with psychosis, adjusting for psychosis symptom severity (Berry et al., 2008). Service users high in avoidant attachment might be more socially and emotionally withdrawn and therefore less likely to develop positive therapeutic relationships. They may also be intepreted as being reluctant to engage with services, but these attachment responses may be understandable based on early difficulties in interpersonal relationships (Barber et al., 2006). Dozier, Lomax, Tyrrell, and Lee (2001) highlight that avoidant individuals may decline help thus creating and reinforcing negative perceptions of others, resulting in a self-perpetuating negative interpersonal dynamic. Staff may find it easier to form therapeutic alliances with anxiously attached individuals because they are more likely to seek care for their difficulties (Vogel & Wei, 2005). Both attachment anxiety and avoidance have been related to interpersonal diffculties in psychosis independent of symptoms, with specific relationships found between attachment anxiety and over demanding behaviour and attachment avoidance and hostility (Berry et al., 2008). It may be that attachment anxiety is related to ruptures in the therapeutic alliance that were not captured in these studies, which relied on self-report measures of working alliance. Repeated involuntary hospital admissions and long periods of time spent in hospital may damage Black Caribbbean service users' attachment relationships in adulthood. Long hospital stays are likely to be difficult for service users as they create interpersonal distance and cut users off from attachment relationships within the community and families (Bucci et al., 2015). Repeated hospital admissions may also disrupt the development of new attachments, reducing the likelihood of service users maintaining stable relationships with service users and staff on the ward (Schuengel & van Ijzendoorn, 2001).

To the authors' knowledge, there is little to no previous research examining links between attachment and service-related factors in Black Caribbean people with psychosis. Findings from the current authors' recent UK-based longitudinal study in a small sample (n=51) of Black African and Caribbean service users with psychosis and their healthcare professionals showed that higher attachment avoidance was negatively related to poorer staff-rated overall working alliance and goal and task agreement, but not service-user ratings of alliance. Attachment anxiety was not associated with working alliance or its components, as rated by service users and staff members. These findings must be interpreted with caution as the small sample size meant there may have been limited power to detect an effect for attachment anxiety. For the same reason, ethnic differences between Black African and Black Caribbean people were not examined. Although individuals of Black ethnicity have similar negative experiences and poorer outcomes of mental health services in the UK (Bhui et al., 2003; Morgan et al., 2017), it is important not to homogenise culturally distinct ethnic groups.[3] There is considerable cultural diversity across African and Caribbean-descended populations in the UK in terms of factors such as spiritual or religious orientation, levels of ethnic identification or acculturation, and degree of interdependency and collectivism. Cultural variations such as these may have an influence on maternal

201

sensitivity, attachment expression, interpersonal dynamics and patterns of engaging with services. Additionally, it is important to consider length of time an individual has resided in the UK as recent migrants may have had different experiences in the mental health services, in terms of pathways to care and treatment by police and healthcare professionals, to those who were born in or have been living in the UK for a long time. This is likely to be influenced by structural changes to NHS mental health provision over the past few decades, such as the introduction of Early Intervention Services and transformation from hospital to multi-disciplinary community-based services (Kreyenbuhl, Nossel, & Dixon, 2009).

Notwithstanding these considerations, Black African and Caribbean people high in attachment avoidance may be reluctant to seek support from or depend on staff members who, in many areas of the UK outside of London are predominantly White. They may also conceal their feelings or avoid social contact all together. Avoidant interpersonal processes are likely to create difficulties in developing and maintaining positive therapeutic alliances; they may be reinforced by negative perceptions and past experiences of mental health services that are pertinent in this population (e.g. Henderson et al., 2015). Developing positive working alliances with service users with avoidant attachment may therefore require time to build trust and engagement, and support to feel comfortable with emotional expression. The relationship between greater attachment avoidance and lower staff-reported alliance related to goal and task agreement in Black African and Caribbean service users diagnosed with psychosis suggests staff may benefit from considering attachment style when developing goals and intervention plans; meeting service users' interpersonal needs may improve collaboration and ensure that planned goals and tasks reflect a shared understanding of their difficulties. Dissonance between staff and service users' explanatory models may reflect intercultural misunderstandings and culturally insensitive practice (Bhui & Bhugra, 2002; Islam et al., 2015). Staff often resist having conversations with service users regarding race and culture for fear of 'getting it wrong' (Keating, 2009). Training in culturally-sensitive clinical practice can improve service users' experiences of care (Bhui et al., 2015). Enhancing cultural curiosity and confidence may help to build relationships and challenge the mistrust existing in Black Caribbean families and communities, but also among healthcare professionals and within mental health services. Therapists may be encouraged to work with their own assumptions and prejudices, and consider how they may be reacting to clients that withdraw or disengage in attachment related situations. It may be that a lack of confidence, fear and uncertainty when dealing with inter-ethnic differences contributes to clinicians' own attachment-related anxiety and defensive activation of their attachment systems.

Between 80 and 90 per cent of the NHS workforce identify as White British (Health and Social Care Information Centre, 2015). Cultural differences between staff and service users might result in different interpersonal and communication patterns and mean it is more difficult for staff to meet service users' attachment needs and develop positive therapeutic alliances. Fear of causing offence, lack of cultural awareness and reduced cultural confidence among staff may lead to a lack of containment and compassion in their relationships with service users. Negative emotional reactions experienced by staff, or 'countertransference' in psychodynamic terms, may be more apparent when working with people with insecure attachment styles (Bucci et al., 2015). Considering cultural, systemic and attachment issues in therapeutic formulations and sharing these with staff teams may increase staff understanding of service users' problems and confidence in working with service users (Berry et al., 2009), including those of different ethnic background to their own. In therapy, conversations to understand culturally-informed aspects of mental health such as causal beliefs and coping strategies may highlight service user strengths and resources as well as moving towards mutually-agreed intervention and recovery goals.

Family intervention in the context of attachment theory

Family intervention (FI) is one area where attachment theory may provide a useful framework for understanding interpersonal difficulties in psychosis across different cultures in psychosis. Over the past few decades, multiple family theories, interventions and training programmes have been developed for people who experience psychosis (Pharoah, Mari, Rathbone, Wong, 2010). However, few have addressed issues of cultural-appropriateness. Contemporary FI models need to recognise that families in the UK come from a wide range of different backgrounds and cultures. This final section of the chapter will draw on a particular model of Culturally-adapted Family Intervention (CaFI), which has been developed to meet the needs of Black Caribbean families in the UK. CaFI has been derived from previous family work (Barrowclough & Tarrier, 1997; Falloon et al., 1984), the authors' research and clinical experience as well as the literature on cultural-adaptation. In doing so, we acknowledge that this is not the only approach to family work and the principles offered could be applied to other systematic approaches in different cultural contexts in psychosis.

FI was largely influenced by pioneering research showing that high *expressed emotion (EE);* high levels of hostility, criticism or emotional over-involvement (Expressed Emotion: Brown, Wing, Carsteir, & Monck, 1962) in the family environment predicts relapse in schizophrenia (Butzlaff & Hooley, 1998). EE has been used as a concept for understanding interactions between service users and their carers or relatives in the home environment and to better understand relationships with professionals in healthcare contexts (Wearden, Tarrier, Barrowclough, Zastowny, & Rahill, 2000). Akin to attachment, there are likely to be cultural variations in the construct of

EE. High emotional over-involvement (e.g. overprotectiveness and self-sacrifice) is a socially acceptable expression of care in certain cultures, such as in South Asian contexts, and would not necessarily be regarded as pathological (Bhugra & McKenzie, 2003). Similarly, critical comments may be the norm in certain cultures, such as in Jewish families (Bhugra & McKenzie, 2003). There is limited evidence for the utility of EE and its cultural relevance in Black Caribbean families, but it could be hypothesised that more collectivist and extended family environments would be more likely to score high on Western measures of emotional over-involvement which poses further questions relating to the cross-cultural validity of the construct.

FI is recommended in current clinical guidelines for psychosis (Dixon et al., 2010; National Institute for Health and Care Excellence, 2014), based on meta-analytic evidence of its clinical- and cost-effectiveness (Pharoah, Mari, Rathbone, & Wong, 2010; Pilling et al., 2002). Despite this, implementation of FI is low in mental health services and is rarely offered to service users experiencing psychosis (Berry & Haddock, 2008; Bucci, Berry, Barrowclough, & Haddock, 2016; Haddock et al., 2014). Although implementation and uptake are often sub-optimal (Berry & Haddock, 2008), there is consistent evidence that engaging with service users with psychosis and their families improves service delivery and outcomes (Addington, Collins, McCleery, & Addington, 2005; Morgan et al., 2006; Onwumere, Smith, & Kuipers, 2010; Pilling et al., 2002). The aim of FI is to support service users and their families by improving understanding of mental health problems and strengthening coping mechanisms. Common principles include developing positive working alliances, setting realistic and achievable shared goals, reducing family stress and tension, and maintaining gains in the family environment. More secure and stable attachment relationships can be developed through family work. Developing a shared understanding, communication skills practice and collaborative problem solving can strengthen family ties and emotional bonds, repair ruptures and prevent future relationship break down. There is evidence to suggest that changes in attachment responses can occur through changes in interpersonal relationships (Waters, Merrick, Treboux, Crowell, & Albersheim, 2000; Waters, Weinfield, & Hamilton, 2000), and that service users can develop more secure attachment styles following therapy (Taylor, Rietzschel, Danquah, & Berry, 2015).

There has been increasing interest in adapting psychological therapies (Degnan et al., 2017) and measures (Degnan, Berry, James, & Edge, 2018) in psychosis to meet the needs of specific ethnic and cultural groups. Most psychosocial interventions for psychosis have been developed in the West (i.e. USA and Europe) and are based on Western belief systems and cultural values. Research suggests that people are more likely to engage with mental health services and treatment when their cultural beliefs and explanatory models are considered (Bhui & Bhugra, 2004; Carter, Read, Pyle, & Morrison, 2016; Rathod, Kingdon, Phiri, & Gobbi, 2010). The present authors' recent systematic review of randomised controlled trials (RCTs) of culturally-adapted psychosocial interventions in psychosis showed that most interventions were adapted to acknowledge the pivotal role of the family unit in service users' care and recovery, ensuring their continued involvement in treatment and decision making (Degnan et al., 2017). Modifications were made to Western-derived psychological interventions to consider the inter-dependent family structures and shared responsibility valued in certain non-Western cultures (Degnan et al., 2017). At the time of the review, there was only one UK trial of culturally-adapted cognitive behavioural therapy (CBT) for minority ethnic groups (Rathod et al., 2013), and no interventions in psychosis specifically adapted for Black Caribbean culture.

Familial and caregiver burden is likely to be compounded in Black UK groups due to long periods of untreated psychosis and negative experiences in mental health services that can be extremely stressful (Keating & Robertson, 2004). The National Institute for Health and Care Excellence (NICE, 2009, 2014) highlights the need to improve access to effective care, experiences of services and outcomes for Black and minority groups in the UK. In response, the current authors developed a Culturally-adapted Family Intervention (CaFI) for Black Caribbean people diagnosed with schizophrenia (Edge et al., 2018; Edge et al., 2016). CaFI is derived from the Barrowclough and Tarrier (1992) model of FI and is delivered over ten sessions with four key phases: assessment and engagement; shared learning; communication; stress management, problem-solving and coping; and maintaining gains and staying well. Cultural adaptations were made to the content and delivery of FI, complimented by bespoke 'cultural confidence' training programmes for therapists. Training aimed to improve therapist confidence in (and reduce anxieties related to) working with people of different ethnic and cultural backgrounds to their own. CaFI is based on a 'shared learning' ethos where therapist, acknowledge relatives and service users' strengths and learn from their experiences, developing individualised formulations that consider their cultural values and explanatory models. Consideration of attachment needs in assessment and formulation would have been beneficial in this context, particularly given the experiences of trauma, separation and loss that may be common in Black Caribbean families.

One key finding in the development phase of the trial was the lack of bio-logical family members available for participation in therapy due to mistrust of services or breakdown in family relationships. To enable service users to take part who would otherwise be excluded, a novel concept of Family Support Members (FSMs) was introduced (Edge et al., 2016). FSMs were either community volunteers recruited by the research team or individuals nominated by service users, including friends, mental health professionals or significant others involved in their care. Bowlby (1988) suggested that the therapeutic relationship can provide a corrective emotional experience to disconfirm insecure internal working models and enable the service user to transition to secure attachment responses. Similarly, the FSMs might act as attachment figure by providing a consistent and 'secure base' by which service users can build trusting relationships with services and extend their social ties in the community.

Case example of Culturally-adapted Family Intervention (CaFI)

The following case example is a fictitious case from the CaFI trial (Edge et al., 2018) but provides a typical account of the experiences of a service user who was supported by an FSM in therapy. Contextual information will be provided, followed by reflections on each stage of the culturally-adapted family work in relation to attachment theory.

Context of referral

Angela was a 38-year-old woman living in supported accommodation in an urban inner-city area. Angela self-identified as Black British. She was born and raised in the UK with an African-Caribbean heritage. She had a long-standing diagnosis of schizophrenia and had been receiving treatment from mental health services for around 20 years. Angela had recently been discharged from a rehabilitation hospital ward and had experienced numerous involuntary hospital admissions throughout her adulthood. Angela had never been offered psychological therapy and was ambivalent about receiving the Culturally-adapted Family Intervention (CaFI). It was initially thought by her care team that Angela might not feel motivated to engage in thera-peutic work. Angela held some negative views of services and 'the system'[4] in general and experienced some difficulties in her relationship with healthcare professionals including her lead mental health worker, Pauline (pseudonym), who had been managing her care in the NHS for the past four years.

Angela had limited contact with her family. She had lost contact with her mother and father. She had two younger sisters, each with their own mental health difficulties. Angela had maintained a relationship with her youngest sister who also had a diagnosis of schizophrenia and was living nearby in a rehabilitation unit. She did not see her regularly but remained in contact over the phone. Angela did not have any close friends and did not converse with other residents, spending most of her time on her own in her room. Angela did not wish to approach her sister about participating in CaFI as she felt it would be 'too much' for her given the current problems she was experiencing. She was supported to invite her mental health worker to take part with her (i.e. nominated family support member (FSM)).

Assessment and engagement

Angela attended a total of ten therapy sessions with her mental health worker. Sessions were facilitated by a lead therapist and co-therapist (clinical psychologist and assistant psychologist) and were carried out weekly in a private room at her supported accommodation. Given Angela's ambivalence about therapy and services, it was crucial to provide a secure and safe place for her to feel able to share her current difficulties and past experiences and to build trust and alliance in therapy. Angela felt that her cultural needs had never previously been considered and she expressed that she wanted to understand more about herself and her culture. Shared therapy goals were for Angela to gain a better understanding of her experiences, and her cultural identity, build her self-esteem and relationship with her mental health worker, and find ways to manage her anxiety. During the first few therapy sessions, Angela was supported to develop a coherent narrative of her life and to understand how her past experiences may have contributed to her difficulties and her internal working model relating to herself, others and her interpersonal environment. She was supported to draw out a timeline which facilitated conversations about her family and themes relating to her cultural identity (e.g. going to Church, social gatherings every Sunday, traditional Caribbean food that her grandmother used to cook), and to sit with and explore any feelings that arose in relation to these experiences.

Angela grew up in an inner-city urban neighbourhood. She described feeling 'rejected' by her 'absent father' who was rarely at home and mother who struggled to raise three children with limited support. She recalled her mother drinking alcohol excessively and regularly witnessing physical fights between her and her father in the family home. Angela's mother often criticised and blamed her for her problems and relationship difficulties, and she felt a huge sense of responsibility for her younger sisters whom she tried to protect. It was hypothesised that Angela developed an avoidant attachment style as a result of her parents being emotionally unavailable and unresponsive to her needs. Angela developed a close relationship with her grandmother who lived next door and was considered to be a secure attachment figure when growing up. She spoke highly of her grandmother and recalled pleasurable memories of her telling stories about her childhood in Jamaica. She described her as a strong-minded woman who was caring but always nagging at her to get a job as 'people like us have to work harder than the others to get anywhere'. Angela always felt like she had let her grandmother down.

Angela described herself as a 'nervous child' and started smoking cannabis to manage her anxiety at the age of 13. She completed her secondary school education and left home to live with her boyfriend when she was 16 years old. Angela experienced her first episode of psychosis at the age of 18 following the death of her boyfriend in a tragic car accident. Angela was frightened that her neighbours were going to harm her and experienced distressing, critical and threatening voices. She became increasingly mistrustful of others, withdrawn and socially isolated. Soon after, Angela was sectioned under the Mental Health Act (2007) and admitted to hospital in the context of intensive anxiety, hearing voices and paranoia.

Angela described feeling stigmatised about her mental health problems by people in her community. She reported that her diagnosis of 'schizophrenia' brought shame on her family as mental health difficulties were not accepted or normalised in her culture. Angela felt misunderstood by her friends and family, particularly her grandmother who attributed her problems to 'not working hard enough' and smoking cannabis. She recalled feeling a great sense of loss when she first became unwell. Angela's formulation made links between her past experiences and negative beliefs about herself ('I am unlovable, worthless, not good enough'), others ('others cannot be trusted, are abusive and rejecting') and the world ('the world is unsafe and unreliable'). Her experiences of her grandmother and peers as rejecting reinforced these beliefs after which she continued to be mistrustful of and avoid social relationships with others. Angela struggled in relationships because of her low self-confidence and beliefs that others were abusive, rejecting and abandoning. She was suspicious of staff and service users in her supported accommodation and kept her 'guard up' and others at a distance. Angela often felt controlled and frustrated and responded with agitation when she was asked to do something. She did not engage in daily activities and would withdraw from others, spending most of her time in her bedroom. Angela felt let down by 'the system' and described being treated unfairly by the police and healthcare staff in the past, which contributed to her mistrust of professionals involved in her care and mental health services in general.

Shared learning

The therapists did not find the explanatory model Angela held for her mental health problems to be a clear one. She was unsure how her problems began, though she believed that they were worsened by her previous negative treatment in services. Angela said she felt blamed by her family as they thought that her problems were caused by her 'getting up to no good' and smoking cannabis. She described having little understanding of her diagnosis of 'schizophrenia' as the meaning had never been explained to her. Therapy supported Angela and her mental health worker, Pauline, to understand Angela's problems in the context of her life experiences, highlighting the impact of stress and vulnerability factors on her beliefs (about herself and others) and experiences of hearing voices, anxiety and mistrust of others. Normalising information was shared to challenge some of the stigmatising views and negative stereotypes Angela had experienced related to her diagnosis and hearing voices. A psychoeducational pamphlet was provided on 'understanding psychosis and schizophrenia' (developed in collaboration with a service user and carer advisory group of Black Caribbean background, specifically for the CaFI trial), which included information to generate discussions around culturally relevant issues (e.g. alternative explanatory models and coping, case study highlighting experiences of racial discrimination, fear and stigma), meaning and labelling, guidelines and interventions for psychosis, and how the 'system' works (i.e. role of healthcare professionals and police, service structure and pathways to care). Pauline was encouraged to share this information with the staff team in Angela's supported accommodation to enhance their understanding of psychosis and some of the cultural factors that may be important when formulating Angela's difficulties. For example, staff were supported to understand how Angela's past experiences of rejection, shame and stigma by her family and community may have led to an avoidant attachment style and the need to keep others at a distance to feel safe. Staff were also encouraged to read over the former psychoeducation materials relating to culture and psychosis. The aim was to reduce criticism and further rejection amongst staff, thus creating a more compassionate and secure environment to support Angela's recovery.

Communication

Angela's mental health worker, Pauline, shared that the professionals involved in Angela's care found her aloof and distant, and struggled to find activities that met her needs and aspirations. CaFI helped Pauline to understand Angela's difficulties with staff (her 'negative attitude') and avoidance as a consequence of her mistrusting others and experiencing professionals as judging and attacking in the past. Participating in therapy facilitated an understanding of situations of conflict by drawing out mini-formulations, taking into account the perspectives of Angela and staff members, and highlighting the escalation of difficulties through unhelpful communication or misunderstanding of each other's viewpoints. Angela found it difficult to express her thoughts and feelings to professionals as she did not feel confident that she would be heard, understood or supported. Role playing hypothetical scenarios was used in sessions to support Angela to increase her ability to communicate her needs to professionals and to find helpful ways for staff to respond thus ensuring she felt valued and listened to rather than criticised and rejected. Assertiveness skills helped Angela to feel in control of stressful situations and build more trusting and secure relationships with staff. Pauline supported Angela to share these formulations and practice communication skills outside of the sessions with staff members at her supported accommodation.

Problem-solving, stress management and coping

Angela had a long history of using avoidance as a way of coping with anxiety and mistrust of others and keeping herself safe, consistent with an avoidant attachment style. Therapy supported a shared understanding of Angela's desire to be emotionally distant from others and attempt to cope with threatening situations on her own, relating these behaviours to her previous

209

experiences of abuse and fear of loss and rejection. Verbal reattribution techniques were used to highlight the disadvantages of avoidance as a long-term coping strategy, whilst acknowledging it to be an adaptive response to early childhood trauma. The concept of vicious maintenance cycles were used to introduce Angela to the idea that withdrawing from others can be self-defeating as it reinforced her negative thoughts (e.g. *'There's no point in talking to them, they will only judge you'*, *'Don't trust them, just look after yourself'*) and beliefs about herself, exacerbating her low self-esteem and low mood. These were drawn out collaboratively with Angela and Pauline in sessions to highlight links between thoughts, feelings and behaviours and demonstrate how Angela's thinking biases were based on her past experiences and may not be a helpful interpretation of current (triggering) situations (e.g. difficult interactions with staff members). Angela learned that, although avoidance was protective in the short-term (i.e. relief from anxiety or protection), it prevented her from finding out that some people may be accepting of her and may not reject or criticise her. Pauline phoned Angela outside of sessions at an agreed time once a week to provide any necessary encouragement and support. Mindfulness-based breathing and grounding techniques were practised in and outside of sessions as a means of helping Angela to regulate her anxiety and manage distressing negative thoughts. Positive data logs and self-talk were used in session to highlight Angela's strengths, plan meaningful and pleasurable activities, and to build his self-confidence. Visual imagery was practised in sessions to support Angela to play out feared scenarios and to introduce more accepting and non-critical images of others. Imagery techniques were also used to bring to life aspects of Angela's culture that she felt had been lost over the years not seeing her family, such as replacing images related to feeling rejected by her grandmother with more pleasurable memories of her family home in Jamaica. These therapeutic strategies encouraged Angela to adopt a more compassionate and balanced view of herself and others. Following therapy, Pauline facilitated a meeting with Angela and a staff member at her supported accommodation to hand over a summary of the therapy blueprint and share key learning points.

Conclusion

As discussed in the preceding chapters, attachment theory provides a useful framework for understanding interpersonal relationships in psychosis (Berry et al., 2008) and relationships with mental health services (Bucci et al., 2015). The current chapter highlights the need to consider differences in the development and expression of attachment styles when working therapeutically with people from different ethnic and cultural groups. There is a growing body of research highlighting cultural differences in the expression of attachment, but further work is required to understand the social and psychological mechanisms mediating the association between culture and attachment

(Agishtein & Brumbaugh, 2013). Black Caribbean people in the UK may be more likely to experience disrupted attachment relationships because of trauma and adversity in childhood and adulthood related to parental separation and loss, fragmented social networks, social disadvantage and racial discrimination (e.g. Morgan et al., 2017). Mental health professionals would benefit from considering culturally-informed attachment issues in therapeutic formulations and interventions with Black Caribbean people experiencing psychosis. Adaptations may include staff training in culturally sensitive practices, building trusting and secure relationships with families and local communities, and increased awareness and understanding of culturally-specific explanatory models and interpersonal structures and processes. Attachment theory may be useful in supporting our understanding of complex and difficult interpersonal dynamics existing between Black service users and staff involved in their care, help to challenge any fear and mistrust on both sides, improve staff confidence and compassion, and reduce any attachment-related anxieties related to working with people from diverse cultural backgrounds.

Notes

1 'Western' and 'non-Western' cultures are defined as ideological, not geographical, constructs and it is recognised that cultures are often heterogeneous and may not be purely 'Western' or 'non-Western', such as the cultures of South and Central America.

2 The present chapter refers to people of Black Caribbean origin in the UK. The term 'Black Caribbean' refers to individuals of Caribbean origin who can trace at least part of their heritage to Africa, including people who regard themselves of being of Mixed heritage or ethnicity. People of Caribbean origin in the UK may also choose to self-identify as 'Black British' in recognition of their British nationality and identification with British culture. Similarly, some Black Caribbean people may prefer 'African-Caribbean' in recognition of their African ancestry.

3 The use of broad ethnic categories in research can conceal marked heterogeneity within these groups and ultimately reduce the applicability of research findings and provision of culturally-appropriate healthcare (Agyemang, Bhopal, & Bruijnzeels, 2005).

4 Term used by some members of Black Caribbean communities to signify institutional racism and resultant 'system' of oppression, subjugation and surveillance with particular reference to the role of the police or Criminal Justice System and mental health services as agents of social control.

References

Addington, J., Collins, A., McCleery, A., & Addington, D. (2005). The role of family work in early psychosis. *Schizophrenia Research*, *79*(1), 77–83. doi: 10.1016/j.schres.2005.01.013

Agishtein, P., & Brumbaugh, C. (2013). Cultural variation in adult attachment: The impact of ethnicity, collectivism, and country of origin. *Journal of Social, Evolutionary, and Cultural Psychology, 7*(4), 384–405.

Agyemang, C., Bhopal, R., & Bruijnzeels, M. (2005). Negro, Black, Black African, African Caribbean, African American or what? Labelling African origin populations in the health arena in the 21st century. *Journal of Epidemiology and Community Health, 59*(12), 1014–1018.

Ainsworth, M. D. S. (1967). *Infancy in Uganda: Infant care and the growth of love.* Baltimore: John Hopkins Press.

Ainsworth, M. D. S., Blehar, M. C., Water, E., & Wall, S. (1978). *Patterns of Attachment: A psychological study of the strange situation.* Hillsdale, New Jersey: Erlbaum.

Arnold, E. (2012). *Working with Families of African Caribbean Origin: Understanding issues around immigration and attachment.* London: Jessica Kingsley Publishers.

Barber, M., Short, J., Clarke-Moore, J., Lougher, M., Huckle, P., & Amos, T. (2006). A secure attachment model of care: meeting the needs of women with mental health problems and antisocial behaviour. *Criminal Behaviour and Mental Health, 16*(1), 3–10.

Barrowclough, C., & Tarrier, N. (1992). *Families of Schizophrenic Patients: Cognitive Behavioural Intervention.* London: Chapman & Hall.

Bartholomew, K., & Horowitz, L. M. (1991). Attachment styles among young adults: a test of a four-category model. *Journal of Personality & Social Psychology, 61*(2), 226–244.

Becares, L., Nazroo, J., & Stafford, M. (2009). The buffering effects of ethnic density on experienced racism and health. *Health Place, 15*(3), 670–678. doi:10.1016/j.healthplace.2008.10.008

Bentall, R. P., Wickham, S., Shevlin, M., & Varese, F. (2012). Do specific early-life adversities lead to specific symptoms of psychosis? A study from the 2007 the Adult Psychiatric Morbidity Survey. *Schizophrenia Bulletin, 38*(4), 734–740. doi:10.1093/schbul/sbs049

Berry, K., Barrowclough, C., & Wearden, A. (2008). Attachment theory: A framework for understanding symptoms and interpersonal relationships in psychosis. *Behaviour Research and Therapy, 46*(12), 1275–1282. doi: 10.1016/j.brat.2008.08.009

Berry, K., Barrowclough, C., & Wearden, A. (2009). Adult attachment, perceived earlier experiences of care giving and trauma in people with psychosis. *Journal of Mental Health, 18*(4), 280–287.

Berry, K., & Bucci, S. (2016). What does attachment theory tell us about working with distressing voices? *Psychosis, 8*(1), 60–71.

Berry, K., & Haddock, G. (2008). The implementation of the NICE guidelines for schizophrenia: Barriers to the implementation of psychological interventions and recommendations for the future. *Psychology and Psychotherapy-Theory Research and Practice, 81*, 419–436. doi: 10.1348/147608308x329540

Bhugra, D., & Bhui, K. (2001). African-Caribbeans and schizophrenia: contributing factors. *Advances in Psychiatric Treatment, 7*(4), 283–291.

Bhugra, D., & McKenzie, K. (2003). Expressed emotion across cultures. *Advances in Psychiatric Treatment, 9*(5), 342–348.

Bhui, K., Aslam, W., Palinski, A., McCabe, R., Johnson, M., Weich, S., … Szczepura, A. (2015). Interventions to improve therapeutic communications between Black and minority ethnic patients and professionals in psychiatric services: systematic review. *The British Journal of Psychiatry*, *207*(2), 95–103. doi:10.1192/bjp.bp.114.158899

Bhui, K., & Bhugra, D. (2002). Explanatory models for mental distress: implications for clinical practice and research. *The British Journal of Psychiatry*, *181*(1), 6–7. doi:10.1192/bjp.181.1.6

Bhui, K., & Bhugra, D. (2004). Communication with patients from other cultures: the place of explanatory models. *Advances in Psychiatric Treatment*, *10*(6), 474–478.

Bhui, K., Stansfeld, S., Hull, S., Priebe, S., Mole, F., & Feder, G. (2003). Ethnic variations in pathways to and use of specialist mental health services in the UK. Systematic review. *British Journal of Psychiatry*, *182*, 105–116.

Bowlby, J. (1982). *Attachment and Loss: Vol 1. Attachment (2nd ed.)*. New York, USA: Basic Books (Original work published in 1969).

Bowlby, J. (1988). *A Secure Base: Clinical applications of attachment theory*. London, UK: Routledge.

Brennan, K. A., Clark, C. L., & Shaver, P. R. (1998). Self-report measurement of adult romantic attachment: An integrative overview. In J. A. Simpson & W. S. Rholes (Eds.), *Attachment Theory and Close Relationships* (pp. 46–76). New York: The Guilford Press.

Broome, M. R., Woolley, J. B., Tabraham, P., Johns, L. C., Bramon, E., Murray, G. K., … Murray, R. M. (2005). What causes the onset of psychosis? *Schizophrenia Research*, *79*(1), 23–34. doi:10.1016/j.schres.2005.02.007

Brown, G. W., Wing, J. K., Carsteir, G. M., & Monck, E. M. (1962). Influence of family life on course of schizophrenic illness. *British Journal of Preventive & Social Medicine*, *16*(2), 55.

Brugha, T. S. (2010). Social support. In C. Morgan & D. Bhugra (Eds.), *Principles of Social Psychiatry* (2nd ed., pp. 461–476). Oxford: Wiley-Blackwell.

Bucci, S., Berry, K., Barrowclough, C., & Haddock, G. (2016). Family interventions in psychosis: a review of the evidence and barriers to implementation. *Australian Psychologist*, *51*(1), 62–68.

Bucci, S., Roberts, N. H., Danquah, A. N., & Berry, K. (2015). Using attachment theory to inform the design and delivery of mental health services: A systematic review of the literature. *Psychology and Psychotherapy: Theory, Research and Practice*, *88*(1), 1–20. doi:10.1111/papt.12029

Butzlaff, R. L., & Hooley, J. M. (1998). Expressed emotion and psychiatric relapse – A meta-analysis. *Archives of General Psychiatry*, *55*(6), 547–552. doi: 10.1001/archpsyc.55.6.547

Campbell, C., Cornish, F., & McLean, C. (2004). Social capital, participation and the perpetuation of health inequalities: Obstacles to African-Caribbean participation in 'partnerships' to improve mental health. *Ethnicity & Health*, *9*(4), 313–335. doi:10.1080/1355785042000302799

Cantor-Graae, E., & Selten, J. P. (2005). Schizophrenia and migration: a meta-analysis and review. *American Journal of Psychiatry*, *162*(1), 12–24. doi:10.1176/appi.ajp.162.1.12

Care Quality Commission. (2011). *Count me in 2010: Results of the 2010 national census of inpatients and patients on supervised community treatment in mental health and learning disability services in England and Wales*. London: Care Quality Commission.

Carlson, E. A., Hostinar, C. E., Mliner, S. B., & Gunnar, M. R. (2014). The emergence of attachment following early social deprivation. *Development and Psychopathology, 26*(2), 479–489.

Carter, L., Read, J., Pyle, M., & Morrison, A. P. (2016). The impact of causal explanations on outcome in people experiencing psychosis: a systematic review. *Clinical Psychology & Psychotherapy, 2*, 332–347. doi:10.1002/cpp.2002

Cheng, S.-T., & Kwan, K. W. (2008). Attachment dimensions and contingencies of self-worth: The moderating role of culture. *Personality and Individual Differences, 45*(6), 509–514.

Commission for Healthcare Audit and Inspection. (2005). Count me in. Results of a national census of inpatients in mental health hospitals and facilities in England and Wales. *Commission for Healthcare Audit and Inspection.* London.

Cowan, P. A., & Cowan, C. P. (2007). Attachment theory: Seven unresolved issues and questions for future research. *Research in Human Development, 4*(3–4), 181–201.

Das-Munshi, J., Becares, L., Boydell, J. E., Dewey, M. E., Morgan, C., Stansfeld, S. A., & Prince, M. J. (2012). Ethnic density as a buffer for psychotic experiences: findings from a national survey (EMPIRIC). *British Journal of Psychiatry, 201*(4), 282–290. doi:10.1192/bjp.bp.111.102376

Degnan, A. J. (2017). *Social networks and engagement with mental health services among Black African and Caribbean people with psychosis.* Unpublished doctoral dissertation. University of Manchester.

Degnan, A., Berry, K., James, S., & Edge, D. (2018). Development, validation and cultural-adaptation of the knowledge about psychosis questionnaire for African-Caribbean people in the UK. *Psychiatry Research, 263*, 199–206. doi:10.1016/j.psychres.2018.03.013

Department of Health. (2005). *Delivering Race Equality in Mental Health Care: an action plan for reform inside and outside services and the Government's response to the independent inquiry into the death of David Bennett.* London: Department of Health. Retrieved from www.nmhdu.org.uk/silo/files/delivering-race-equalityin-mental-health-care.pdf

Dixon, L., Dickerson, F., Bellack, A. S., Bennett, M., Dickinson, D., Goldberg, R. W., ... Pasillas, R. M. (2010). The 2009 schizophrenia PORT psychosocial treatment recommendations and summary statements. *Schizophrenia Bulletin, 36*(1), 48–70.

Dozier, M., Lomax, L., Tyrrell, C. L., & Lee, S. W. (2001). The challenge of treatment for clients with dismissing states of mind. *Attachment & Human Development, 3*(1), 62–76.

Edge, D., Degnan, A., Cotterill, S., Berry, K., Baker, J., Drake, R., & Abel, K. (2018). Culturally-adapted Family Intervention (CaFI) for African-Caribbean people diagnosed with schizophrenia and their familes: A mixed methods feasibility study of development, implementation and acceptability. *Health Services and Delivery Research (NHR Journals), 6*(32). doi: https://doi.org/10.3310/hsdr06320.

Edge, D., Degnan, A., Cotterill, S., Berry, K., Drake, R., Baker, J., ... Bhugra, D. (2016). Culturally-adapted Family Intervention (CaFI) for African-Caribbeans diagnosed with schizophrenia and their families: a feasibility study protocol of implementation and acceptability. *Pilot and Feasibility Studies, 2*(1), 2–39.

Eliacin, J. (2013). Social capital, narratives of fragmentation, and schizophrenia: an ethnographic exploration of factors shaping African-Caribbeans' social capital and mental health in a North London community. *Culture & Medical Psychiatry*, *37*(3), 465–487. doi:10.1007/s11013-013-9322-2

Fearon, P., Kirkbride, J. B., Morgan, C., Dazzan, P., Morgan, K., Lloyd, T., ... Group, A. S. (2006). Incidence of schizophrenia and other psychoses in ethnic minority groups: results from the MRC AESOP Study. *Psychological Medicine*, *36*(11), 1541–1550.

Foster, J. S. (2013). Mothering, migration and the global village: Understanding support for mothering in the 21st century Caribbean. *Journal of the Motherhood Initiative for Research and Community Involvement*, *4*(2).

Fox, N. A., Nelson, C. A., 3rd, & Zeanah, C. H. (2017). The effects of psychosocial deprivation on attachment: lessons from the Bucharest early intervention project. *Psychodynamic Psychiatry*, *45*(4), 441–450. doi:10.1521/pdps.2017.45.4.441

Fung, W. L. A., Bhugra, D., & Jones, P. B. (2009). Ethnicity and mental health: the example of schizophrenia and related psychoses in migrant populations in the Western world. *Psychiatry*, *8*(9), 335–341.

Goodwin, I., Holmes, G., Cochrane, R., & Mason, O. (2003). The ability of adult mental health services to meet clients' attachment needs: The development and implementation of the Service Attachment Questionnaire. *Psychology and Psychotherapy: Theory, Research and Practice*, *76*(2), 145–161.

Gumley, A. I., Taylor, H. E., Schwannauer, M., & MacBeth, A. (2014). A systematic review of attachment and psychosis: measurement, construct validity and outcomes. *Acta Psychiatrica Scandinavica*, *129*(4), 257–274. doi:10.1111/acps.12172

Haddock, G., Eisner, E., Boone, C., Davies, G., Coogan, C., & Barrowclough, C. (2014). An investigation of the implementation of NICE-recommended CBT interventions for people with schizophrenia. *Journal of Mental Health*, *23*(4), 162–165. doi:10.3109/09638237.2013.869571

Health and Social Care Information Centre. (2015). Healthcare Workforce Statistics. Retrieved 29 April 2017 www.hscic.gov.uk

Henderson, R., Williams, P., Gabbidon, J., Farrelly, S., Schauman, O., Hatch, S., ... Group, M. S. (2015). Mistrust of mental health services: ethnicity, hospital admission and unfair treatment. *Epidemiology and Psychiatric Sciences*, *24*(3), 258–265.

Islam, Z., Rabiee, F., & Singh, S. P. (2015). Black and minority ethnic groups' perception and experience of early intervention in psychosis services in the United Kingdom. *Journal of Cross-Cultural Psychology*, *46*(5), 737–753. doi:10.1177/0022022115575737

Keating, F. (2009). African and Caribbean men and mental health. *Ethnicity and Inequalities in Health and Social Care*, *2*(2), 41–53.

Keating, F., Roberson, E. D., McCulloch, A., & Francis, E. (2002). *Breaking the circles of fear: A review of the relationship between mental health services and African and Caribbean communities*. The Sainsbury's Centre for Mental Health, London.

Keating, F., & Robertson, D. (2004). Fear, black people and mental illness: a vicious circle? *Health and Social Care Community*, *12*(5), 439–447. doi:10.1111/j.1365-2524.2004.00506.x

Kirkbride, J. B., Coid, J., Morgan, C., Fearon, P., Dazzan, P., Yang, M., ... Jones, P. (2010). Translating the epidemiology of psychosis into public mental health: evidence, challenges and future prospects. *Journal of Public Mental Health*, *9*(2), 4–14.

Kirkbride, J. B., Errazuriz, A., Croudace, T. J., Morgan, C., Jackson, D., Boydell, J., ... Jones, P. B. (2012). Incidence of schizophrenia and other psychoses in England,

1950–2009: A systematic review and meta-analyses. *PLoS ONE, 7*(3), e31660. doi:10.1371/journal.pone.0031660

Kirkbride, J. B., Jones, P. B., Ullrich, S., & Coid, J. W. (2014). Social deprivation, inequality, and the neighborhood-level incidence of psychotic syndromes in East London. *Schizophrenia Bulletin, 40*(1), 169–180.

Kirkbride, J. B., Morgan, C., Fearon, P., Dazzan, P., Murray, R. M., & Jones, P. B. (2007). Neighbourhood-level effects on psychoses: re-examining the role of context. *Psychological Medicine, 37*(10), 1413–1425. doi:10.1017/S0033291707000499

Kreyenbuhl, J., Nossel, I. R., & Dixon, L. B. (2009). Disengagement from mental health treatment among individuals with schizophrenia and strategies for facilitating connections to care: a review of the literature. *Schizophrenia Bulletin, 35*(4), 696–703. doi:10.1093/schbul/sbp046

Littlewood, R., & Lipsedge, M. (1981). Some social and phenomenological characteristics of psychotic immigrants. *Psychological Medicine, 11*(2), 289–302.

Longden, E., Madill, A., & Waterman, M. G. (2012). Dissociation, trauma, and the role of lived experience: toward a new conceptualization of voice hearing. *Psychology Bulletin, 138*(1), 28.

Magai, C., Cohen, C., Milburn, N., Thorpe, B., McPherson, R., & Peralta, D. (2001). Attachment styles in older European American and African American adults. *The Journals of Gerontology Series B: Psychological Sciences and Social Sciences, 56*(1), S28-S35.

Mallett, R., Leff, J., Bhugra, D., Pang, D., & Zhao, J. H. (2002). Social environment, ethnicity and schizophrenia A case-control study. *Society of Psychiatry Psychiatry Epidemiology, 37*(7), 329–335.

Markus, H. R., & Kitayama, S. (1991). Culture and the self: Implications for cognition, emotion, and motivation. *Psychological Review, 98*(2), 224.

McConnell, M., Moss, E. J. A. J. o. E., & Psychology, D. (2011). Attachment across the life span: factors that contribute to stability and change, *Australian Journal of Education and Developmental Psychology. 11*, 60–77.

Mclean, C., Campbell, C., & Cornish, F. (2003). African-Caribbean interactions with mental health services in the UK: experiences and expectations of exclusion as (re) productive of health inequalities. *Social Science & Medicine, 56*(3), 657–669.

Mental Health Taskforce. (2016). *The five year forward view of mental health: A report from the independent Mental Health Taskforce to the NHS England.* Retrieved from www.england.nhs.uk/mental-health/taskforce

Mikulincer, M., Shaver, P. R., & Pereg, D. (2003). Attachment theory and affect regulation: The dynamics, development, and cognitive consequences of attachment-related strategies. *Motivation and Emotion, 27*(2), 77–102.

Morgan, C., Abdul-Al, R., Lappin, J. M., Jones, P., Fearon, P., Leese, M., ... Murray, R. (2006). Clinical and social determinants of duration of untreated psychosis in the AESOP first-episode psychosis study. *British Journal of Psychiatry, 189*, 446–452. Doi:10.1192/bjp.bp.106.021303

Morgan, C., Charalambides, M., Hutchinson, G., & Murray, R. M. (2010). Migration, ethnicity, and psychosis: toward a sociodevelopmental model. *Schizophrenia Bulletin, 36*(4), 655–664. doi:10.1093/schbul/sbq051

Morgan, C., & Fearon, P. (2007). Social experience and psychosis. Insights from studies of migrant and ethnic minority groups. *Epidemiologia e Psichiatria Sociale, 16*(2), 118–123.

Morgan, C., Fearon, P., Lappin, J. M., Heslin, M., Donoghue, K., Lomas, B., ... Jones, P. B. (2017). Ethnicity and long-term course and outcome of psychotic disorders in a UK sample: the AESOP-10 study. *British Journal of Psychiatry, 211*(2), 88–94.

Morgan, C., & Hutchinson, G. (2010). The social determinants of psychosis in migrant and ethnic minority populations: a public health tragedy. *Psychological Medicine, 40*(5), 705–709.

Morgan, C., Kirkbride, J. B., Hutchinson, G., Craig, T., Morgan, K., Dazzan, P., ... Fearon, P. (2008). Cumulative social disadvantage, ethnicity and first-episode psychosis: a case-control study. *Psychological Medicine, 38*(12), 1701–1715. doi:10.1017/S0033291708004534

Morgan, C., Kirkbride, J. B., Leff, J., Craig, T., Hutchinson, G., McKenzie, K., ... Jones, P. (2007). Parental separation, loss and psychosis in different ethnic groups: a case-control study. *Psychological Medicine, 37*(4), 495–504.

Morgan, C., Mallett, R., Hutchinson, G., Bagalkote, H., Morgan, K., Fearon, P., ... Group., A. S. (2005a). Pathways to care and ethnicity. 1: Sample characteristics and compulsory admission. Report from the AESOP study. *British Journal of Psychiatry, 186*, 281–289. doi:10.1192/bjp.186.4.281

Morgan, C., Mallett, R., Hutchinson, G., Bagalkote, H., Morgan, K., Fearon, P., ... Group., A. S. (2005b). Pathways to care and ethnicity. 2: Source of referral and help-seeking – Report from the AESOP study. *British Journal of Psychiatry, 186*, 290–296. doi:10.1192/bjp.186.4.290

Morgan, C., Mallett, R., Hutchinson, G., & Leff, J. (2004). Negative pathways to psychiatric care and ethnicity: the bridge between social science and psychiatry. *Social Science & Medicine, 58*(4), 739–752. doi:10.1016/S0277-9536(03)00233-8

Murphy, M. (1996). Household and family structures among ethnic groups. In D. Coleman & J. Salt (Eds.), *Ethnicity in the 1991 Census: demographic characteristics of the ethnic minority population*. London: HMSO.

National Institute for Health and Care Excellence. (2009). *Schizophrenia: The NICE Guideline on Core Interventions in the Treatment and Management of Schizophrenia in Adults in Primary and Secondary Care*. London: The British Psychological Society and the Royal College of Psychiatrists.

National Institute for Health and Care Excellence. (2014). *Psychosis and schizophrenia in adults: prevention and management. Clinical guideline [CG178]*. Leicester and London (UK): British Psychological Society and The Royal College of Psychiatrists.

National Institute for Mental Health. (2003). *Inside out: improving mental health services for Black and Minority Ethnic communities in England*. Retrieved from Department of Health, London

Office for National Statistics. (2011). *2011 Census: Special Migration Statistics (United Kingdom). UK Data Service Census Support*. Retrieved from: https://wicid.ukdataservice.ac.uk

Onwumere, J., Smith, B., & Kuipers, E. (2010). Families and psychosis. In D. Bhugra & C. Morgan (Eds.), *Principles of Social Psychiatry* (2 ed., pp. 103–116): John Wiley & Sons Ltd.

Pharoah, F., Mari, J., Rathbone, J., & Wong, W. (2010). Family intervention for schizophrenia. *Cochrane Database of Systematic Reviews* (12), Cd000088. doi:10.1002/14651858.CD000088.pub2

Pilling, S., Bebbington, P., Kuipers, E., Garety, P., Geddes, J., Orbach, G., & Morgan, C. (2002). Psychological treatments in schizophrenia: I. Meta-analysis of family intervention and cognitive behaviour therapy. *Psychological Medicine, 32*(5), 763–782.

Pinto, R., Ashworth, M., & Jones, R. (2008). Schizophrenia in black Caribbeans living in the UK: an exploration of underlying causes of the high incidence rate. *British Journal of General Practice, 58*(551), 429–434. doi:10.3399/bjgp08X299254

Rathod, S., Kingdon, D., Phiri, P., & Gobbi, M. (2010). Developing culturally sensitive cognitive behaviour therapy for psychosis for ethnic minority patients by exploration and incorporation of service users' and health professionals' views and opinions. *Behavioural and Cognitive Psychotherapy, 38*(5), 511–533.

Rathod, S., Phiri, P., Harris, S., Underwood, C., Thagadur, M., Padmanabi, U., & Kingdon, D. (2013). Cognitive behaviour therapy for psychosis can be adapted for minority ethnic groups: A randomised controlled trial. *Schizophrenia Research, 143*(2–3), 319–326.

Reininghaus, U. A., Craig, T. K., Fisher, H. L., Hutchinson, G., Fearon, P., Morgan, K., ... Morgan, C. (2010). Ethnic identity, perceptions of disadvantage, and psychosis: findings from the AESOP study. *Schizophrenia Research, 124*(1–3), 43–48. doi:10.1016/j.schres.2010.08.038

Rothbaum, F., Weisz, J., Pott, M., Miyake, K., & Morelli, G. (2000). Attachment and culture: Security in the United States and Japan. *American Psychologist, 55*(10), 1093.

Schofield, P., Ashworth, M., & Jones, R. (2011). Ethnic isolation and psychosis: re-examining the ethnic density effect. *Psychological Medicine, 41*(6), 1263–1269. doi:10.1017/s0033291710001649

Schuengel, C., & van Ijzendoorn, M. H. (2001). Attachment in mental health institutions: A critical review of assumptions, clinical implications, and research strategies. *Attachment & Human Development, 3*(3), 304–323.

Sharpley, M. S., Hutchinson, G., Murray, R. M., & McKenzie, K. (2001). Understanding the excess of psychosis among the African–Caribbean population in England Review of current hypotheses. *The British Journal of Psychiatry, 178*(40), s60–s68.

Taylor, P., Rietzschel, J., Danquah, A. N., & Berry, K. (2015). Changes in attachment representations during psychological therapy. *Psychotherapy Research, 25*(2), 222–238.

The Schizophrenia Commission. (2012). *The Abandoned Illness: A Report from the Schizophrenia Commission.* London: Rethink Mental Illness.

Thomas, L. K. (2013). Attachment in African Caribbean Families. In A. N. Danquah & K. Berry (Eds.), *Attachment Theory in Adult Mental Health: A Guide to Clinical Practice.* London: Routledge.

Tortelli, A., Errazuriz, A., Croudace, T., Morgan, C., Murray, R. M., Jones, P. B., ... Kirkbride, J. B. (2015). Schizophrenia and other psychotic disorders in Caribbean-born migrants and their descendants in England: systematic review and meta-analysis of incidence rates, 1950–2013. *Society of Psychiatry Epidemiology, 50*(7), 1039–1055. doi:10.1007/s00127-015-1021-6

van Ijzendoorn, M. H., & Sagi-Schwartz, A. (2008). Cross-cultural patterns of attachment: Universal and contextual dimensions. In J. Cassidy & P. R. Shaver (Eds.), *Handbook of Attachment: Theory, Research, and Clinical Applications* (pp. 880–905). New York: Guildford Press.

Varese, F., Smeets, F., Drukker, M., Lieverse, R., Lataster, T., Viechtbauer, W., ... Bentall, R. P. (2012). Childhood adversities increase the risk of psychosis: a meta-analysis of patient-control, prospective-and cross-sectional cohort studies. *Schizophrenia Bulletin, 38*(4), 661–671.

Veling, W., Hoek, H. W., Wiersma, D., & Mackenbach, J. P. (2010). Ethnic identity and the risk of schizophrenia in ethnic minorities: a case-control study. *Schizophrenia Bulletin, 36*(6), 1149–1156. doi:10.1093/schbul/sbp032

Vogel, D. L., & Wei, M. F. (2005). Adult attachment and help-seeking intent: The mediating roles of psychological distress and perceived social support. *Journal of Counseling Psychology, 52*(3), 347–357. doi:10.1037/0022-0167.52.3.347

Wang, C.-C. D. C., & Mallinckrodt, B. (2006a). Acculturation, attachment, and psychosocial adjustment of Chinese/Taiwanese international students. *Journal of Counseling Psychology, 53*(4), 422.

Wang, C.-C. D. C., & Mallinckrodt, B. (2006b). Differences between Taiwanese and US cultural beliefs about ideal adult attachment. *Journal of Counseling Psychology, 53*(2), 192.

Waters, E., Merrick, S., Treboux, D., Crowell, J., & Albersheim, L. (2000). Attachment security in infancy and early adulthood: A twenty-year longitudinal study. *Child Development, 71*(3), 684–689.

Waters, E., Weinfield, N. S., & Hamilton, C. E. (2000). The stability of attachment security from infancy to adolescence and early adulthood: General discussion. *Child Development, 71*(3), 703–706.

Wearden, A. J., Tarrier, N., Barrowclough, C., Zastowny, T. R., & Rahill, A. A. (2000). A review of expressed emotion research in health care. *Clinical Psychology Review, 20*(5), 633–666.

Wei, M., Russell, D. W., Mallinckrodt, B., & Zakalik, R. A. (2004). Cultural equivalence of adult attachment across four ethnic groups: factor structure, structured means, and associations with negative mood. *Journal of Counseling Psychology, 51*(4), 408.

Weinfield, N. S., Sroufe, L. A., & Egeland, B. (2000). Attachment from infancy to early adulthood in a high-risk sample: continuity, discontinuity, and their correlates. *Child Development, 71*(3), 695–702.

Part III

INDIVIDUAL AND
ORGANISATIONAL
PERSPECTIVES

13

MAKING SENSE OF VOICES

Perspectives from the hearing voices movement

Eleanor Longden and Dirk Corstens

Introduction

In recent decades the experience of voice-hearing (or 'auditory hallucinations') has increasingly been framed as a biogenetic abnormality with negligible emotional meaning: "a symptom of brain disease just like blindness or hemiplegia" (Stephane et al., 2003, p.186). Nevertheless, growing research supports the proposition that voice-hearing (including that in the context of psychosis/schizophrenia) is explicable in psychological terms; together with the corresponding claim that voice presence and content are significantly associated with adversity exposure (particularly, but not exclusively, childhood abuse: e.g., Bentall et al., 2012; Longden et al., 2012a; Romme et al., 2009; Varese et al., 2012). In turn, this awareness has augmented interest in the possibility of applying therapeutic interventions to voice-hearing that utilise psychological principles like formulation (e.g., Romme & Escher, 2000), dialogical engagement (e.g., Leff et al., 2014), trauma-informed frameworks (e.g., Steel, 2017), and working with interpersonal attributions of threat and self-criticism (e.g., Mayhew & Gilbert, 2008). Other chapters in this volume describe therapeutic approaches to working with voices and psychosis more generally (e.g., Berry et al., this volume; Heriot-Mailand & Kennedy, this volume; Taylor & Seddon, this volume). In this chapter, we explore specific strategies for supporting voice hearers that are derived from the work of the International Hearing Voices Movement, a survivor-led coalition of voice hearers, academics and clinicians which promotes approaches to hearing voices that emphasise accepting and making sense of the experience, providing frameworks for coping and recovery, and exploring the role of psychosocial adversity in voice-hearing onset and maintenance. Firstly, we discuss a method for understanding and interpreting voices in the context of life events, known as 'the construct,' and examine how it can be combined with knowledge from the attachment literature to explicate the psychosocial origins of voice-hearing. Consideration is also given to the role of peer support, in combination with relational therapeutic approaches, for providing a 'secure base'

for voice-hearers to make sense of their experiences and develop more positive and empowered relationships with the voices that they hear.

Making sense of voices: 'The Construct'

A key influence in reconstructing voice-hearing as an intelligible sign of distress rather than a random symptom of disease is the work of Marius Romme
and Sandra Escher (1989, 1993, 2000) whose theories and research underlie the
International Hearing Voices Movement and which, in the past few decades,
has forced fundamental shifts in the way that voice-hearing is conceptualised
and understood (Corstens et al., 2014; Longden et al., 2013; Woods, 2013).
Amongst other work, Romme and Escher (2000) have promoted the construct
method (also known as 'voice profiling'), a form of psychological formulation
that acts as a systematic assessment model for investigating and deciphering
associations between voice(s)' content/characteristics and emotionally significant events in the hearer's life (for case examples of the method, see Corstens
et al., 2019; Longden et al., 2012b; Romme & Escher, 2000; Romme et al.,
2009). In order to develop a construct, five key areas of enquiry are examined:

(1) voice identity (e.g., their name, gender, age);
(2) characteristics and content (e.g., whether they are negative or posi-
    tive, their exact utterances, how they relate to one another and to the
    voice-hearer);
(3) triggers (emotions, situations and/or people that provoke the voices);
(4) history of voice-hearing (what was occurring in the person's life when
    each voice first appeared; how the voices may have changed since then);
(5) personal history (adversity exposure, attachment relationships and sig-
    nificant developmental events in the person's life before they started
    hearing voices).

This information is used to explore two central questions in order to formulate the construct: (1) who or what might the voices represent; and (2) what
social and/or emotional problems may be embodied by the voices. In contrast to psychiatric diagnoses, which generally decontextualise voice-hearing,
the construct therefore aims to *deconstruct* voices from generic symptoms,
and *reconstruct* them into subjectively meaningful events that emerged in specific psychosocial circumstances (Romme & Escher, 2000). Correspondingly,
once such themes are identified, the construct can be applied in developing
a customised recovery plan. This typically follows phase-orientated trauma-
focused models of healing, broadly defined as: (1) establishing safety,
(2) making sense of one's experiences, and (3) social reconnection (Herman,
1992; see also Corstens et al., 2019; Longden et al., 2013). However, an
important consideration in devising a construct is that the process should
not entail an expert therapist 'telling' a client what their voices mean. As

224

with guidelines for best practice formulation (Johnstone & Dallos, 2013), the procedure should be one of collaboration and mutual exploration, which constantly respects and accedes to the voice-hearer's views on its precision, accuracy and helpfulness. For example, the construct can accommodate non-psychological explanations for voices (i.e., spiritual, cultural, paranormal) if this is something the voice-hearer deems relevant.

Attachment and voice representations

How might wisdom from the attachment field be combined with the construct method to promote understandings of voice-hearing? In the past, attachment literature was not commonly applied to so-called 'psychotic' phenomena due to prevailing views of them as primarily biogenetic in origin. In the past decade this has begun to change, with recent research demonstrating that adulthood-assessed attachment styles partially mediate between trauma and hallucinations (Sitko et al., 2014; Read & Gumley, 2010), and in some cases are associated with hallucination presence and/or severity (e.g., Arbuckle et al., 2012; Berry et al., 2008; Korver-Nieberg et al., 2015; Ponizovskyet al., 2007). (Although see Chapter 2 in this volume for a slightly different inter-pretation of these findings). Advanced understandings of the developmental impact of victimisation, relational trauma, and attachment disruption have provided neurological evidence for how childhood adversity and adulthood mental health problems (including psychosis) may be linked (e.g., Perry & Szalavitz, 2006; Read et al., 2008, 2014; Schore, 2002). Furthermore, the growing emphasis on dissociation as an important psychological mechanism for understanding voice-hearing (including that which occurs in the context of psychosis/schizophrenia: for review see Pilton et al., 2015) is creating dynamic new avenues for understanding how disrupted attachment may set a precedent for responding to adversity exposure with dissociated mental representations, wherein "a prototype of psychic collapse or segregating experience [is] established" (Sroufe, 2005, p.361; see also Berry et al., this volume; Heriot-Maitland & Kennedy, this volume; Liotti & Gumley, 2008).

As such, exploration of the voice-hearing experience with a tool like the con-struct can lead to therapeutically useful insights about the dynamics between hearer and voice(s), and how these can be interpreted in terms of current or historical attachment relationships (see Figure 13.1). For example, a con-struct can reveal important information about the types of developmental precursors that may have disposed clients towards hearing voices (as well as identifying increased vulnerability to associated factors like affective distress/dysregulation, autonomic reactivity, meta-cognitive distortions, and impaired resilience and coping ability). In this regard, preliminary evidence for the utility of the method comes from an analysis of 100 completed constructs, which recruited voice-hearers with diagnoses predominantly of psychosis/schizophrenia (80%) who had heard voices for a mean of 18.2 years (Corstens

& Longden, 2013). Social/emotional conflicts embodied by the voices (i.e., 'what problems the voices represent') could be formulated in 94 per cent of cases, most commonly issues with self-esteem (93%), anger (60%), shame/ guilt (60%), and adulthood difficulties with attachment and intimacy (45%). In turn, participants identified a range of formative adversities that pre-dated voice onset and which were relatable to attachment disturbance: emotional abuse (72%), family conflict (65%), neglect (45%), physical (41%) or sexual abuse (30%), witnessing domestic violence (23%) and being subject to excessively high expectations (18%).

Another key area of enquiry within the construct ('who or what the voices represent') also has important implications for the impact of attachment on voice-hearing. In this regard it has been shown that thematic or semantic congruence can often exist between voice content and previous adversity exposure (e.g., Hardy et al., 2005; Raune et al., 2006; Romme et al., 2009; Thompson et al., 2012). However, descriptive analysis of the 100 constructs also indicated that after voices representing aspects of self (e.g., oneself at a different age: 48%), the most common personification for voices was attachment figures. Specifically, this included abusive family members (45%), most frequently a parent (31% father; 23% mother) or grandparent (7%). These could be either literal (i.e., the voice sounds like the real person and is identified as such by the voice-hearer), or figurative/symbolic representations (i.e., voice utterances are consistent with a real-life individual, but are identified metaphorically by the voice-hearer, for example, as 'The Devil'). Importantly, however, 30 per cent of the sample also reported voices that represented non-abusive attachment figures, most often a parent (10% father; 5% mother), sibling (5%), or grandparent (4%). In this regard, it is notable

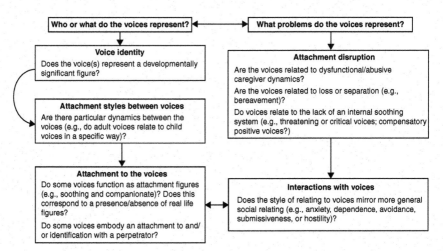

Figure 13.1 Attachment related issues to consider when developing and interpreting a construct for voice-hearers.

that non-patient groups in conditions of extreme stress and isolation (e.g., prisoners of war) have reported benevolent, caring voices that can be understood within the framework of attachment theory in the sense of compensating for a lack of supportive social contact (Stein et al., 2016). Despite this, compassionate and reassuring voices are generally not acknowledged within clinical practice, even though the "protective power and problem-solving capacity" (Jenner et al., 2008, p.244) attributed to them can, in some cases, render them a valuable therapeutic resource that can be utilised for coping enhancement.

In contrast, the relative frequency with which abusive caregivers were embodied via voice representations has significance in terms of the severe psychological impact that such maltreatment is believed to constitute. Specifically, abusive carers violate "a fundamental ethic" (Freyd, 1994, p.307) of their relationship with a child, who is subsequently faced with an insoluble dilemma in which dissociation permits the maintenance of an attachment that is essential for survival and meeting of developmental needs (DePrince & Freyd, 2002). In this respect a greater sense of betrayal also may be experienced as more traumatic, and Freyd et al. (2005) found that adversities high in betrayal trauma (e.g., abuse by a close other) were significant predictors of anxiety, depression and dissociation relative to those low in betrayal but high in threat to life (e.g., accidents) amongst 99 non-patient adults.

Therapeutic implications

A central application of the construct is its capacity to assist in identifying strategies for coping with the voices themselves, as well as the psychosocial conflicts that are implicated in their onset and maintenance. Indeed, seeking comprehensible links between adversity exposure and symptom content (including other psychotic phenomena, such as delusions) is an intervention that is emphasised in numerous therapeutic modalities on the basis that "[s]uch links often provide indications of...unresolved difficulties and associated negative self-evaluations...which may be closely intertwined with processes maintaining delusional beliefs and voices and may underpin aspects of the emotional reaction" (Fowler et al., 1998, p.127; see also British Psychological Society: Division of Clinical Psychology, 2011; 2014). In this respect, the construct can be used to understand the impact of formative attachment relationships on clients' experiences of hearing voices, both in terms of historical loss/stress and contemporary interpersonal difficulties, thus signposting critical issues to address in therapy.

In addition to working with other symptoms that can result from adversity exposure (e.g., dissociation, hypervigilance, sleep problems: Bacon & Kennedy, 2015; Romme et al., 2009; Ross & Halpern, 2009), clinical intervention might also include finding ways to understand the dynamics of voice-hearing as an interpersonal exchange between hearer and voice (Benjamin,

1989). An emergent therapeutic strategy consistent with this principle is 'Talking With Voices' (e.g., Corstens et al., 2012a; Corstens et al., 2012b) an exploratory process that directly engages with voices in a manner intended to instigate integration and reconciliation, examine relevant factors in voice emergence and maintenance, and redress unequal power dynamics between hearer and voice. In theoretical terms, the approach is derived from the model of Voice Dialogue (Stone & Stone, 1989), which suggests that 'normal' personality is comprised of different components that exist simultaneously; and structural models of dissociation (van der Hart et al., 2006), which posits that the personality of traumatised individuals is fragmented into independent subsystems. Talking With Voices thus blends two central premises of Romme and Escher's (1993) 'Accepting Voices' approach: that voice-hearing lies on a continuum with 'normal' human experience; and, in conjunction with adversity, can embody unbearable, yet psychologically meaningful material, that it is important to acknowledge and process. As such, Talking With Voices does not focus on eradication or suppression, but endeavours to establish a more positive relationship by helping the person gain a different perspective on what the voices are trying to say. An important aspect of this is the concept of voices (although not the real-world perpetrators which they may represent) offering a 'protective' function, in the sense that they can provide insights into previous social-emotional conflicts that the person has faced (Romme & Escher, 2000). Furthermore, the perspective of the voice(s) is also explored; for example, trying to understand why a malevolent voice expresses itself so negatively, or the source of a voice's anger or sadness (i.e., what has happened in the hearer's life to make the voices appear this way). On one hand, the method strives for a transformation of the voice(s) (1) into a supportive and meaningful experience that is taken seriously by the voice-hearer (without submission) and (2) to support the voice-hearer to distance herself from the voice's emotional content by relating to it in a more compassionate, curious way and from the perspective that the voice(s) contains knowledge that has helped her survive in the world. Although the method currently awaits systematic, controlled evaluations, it can be positioned within the growing research interest in the role of relational dynamics for understanding voice-hearing (e.g., Hayward et al., 2009; Hayward et al., 2011; Leff et al., 2014; Pérez-Álvarez et al., 2008). Examples of the method are described by Corstens et al. (2012a-b) and Moskowitz and Corstens (2007). However, an abbreviated case is presented here:

> Charles (C), along with his support worker, attended a four-day 'Working With Voices' course co-facilitated by the second author. Within these courses, voice-hearers and their allies (usually a healthcare worker or family member) work together to develop a mutual understanding of the voice-hearing experience and devise positive frameworks to create a better relationship with the voices.

Charles heard three voices. One of them, Felix (F), was predominantly negative and regularly told Charles to kill himself. Charles was afraid of this voice and felt desperate about his inability to cope with it. The therapist (T) who developed the construct with Charles during the course subsequently explained the Talking With Voices approach then asked permission from both Charles and his voices to begin a session. The therapist emphasised that his intention was to improve the relationship between Felix, Charles, and the other voices rather than trying to get rid of them. Charles was then asked if he would like to take another seat in the room from which to speak from the position of the voice; but to also remain aware and in control so that he could 'come back' if the therapist should ask for it, or if Charles himself wanted to 'return.'

T: Hi, Charles told me your name is Felix.
F: That's right.
T: Is there something you want to discuss?
F: Sure, it's the behaviour of Charles – he's a wimp!
T: Please could you explain that a bit more?
F: He's weak, he never stands up for himself. It drives me crazy.
T: So, you want him to be more confident?
F: Yes, that's what I'm trying to achieve.
T: Have you been successful?
F: No, not at all, he just becomes more and more anxious.
T: Shall we discuss how you can be more effective?
F: That sounds great!
   [At this point the therapist shared some of his own experiences of supporting anxious people, and suggested similar strategies for the voice to try.]
T: Felix, Charles told me he hears two other voices. Do you know them?
F: I only know one other voice. Not very well, but she is called Jo-Anne [J-A]. I don't like her.
T: Why not?
F: She's too nice to Charles, she never criticises him.
T: Do you talk with her?
F: No, she won't.
T: Does Charles like her?
F: I suppose so.
T: Do you want to relate to her?
F: Yeah, I would like to work together with her to support Charles in the new way I've learned. We could be a team.
T: That sounds great.
   [The therapist says goodbye to Felix and reflects on the conversation with Charles. After a while, the therapist asks to speak to Jo-Anne. The

therapist explained to this voice what Felix's intentions were and his aspiration to become a team. Jo-Anne was surprised, and initially suspicious, but ultimately agreed.]

T: Felix and Jo-Anne, I'm very pleased that you intend to work together; I'm sure Charles will be very grateful. I want to thank you both for relating with me in this way and I hope to have more positive conversations with you.

J-A: I'm glad Felix wants to work with me. We'll certainly have disagreements, but I know we both want to support Charles. And thank you for that.

T: You're welcome Jo-Anne. And I now want to ask you to leave and Charles to come back.

(...)

T: Hi, Charles. Did you hear what I discussed with Jo-Anne and Felix?

C: Yeah, it's amazing. I now have two people working together to support me!

Although this appears a brief intervention, it is important to consider it within the context of an established therapeutic relationship in which time had already been invested in working towards the type of safe and hopeful setting in which the dialogue could take place. In this respect, conversations with voices should be carefully and thoroughly planned so that all parties (voice-hearer, voices and facilitator) feel comfortable and the situation is conducive to conducting a safe and respectful discussion (see Corstens et al. 2012a, 2012b). Creating such conditions can be time-consuming, and may not always be possible, but in some instances it can also occur easily and even naturally; particularly amongst individuals who already have experience of conversing with their voices.

Peer support

In addition to relationships between hearer and voice, we believe that it is also important to consider attachment dynamics that voice-hearers experience in their interactions with other people. In terms of clinical services, this includes the role of relational factors that are known to promote a strong therapeutic alliance, such as collaboration, consistency, empathy, responsiveness and availability (Goodwin et al., 2003; Norcross, 2002; Perrin, 2012). A particular issue promoted by the Hearing Voices Movement, once again inspired by Romme and Escher's (1993, 2000) research, is the valuable role of peer support groups. Such groups are a central component of the Movement's work, and have been characterised as "safe spaces" (Dillon & Longden, 2011, p.129) – in attachment terms, *a secure base* – in which distressed voice-hearers can share experiences, develop meaningful connections with one another, and cultivate a sense of hope and empowerment. This is an important consideration, because in addition to processes with a more ostensibly 'clinical' focus (e.g., devising explanatory frameworks for one's voices, developing coping strategies and recovery goals; Oakland & Berry, 2015; Romme et al., 2009), such groups are also capable of offering a consistency and continuity in relationships that are not necessarily available within statutory services (Dillon & Hornstein, 2013).

Attending peer support groups can therefore offer an immediate sense of sanctuary and attachment potential in which one's experiences are respected, validated and acknowledged. Voice-hearing can be a deeply isolating event, not only due to the solitude in which one hears one's voices, but the fact that the stigmatised nature of the experience can often limit opportunities to safely confide. As such, it can be affirming and comforting to recognise one's own situation in the experiences of other members "without having to put on a mask'" (Bullimore quoted in Downs, 2005, p.5). In turn, these opportunities for companionship and solidarity can provide valuable access to a supportive, collaborative and non-hierarchal community in which voice-hearers seek to assist both other members as well as themselves (Dillon & Hornstein, 2013). The relational value of such groups has been referred to in various ways within the literature, including "mutual acceptance through shared experience" (Hendry, 2011; p.76), a "safe-haven" (Downs, 2005; p.5) and "the veil being lifted" (Oakland & Berry, 2015; p.123), and is powerfully described by one young woman with experience of group participation in the following way: "Creating a 'fellowship' around voice hearing gives the experience the recognition, the weight of reality, the value, that it truly has to every voice hearer" (quoted in Romme et al., 2009; p.82).

In addition to the peer support dynamics within actual groups, the communication opportunities made possible by the Internet have also enabled a powerful sense of collective identity for members of the Hearing Voices Movement. For example, Intervoice (the Movement's organisational body), as well as many national hearing voices networks, host their own websites and social media pages. In this context, 'collective identity' can be used to refer to an individual's sense of shared status: "a cognitive, moral, and emotional connection with a broader community, category, practice, or institution" (Polletta & Jasper, 2001, p.85), which in the case of the Hearing Voices Movement has been positioned in terms of reformative social action (Longden et al., 2013). Specifically, the Movement seeks to achieve a number of progressive goals, including reclaiming 'voice-hearer' as a valuable, non-stigmatised identity; challenging reductive biogenetic explanations for voice-hearing; and promoting greater awareness and understanding of the experience amongst the general public and media. Intervoice, is now active within 32 countries; and since its inception in 1997 has provided a locus for its members (including voice-hearers, their friends and family, and clinicians and academics) to congregate and share support and perspectives. Although no formal research exists around voice-hearers' perceptions of these activities, it makes intuitive sense to us that access to a forum in which individuals assemble to share coping strategies, validate one another's stories, and exchange wisdom and insights, could help to reduce shame and isolation and expedite a greater sense of acceptance for an experience that is both distressing and highly stigmatised. Indeed, as stated by the mental health activist and voice-hearer Kellie Comans during an address to the 2014 World Hearing Voices Congress: "I've come home, to my people and my tribe. It's an unexplainable feeling to be so accepted and embraced by so many people and to feel like finally I belong somewhere. Like I have a real place in the world."

Conclusions

A recurring premise, both in clinical research and survivor testimony, is that many individuals experience hearing voices – including in the context of psychosis – as a meaningful defensive response to overwhelming events. In addition, early attachment relationships can often influence the way individuals respond towards both positive and negative voice(s). The personal construct approach to psychological formulation can be applied to systematically explore the identity, characteristics and content of the voice(s) and how they are related to significant life events, including both adversity exposure and indications of (disrupted) attachment relationships. Such formulations may provide valuable insights into how significant others have influenced the role of the voice in the hearer's internal world and what kind of developmental themes (often derived from disturbed attachment relationships) are relevant for improving the dynamics between hearer and voice. We have suggested that the relational psychotherapy approach of Talking With Voices is promising in that it tries to improve the interactions between individuals and their voices and address underlying psychosocial conflicts that need to be acknowledged and resolved. In addition, national and international peer support networks offer further safe spaces in which individuals can share their experiences in an atmosphere of fellowship and solidarity.

References

Arbuckle, R., Berry, K., Taylor, J. L., & Kennedy S. (2012). Service user attachments to psychiatric key workers and teams. *Social Psychiatry and Psychiatric Epidemiology*, 47(5), 817–825.

Bentall, R. P., Wickham, S., Shevlin, M., & Varese, F. (2012). Do specific early-life adversities lead to specific symptoms of psychosis? A study from the 2007 the Adult Psychiatric Morbidity Survey. *Schizophrenia Bulletin*, 38(4), 734–740.

Bacon, T., & Kennedy, A. (2015). Clinical perspectives on the relationship between psychosis and dissociation: Utility of structural dissociation and implications for practice. *Psychosis: Psychological, Social and Integrative Approaches*, 7(1), 81–91.

Benjamin, L. S. (1989). Is chronicity a function of the relationship between the person and the auditory hallucination? *Schizophrenia Bulletin, 15*(2), 291–310.

Berry, K., Barrowclough, C., & Wearden, A. (2008). Attachment theory: A framework for understanding symptoms and interpersonal relationships in psychosis. *Behavior Research and Therapy, 46*(12), 1275–1282.

British Psychological Society: Division of Clinical Psychology. (2011). *Good Practice Guidelines on the Use of Psychological Formulation.* Leicester, England: British Psychological Society.

British Psychological Society: Division of Clinical Psychology. (2014). *Understanding Psychosis and Schizophrenia. A Report by the Division of Clinical Psychology.* Leicester, England: British Psychological Society.

Corstens, D., Escher, S.,Romme, M., & Longden, E. (2019). Accepting and working with voices: The Maastricht Approach. In A. Moskowitz (ed.) *Psychosis, Trauma and Dissociation: Evolving perspectives on severe psychopathology.* 2nd revised edition (pp. 381–396). Chichester, England: Wiley & Sons.

Corstens, D., & Longden, E. (2013). The origins of voices: Links between voice hearing and life history in a survey of 100 cases. *Psychosis: Psychological, Social and Integrative Approaches, 5*(3), 270–285.

Corstens, D., Longden, E., & May, R. (2012a). Talking with voices: Exploring what is expressed by the voices people hear. *Psychosis: Psychological, Social and Integrative Approaches, 4*(2), 95–104.

Corstens, D., Longden, E., McCarthy-Jones, S., Waddingham, R., & Thomas, N. (2014). Emerging perspectives from the Hearing Voices Movement: Implications for research and practice. *Schizophrenia Bulletin, 40*(S4), S285–S294.

Corstens, D., May, R., & Longden, E. (2012b). Talking with voices. In M. Romme & S. Escher (Eds.), *Psychosis as a Personal Crisis: An experience based approach* (pp. 166–178). London, England: Routledge.

DePrince, A. P., & Freyd, J. J. (2002). The harm of trauma: Pathological fear, shattered assumptions, or betrayal? In J. Kauffman (Ed.), *Loss of the Assumptive World: A theory of traumatic loss.* (pp. 71–82). New York, NY: Brunner-Routledge.

Dillon, J., & Hornstein, G. A. (2013). Hearing voices peer support groups: A powerful alternative for people in distress. *Psychosis: Psychological Social and Integrative Approaches, 5*, 286–295.

Dillon, J., & Longden, E. (2011). Hearing voices groups: Creating safe spaces to share taboo experiences. In M. Romme & S. Escher (Eds.), *Psychosis as a Personal Crisis: An experience based approach* (pp. 129–139). London, England: Routledge.

Downs, J. (2005). *Coping with Voices and Visions: A guide to helping people who experience hearing voices, seeing visions, tactile or other sensations.* Manchester, England: The Hearing Voices Network.

Fowler, D., Garety, P., & Kuipers, E. (1998). Cognitive therapy for psychosis: Formulation, treatment, effects and service implications. *Journal of Mental Health, 7*(2), 123–133.

Freyd, J. (1994). Betrayal trauma: Traumatic amnesia as an adaptive response to childhood abuse. *Ethics & Behavior, 4*(4), 307–330.

Freyd, J., Klest, B., & Allard, C. B. (2005). Betrayal trauma: Relationship to physical health, psychological distress, and a written disclosure intervention. *Journal of Trauma and Dissociation, 6*(3), 83–104.

Goodwin, I., Holmes, G., Cochrane, R. & Mason, O. (2003). The ability of adult mental health services to meet clients' attachment needs: The development and implementation of the Service Attachment Questionnaire. *Psychology and Psychotherapy: Theory, Research and Practice, 76*(2), 145–161.

Hardy, A., Fowler, D., Freeman, D., Smith, B., Steel, C., Evans, J.,...Dunn, G. (2005). Trauma and hallucinatory experience in psychosis. *The Journal of Nervous and Mental Disease, 193*(8), 501–507.

Hayward, M., Berry, K., & Ashton, A. (2011). Applying interpersonal theories to the understanding of and therapy for auditory hallucinations: a review of the literature and directions for further research. *Clinical Psychology Review, 31*(8), 1313–1323.

Hayward, M., Overton, J., Dorey, T., & Denney, J. (2009). Relating therapy for people who hear voices: a case series. *Clinical Psychology & Psychotherapy, 16*(3), 216–227.

Herman, J. L. (1992). *Trauma and Recovery*. New York, NY: Basic Books.

Jenner, J. A., Rutten, S., Beuckens, J., Boonstra, N., & Sytema, S. (2008). Positive and useful auditory vocal hallucinations: Prevalence, characteristics, attributions, and implications for treatment. *Acta Psychiatrica Scandinavica, 118*(3), 238–245.

Johnstone, L., & Dallos, R. (2013). *Formulation in Psychology and Psychotherapy: Making sense of people's problems*. London, England: Routledge.

Korver-Nieberg, N., Berry, K., Meijer, C., de Haan, L., & Ponizovsky, A. M. (2015). Associations between attachment and psychopathology dimensions in a large sample of patients with psychosis. *Psychiatry Research, 228*(1), 83–88.

Leff, J., Williams, G., Huckvale, M., Arbuthnot, M., & Leff, A. P. (2014). Avatar therapy for persecutory auditory hallucinations: What is it and how does it work? *Psychosis: Psychological, Social and Integrative Approaches, 6*(2), 166–176.

Liotti, G., & Gumley, A. (2008). An attachment perspective on schizophrenia: The role of disorganised attachment, dissociation and mentalisation. In A. Moskowitz, I. Schäfer & M. J. Dorahy (Eds.), *Psychosis, Trauma and Dissociation: Emerging perspectives on severe psychopathology* (pp.117–134). Chichester, England: Wiley-Blackwell.

Longden, E., Corstens, D., & Dillon, J. (2013). Recovery, discovery and revolution: The work of Intervoice and the hearing voices movement. In S. Coles, S. Keenan & B. Diamond (Eds.), *Madness Contested: Power and practice* (pp. 161–180). Ross-on-Wye, England: PCCS Books.

Longden, E., Madill, A., & Waterman, M. G. (2012a). Dissociation, trauma, and the role of lived experience: Toward a new conceptualization of voice hearing. *Psychological Bulletin, 138*(1), 28–76.

Longden, E., Corstens, D., Escher, S., & Romme, M. (2012b). Voice hearing in a biographical context: A model for formulating the relationship between voices and life history. *Psychosis: Psychological, Social and Integrative Approaches, 4*(3), 224–234.

Norcross, J. C. (Ed.). (2002). *Psychotherapy Relationships That Work: Therapist contributions and responsiveness to patient needs*. New York, NY: Oxford University Press.

Mayhew, S., & Gilbert, P. (2008). Compassionate mind training with people who hear malevolent voices: A case series report. *Clinical Psychology and Psychotherapy, 15*(2), 113–138.

Moskowitz, A., & Corstens, D. (2007). Auditory hallucinations: Psychotic symptom or dissociative experience? *The Journal of Psychological Trauma, 6*(2/3), 35–63.

Oakland, L., & Berry, K. (2015). "Lifting The Veil"; a qualitative analysis of experiences in Hearing Voices Network groups. *Psychosis: Psychological, Social and Integrative Approaches, 7*(2), 119–129.

Pérez-Álvarez, M., García-Montes, J.M., Perona-Garcelán, S., & Vallina-Fernández, O. (2008). Changing relationship with voices: New therapeutic perspectives for treating hallucinations. *Clinical Psychology and Psychotherapy, 15*(2), 75–85.

Perrin, A. (2012). Now you see it, now you don't: Mental health services' struggle to provide safe attachment relationships for traumatised clients. *The Journal of Critical Psychology, Counselling and Psychotherapy,* 12(3), 164–175.

Perry, B. & Szalavitz, M. (2006). *The Boy Who Was Raised As A Dog.* New York, NY: Basic Books.

Pilton, M., Varese, F., Berry, K., & Bucci, S. (2015). The relationship between dissociation and voices: A systematic literature review and meta-analysis. *Clinical Psychology Review.* Advanced online publication doi: 10.1016/j.cpr.2015.06.004

Polletta, F., & Jasper, J. (2001). Collective identity and social movements. *Annual Review of Sociology, 27,* 283–305.

Ponizovsky, A. M., Nechamkin, Y., & Rosca, P. (2007). Attachment patterns are associated with symptomatology and course of schizophrenia in male inpatients. *The American Journal of Orthopsychiatry, 77*(2), 324–331.

Raune, D., Bebbington, P., Dunn, G., & Kuipers, E. (2006). Event attributes and the content of psychotic experiences in first-episode psychosis. *Psychological Medicine, 36*(2), 221–230.

Read, J., Fosse, R., Moskowitz, A., & Perry, B. (2014). The traumagenic neurodevelopmental model of psychosis revisited. *Neuropsychiatry, 4*(1), 65–79.

Read, J., & Gumley, A. (2010). Can attachment theory help explain the relationship between childhood adversity and psychosis? In S. Benamer (Ed.), *Telling Stories? Attachment based approach to the treatment of psychosis* (pp.51–94). London, England: Karnac Books.

Read, J., Perry, B. D., Moskowitz, A., & Connolly, J. (2001). The contribution of early traumatic events to schizophrenia in some patients: A traumagenic neurodevelopmental model. *Psychiatry, 64*(4), 319–345.

Romme, M. A. J., & Escher, A. D. M. A. C. (1989). Hearing voices. *Schizophrenia Bulletin, 15*(2), 209–216.

Romme, M. & Escher, S. (1993). *Accepting Voices.* London, England: Mind Publications.

Romme, M., & Escher, S. (2000). *Making Sense of Voices.* London, England: Mind Publications.

Romme, M., Escher, S., Dillon, J., Corstens, D., & Morris, M. (Eds.). (2009). *Living with Voices: Fifty stories of recovery.* Ross-on-Wye, England: PCCS Books.

Ross, C.A., & Halpern, N. (2009). *Trauma Model Therapy: A treatment approach for trauma, dissociation and complex comorbidity.* Richardson, TX: Manitou Communications Inc.

Schore, A. (2002). Dysregulation of the right brain: A fundamental mechanism of traumatic attachment and the psychopathogenesis of posttraumatic stress disorder. *Australian and New Zealand Journal of Psychiatry, 36,* 9–30.

Sitko, K., Bentall, R. P., Shevlin, M., & Sellwood, W. (2014). Associations between specific psychotic symptoms and specific childhood adversities are mediated by attachment styles: An analysis of the National Comorbidity Survey. *Psychiatry Research, 217*(3), 202–209.

Sroufe, L.A. (2005). Attachment and development: A prospective, longitudinal study from birth to adulthood. *Attachment & Human Development, 7*(4), 349–367.

Steel, C. (2017). Psychological interventions for working with trauma and distressing voices: The future is in the past. *Frontiers in Psychology, 7*, 2035. http://journal.frontiersin.org/article/10.3389/fpsyg.2016.02035

Stein, J.Y., Crompton, L., Ohry, A., & Solomon, Z. (2016). Attachment in detachment: The positive role of caregivers in POWs' dissociative hallucinations. *Journal of Trauma & Dissociation, 17*(2), 186–198.

Stephane, M., Thuras, P., Nasrallah, H., & Georgopoulos, A. P. (2003). The internal structure of the phenomenology of auditory verbal hallucinations. *Schizophrenia Research, 61*(2–3), 185–193.

Stone, H., & Stone, S. (1989). *Embracing Our Selves: The voice dialogue training manual*. New York, NY: Nataraj Publishing.

Thompson, A., Nelson, B., McNab, C., Simmons, M., Leicester, S., McGorry, P.,… Yung, A.R. (2010). Psychotic symptoms with sexual content in the "ultra high risk" for psychosis population: Frequency and association with sexual trauma. *Psychiatry Research, 177*(1–2), 84–91.

Woods, A. (2013). The voice hearer. *Journal of Mental Health, 22*(3), 263–270.

Varese, F., Smeets, F., Drukker, M., Lieverse, R., Lataster, T., Viechtbauer W.,…Bentall, R.P. (2012). Childhood trauma increases the risk of psychosis: A meta-analysis of patient-control, prospective- and cross sectional cohort studies. *Schizophrenia Bulletin, 38*(4), 661–671.

14

HOW CAN ATTACHMENT THEORY INFORM THE DESIGN AND DELIVERY OF MENTAL HEALTH SERVICES?

*Sandra Bucci, Katherine Berry, Adam N. Danquah
and Lucy Johnstone*

In light of the Winterbourne View case and the Mid Staffordshire Public Inquiry (Francis, 2013a), there is no better time to think about how attachment theory can be applied in the design and delivery of mental health services offering support and interventions to vulnerable populations. At its heart, attachment emphasises the importance of safe and secure relationships. To date, there has been a paucity of empirical research examining how attachment ideas can be applied in the context of service delivery models, and the impact of implementing an attachment-informed service model. Perhaps this has been due to the additional costs services would incur in implementing attachment ideas in routine clinical practice. Regardless of the reason, we urge services to consider attachment ideas when working in mental health settings.

In this chapter, we propose ways in which mental health services might provide an attachment-informed response to users of mental health services, including people who access interventions for psychosis. We also provide a brief overview of the work on trauma-informed care for psychosis and discuss ideas for attachment-informed ways of responding to trauma. As discussed in previous chapters, interpersonal trauma is a well-established vulnerability factor in psychosis, and the experience of psychosis itself can be traumatic for service users and caregivers. In the remainder of the chapter, we highlight the importance of attachment processes in team formulations and therapeutic relationships. Bowlby (1988) himself likened the therapeutic relationship to an attachment relationship, such that a clinician might act as an attachment figure by providing a safe and consistent platform by which the service user can experience a more positive and reparative interpersonal relationship (a 'corrective experience' in attachment terms).

According to attachment theory, early caregiving experiences, initially formed with one's primary caregiver, establish and guide mental representations about the self in relation to others. These so called 'internal working models' create expectations about future relationships (Bowlby, 1982). Caregivers can provide a coherent and safe and secure environment by being sensitive and responsive to distress, being available and flexible, and intervening when needed. This in turn helps the individual develop a positive self-image, provides a platform for the individual to form emotionally close relationships with others, helps the individual regulate emotional distress and fosters a sense of autonomy. The attachment system is designed to be a help-seeking system (Bowlby, 1982) and as such there are clear links that can be made with the ways in which service users seek help when they present to mental health services, and the ways in which service providers care for, and respond to, service users during times of distress.

Research has shown that individuals with experience of psychosis who present to mental health services in times of distress frequently display inse-cure attachment styles, and in some cases, a disorganised attachment style (MacBeth et al., 2011). Attachment-informed work suggests that service users will react to clinical staff based on their attachment history. For example, ser-vice users with a dismissing attachment style may find it difficult to engage in the therapeutic process. This can be interpreted by staff as failure to engage but is often understandable in the context of difficult past relationships many service users' have often experienced (Barber et al., 2006). Alternatively, service users with anxious ambivalent attachment styles tend to develop attachment relationships to staff/others that are often unstable, with rapid changes of mood and behaviour. Service users' attempts to seek proximity with caregivers can lead to their being viewed by clinicians as demanding and emotionally draining (Barber et al., 2006).

Bowlby (1982) envisaged his developmental theory of attachment to be clin-ical in its application. Accordingly, attachment theory has been proposed as a framework to inform the design and delivery of mental health services (Barber et al., 2006; Bucci et al., 2015; Goodwin, 2003; Goodwin et al., 2003). There have been a number of positive developments, such as the UK Department of Health national advisory group on mental health, safety and well-being (Seager et al., 2007) agreeing that secure attachments and relationships are key to mental well-being. The concept of recovery is also important in this context. Recovery from service users' perspectives usefully emphasises safety, consistency, hope, building a meaningful life and provision of choice (Pitt et al., 2007), ideas that are consistent with the central tenets of attachment theory. Similarly, 'relational security', a concept developed in secure mental health settings (Drennan & Aldred, 2013), emphasises the importance of safe and secure staff-service user relationships. Despite these developments, there has been comparatively little application of how attachment theory might be applied to mental health service delivery and limited change in the commissioning and delivery of mental health services, which across the world remain dominated by the diagnostically driven 'medical model' (Bloom & Farragher, 2010).

Attachment-informed care is particularly relevant in the current UK NHS landscape as financial pressures and the drive to privatise healthcare in the UK is undoubtedly resulting in a state of insecurity, unease and a sense of threat to staff job security and quality of care, factors that are fundamentally inimical to the security and stability staff need in order to provide containment and safety to service users. Safe and responsive caregiving is vital in any healthcare setting and is in keeping with many healthcare systems' values. Attachment is one of the few social psychological theories validated across cultures, but it is important to bear in mind that more data are still required on ethnic and cultural variation in adult attachment (Agishtein & Brumbaugh, 2013). Beyond cross-cultural differences in expression (e.g. Grossman, Grossman, & Kepler, 2005), Agishtein and Brumbaugh (2013) argue it is important to consider intercultural differences in the distribution of patterns and 'ideal' versions of attachment behaviours. Clinically, insecure attachment may be more normative in certain cultures, for example, and thus less associated with stigma and psychological burden. We always have to ask ourselves what the service user has had to adapt to, and how their resulting attachment pattern or 'solution' sits within their wider frame of ethnic and cultural reference. In this way, attachment measures have to be interpreted with particular caution when the service user's culture is not primarily 'Western' (Wang & Mallinckrodt, 2006). We have to hold in mind not only issues around the respondent's interpretation of the items *per se*, but also what ideals of attachment might be guiding responses, in order not to pathologise diverse ways of expressing attachment across cultures (Wang & Mallinckrodt, 2006). As ever, the clinician's consideration of context and curious, questioning attitude is vital.

The aim of the current chapter is to: i) describe areas in which services for psychosis in particular can draw on attachment ideas and the related body of literature on trauma and adversity; ii) highlight the importance of the therapeutic relationship and how attachment theory can help with understanding these; and iii) give examples of strategies for implementing these ideas in practice, despite the many very real pressures facing staff and services in the current political climate.

Factors to consider when developing an attachment-informed mental health service

To develop a successful attachment-informed mental health service, all aspects of the service need to be considered (Berry & Drake, 2010; Seager, 2006, 2013). An attachment-informed service is one that works in a way that reflects styles of caregiving known to foster secure attachment. In practice, the organisation of an attachment-informed service would model caregiving by providing individual services the freedom and autonomy to be creative and flexible in making decisions about delivery of care at a local level, but offering support when needed. Lack of containment for staff working in a service undergoing re-organisation or change can put staff in a vulnerable situation. This highlights the need for organisations to provide adequate care to staff so that staff do not re-enact any potential lack of compassion they might have experienced themselves as workers (Wainwright, 2014).

The attachment literature overlaps with the growing body of evidence on the long-term mental health impact of trauma and adversity of all kinds, including within presentations termed 'psychosis' (e.g. Read & Bentall, 2012; Read & Gumley, 2008; BPS, 2014; Varese et al., 2012). As described in numerous other chapters in this book, insecure early attachment relationships may be the result of traumas such as parental maltreatment (e.g. neglect, abuse), witnessing domestic violence and/or subtle but frequent parental misattunement. Insecure relationships also set the scene for emotional dysregulation, which leave vulnerable individuals less well equipped to survive subsequent traumatic experiences. A well-established body of evidence from neuroscience demonstrates the profound impact of these early traumas and attachment disturbances on the development of the brain, and the damaging consequences of remaining hyper-alert to threat (useful summaries can be found in Van Der Kolk, 2014 and Chapter 7. In the psychiatric literature, such effects of adverse experiences have traditionally often been diagnosed under the umbrella term 'psychosis'; although, within the trauma literature, they may be understood as originating in an adaptive response to threat, mediated by dissociation and other putative psychological processes (see Chapters 3 and 11), with traumatic memories re-appearing in the form of flashbacks, nightmares, voice-hearing and unusual beliefs (Dillon et al., 2012). Trauma-informed services are, like attachment-based services, based on the assumption that the core role of the staff and the system is to provide secure and consistent relationships within which traumatic experiences can be heard, understood and processed safely. They recognise that 'the majority of people treated by public mental health and substance abuse services have trauma histories' ("Adults |Surviving Child Abuse (ASCA) 'The last frontier': Practice Guidelines for treatment of complex trauma and trauma-informed care and service delivery. Available at www.asca.org.au," p.xxvviii) and that the first duty of any healthcare service is not to re-traumatise the people it sets out to help (Fallot & Harris, 2009).

Based on a synthesis of the literature examining attachment-informed general mental health service delivery, we have previously proposed a series of ideas and recommendations regarding ways in which mental health services can draw on attachment and trauma theory to inform the design and delivery of mental healthcare and summarise them here (Bucci et al., 2015).

Using attachment theory to inform the design and delivery of mental healthcare

1. Referral pathways

An attachment-informed mental health model should consider individual needs, starting with referral pathways. In the UK and elsewhere, many service referral criteria rely on an individual's diagnosis, severity and risk, which may be centered around service and societal concerns rather than the need perceived by the individual, to decide whether the individual fits into the existing service framework or qualifies for treatment (Seager, 2006). Seager (2006) recommends services adapt their method of delivery to meet the needs of service users in the same way an effective caregiver is flexible, adaptive and responsive in meeting their loved one's needs; this needs to happen from the point of referral onwards.

In discussing attachment-informed care, we acknowledge the difficulties in providing 'ideal' care. Resource pressures, demanding caseloads and organisational restructures, to name a few, may render it almost impossible to provide stable and consistent caregiving. The concept of 'good-enough care' may therefore be a helpful way to conceptualise attachment-informed care. This concept is drawn from Donald Winnicott (1973) who coined the term in relation to the 'good-enough mother'. Winnicott recognised that it was both unhelpful and unrealistic to expect the primary caregiver to provide perfect parenting when most caregivers provide 'good enough' care to meet an infant's needs. This is a helpful framework when considering attachment-informed care in the current context. In terms of service delivery, it is unrealistic to expect a service to provide the support an individual requires in its entirety. Rather, creating a facilitating environment that incorporates attachment ideas in care plans and all aspects of contact with a service means 'good-enough' care can be provided to service users in a way that eases distress, provides security and safety, and offers the support required at a given point in time.

Inpatient admissions and referrals to mental health services often occur at a time of extreme distress and upheaval in an individual's life, and, especially in the case of inpatient admissions, individuals can be separated from attachment figures and attachment relationships in the community. Schuengel and van Ijzendoorn (2001) proposed that attachment theory should inform decisions about the appropriateness of referrals to inpatient services (although this is also relevant to services more widely) given the distress for both the service user and caregivers at these times and the impact on the service user's attachment system. As the stressors associated with inpatient treatment might exceed a service user's coping abilities, service resources and staffing need to be adequate to provide at least one staff relationship that is stable enough to be a proxy attachment relationship. If the staff-service user ratio is too large, and staff turnover is too frequent, or if the service user is likely to be transferred multiple times between beds, wards, units or even hospitals, inpatient admissions are likely to increase distress and, wherever possible, should be avoided (Schuengel & van Ijzendoorn, 2001). At a minimum, staff members need to feel sufficiently supported and secure in their work in order to provide the consistent and reliable support that is necessary to facilitate the formation of a safe and secure staff/service-service user relationship. Indeed, service user satisfaction surveys carried out worldwide show that consistent and reliable relationships with staff are the most valued aspect of care, yet sadly opportunities to develop such relationships are often lacking (Schizophrenia Commission, 2012).

2. *Assessment and formulation*

Staff should follow national guidance in asking about possible abuse and should be informed and confident about the steps that may need to be taken following a disclosure. In addition, attachment issues need to be considered during routine assessment and formulation. An attachment-informed service would need to take into account the quality of clients and staff attachment relationships. Clinicians might use various approaches, including structured clinical interviews, questionnaires and drawing on their own observations and the individual's history. While the Adult Attachment Interview (AAI; George et al., 1985) is the most commonly used clinical interview assessment of adult attachment, administration of the measure is time consuming and resource intensive. If time is problematic, self report measures are also available: i) the Relationship Questionnaire (RQ; Bartholomew & Horowitz, 1991) and the Experiences of Close Relationships Scale-Revised (ECR-R; Fraley et al., 2011; Fraley et al., 2000) can be used to assess the quality of individual attachment relationships; ii) the Parental Bonding Instrument (PBI; Parker, 1990) has also been widely used to assess perceived warmth and over control in relationships with parents in childhood. Adshead and colleagues (2005) argued that attachment assessments could be supplemented by clinicians paying attention to their own responses to service users (*countertransference* in the psychoanalytic literature). Findings from questionnaires, and attachment theory more generally, can also inform formulations by providing an understanding of challenging/risky behaviour and predicting engagement and responses to staff and potential pressures on staff to respond in particular ways.

A formulation of a service user's difficulties helps the service user develop a personally meaningful and coherent narrative of their distress. Formulation is an attempt to explain why a person's difficulties have arisen and what might be helping to maintain them. Formulation provides a framework for thinking together with the service user about how to understand their experiences and for drawing up an individual intervention plan tailored to their particular needs (Johnstone et al., 2011). Formulation draws on two equally important sources of evidence: the clinician brings knowledge derived from theory, research and clinical experience, while the service user brings expertise about their own life and the meanings and impact of their relationships and circumstances. Of particular interest is the recent acknowledgement in the NICE Guidelines on psychosis and schizophrenia (National Institute for Clinical Excellence; NICE, 2014), that some professionals and service users and families prefer a narrative or psychological formulation-driven approach to an individual's experiences because of the toxicity of diagnostic labels such as schizophrenia. A formulation-driven model of understanding emotional distress has been shown to counter some of the negative consequences of receiving a psychiatric diagnosis, including reducing service users' sense of powerlessness and worthlessness (Honos-Webb & Leitner, 2001), increasing psychiatric staff's understanding of service users' problems resulting in more optimism about treatment (Berry et al., 2009) and decreasing challenging behaviour (Ingham, 2011). A formulation that seeks to understand an individual's attachment needs can provide helpful pointers in tailoring appropriate interventions that take into account the attachment needs of the service user. Assessing attachment styles can also inform a formulation by providing an understanding of the psychological function of challenging behaviour. For example, deliberate self-harm, suicide, aggression and violence can be understood as attachment behaviours that are triggered by threats to an individual's safety. They can also be understood as desperate attempts to regulate overwhelming feelings arising out of traumatic experiences that were not validated or processed at the time the trauma occurred. Understanding the functions of problematic behaviours and distress more generally is vitally important as understanding helps to develop staff empathy as well as provide an insight into ways of reducing risk (Berry et al., 2016).

3. Intervention

To ensure they can offer an attachment informed response to service users, services might consider a number of key aims, such as fulfilling the function of a secure base or safe haven at a time of distress through attention to supportive and meaningful relationships, consistency, provision of both physical and emotional safety, and validation of individuals' distress by careful and attentive listening. All of these are key factors in facilitating a secure base or safe haven. There is also a need to set and manage boundaries so that staff do not become overinvolved or enact conflicted relationships with service users. Boundaries can be maintained by carefully balancing dependence and independence, creating a therapeutic structure that provides order and consistency, and defining roles and expectations. Establishing an accessible place of safety for both staff and service users is fundamental to service users and staff developing attachment-informed relationships. Physical safety, such as feeling safe in the service setting, and psychological safety through a sense of belonging to a team or service, are vital in this process. Developing meaningful relationships with staff members is a key factor in creating a secure environment for individuals; this approach has been shown to aid the recovery process regardless of the type of therapy offered (Horvath et al., 2011). Where possible, staff members should consider how they might draw on the existing attachment relationships clients have outside services in order to help service users optimise these. Furthermore, staff members should engage with service users on a one-to-one basis to facilitate the development of a secure relationship whilst simultaneously keeping in mind that they may come to represent attachment figures to service users and that they thus need to be mindful of becoming over-involved or developing conflicted relationships (Schuengel & van Ijzendoorn, 2001). It is important to maintain a therapeutic structure that provides order and consistency with clearly defined roles and expectations (Rich, 2006a).

As mentioned previously, attachment-informed services need to be available consistently over time; providing continuity of care through building a consistent relationship between staff member or team and service user is imperative (Berry & Drake, 2010; Seager, 2013). Ways of achieving this include assigning dedicated key workers to work with each service user and minimising the number of other staff working with an individual service user (Adshead, 2001; Berry & Drake, 2010). Avoiding unnecessary re-organisation in services and ensuring staff retention by creating a positive working environment with good support mechanisms in place, as well as appropriate remuneration, also facilitates continuity of care and stability in the system (Berry & Drake, 2010; Schuengel & van Ijzendoorn, 2001). Services should also consider service users' attachments to all employees of the service, including cleaners, receptionists and cooks (Department of Health, 2010), with the implication that services should attempt to retain stability in these workforces too. In terms of flexibility and availability, Seager (2006) advocates that services should offer a more diverse range of intervention options, including briefer sessions, telephone contacts, written contacts, and on-demand services, not just structured doses of therapy sessions. Support outside normal working hours, when people are particularly vulnerable and are most in need of help and most at risk (Seager, 2013), is essential in ensuring continuity of care. The promise of digital technologies, such as Smartphone apps, that can extend the reach of service delivery by providing service users with access to mental health support at the time of need, is encouraging (Bucci et al., 2015).

Bowlby (1982) suggests caregivers need to be sensitive and responsive when responding to individuals' emotional needs. Research suggests that sensitive appropriate responses to service user distress can be achieved through good professional listening, demonstrating care and concern, emotional containment, empathic listening and warmth and attunement to an individual's emotions and needs (Goodwin et al., 2003). Furthermore, service users benefit from relationships that provide new opportunities for learning. Whether or not this is the focus of the therapeutic model, providing service users with positive relational experiences that may challenge and modify insecure internal working models is important in all therapeutic approaches. For example, staff members who show confidence in a service user, who focus on their strengths and recognise their value and worth can go some way in deconstructing negative and unhelpful mental representations that service users may hold about themselves and others.

Finally, service user dependence on services, and attachment behaviours that may be viewed as 'attention seeking', should also be de-stigmatised. Bowlby (1982) asserted that attachment behaviour should be viewed as a positive behavioural concept and should not be confused with dependence. To modify insecure internal working models, Rich (2006a) suggested that staff should provide non-contingent positive interaction with service users, rather than interacting only when there are problems. Conflict within staff–service user relationships might also be viewed as a therapeutic opportunity; conflict that arises in relationships with staff might mean that some aspect of the service user's internal working model is activated, affording the clinician the opportunity for potential reparation (Moore et al., 1997), reflecting the importance of relational conflict in bringing about therapeutic change. In contrast, for those who display a dismissing attachment style, staff should persevere with efforts to connect with these service users.

4. Support for staff

Implementing an attachment based and trauma-informed service will indeed test the internal resources of staff as many users of mental health services will present with difficult attachment experiences and bring into relationships staff patterns of behaviour that result from these experiences (Adshead et al., 2005; Barber et al., 2006; Berry & Drake, 2010). Moreover, the acknowledgement, witnessing and validation of trauma experiences place very heavy emotional demands on staff. One consequence of this may be a temptation to retreat behind psychiatric labels rather than face the reality of people's lives (Herman, 2001; Van Der Kolk, 2014). Another consequence may be the potential activation of practitioner's own attachment responses. There are a number of ways in which staff can be supported to manage attachment relations and clients suffering after consequences of trauma, including (but not limited to): staff training, supervision and consultation (Adshead et al., 2005; Seager, 2013); staff reflective practice groups that focus on understanding service users' and clinicians' attachment styles, behaviours and needs (Barber et al., 2006; Berry & Drake, 2010); and maintaining boundaries (Schuengel & van Ijzendoorn, 2001). Furthermore, supporting caregivers to identify their role in maintaining unhelpful cycles by helping them recognise their own attachment styles and how these influence their perceptions of, and relationships with, service users, is also important. As Wallin (2013) has highlighted, difficult attachment histories may in part motivate involvement in caregiving work. Personal therapy or carefully conducted attachment-informed clinical supervision are two ways in which staff can be supported to understand how their own attachment style might contribute to interpersonal relationships.

One strategy for offering staff support to manage these demands and aims and avoid the therapeutic traps is the increasingly popular practice of team formulation. This is the process of facilitating a group or team of staff to develop a shared formulation about a service user (Johnstone, 2014b). The Division of Clinical Psychology 'Good practice guidelines on the use of psychological formulation' recommend, in line with trauma-informed practice, that all formulations should consider "the possible role of trauma and abuse along with the possible role of services in compounding the difficulties" (Johnstone et al., 2011, p. 29). Practitioners have developed models of team formulation that include attachment styles and relationships on the part of both staff and service users as a central feature of the discussion (Berry et al., 2016; Johnstone, 2014b). Attachment-informed team formulations, along with education about the impact of trauma and adversity, help staff to provide the containing emotional environment that is so central to healing from trauma (Clarke, 2015).

One advantage of a team formulation over individual formulation is that this process can begin even if the service user is not yet ready or able to be an active participant, which enables the identification of potentially unhelpful staff reactions right from the start. This is particularly important in the face of the profound confusion, chaos and disturbance that may characterise a 'psychotic' reaction to complex trauma. There is some empirical evidence that developing psychological formulations with staff teams, in relation to service users' problems, can increase staff members' understanding and confidence in supporting service users (Berry et al., 2009). Furthermore, psychological formulations with staff have been shown to help staff feel more connected with service users and made service users feel less criticised by staff (Berry et al., 2016). While research in this area is still limited, there is a growing consensus that multi-disciplinary team (MDT) staff very much value the team formulation approach (Cole et al., 2015; Hollingworth & Johnstone, 2014) and that it may confer general benefits such as understanding attachment issues, raising staff morale, processing staff counter-transference reactions, and increasing team empathy and reflectiveness (Johnstone et al., 2011). This might be expected to have a positive impact on the service as a whole, as a good formulation can be a powerful intervention in itself, changing the meaning of a service user's subjective experiences and a team's thinking about presenting difficulties or challenging behaviours (Kennedy et al., 2003).

Formulations are, of course, not the only way in which staff can be offered support when working with service users with attachment-related difficulties. Balint groups, where a group of clinicians meet regularly to discuss cases with one another; forms of supervision that focus on relationships issues; Schwartz rounds, where healthcare providers regularly scheduled time to openly discuss the social and emotional issues they face in offering compassionate care, are among other strategies staff can use to support each other. Organisational factors can also impact on staff's ability to manage emotionally difficult work. It is important for staff to feel supported in their work not only by the organisation more broadly but also by their immediate managers. Manageable workloads, feeling part of a team and feeling that one's concerns are heard and taken seriously are important factors in ensuring staff them-selves feel stable and secure in their working environment.

5. *Endings and transitions*

Acknowledging the impact of endings and transitions and planning for these events can be particularly problematic for individuals with attachment dif-ficulties. The issue of discharge planning is also important in the light of the known high suicide rates following discharge from inpatient care par-ticularly (Crawford, 2004). An attachment-informed mental health service model must support careful planning for transitions and endings in advance, as these are times when an individual's attachment system, or bond with the service/member of staff, is threatened. Problems evident around discharge or transitions could be reduced, or sometimes even prevented by graded dis-charge or outreach work (Seager, 2013), arranging ongoing professional and lay support for the service user (Barber et al., 2006), and/or by ensuring, where possible, that service users are discharged into the care of an attachment figure to minimise the possible risk of self-harm, suicide, aggression and violence. Endings and transitions have been shown to be especially significant for ser-vice users who may have suffered multiple past losses (Adshead et al., 2005).

Introducing attachment and trauma-informed models of care

Attachment- and trauma-informed models of care undoubtedly require additional commissioning commitment over and above usual service costs, at least at the outset. Extra resources in terms of workforce numbers and planning, staff training, formal and informal support for staff and caregivers, flexible service inclusion and delivery, and the development of appropriate attachment assessments are needed. Interestingly, studies have shown that investment in the mental health service workforce has the potential to lead to savings and improved quality of life for service users. For example, Olfson and colleagues (1995) reported resource savings and benefits over time, including reduced absenteeism and less staff turnover, when they examined the benefits of investing in the mental health workforce. Furthermore, evidence-based Early Intervention Services (EIS) for early psychosis have been shown to be cost saving and preferred by service users and carers over generic mental health service support. EIS reduce overall costs to the health service despite the extra investment in staff and training. A recent study also found that in a small sample of service users who had received a psychosis-related diag-nosis, insecure attachment styles were associated with higher service util-isation independent of the severity of distress. In the same study, insecure attachment styles were also associated with higher service costs, suggesting that investing in services that facilitate the development of secure attachments could be cost effective (Berry et al., 2015). These findings indicate possible economic benefits to attachment- and trauma-informed models of care, but more research is needed to clarify the potential economic impact and longer-term benefits of developing such services.

Conclusions

Effort and involvement is required by all stakeholders to ensure successful implementation of new practice (Drake et al., 2003; Proctor et al., 2009), including an attachment-informed way of working. It takes time for changes to practice to be operationalised and embedded within service delivery. Considering the continual obligation for commissioners to develop effective services that provide value for money, an attachment-informed service model may need to demonstrate the potential to recoup any extra initial investment in the long term. However, developing an attachment-informed mental health service will have serious implications for the support needs of staff. Supervision, training, consultation, reflective groups, caseload management, team building, team formulation and additional managerial support are among the methods that can be used to enable staff to offer compassionate caregiving. Attachment theory provides a universal evidence-based theory that we believe should inform mental health policy to promote psychologically 'safe' services (Seager et al., 2007).

References

Adshead, G. (2001). Attachment in mental health institutions: A commentary. *Attachment and Human Development, 3*, 324–329.

Adshead, G., Charles, S., & Pyszora, N. (2005). Moving on: A group for patients leaving a high security hospital. *Group Analysis, 38*, 380–394.

Adults |Surviving Child Abuse (ASCA) 'The last frontier': Practice Guidelines for treatment of complex trauma and trauma-informed care and service delivery. Available at www.asca.org.au.

Agishtein, P., & Brumbaugh, C. (2013). Cultural variation in adult attachment: the impact of ethnicity, collectivism, and country of origin. *Journal of Social, Evolutionary, and Cultural Psychology, 7*, 384–405.

Barber, M., Short, J., Clarke-Moore, J., Lougher, M., Huckle, P., & Amos, T. (2006). A secure attachment model of care: meeting the needs of women with mental health problems and antisocial behaviour. *Criminal Behaviour and Mental Health, 16*, 3–10.

Bartholomew, K., & Horowitz, L. M. (1991). Attachment styles among young adults: a test of a four-category model. *Journal of Personality and Social Psychology, 61*, 226–244.

Berry, K., Barrowclough, C., & Wearden, A. (2009). A pilot study investigating the use of psychological formulations to modify psychiatric staff perceptions of service users with psychosis. *Behavioural and Cognitive Psychotherapy, 37*, 39–48.

Berry, K., & Drake, R. (2010). Attachment theory in psychiatric rehabilitation: informing clinical practice. *Advances in Psychiatric Treatment, 16*, 308–315.

Berry, K., Haddock, G., Kellett, S., Roberts, C., Drake, R., & Barrowclough, C. (2016). Feasibility of a ward-based psychological intervention to improve staff and patient relationships in psychiatric rehabilitation settings. *British Journal of Clinical Psychology*, *55*, 236–352.

Berry, K., Roberts, N., Danquah, A. N., & Davies, L. (2015). An exploratory study of associations between adult attachment, health service utilisation and health service costs. *Psychosis*, *6*, 355–358.

Bloom, S. L., & Farragher, B. (2010). *Destroying Sanctuary: The crisis in human service delivery systems.* Oxford: Oxford University Press.

Bowlby, J. (1969). *Attachment. Attachment and Loss Vol. I.* London: Hogarth.

Bowlby, J. (1982). Attachment and loss: retrospect and prospect. *American Journal of Orthopsychiatry*, *52*, 664–678.

Bucci, S., Barrowclough, C., Ainsworth, J., Morris, R., Berry, K., Machin, M., Emsley, R., Lewis, S., Edge, D., Buchan, I. and Haddock, G., 2015. Using mobile technology to deliver a cognitive behaviour therapy-informed intervention in early psychosis (Actissist): study protocol for a randomised controlled trial. *Trials*, *16*(1), 404.

Bucci, S., Roberts, N. H., Danquah, A. N., & Berry, K. (2015). Using attachment theory to inform the design and delivery of mental health services: A systematic review of the literature. *Psychology and Psychotherapy: Theory, Research and Practice*, *88*, 1–20.

Butler, G. (1998). Clinical formulation. In A. S. Bellack & M. Hersen (Eds.), *Comprehensive Clinical Psychology* (pp. 1–23). Oxford: Pergamon.

Clarke, I. (2015). The emotion focused formulation approach: bridging individual and team formulation. *Clinical Psychology Forum*, *275*, 28–32.

Cole, S., Wood, K., & Spendelow, J. (2015). Team formulation: A critical evaluation of current literature and future research directions. *Clinical Psychology Forum*, *275*, 13–19.

Crawford, M. J. (2004). Suicide following discharge from in-patient psychiatric care. *Advances in Psychiatric Treatment*, *10*, 434–438.

Daly, K. D., & Mallinckrodt, B. (2009). Experienced therapists' approach to psychotherapy for adults with attachment avoidance or attachment anxiety. *Journal of Counseling Psychology*, *56*, 549.

Department of Health (2010). Your guide to relational security. In t. See, act. (Ed.), *Crown*. London, UK.

Dillon, J., Johnstone, L., & Longden, E. (2012). Trauma, dissociation, attachment and neuroscience: A new paradigm for understanding severe mental distress. *Journal of Critical Psychology, Counselling and Psychotherapy*, *12*, 145–155.

Drennan, G. and Alred, D. eds., 2013. *Secure Recovery: Approaches to recovery in forensic mental health settings.* Willan.

Drake, R. E., Torrey, W. C., & McHugo, G. J. (2003). Strategies for implementing evidence-based practices in routine mental health settings. *Evidence Based Mental Health*, *6*, 6–7.

Fallot, R., & Harris, M. (2009). *Creating cultures of trauma-informed care.* Washington DC: Community Connections.

Fraley, C. R., Heffernan, M. E., Vicary, A. M., & Brumbaugh, C. C. (2011). The experiences in close relationships—Relationship Structures Questionnaire: A method for assessing attachment orientations across relationships. *Psychological Assessment, 23*, 615–625.

Fraley, C. R., Waller, N. G., & Brennan, K. A. (2000). An item response theory analysis of self-report measures of adult attachment. *Journal of Personality and Social Psychology, 78*, 350–365.

Francis, R. (2013a). Report of the Mid Staffordshire NHS Foundation Trust Public Inquiry. The Stationery Office.

George, C., Kaplan, N., & Main, M. (1985). Attachment interview for adults. In *Unpublished manuscript*, University of California, Berkeley.

Goodwin, I. (2003). The relevance of attachment theory to the philosophy, organization, and practice of adult mental health care. *Clinical Psychology Review, 23*, 35–56.

Goodwin, I., Holmes, G., Cochrane, R., & Mason, O. (2003). The ability of adult mental health services to meet clients' attachment needs: The development and implementation of the Service Attachment Questionnaire. *Psychology Psychotherapy, 76*, 145–161.

Grossmann, K. E., Grossman, K., & Kepler, A. (2005). Universal and culture-specific aspects of human behavior: The case of attachment. In W. Friedlmeier, P. Chakkarath, & B. Schwarz (Eds.), *Culture and Human Development: The importance of cross-cultural research for the social sciences* (pp. 75–97). Hove, England: Taylor & Francis.

Herman, J. (2001). *Trauma and Recovery*. London: Pandora.

Hollingworth, P., & Johnstone, L. (2014). Team formulation: what are the staff views? *Clinical Psychology Forum, 257*, 28–34.

Honos-Webb, L., & Leitner, L. M. (2001). How using the DSM causes damage: A client's report. *Journal of Humanistic Psychology, 41*, 36–56.

Horvath, A. O., Del Re, A. C., Flückiger, C., & Symonds, D. (2011). Alliance in individual psychotherapy. *Psychotherapy, 48*, 9–16.

Ingham, B. (2011). Collaborative psychosocial case formulation development workshops: a case study with direct care staff. *Advances in Mental Health and Intellectual Disabilities, 5*, 9–15.

Johnstone, L. (2014b). Using formulation in teams. In L. Johnstone & R. Dallos (Eds.), *Formulation in Psychology and Psychotherapy: Making Sense of people's problems* (2nd ed., pp. 216–242). New York: Routledge.

Johnstone, L., Whomsley, S., Cole, S., & Oliver, N. (2011). Good practice guidelines on the use of psychological formulation. In *Leicester: British Psychological Society*.

Kennedy, F., Smalley, M., & Harris, T. (2003). Clinical psychology for inpatient settings: principles for development and practice. *Clinical Psychology Forum, 30*, 21–24.

MacBeth, A., Gumley, A., Schwannauer, M., & Fisher, R. (2011). Attachment states of mind, mentalization, and their correlates in a first-episode psychosis sample. *Psychology and Psychotherapy: Theory, Research and Practice, 84*, 42–57.

Mikulincer, M., & Shaver, P. R. (2010). *Attachment in Adulthood: Structure, dynamics, and change*. New York: Guilford Press.

Moore, K., Moretti, M. M., & Holland, R. (1997). A new perspective on youth care programs: Using attachment theory to guide interventions for troubled youth. *Residential Treatment for Children and Youth, 15*, 1–24.

NICE (National Institute of Clinical Excellence) (2014). Psychosis and schizophrenia in adults: Treatment and management National Clinical Guideline no. 178, February.

Olfson, M., Gorman, J., & Pardes, H. (1995). Investing in mental health research. *The Journal of Nervous and Mental Disease, 183*, 421–424.

Pitt, L., Kilbride, M., Nothard, S., Welford, M. and Morrison, A. P., 2007. Researching recovery from psychosis: a user-led project. *The Psychiatrist, 31*(2), 55–60.

Proctor, E. K., Landsverk, J., Aarons, G., Chambers, D., Glisson, C., & Mittman, B. (2009). Implementation research in mental health services: An emerging science with conceptual, methodological, and training challenges. *Administration and Policy in Mental Health and Mental Health Services Research, 36*, 24–34.

Read, J., & Bentall, R. P. (2012). Negative childhood experiences and mental health: theoretical, clinical and primary prevention implications. *The British Journal of Psychiatry, 200*, 89–91.

Read, J., & Gumley, A. (2008). Can attachment theory help explain the relationship between childhood adversity and psychosis? *Attachment: New Directions in Psychotherapy and Relational Psychoanalysis, 2*, 1–35.

Rich, P. (2006a). *Attachment and Sexual Offending: Understanding and applying attachment theory to the treatment of juvenile sexual offenders* (1st ed.). Chichester: John Wiley & Sons.

Schizophrenia Commission. (2012). *The Abandoned Illness: A report from the Schizophrenia Commission*. London: Rethink Mental Illness.

Schuengel, C., & van Ijzendoorn, M. H. (2001). Attachment in mental health institutions: A critical review of assumptions, clinical implications, and research strategies. *Attachment and Human Development, 3*, 304–323.

Seager, M. (2006). The concpet of 'psychological safety' – a psychoanalytically-informed contribution towards 'safe, sound & supportive' mental health services. *Psychoanalytic Psychotherapy, 20*, 266–280.

Seager, M. (2013). Using attachment theory to inform psychologically minded care services, systems and environments. In A. N. Danquah & K. Berry (Eds.), *Attachment Theory in Adult Mental Health: A guide to clinical practice* (pp. 213–224). London: Routledge.

Seager, M., Orbach, S., Sinason, V., Samuels, A., Johnstone, L., Fredman, G., Kinderman, P., Wilkinson, M., & Hughes, R. (2007). 'National advisory group on mental health, safety and well-being–towards proactive policy: five universal psychological principles. In *unpublished advisory paper commissioned by the Secretary of State for Health, Patricia Hewitt*.

Society, B. P. (2014). Understanding psychosis and schizophrenia. Leicester: British Psychological Society. In. Available from www.understandingpsychosis.net

Van Der Kolk, B. (2014). *The Body Keeps the Score: Mind, brain and body in the healing of trauma*. New York: Penguin.

Varese, F., Smeets, F., Drukker, M., Lieverse, R., Lataster, T., Viechtbauer, W., Read, J., van Os, J., & Bentall, R. P. (2012). Childhood adversities increase the risk of psychosis: a meta-analysis of patient-control, prospective-and cross-sectional cohort studies. *Schizophrenia Bulletin, 38*, 661–671.

Wainwright, A. (2014). The governance and influence of clinical psychology: professional ethics and the Francis report Clin Psy Forum. *Clinical Psychology Forum, 263*, 5–7.

Wallin, D. (2013). We are the tools of our trade: the therapist's attachment history as a source of impasse, inspiration and change. In A. N. Danquah & K. Berry (Eds.), *Attachment Theory in Adult Mental Health: A guide to clinical practice* (pp. 225–239). London: Routledge.

Wang, C-C., & Mallinckrodt, S. (2006). Differences between Taiwanese and U.S. cultural beliefs about ideal adult attachment. *Journal of Counselling Psychology, 53,* 192–204.

Winnicott, D. W. (1973). *The Child, the Family, and the Outside World.* Penguin. p. 173.

15

THE SIGNIFICANCE OF THE CLINICIAN'S FELT EXPERIENCE

Using attachment theory to understand the therapist's emotional experience when working with someone with psychosis

Mark Linington

Introduction

One of the most important and interesting aspects of many psychotherapies is its recognition, understanding and careful use of the felt experiences of the therapist. From an attachment perspective, being able to register and reflect on such feelings in oneself – including sometimes the lack of feelings (Alvarez, 2012) – rather than excluding them defensively, is crucial in understanding and working effectively with a person who experiences psychosis. In this chapter I will discuss the therapist's experience in therapy (their 'countertransference') from the perspective that understanding this can make a significant contribution to the understanding of the client. This perspective is supported by attachment theory, as the chapter will highlight. It is also in line with psychoanalytic theory (see Summers & Adshead in this volume). With this perspective, the therapist's feelings and thoughts can be understood as potential unconscious communications of the client's internal working models of relationships. Such communications can provide important insights into the real traumatic experiences of the client's attachment-caregiving relationships, including sometimes experiences of abuse by caregivers, and/or aspects of insecurity in those childhood relationships.

In addition to being able to make use of this countertransferential form of communication to understand the client and the work with them; we must also equally be able to acknowledge, reflect on and work with the presence and impact of our own subjectivity in the therapy (Aaron, 1991, Renik, 1993). Who we are as professionals is rooted in our attachment histories. This history may include unresolved, perhaps unconscious, experiences of insecurity and trauma. Such experiences can leave us with a variety of relational vulnerabilities and potentially fearful responses in certain relational contexts or interactions. It is probably inevitable that such patterns of our relating emerge in different ways in our work, even if, relatively speaking, we are able to hold these feelings inside ourselves. Even responses felt inside ourselves, but not communicated explicitly, are likely to be communicated implicitly (for example, in our gestures, tone, silence and demeanour), and our containment of these internal responses in itself is likely to become a significant therapeutic communication.

Knowing how to recognise and make use of these different felt responses in a reflective and clinically effective way is vital to the progress of any therapy. As Wallin (2013) puts it:

'Our authentic personal involvement, emotional responsiveness, and unavoidable subjectivity, far from interfering, are essential features of every successful psychotherapy'.

p.171

Arguably, understanding the practitioner's experience as having these two aspects, (the communication from the client and the subjective response of the practitioner), is relevant to all caregiving professionals, including social workers, doctors, nurses, teachers and others. The theory underpinning attachment-based psychotherapies can perhaps offer something helpful to the understanding of this area.

In this chapter I describe my work as a psychotherapist with a woman, Joan, who experienced psychotic episodes. I show how what was evoked internally in me in the work with her could be understood and used therapeutically. The use of attachment theory has been especially helpful in reflecting on this work, with its acknowledgement and understanding of the impact of real caregiving relationships, of attachment trauma and the ways in which these early experiences are repeated emotionally and relationally in the therapeutic interactions (Wallin, 2007, Herman, 1992). Joan consented to me writing about our work together and I have also made alterations to the material to protect her confidentiality.

Joan

Joan was referred for weekly attachment-based psychoanalytic psychotherapy by her psychiatrist. Attachment-based psychoanalytic psychotherapy is a form of psychotherapy that applies different aspects of attachment theory and research, including a relational psychoanalytic approach (for example, the significance of the secure base, the role of the fear system and the impact of attachment trauma) (Linington, M. & Settle, V., 2017). The psychiatrist was deeply concerned that Joan did not seem able to free herself from a damaging and sometimes violent attachment to her long-term male partner. The psychiatrist said she was worried for Joan's safety in her relationship with her partner and described her own angry frustration at not being able to persuade

Joan to leave him. The psychiatrist said these feelings had been especially difficult for her: playing on her mind at home, and leaving her feeling hopeless about the situation and being fiercely annoyed with Joan in a way she could not understand. As an experienced psychiatrist she was surprised at the strength of these feelings and the way they were getting inside her. She said she felt relieved that she was able to refer Joan over to me.

Joan was a white woman, in her sixties when she was referred. She was described as having a history of infrequent positive psychotic symptoms (auditory and visual hallucinations) and more frequent negative symptoms (a lack of feeling, motivation and engagement with others). She had tried different medications over the years to try and help her with these symptoms. At the time of the referral she was taking an anti-depressant, which she said helped her feel calmer. No aspect of her attachment or life history was described by the psychiatrist as contributing to these psychotic symptoms. However, the referral did note that both her mother and father were dead and that Joan's relationship with her brothers was frequently acrimonious. She was in part-time employment as a cleaner at a school, where she had worked for several years – she reported enjoying her work. Social services were involved in her life because she was seen as a vulnerable adult. Joan's social worker got in contact at the time of the referral to add further information. She said she had, like the psychiatrist, tried hard to persuade Joan to move out of the flat she shared with her partner, into a flat of her own. Joan had said that she would do this, when speaking with her face-to-face, but then had been "non-compliant" and avoided any contact with her after that conversation. Little was known of the specifics of Joan's childhood history by social services, but the social worker said that she had first come into contact with Joan many years before after she had a breakdown following the death of her mother. At that time she had been arrested when living on the street. Joan was sectioned, as she had become aggressive and violent. Something similar had happened when her father died some years later. Like the psychiatrist, the social worker said how angry she felt towards Joan, describing her as "manipulative" and "untrustworthy". The social worker said Joan had not been keen to be referred for psychotherapy, but that she had been insistent.

When I first read through the referral, I noticed that a strong and disturbing personal association came to mind, linking Joan to my father's side of the family. I was puzzled by this association and noticed the feeling of discomfort and anxiety that came with it. I had made a link in my mind between Joan and an aunt, whom I knew had been in several violent relationships and had also experienced sexual abuse in her family as a child. I was certainly unsettled by this out-of-nowhere 'reverie' (Bion, 1962a, Ogden, 1999) appearing like a ghost in my mind. I felt guilty and ashamed as though I had transgressed a boundary, while at the same time I felt intruded upon by these thoughts, which felt alien to the context. I saw that there was a tendency for

255

those working with Joan to have strangely intense feelings, apparent not only in this association in myself, but also in the strikingly strong feelings of both the psychiatrist and social worker.

The strength and immediacy of these feelings that were aroused at taking on the referral interested me, but also brought some anxiety. I was, however, fortunate to have secure enough relationships with some of my colleagues and my clinical supervisor to be able to think about these feelings and their significance. This is not always easy to do in our professional groups. As Ogden (1999, p. 159) says:

'The thoughts and feelings constituting reverie are rarely discussed with our colleagues. To attempt to hold such thoughts and feelings, and sensations in consciousness is to forego a type of privacy that we ordinarily unconsciously rely on as a barrier separating inside from outside, public from private. In our efforts to make analytic use of our reveries, "I" as unselfconscious subject is transformed into "me" as object of analytic scrutiny'.

Such uncanny emotive complex responses to referral information are not uncommon when coming into contact with individuals who experience psychosis. Psychosis is about the crossing of spatial and temporal barriers: the "barrier separating inside from outside", as well as the barrier separating past from present (Ogden, 1999). As is described elsewhere in this book, people with psychotic symptoms will often have had experiences of early abusive attachment trauma (Bowlby, 1988, Read, 2004). Where the individual who has experienced such trauma has not had an opportunity to process such an experience, not infrequently, the un-narrated attachment trauma is exported (Bowlby, 1980) into the professional caregiving system. It is not uncommon for there to be widespread re-enactments of different family roles across the multi-disciplinary professional systems working with individuals with such experiences. The unconscious intrusion of such projected communications into the caregiving system parallels the individual's experience of psychosis in which aspects of the past trauma are represented. In both instances, there is the experience of something which does not belong to the current context, which can elicit a strong set of powerful mixed feelings in professionals and which can lead to relational responses that echo an original relationally traumatic (often abusive) situation (Brown, 2015).

However, despite my thoughts and feelings, there was no mention in Joan's case of abusive trauma in earlier life. She had experienced disturbing reactions to the loss of both parents when she was an adult, but it was unclear whether this trauma of loss was aetiological in her psychosis, or linked to the evoking of these responses in me as a clinician, as well as the emotional-relational responses of the psychiatrist and social worker, or whether there was more trauma that was not yet known.

The first appointment

Joan did not arrive for her first appointment. As I waited for her I moved through a series of intense feelings. I felt *angry and attacked*: how could she be rejecting my help in this way? I felt *worried, but not so much for her as for myself* – that something bad had happened to her and somehow I was going to be held responsible and get blamed for this incident. I felt *relief*. I had from the time that the referral was allocated to me experienced a growing *dread* at the prospect of our meeting, which now vanished when I knew she was not going to arrive.

I received a telephone message from Joan to say she was sorry to have let me down. I spoke with her on the telephone: she had forgotten about her appointment and fallen asleep, woken in a panic, and then lost her way coming to see me and finally gone back to her flat. She asked if she could have another appointment. She said she felt scared coming to see me. I noticed I had an *uncomfortable feeling* when she said this, as though I had done something wrong in asking her to come and meet me. I acknowledged how it was scary coming to see someone for help. My feeling of discomfort linked to her fear passed when I said this to her, but I was left with a horrible feeling of having somehow manipulated her.

When Joan arrived for her next appointment she sat in the waiting area, holding a life-sized baby doll. She had arrived an hour early. I went to tell her I would not be able to see her until her appointment time. Joan cradled the doll in her arms, rocking and talking to it as though it were a real baby. Indeed her treatment of the doll made it seem so real that as I approached and stood speaking with her, I had moments when I felt unsure: unsure whether this was a real baby, and unsure whether Joan was experiencing this as a real baby. I felt that were I to treat this baby doll as anything other than real, I would be killing the baby. She introduced me: "This is baby Joanie, Mark". I said I was glad she had been able to bring her baby, who must be so important to her. I had a surge of fearful feelings as I stood there talking with her – a fear of her "madness", a fear of being near to her, and a fear that she might attack me in a frenzy. I sat down next to her and I managed to ground myself. I said I could not see her until our appointment time, but I would come back and see her then. She spoke in a different hollow sounding voice like that of a young child, looking at me and smiling, while she rocked her baby, holding it in against her breast, saying "That's all right dear, we don't mind waiting".

When I returned at the appointment time – having had these fearful feelings dominating my mind since that time – I had a strong urge to help her as she struggled to stand and walk, being unsteady on her feet. I noticed how this desire to move towards her and help, immediately triggered again a feeling of fear in me that made me pull myself back; Joan looked up at me as she stood and said "hello dear; how are you now?"

As we walked to the therapy room, I again felt self-conscious at being seen with her by other people in the waiting area – whom I imagined were looking at us, *wondering about the nature of our relationship*, as though I were in an improper relationship with her. At the same time I felt *protective* of her – wanting to shield her from what I thought was the critical attacking gaze of the other.

Joan was silent as we walked slowly to the consulting room, and I sensed in her a growing apprehension. I said a couple of things to ease the process of getting to the room. It was as though the transition between places was evoking a fear I wanted to soothe. I said we could talk once we got to the room and that the room was just along the corridor. She did not respond to me and seemed to be managing to get to the room by being in a form of trance.

All of these feelings, in these moments of first contact are helpful for understanding Joan and what she had experienced in her life, especially the traumatic elements of her relational history. Such an intensity of feeling, particularly fear, is common in work with people who experience psychosis. In my clinical experience, such an intense and confusing mixture of feelings experienced at the beginning of the therapeutic relationship can be an indication of a history of a severe level of interpersonal complex trauma (Herman, 1992), with a resulting ongoing disorganised attachment pattern. The nature of the emotions one feels as a clinician can be a way of understanding the attachment world of the client: not just in the present situation, but in their early attachment relationships.

Understanding fear

In cases where the person with whom one is working has features of psychosis originating in early attachment trauma, there is often a significant level of fear operating both intrapsychically (within the internal environments of client and clinician) and interpersonally (in the relationship between them, as well as in other relationships external to the therapy) (Slade, 2013). With Joan, I did not know much about the nature of her attachment trauma, but I noticed the characteristics in my emotional responses which suggested she might have experienced such trauma. These included the presence and level of fear, the mixture of feelings and the haphazard movement between these feelings.

Figure 15.1 shows how fear, including the fear "aroused in situations that are not, in fact, the least dangerous" (Bowlby, 1973, p.139), functions as part of the self defence system (Heard & Lake, 1997, McCluskey, 2005)

In this diagram, we see how a threat evokes two sorts of self-defensive response: a fear response, and/or a careseeking response. The fear response

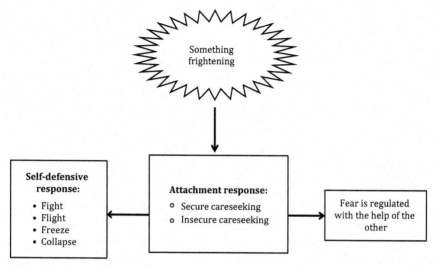

Figure 15.1 The Self Defence System

is characterised by fighting, fleeing or freezing. Careseeking (attachment behaviour) can be either secure or insecure. In its secure-effective form the careseeker, feeling under threat, can approach the available attachment figure and expects a protective, empathic and comforting response. In later life this figure, having been internalised, can be evoked as a companion in frightening situations where an attachment figure is unavailable. In its insecure form, where the attachment figure may be unavailable or unresponsive or a source of the threat, careseeking takes the different forms of insecure attachment patterns (for example, and most simply: ambivalent, avoidant, disorganised). The way the system of self defence operates throughout the life cycle is based significantly upon experiences in early attachment relationships. When attachment relationships have been the source of the trauma, then adult care-giving moments (such as the offer of help from a psychotherapist) are likely to activate fearful aspects of the self-defence system, such as internal working models where careseeking is associated with fear. This evoking of internal working models can emerge in the form of psychotic symptoms, which are based on real events, displaced in time and space (Bowlby, 1988). This seemed to be the case with Joan. For Joan it did seem – in her difficulties in coming to the session – that some sort of experience was evoked, which contained elements of flight, freeze and collapse. Furthermore, when an internal working model is active, aspects of this may be exported as an emotional response into the clinician. This felt experience in the therapy originates in the traumatising dynamics of the original client-caregiver relationship. In addition to this projective aspect, the psychotherapist may also find their own fear system is activated, according to their own relational history and vulnerabilities.

We can understand Joan's behaviour in regard to this attachment-based system of self defence. My letter offering the prospect of a meeting with me – as a stranger, a man and a caregiver – triggered her self-defence system into a fearful and disorganised response. Joan was able to describe later how she had felt frightened on the journey as she came nearer to the clinic. She said she felt taken over, things went blank and she found herself in a different part of town away from the clinic and decided to go home where she felt safer.

Joan's history of relational trauma

A number of writers have recognised how clients with psychosis can often have their relational history – particularly early abusive trauma – disregarded, when considering the aetiology and relational function of their psychosis (Brown, 2015; Taylor, 2014). Ignoring the relational context of a person's psychosis can infect present relationships, including the professional network, and may serve to defend the client and others against difficult emotional experience (Bowlby, 1980). This tendency to ignore the relational aspects of psychosis can be understood as a repetition of an earlier abusive relational situation (Frawley & Davis, 1999), in which the perpetrator of the abuse gave powerful injunctions to the child not to speak of what was being done to them. The taking into the self of the responsibility for the abuse, as a way of preserving the sense of a good caregiver, is not uncommon, as are explicit messages from the abusing caregiver that the responsibility for the abuse lies with the victim (Herman, 1992). Each of these features of abuse potentially leads to an individualised (excluding the role of the other), rather than attachment-based focus in the work with people with such histories. I suggest that the failure to recognise the significance of the specific attachment origins of such trauma may be detrimental to the effectiveness of the therapy in supporting a client's recovery.

Over the course of her long-term weekly psychotherapy it became clear that Joan's psychotic symptoms had their origins in experiences of "complex trauma" (Herman, 1992). Complex trauma includes trauma where there is early and chronic emotional, physical and sexual abuse by a caregiver or caregivers, often including experiences of neglect and often combined with several other experiences of severe trauma and abuse throughout life. Many of the things that had happened and been done to Joan, she talked about for the first time in her psychotherapy. It seems likely that in a situation when aspects of attachment trauma are being named for the first time, the feelings and the self-preserving and relational strategies developed in response to such abuse will emerge more strongly and less consciously. As a result, the clinician is also likely to have stronger and more disregulating emotional experiences in relation to such work.

At the beginning of the psychotherapy, Joan's way of saying what had happened to her throughout life was conveyed with many of the features of a traumatised narrative (Holmes, 1999; Herman, 1992). These features in Joan's case included those associated with both the *intrusive* aspects of trauma, such as extreme fear, flashbacks, visual and auditory hallucinations, emotional hyper-arousal and fragmented thinking easily triggered by her current environment, and the more *constrictive (numbing)* post-traumatic responses, including blankness in her mind, an increased dissociation between different aspects of herself and a withdrawing from help. These constrictive symptoms often seemed to be her way of trying to regulate the impact of the intrusive symptoms on her.

For the first six months of Joan's psychotherapy she would switch erratically between these two forms of being (being intruded upon and being constricted), in what Herman (1992) has called "the dialectic of trauma". In this period of the psychotherapy, in which I was working to establish a sense of safety with Joan, I found myself undergoing parallel intrusive and constrictive experiences (Searles, 1979). When I was "near" to the work with Joan (having or about to have sessions, discussing the work with colleagues, writing notes), I sometimes found myself feeling intensely frightened, feeling a sense of dread (Bion, 1962), having nightmarish dreams and experiencing a range of somatic symptoms (feeling sick, sweating). At other times I felt distant. I would forget things associated with the work, find my mind going blank, be unable to write notes, become paralysed in my office chair and drift into a sort of trance.

Joan was the second youngest of five children. She was raised by her mother and father, and to some extent by two of her older brothers. From when she was a young child, her father had been repeatedly physically violent and threatening to her – in a way she said he was not with her brothers. At times she seemed to become the family scapegoat and her brothers would also join in with the father's violence. Some of her earliest memories from when she was a toddler, about which it took her several weeks to speak, were of her father calling her a "dummy" and "retard". He hit her round the head frequently. She thought that many of the difficulties she now had with her mind were to do with this violence. When she described this aspect of the father's violence to me, motioning the swipe he would take at her head and the shoves he would give to her body, I noticed how real these hits seemed. I could almost feel the blows on my own body – I had images come to me from my own childhood of *my* father's physically threatening way of relating. Not unlike a sort of psychotic experience, the boundaries separating time, place, person and physicality were giving way. In these experiences I had to frequently re-centre and re-ground myself.

At school Joan was frequently excluded for being aggressive and violent, often in response to insults and violence from the teachers and other pupils, which reminded her of how things were at home. She described how in these moments of violence she felt everything go dark and it was as if someone took over. From when she was fourteen years old her father began to come to her bedroom at night to sexually assault and rape her. He continued this over a number of years. When she was sixteen, Joan was raped by a neighbour. She became pregnant following the rape. She decided that she wanted to have the baby, because she thought it was not right to have an abortion. She had a miscarriage two months into the pregnancy. In her early twenties, her mother became ill with lung cancer and over several months became more and more unwell, until she eventually died. At this time, in response to a terrible grief, Joan had a serious psychotic breakdown – she said she would see her mother in different places, follow her and then her mother would disappear. She said she began to hear voices of a highly self-attacking nature. She ran away from the family home and lived on the street for several months. She became involved with social services and mental health services and was briefly sectioned in hospital, before living in a refuge. She had periods of time where she went back to live with her father, but found that her mental state would deteriorate when she did. He would continue to rape her when she returned to him, which she did not reveal to anyone. One day when he was out at work, he collapsed with a heart attack and later died in hospital. Joan had a further breakdown and after another period in hospital, moved into a flat of her own. Soon afterwards she met an older man on the street and began living with him. They had a relationship for a number of years. One day she came home and found he had left her without any communication, or indication of his whereabouts. She experienced another psychotic episode and started "blacking out" when she was out in public and finding herself in places, not knowing how she had got there. At her work as a school cleaner, she was increasingly bullied. Her colleagues began to tease her about being stupid. They locked her in a cupboard, hit her and stole things from her. A few years later she met another man who was 15 years older than her – again when she was sleeping out on the street – and began a romantic relationship with him. This was the partner she was with when she was referred to me for psychotherapy, who was threatening her and sometimes beating her.

The clinical work

I worked with Joan for five years in weekly psychotherapy. Reflecting on Joan's response to the invitation to come and see me for an initial session, it seems as she approached me that the internal model of her relationship with her father was unconsciously activated. Such fear-based difficulties in approaching help – an aspect of disorganised attachment – are common for people who have experienced complex attachment trauma (Linington, 2016). She was later to tell me that her father had first sexually abused her when she was asleep in her bed, and she had awoken in a fearful panic to find him abusing her. In our work in the therapy, Joan was later to re-experience and recall this intense feeling of panic.

These feelings, with their associated traumatic relational models, were at work in the process of her coming to see me for the first time. When Joan set off on her journey towards me there was both the *compliance* that was associated with her abuse and the *careseeking* behaviour looking for help when under attack. There are different points in her approach at which the fearful responses that form part of the self defence system begin to operate: she has a psychotic experience, she runs away, she dissociates. These fearful responses occurred not only on Joan's first journey, but also throughout our work, often when we were involved in working on her traumatic experiences with men. It is also significant that powerful emotional-relational models both from my own history and also those that seem connected to her attachment trauma also intruded into my experience. In our work together we were able to think about her experience together and to gradually build up a narrative about what had happened to her internally, from the psychiatrist suggesting that she might have psychotherapy, to receiving my appointment letter, to forgetting, to falling asleep to having the phone call and further letter from me, to beginning to make the journey and getting there.

There were three areas of the clinical work with Joan which were especially evocative of feelings in me as a clinician:

1. Loss

Perhaps all clinicians are likely to bring a history of their own loss as an influence on their work. One important aspect of therapeutic training is the opportunity in one's own therapy to reflect on the impacts of losses on one's life, relationships and sense of self, and to work on one's own grief and recovery from distress. As professional caregivers, in acknowledging and understanding this aspect of our own history, we hope to become more conscious of how aspects of our own still painful mourning might be triggered by work with clients. Bowlby (1980) has described how experiences of loss (particularly those of childhood, and those of an attachment figure in childhood) can have a lifelong significance.

As I engaged with Joan – in the area of her awful and frightening experiences of loss – I became aware of two aspects of my own history of loss that were relevant to the work with her. One was my tendency to cope with distressing loss through a dissociative type process, like the "detachment" described by Robertson (1952). Given Joan's propensity for dissociation as a way of coping with frightening relational situations, I thought my coping strategy might well emerge in the psychotherapy. Secondly, having also experienced some frightening caregiving in my life, I identified with the approach or flee dilemma that Joan faced in many relationships: most powerfully in regard to her father, but also in her partner relationship and other family relationships.

Joan's life is a history of multiple losses in a relational context of ongoing intimate violence. Bowlby (1980) and others (Brown et al., 1978) have identified the connection between loss and mental health problems, including depression and psychosis, especially in an unfavourable caregiving environment. Psychosis can be understood as part of a mourning process. Often, as in Joan's case, it can be understood as the searching for the lost attachment figure, bound together with a returning of the persecuting/abusive object. It can be a form of stuckness in grief, where it is not possible to move through the mourning process in the usual way, but there is, I think, an "entrappedness" that develops. Such an "entrappedness" is I think more likely to emerge where there have been experiences of long term abuse from which there is no escape, linked to an experience of loss.

The most significant of Joan's bereavements were her mother, her baby and her father. These experiences of loss, each with its own painful and difficult aspects, seem to have frequently overwhelmed Joan's ability to function. However, there were in addition two other losses, which were less tangible, but which were also an important part of our work together: her hope and desire for a safe and loving family, and her loss of her self in her own potential as a person in the world. Each of these losses needed careful attention as part of the psychotherapy and each began as too frightening for Joan to explore. The psychotherapy began with an exploration of her fear of losing her current partner, often linked together with her anger and threats of violence towards those whom she saw as trying to separate her from him. Identifying such fearfulness and understanding it in relation to each of her losses was an important part of the safety enhancing clinical work with her. Since the death of her mother Joan had continued to hear her voice and on occasions would have visions of her. At first she was too anxious to tell me about these experiences: she was frightened that I would not believe her, that I would think she was mad and have her "locked up in hospital" or that somehow by talking about these experiences they would be taken away from her: that I would destroy her safe haven mother: the representation of her good protective mother that she held inside herself. Each of these fears needed to be understood. I noticed when we engaged in the detail of these experiences; for example, the conversation she had with her mother in her flat, how my own experiences of loss came back to me in a near-psychotic way. In one session, when Joan was sobbing, describing her feelings at being in her flat with her mother, and how important her mother was to her, I had the physical feeling of my dead grandfather grasping my hand (an event which had really taken place many years ago, when he was delirious in the last stages of brain cancer). This uncanny psychosomatic event, a form of identification with Joan, provided me with some important empathic connection to her. I was able to say, with something more than a cognitive understanding, that when someone very important to us dies they can stay with us. As a person, I do not believe in life after death, in the other being a separate surviving entity. There was a risk in this clinical work that this difference in belief might be experienced by Joan as "disbelief", which would severely undermine the sharing of her experience of her mother as a continuing safe haven. This moment in which my subjective experience of loss was evoked, in a way that was not too frightening, but one from which I could manage to speak in a way that met with Joan's experience, allowed for the forming of significant relational connection between us.

Joan's feelings about the death of her father were understandably complex. During the beginning period of the psychotherapy, when Joan talked about her father, she was often overcome by such a powerful hatred that she lost the ability to speak coherently. Her face would contort with simultaneous rage and fear, she would clench her fists tightly, punch out into the air and shout "get off me". I sought to sit with Joan's expression of such feelings and not allow the fear (mine and hers) to push me to a frightened interaction (fight, flight, freeze). This took some practice on my part, some failings (for example, going numb and frozen, trying to control rather than contain her feelings). However, I was gradually able to find a way to meet, understand and explore these feelings with her. My learning to bear and think about such felt experiences was, I think, fundamental to Joan's healing from such awful trauma. (For example the experiences of being psychosomatically overwhelmed, inadequate to Joan's needs at her most desperate, and terrified of the threat of violence in the room). Our achievement, in working together with the impact on her of her father as a chronically violent sexual abuser, laid the ground for a deeper exploration of her mourning his death. The death of an abusive attachment figure can raise profound internal conflicts, in which there is a complex entanglement of fear linked to attachment trauma and complex grief. With Joan, the therapy became a vital opportunity to think not only about her fear and hatred of her father, but also about her longing for his love. Being able to reflect on these feelings seemed to allow her to free herself from an internal tyranny linked to her traumatic relationship to him, and this in turn seemed to empower her to begin to make transformations in her relationship with her partner, as an external representation of the abusive aspects of her father.

2. Sexual abuse

Having feelings you do not want to feel, and being a person you do not want to be are not uncommon experiences for psychotherapists working with survivors of childhood sexual abuse (Frawley & Davis, 1999). Such experiences can feel like an attack on the values upon which we have securely based our model of ourselves as a caregiver: our view of ourselves as compassionate, empathic, with a desire to help and empower the other, is foundational to our work. Some of the transference-countertransferential positions, which can include being in *concordant* and *complementary* emotional – relational positions (Racker, 1968, Tansey & Burke, 1989), can be disturbing for us as professional caregivers. With concordant experiences the therapist identifies with the client, has feelings and takes relational positions which make sense when understood *as part of the client's experience in the original abusive relationship*. These can include feeling afraid, feeling panic, blaming oneself and dissociating. In my work with Joan, especially when we were working with her experiences of sexual abuse, which began with her father, then included different perpetrators and also the very difficult experience of getting pregnant and having a miscarriage from a rape, I often felt frightened after the sessions with her. I could feel myself being on alert, in a state of tense readiness, as though I expected an attack. I needed longer after the sessions with her before seeing another client. I needed to process the horrible material that I had received, otherwise I found I was likely to use dissociative type mechanisms. Having ordinary everyday contact with colleagues, after the time with Joan, had an important regulating function for me.

Although such concordant experiences are usually deeply unsettling, it can be more difficult for the psychotherapist to feel like the perpetrator of abuse. Having a pernicious complementary felt experience, in which one finds oneself myself *in the position of the perpetrator* can be ontologically disturbing. When one feels for example, disgustingly seductive, manipulative, guilty, cruel, hateful, filled with unbidden images of sexual violence, it can be like having something malignant inside oneself. Being able to regard, hold and then reflect on the traumatic relational significance of such invasive internal experiences, rather than segregating them off (Bowlby, 1980) is probably vital to the effectiveness of therapeutic work with survivors of such abuse. With Joan, it was vital to acknowledge such felt experience, to think about it in myself and in supervision, and then to use it in relation to the work with her. The reflective acknowledgement of such experience allowed me to have a much greater understanding of Joan's fear, her relationship with her father and other men, and the horrible feeling of longing for love from someone who is abusing you.

3. Dissociation

I noticed when Joan attended her psychotherapy sessions that she sometimes dressed in different ways and that she had different ways of talking and being with me. Sometimes she seemed and sounded like a little girl, often at the point at which she said goodbye to me at the end of a session, and at times when she was talking about her feelings about her mother. At other times she seemed to want to have a fight, where everything I said was experienced as an attack and she had to aggressively defend herself. Also, there was a more adult caregiving identity, who would come with the baby doll and talk more maturely. Each of these different identities, to whom Joan had given different names (Joanie, Jo and Joan) can be understood in relation to the attachment trauma which Joan had experienced. Joan struggled at first to talk about these different selves/aspects of herself, which seemed disconnected from each other. She thought they might be another indication of her "madness". There seemed an important relationship between these different identities and the psychotic states that Joan experienced. She (Joan) was sometimes unaware of what she had done as Joanie or Jo. In this aspect of the work I would experience a sense of fragmentation in my own feelings and in my sense of self, which paralleled the dissociative relations between these different identities. For Joan there was a marked relief in being able to reveal these different selves to another person, for each of them to be met empathically and to come to an understanding of how they functioned internally and in the external world. Each identity evoked in me a different set of feelings and relational responses. The different countertransferential meanings implicit in these responses not only required attention in themselves, but also the need to be understood and worked with in a more holistically interconnected way.

Conclusion

In this chapter I have described the importance and significance of the clinician's felt experience for effective attachment-based psychotherapeutic work with people who experience psychosis. Furthermore, I hope I have shown how these feelings can be used in a reflective and meaningful way to inform effective therapeutic thinking and work with the client. The main aspects of the work with clinician's felt experience are:

1. *Containing and understanding the complexity of emotional experience in us as clinicians.*
   Our feelings with clients who have experienced such complex trauma are likely to be pervaded by fear that is more intensely felt, fragmented, out of keeping with the present moment, muddled and contradictory. Such feelings are important to recognise rather than censor in ourselves. This recognition, together with our knowledge of how and when these feelings emerge in the clinical work, are important ways to contain (Bion, 1962) these feelings and begin to understand their significance for the clinical work. Recognising these feelings, catching their place in the therapeutic interaction, and being able to reflect on and distinguish their potential meaning in relation to our own history and/or that of the client, are tasks often only accomplished with the help of another, such as our supervisor or a colleague.
2. *Knowing and exploring the impact of our own vulnerabilities.*
   Being able to acknowledge our own relational vulnerabilities, with an awareness of the feelings that accompany them, is a key ability for all psychotherapists (and perhaps for all professional caregivers). Understanding the impact of our own attachment history is a therapeutic task which requires attention throughout all of our clinical work. However, with clients who experience psychosis – where fear will have a very significant presence – it is especially important to ensure we receive

267

adequate secure caregiving, including personal therapy, clinical supervision, peer support and ongoing professional development.

3. *Exploring the connections between the felt experience of the clinician and attachment trauma experienced by the client.*

It seems evident that when working with people who have experienced severe and complex trauma we will have feelings as clinicians that are connected to those experiences. This is more likely where the person has not had the opportunity to begin to recover from such horrible experiences. Sometimes such feelings get enacted between the therapist and client in a manner that parallels the relational positions of the original attachment trauma (Frawley & Davies, 1994). Such feelings and parallel re-enactments fall into the two broad categories of those of the client themselves in the original traumatic situation ("concordant"), and those of the caregiver/perpetrator ("complementary"). It can be especially challenging for our sense of ourselves as "good caregivers" when we find ourselves experiencing feelings and behaving in a way towards the client which echoes the abusive caregiver. Catching these repetitions in their emotional and interactive forms has an important value in safeguarding the relationship from uncontained re-enactment.

As with all aspects of clinical felt experience, a clinical supervisor who understands the link between such countertransferential material and the client's relational trauma, together with the importance of reflecting on and containing re-enactments, is essential for effective therapeutic work. Given such holding by another, one's own ability to reflect within oneself (Casement, 1985) can also be developed progressively over time.

References

Aaron, L. (1991). The patient's experience of the analyst's subjectivity. In: Mitchell, S. A., Aron, L. (Eds.), *Relational Psychoanalysis: The emergence of a tradition* (pp. 243–268). Hillsdale, NJ: The Analytic Press.

Alvarez, A. (2012). *The Thinking Heart: Three levels of psychoanalytic therapy with disturbed children.* Hove: Routledge.

Bion, W. R. (1967). *Second Thoughts.* London: Karnac.

Bowlby, J. (1973). *Separation: Anxiety and anger.* London: The Hogarth Press and The Institute of Psychoanalysis.

Bowlby, J. (1980). *Loss: Sadness and depression.* London: The Hogarth Press and The Institute of Psychoanalysis.

Bowlby, J. (1988). *A Secure Base: Clinical applications of attachment theory.* London: Routledge.

Brown G. W., & Harris, T. (1978). *The Social Origins of Depression: A study of psyciatric disorder in women.* London: Tavistock Publications.

Brown, K. (2015). Psychosis from an Attachment Perspective. *ATTACHMENT: New Directions in Psychotherapy and Relational Psychoanalysis, 9*(1), 29–52.

Frawley, M. G., & Davies, J. M. (1994). *Treating the Adult Survivor of Childhood Sexual Abuse*. New York: Basic Books.

Heard, D., & Lake, B. (1997). *The Challenge of Attachment for Caregiving*. London: Karnac.

Herman, J. (1992). *Trauma and Recovery*. New York: Basic Books.

Holmes, J. (1999). *The Search for the Secure Base: Attachment theory and psychotherapy*. Hove: Brunner-Routledge.

Linington, M. (2016). Who Cares? Some Applications of Attachment Theory with a Man Abused in Childhood. *ATTACHMENT: New Directions in Psychotherapy and Relational Psychoanalysis*, 9(3), 277–289.

Linington, M. Settle, V (2017). Attachment-based Psychoanalytic Psychotherapy. In: Feltham, C., Hanley, T. & Winter, L. A. (Eds.) *The SAGE Handbook of Counselling and Psychotherapy* (pp. 190–196). London: Sage Publications Ltd.

McCluskey, U. (2005). *To Be Met as a Person*. London: Karnac.

Ogden, T. (1999). *Reverie and Interpretation: Sensing something human*. London: Karnac.

Racker, H. (1968). *Transference and Countertransference*. London: The Hogarth Press and The Institute of Psychoanalysis.

Read, J., Mosher, L. R. & Bentall, R. P. (Eds.) (2004). *Models of Madness: Psychological, social and biological approaches to schizophrenia*. Hove: Routledge.

Renik, O. (1999). Analytic Interaction: Conceptualising Technique in the Light of the Analyst's Irreducible Subjectivity. In: Mitchell, S. A., Aron, L. (Eds.), *Relational Psychoanalysis: The emergence of a tradition* (pp. 407–424). Hillsdale, NJ: The Analytic Press.

Robertson, J. (1952). *A Two Year Old Goes to Hospital*. United Kingdom: Robertson Films.

Searles, H. F. (1979). *Countertransference and Related Subjects*. Madison: International Universities Press Inc.

Slade, A. (2013). The place of fear in attachment theory and psychoanalysis: the fifteenth John Bowlby Memorial Lecture. In: Yellin, J., Badouk Epstein, O. (Eds.), *Terror Within and Without: Attachment and Disintegration: Clinical Work on the Edge*. London: Karnac.

Tansey M. J. & Burke, W. F. (1989). *Understanding Countertranseference: From projective identification to empathy*. Hillsdale: The Analytic Press.

Taylor, B. (2014). *The Last Asylum: A memoir of madness in our times*. London: Hamish Hamilton.

Wallin, D. J. (2007). *Attachment in Psychotherapy*. New York: The Guilford Press.

16

CROSS-CUTTING THEMES AND FUTURE DIRECTIONS

Katherine Berry, Adam N. Danquah and Sandra Bucci

Themes and future directions

1. Search for mechanisms

The over-representation of insecure attachment patterns in people with psychosis is well established. However, the way in which insecure attachment patterns influence psychopathology (i.e. the mechanisms of action) is still relatively poorly understood. Key psychological mechanisms that have been discussed within the book include psychological constructs such as beliefs, affect regulation and dissociation. We need to test the role of these proposed processes, in relation to psychosis, through longitudinal research, which ideally measures attachment and mechanisms of action prior to the onset of psychotic symptoms. In developing psychosocial models of attachment processes and psychosis, it is also important to identify the biological substrates of psychosocial constructs. Attachment theory is a biopsychosocial theory, but empirical research into the neurobiology of psychosis has yet to draw on attachment theory.

2. The importance of trauma and the concept of disorganised attachment

Throughout the book, authors have emphasised the important role of trauma in the development of psychosis. In attachment terms, interpersonal trauma is most closely associated with the concept of disorganised attachment (in infancy) and an unresolved or fearful attachment (in adulthood). Although there are problems associated with the measurement of this attachment pattern in adulthood, it is this pattern – characterised by dissociative phenomena, a confused 'push and pull' style of relating to others, and relationship difficulties – that is likely to be most helpful in understanding the development of psychotic symptoms (and voice-hearing in particular). In order to advance research into disorganised attachment patterns and psychosis, we need more accessible ways of measuring disorganised attachment in adulthood. As it stands, neither the Adult Attachment Interview (George,

270

Kaplan & Main, 1996), which can be used to assess unresolved attachment, nor self-report measures, which can be used to assess fearful attachment in terms of conscious relationship processes, seems to fully capture the concept of disorganised relating that is so neatly captured via the classic behavioural measure of attachment in infancy, the Strange Situation (Ainsworth, Blehar, Waters & Wall, 1978).

3. The concept of dissociation

Relatedly, many of the chapters have highlighted the theoretical import-ance of dissociation in terms of both attachment theory and psychosis. Traditionally, we have understood dissociation as it relates to psychosis rather crudely in terms of a loss of touch of reality. As highlighted within several chapters in this book, dissociation is a much more nuanced concept than this, encompassing compartmentalisation and detachment experiences, such as depersonalisation and derealisation. It is important that researchers working in the dissociation and psychosis fields collaborate with each other to better understand which particular aspects of dissociative phenomena are most relevant to which aspects of psychosis, and how these relate to attachment processes.

4. Importance of secure attachment

Within the fields of both psychology, and mental health more widely, there is a tendency to focus on psychopathology. Yet, there is a growing trend to con-sider positive phenomena, including the concept of resilience. As such, it is reassuring that there have been references to the important concept of secure attachment throughout the book, with a recognition that people who experi-ence psychosis can have secure attachment styles, and that it is possible for people to move from insecure to secure attachment states within the context of a supportive environment or therapeutic relationship. Future research is needed to demonstrate empirically the protective role that secure attachment might play in influencing outcomes in psychosis and what factors are most key to helping people move towards more secure attachments within the con-text of therapy or other types of interventions. One might hypothesise that positive beliefs about the self and others, good affect regulation and support-seeking are key mechanisms that help people with secure attachments to have more positive outcomes following an experience of psychosis. Similarly, one might predict that a therapist who is responsive and attuned, in terms of relating to a client in a way that sensitively matches or challenges their rela-tional style at the right point in time, would be more likely to facilitate the client in moving from an insecure to secure attachment style. However, both of these hypotheses need to be tested empirically.

271

5. *The importance of therapist, staff or carer attachment styles*

We most frequently think or write about attachment styles in relation to people with psychosis but attachment theory is more generally a theory of social relating. As several authors throughout the book have highlighted, it is equally important to consider the attachment styles and attachment needs of those in the person's social environment; be that therapists, other mental health workers, or family and other carers. The attachment system is fundamentally related to the caregiving system, so the mental health worker's or carer's attachment style is going to influence how they provide care and support to the person who experiences psychosis. There is evidence that securely attached mental health workers are more likely to develop positive therapeutic alliances with service users. However, there is relatively limited research on informal carer attachment styles and caregiving styles, together with how these interact with service user attachment styles. In terms of clinical implications, it is also important for mental health services to ensure that staff and carer attachment needs are met, in order to help them function as effective caregivers. In this respect, staff need to feel safe and secure within their job roles and organisations. There needs to be training and supervision in place, which can help workers understand the impact of their own relational history, and consequent attachment styles, on their interactions with others.

6. *Working with diversity and difference*

Thinking about their own attachment histories may enable practitioners to work more effectively in multicultural societies. This is because understanding our own attachment forces us to confront what threatens our sense of safety. While this is different for each individual, there are also commonalities. One of these can be perceived cultural differences in others. If we construe this difference as unfamiliarity, or even strangeness, we can see quickly how our attachment system might be activated, despite ourselves. We believe that people generally want to get on with others and treat them fairly, but that attachment processes are not always readily available for conscious scrutiny and it takes work (and help) to understand our predispositions. This represents a responsibility that all of us have. It is, however, perhaps even more incumbent on practitioners to do this work, because we are working with vulnerability and distress (and, with psychosis, often terror). These powerful feelings, especially when exacerbated by the uncertainties provoked by cultural difference, can make us susceptible to acting as we are disposed to (i.e. as threatened by danger) rather than in more thoughtful ways. Several chapters write about the influence of the therapists' own attachment experiences (most notably Chapter 15) and demonstrate how we might be helped to understand these difficult dynamics in order to do no harm and then go on to work openly and inclusively with all that others have to bring.

7. *Importance of prevention*

As several authors have highlighted, the role of attachment in psychosis emphasises the importance of preventative interventions in infancy to help promote the development of secure attachments to caregivers. There is evidence that such interventions can be effective in terms of reducing the development of mental health problems in childhood and adolescence, but further work is needed to ensure that the most vulnerable groups are targeted and engage with the interventions offer. Given what we know about the transgenerational transmission of attachment difficulties, those parents with their own trauma histories and consequent attachment and emotional problems, in particular, may benefit from psychosocial interventions. These interventions should involve both support in coping with the psychological effects of previous traumas and support and guidance in developing skills in positive parenting. Interventions should also aim to increase social support networks to ensure that the parents are supported by others on both a practical and emotional level on an ongoing basis as parenting can be a demanding task at the best of times.

8. *Attachment-informed mental health services*

As a model of help seeking, attachment theory gives us important insights into how people elicit support from health services and how care systems can foster secure attachments in service users. As highlighted within several chapters, attachment theory does not only tell us how to build effective relationships within the context of psychotherapy but can guide us in the design and delivery of our mental health services. What we now need to do is demonstrate empirically the added value both in terms of cost and well being of an attachment-informed mental health system.

Concluding remarks

The above themes are not an exhaustive list, but have been particularly salient for us as editors during the editorial process. The study and application of attachment theory within the field of psychosis has grown exponentially in the past decade. This body of work has been a fundamental part of a paradigm shift within psychosis, where psychosocial theories of, and treatment for, psychosis are now widely recognised as more useful than purely biological models. It has been a real pleasure, for us as editors, to bring this volume of work together and showcase some excellent examples of research and clinical applications. We look forward to what the next decade will bring in terms of new research findings and theoretical insights.

References

Ainsworth, M. D. S., Blehar, M. C., Waters, E., & Wall, S. (1978). *Patterns of Attachment: A psychological study of the strange situation.* Hillsdale, NJ: Erlbaum.

George, C., Kaplan, N. & Main, M. (1996). *Adult Attachment Interview* (3rd ed.) University of California: Berkeley.

INDEX

Indexer: Dr Laurence Errington.

Note: page numbers in **bold** indicate tables

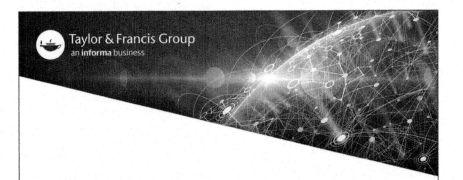